BASEBALL
HACKS™

Other resources from O'Reilly

Related titles

Access Hacks™	PHP Hacks™
Excel Hacks™	Retro Gaming Hacks™
Gaming Hacks™	Spidering Hacks™
Google Hacks™	Programming Perl
Google Maps Hacks™	MySQL Cookbook™

Hacks Series Home

hacks.oreilly.com is a community site for developers and power users of all stripes. Readers learn from each other as they share their favorite tips and tools for Mac OS X, Linux, Google, Windows XP, and more.

oreilly.com

oreilly.com is more than a complete catalog of O'Reilly books. You'll also find links to news, events, articles, weblogs, sample chapters, and code examples.

oreillynet.com is the essential portal for developers interested in open and emerging technologies, including new platforms, programming languages, and operating systems.

Conferences

O'Reilly brings diverse innovators together to nurture the ideas that spark revolutionary industries. We specialize in documenting the latest tools and systems, translating the innovator's knowledge into useful skills for those in the trenches. Visit *conferences.oreilly.com* for our upcoming events.

Safari Bookshelf (*safari.oreilly.com*) is the premier online reference library for programmers and IT professionals. Conduct searches across more than 1,000 books. Subscribers can zero in on answers to time-critical questions in a matter of seconds. Read the books on your Bookshelf from cover to cover or simply flip to the page you need. Try it today.

BASEBALL
HACKS™

Joseph Adler

O'REILLY®

Beijing · Cambridge · Farnham · Köln · Paris · Sebastopol · Taipei · Tokyo

Baseball Hacks™
by Joseph Adler

Copyright © 2006 O'Reilly Media, Inc. All rights reserved.
Printed in the United States of America.

Published by O'Reilly Media, Inc., 1005 Gravenstein Highway North,
Sebastopol, CA 95472.

O'Reilly books may be purchased for educational, business, or sales promotional use. Online editions are also available for most titles (*safari.oreilly.com*). For more information, contact our corporate/institutional sales department: (800) 998-9938 or *corporate@oreilly.com*.

Editors: Tatiana Apandi and
  Andrew Odewahn
Production Editor: Marlowe Shaeffer
Copyeditor: Audrey Doyle
Proofreader: Chris Downey

Indexer: Johnna Dinse
Cover Designer: Hanna Dyer
Interior Designer: David Futato
Illustrators: Robert Romano, Jessamyn
  Read, and Lesley Borash

Printing History:

February 2006:   First Edition.

 This book uses RepKover™, a durable and flexible lay-flat binding.

ISBN: 0-596-00942-9
[M]   [2/06]

Contents

Credits

About the Author

Joseph Adler is a researcher in the Advanced Product Development Group at VeriSign, focusing on problems in user authentication, managed security services, and RFID security. Joe has years of experience analyzing data, building statistical models, and formulating business strategies as an employee and consultant for companies including DoubleClick, American Express, and Dun & Bradstreet. He is a graduate of the Massachusetts Institute of Technology with an Sc.B. and an M.Eng. in computer science and computer engineering. Joe is an unapologetic Yankees fan, but he appreciates any good baseball game. Joe lives in Silicon Valley with his wife, two cats, and a DirecTV satellite dish.

Contributors

The following people contributed their hacks, writing, and inspiration to this book:

- Tom Dierickx is a data analyst specializing in automating data processes and authoring data-driven solutions. He has a wide range of computer programming and database development experience, along with an M.S. in statistics from Arizona State University. All of the languages, tools, and techniques he enthusiastically pursues—whether technical or statistical—are simply an outgrowth of the passion he has for working with data.

- Mark E. Johnson, Ph.D., earned his Ph.D. from Princeton University's Program in Applied and Computational Mathematics in 1998, where his research interests included the visualization and study of chaotic dynamical systems arising in physics and chemical engineering. A cofounder of SportMetrika, Inc., Mark spent the 2004 baseball season as the in-house baseball analyst of the National League Champion St. Louis Cardinals. While pursuing his B.S. in computer science and M.A. in mathematics as an undergraduate at Indiana University, Mark spent four years as a student manager of the men's basketball team under the leadership of Coach Bob Knight.

- Matthew S. Johnson, Ph.D., earned his Ph.D. from the Department of Statistics at Carnegie Mellon in 2001. His research interests lie in the field of psychometrics, estimating abilities from repeated categorical responses, where the responses might be answers to test questions used to measure a student's ability, or wins and losses used to measure a team's talent. Matt is an assistant professor in the Department of Statistics and Computer Information Systems in the Zicklin School of Business at Baruch College, of the City University of New York. Matt received his undergraduate degree in mathematics from Indiana University in 1996, and he is a cofounder of SportMetrika, Inc.

- Ari Kaplan is a leading figure known throughout the major leagues for revolutionizing and modernizing player assessment. Educated at the elite California Institute of Technology, he is a recipient of the university's Alumni of the Decade award for pioneering groundbreaking sabermetrics used to evaluate pitcher talent, including the reliever effectiveness, expected ERA, and save value, while popularizing the inherited runner statistics. Over the past 17 seasons, Ari has worked full time and consulted for 11 MLB organizations, working directly with general managers, presidents, and scouting directors to improve business operations and strategic analytical and technology capabilities dramatically. He comes from a scouting background and is one of the few long-term baseball leaders with a proven track record of successfully running several high-profile companies as CEO. See *http://www.arikaplan.com/baseball.html* for more.

- Pete Palmer is a coauthor of *The Hidden Game of Baseball* (Doubleday) and coeditor of the *ESPN Baseball Encyclopedia* (Sterling), which has a third edition due out next spring. Pete introduced on-base average as an official statistic for the American League in 1979 and invented on-base plus slugging, now universally used as a good measure of batting strength. A member of SABR since 1973, Pete is also a contributor to *The Complete Baseball Record Book & Fact Book* (The Sporting News) as well as *Who's Who in Baseball*.

- Brendan Roberts is a senior editor at *The Sporting News*. He has been with *The Sporting News* since 1996 and was one of the first to work on its fantasy sports web site (*http://fantasy.sportingnews.com*) when it launched in 2000. As part of his duties, he writes weekly baseball columns for the web site during the season, responds to readers' fantasy baseball and football questions, and creates updates for the site's round-the-clock news coverage, from a fantasy perspective. He has been playing fantasy sports for about 15 years against a varied competition level, including public leagues and expert leagues.

Acknowledgments

First, I would like to thank the many sports writers who helped me with this book. Baseball is a competitive sport, but baseball writing is not. Some of this help is visible: Mark Johnson, Tom Dierickx, Brendan Roberts, and Pete Palmer contributed hacks to this book. Additionally, I exchanged email with each of these experts while writing this book, and I received many useful corrections and suggestions on early drafts. I especially would like to thank Pete Palmer for his assistance. His books inspired many of the hacks in this book, and his comments helped me to fix many mistakes.

In addition to these four contributors, I would like to thank Thomas Gorman, Phil Birnbaum, David Tybor, Dean Oliver, Justin Plouffe, Adam Levensohn, Dan Mueller, Dave Carrano, Darren Kelly, Gary Gillette, John Viega, and Roger Magoulas for reviewing early drafts of this book and providing helpful feedback.

Next, I would like to thank the editors and staff at O'Reilly—in particular, editors Andrew Odewahn and Tatiana Apandi. Unless you try to write a book, you do not appreciate how important a good editor is. An editor not only corrects and refines a book's text but also helps the author to define the content and manages the writing process. Andrew and Tatiana made this a much stronger book, and I am grateful for their help.

Additionally, I would like to thank my father for introducing me to probability and data analysis. In college, my dad took a class called Probabilistic Systems Analysis with Professor Al Drake that changed his view of the world, making him see everything as a stochastic process. As I was growing up, my father shared this worldview with me. When I took the same class 30 years later, everything my dad talked about when I was a boy finally made sense.

Finally, I would like to thank my wife, Sarah. For the past year, I have spent most of my free time writing and working on this book. Throughout this process, she has been supportive and encouraging. My love for Sarah has grown while I have written this book; I greatly miss seeing her on evenings and weekends. Now that this book is finished, I hope to spend more time with her, at least until opening day.

Preface

I love baseball. I love going to baseball games and watching games on TV. I love studying player statistics in newspapers and checking them on the Internet. I love reading books about baseball. I wrote this book because of this love.

Many people have written beautifully about baseball. For example, Bill James wrote about baseball statistics, Jim Bouton wrote about what it's like to play baseball, and Michael Lewis wrote about what it's like to run a baseball team. But I don't know of a book that teaches how to take advantage of the many free baseball resources on the Internet. So I decided to write one.

I think this is a unique book. It's a book about how to watch, research, and understand baseball. It's an instruction manual for the free baseball databases. It's a cookbook for baseball research. Every part of this book is designed to teach you how to do something. In short, it's a how-to book.

My goal is to show you all the baseball-related stuff that you can do free of charge (or close to free). Just as open source projects such as Linux, MySQL, Open Office, and R have made great software freely available, collaborative projects such as Retrosheet and Baseball DataBank have made great data freely available. This book shows you how to take advantage of these data sources to research your favorite players, to win your fantasy league, or just to appreciate the game of baseball even more.

When I started writing this book, I thought of it as the baseball book for the person who reads Slashdot (*http://slashdot.org*), but it's become a lot more than that. I wrote about tools. I wrote about data sources. I wrote about formulas. But mostly, I wrote about baseball. I hope that all baseball fans will find something in this book that they like.

Why Baseball Hacks?

Hack means something specific in a baseball context: it means "to take a bad swing at the ball." However, that's not what we mean by *hack* in this book.

The term *hacking* has a bad reputation in the press. They use it to refer to someone who breaks into systems or wreaks havoc with computers as his weapon. Among people who write code, though, the term *hack* refers to a "quick-and-dirty" solution to a problem, or a clever way to get something done. And the term *hacker* is taken very much as a compliment, referring to someone as being *creative*, having the technical chops to get things done. The Hacks series is an attempt to reclaim the word, document the good ways people are hacking, and pass the hacker ethic of creative participation on to the uninitiated. Seeing how others approach systems and problems is often the quickest way to learn about a new technology.

I wrote *Baseball Hacks* for all types of baseball fans—young and old, computer novices and geeks, baseball experts and neophytes. I've tried to resist the temptation to pontificate about baseball, focusing not on which players, strategies, and formulas are good and bad but on how to assess those values. I have years of experience working with data, so I have tried to share tips, tricks, and techniques that will make it easier for you, as a fan, to actively participate in baseball.

How to Use This Book

You can read this book from cover to cover if you like, but each hack stands on its own, so feel free to browse and jump to the different sections that interest you most. If there's a prerequisite you need to know about, a cross-reference will guide you to the right hack.

I've tried to keep the hacks independent, but many hacks require you to start with a baseball database. Baseball is a game of statistics, and many of the hacks in this book deal with those statistics. Before you can try many of the hacks, you'll need to install a baseball database. I've also included some hacks that don't require you to do anything at all. In particular, Chapter 5 of this book explains what formulas mean and how they work. Even if you never plan to calculate a player's DIPS ERA yourself, I hope you'll find the explanation helpful when you see this number listed elsewhere.

How This Book Is Organized

The book is divided into several chapters, organized by subject:

Chapter 1, *Basics of Baseball*
Let's start by warming up with a few easy hacks showing how to watch and score baseball games, and how to find some simple baseball data on the Web.

Chapter 2, *Baseball Games from Past Years*
This chapter shows you where to get databases of career statistics and introduces some tools that you'll find helpful in working with this data.

Chapter 3, *Stats from the Current Season*
In this chapter, I'll show you how to get data on current baseball games. It's easy to get data on old games because they're already in databases. It's hard to get data on this year's games because you have to scrape it off the Web. This chapter shows you how.

Chapter 4, *Visualize Baseball Statistics*
I'm a big fan of R, a free data analysis and visualization tool. This chapter introduces R and shows you a lot of cool tricks that you can use to analyze baseball data with R.

Chapter 5, *Formulas*
Formulas have a special place in baseball history. Many baseball writers have spent months or years searching for the perfect formula to measure some aspect of the game. Thousands of different formulas are available for rating and ranking baseball players. This chapter covers a few of the most popular formulas and a few of my favorites.

Chapter 6, *Sabermetric Thinking*
This chapter discusses many baseball problems, some classic and some new.

Chapter 7, *The Bullpen*
This chapter comprises a few random topics that didn't fit anywhere else: fantasy baseball, widgets, and other sports.

Appendix A, *Where to Learn More Stuff*
This appendix lists resources, such as books and web sites, to supplement what you've learned in this book.

Appendix B, *Abbreviations*
This appendix contains a list of common baseball abbreviations.

Conventions Used in This Book

The following is a list of the typographical conventions used in this book:

Italics

> Used to indicate URLs, filenames and extensions, and directory/folder names. For example, a path in the filesystem will appear as */Developer/ Applications*.

`Constant width`

> Used to show code examples, the contents of files, and console output, as well as the names of variables, commands, and other code excerpts.

`Constant width bold`

> Used to highlight portions of code, typically new additions to old code.

`Constant width italic`

> Used in code examples and tables to show sample text to be replaced with your own values.

Gray type

> Used to indicate a cross-reference within the text.

You should pay special attention to notes set apart from the text with the following icons:

> This is a tip, suggestion, or general note. It contains useful supplementary information about the topic at hand.

> This is a warning or note of caution, often indicating that your money or your privacy might be at risk.

The thermometer icons, found next to each hack, indicate the relative complexity of the hack:

 beginner   moderate   expert

Using Code Examples

This book is here to help you get your job done. In general, you may use the code in this book in your programs and documentation. You do not need to contact us for permission unless you're reproducing a significant portion of the code. For example, writing a program that uses several chunks of code from this book does not require permission. Selling or distributing a CD-ROM of examples from O'Reilly books *does* require permission. Answering a question by citing this book and quoting example code does not require permission. Incorporating a significant amount of example code from this book into your product's documentation *does* require permission.

We appreciate, but do not require, attribution. An attribution usually includes the title, author, publisher, and ISBN. For example: "*Baseball Hacks* by Joseph Adler. Copyright 2006 O'Reilly Media, Inc., 0-596-00942-9."

If you feel your use of code examples falls outside fair use or the permission given above, feel free to contact us at *permissions@oreilly.com*.

How to Contact Us

We have tested and verified the information in this book to the best of our ability, but you may find that features have changed (or even that we have made mistakes!). As a reader of this book, you can help us to improve future editions by sending us your feedback. Please let us know about any errors, inaccuracies, bugs, misleading or confusing statements, and typos that you find anywhere in this book.

Please also let us know what we can do to make this book more useful to you. We take your comments seriously, and we will try to incorporate reasonable suggestions into future editions. You can write to us at:

O'Reilly Media, Inc.
1005 Gravenstein Highway North
Sebastopol, CA 95472
(800) 998-9938 (in the U.S. or Canada)
(707) 829-0515 (international/local)
(707) 829-0104 (fax)

To ask technical questions or to comment on the book, send email to:

bookquestions@oreilly.com

The web site for *Baseball Hacks* lists examples, errata, and plans for future editions. You can find this page at:

http://www.oreilly.com/catalog/baseballhks

For more information about this book and others, see the O'Reilly web site:

http://www.oreilly.com

Got a Hack?

To explore Hacks books online or to contribute a hack for future titles, visit:

http://hacks.oreilly.com

Safari® Enabled

 When you see a Safari® Enabled icon on the cover of your favorite technology book, that means the book is available online through the O'Reilly Network Safari Bookshelf.

Safari offers a solution that's better than e-books. It's a virtual library that lets you easily search thousands of top tech books, cut and paste code samples, download chapters, and find quick answers when you need the most accurate, current information. Try it for free at *http://safari.oreilly.com*.

Basics of Baseball
Hacks 1–7

More than most other sports, baseball is a game of numbers. Everything that happens can be measured, and people try to measure everything that can happen. They've done this for a long, long time. If you are so inclined, you can find detailed descriptions of games played when Ulysses S. Grant was president of the United States. It is the sense of endless possibilities for exploration and discovery in this data, along with the sheer love of the game, that drives passionate fans to devote countless hours to the smallest details of baseball.

Many fans love the history of baseball and want to compare the top players of today to the top players of the past. Some fans like to look up specific games from many years ago, maybe looking for the play-by-play for Sandy Koufax's perfect game or the box score for the first game their dad brought them to. Others wonder about how the game works, wanting to know if clutch hitters really exist, if sacrifice bunts are a good strategy, or if platooning batters is a good idea. Another group of fans just wants to know how their favorite players are doing this year, or they want to pick a winning fantasy team for next year.

This book will help you do these things, and it will tell you where to find the answers to questions like these. It will tell you where to find stats on past games, from wins and losses by teams all the way down to specific pitches. Many diligent fans from places like Retrosheet and Baseball DataBank work hard to collect historical data, and they make it available free of charge. This book shows you how to find and use their data, and how to analyze it with powerful and—thanks to the open source software movement—free tools that would have cost thousands of dollars just a few years ago.

Before diving headfirst into baseball statistics, databases, and programming, this chapter starts with the fundamentals: the rules of the game and of scoring a baseball game. I'll also give a few tips for easily getting baseball information off the Internet.

Baseball 101

I think that most readers of this book will know the rules of baseball. Many readers will know them better than I do. But it didn't seem right to dive into databases, formulas, and statistics without explaining the basics of the game. If you're not familiar with baseball or you want a quick refresher, keep reading. If you know the rules, feel free to skip to the first hack.

Here's a short description of how baseball works. At the game level, there are two competing teams. Each team has 25 players on its roster during most of the season, and 40 players in September. During the game, only nine players can be on the field at any time. In the National League, the same nine players bat and play defense. In the American League, the pitcher does not bat; he is replaced by a 10th player, called a *designated hitter*.

The game is divided into nine innings. During each inning, each team can bat until it makes three outs. The away team always bats first and the home team bats second. If the score is tied at the end of the ninth inning, the game will continue until one team gets the lead and holds it through the end of the inning. Incidentally, if the home team gets a lead during any inning when it can win the game at the end of the inning, the game ends. (Umpires can call games because of weather, mechanical difficulties, or other reasons; see the official rules for more about what can happen here.)

Each player bats in a specific order, cycling through players until the end of the game. The manager can choose the batting order before each game but cannot change the order after it has been set. A manager can make substitutions during the game, changing batters, runners, or fielders. However, once a player is removed from the game, he cannot reenter the game.

Each at bat is a little game in itself. The pitcher throws the ball to the batter, and the batter attempts to put the ball into play. The pitcher tries to throw the ball into the batter's *strike zone*. The strike zone is a region over home plate, as wide as the plate and extending from the player's knees to the letters on his jersey. A ball just needs to touch an edge of this zone to be considered a strike. If the pitch is thrown within the strike zone and the player does not swing at the pitch, this is a *called strike*. If the batter swings and misses, this is a *swinging strike*, even if the pitch is not thrown within the strike zone. Finally, if the pitch is thrown outside the strike zone and the player does not swing, this is called a *ball*. Each time a player comes to the plate to face a pitcher, a batter is allowed three strikes to put the ball in play, and the pitcher is allowed four balls to try to throw a strike.

If the batter makes contact with the ball, it must land within *fair territory*, or it is considered a *foul ball*. Fair territory extends from home plate down the third base line to a foul pole approximately 300 feet away (though usually farther), and down the first base line to a foul pole approximately 300 feet away. If a player has no strikes or one strike, a foul ball is considered a strike. If a player has two strikes, the number of strikes does not increase.

The defensive team can *put out* a player in several ways. First, on two strikes, the batter can strike out on a called strike or a swinging strike, giving the catcher a putout. Second, a player can catch a ball in the air (before it hits the ground), in fair or foul territory. Third, a defensive player can tag a runner with the ball. Finally, there are *force plays*. The batter is required to run to first base when a ball is put into play. If a base runner is on first base, this player is required to run as well. (In turn, batters on other bases are also required to run.) In these situations, a defensive player holding the ball can simply tag a base before a base runner does to put out that player.

A base runner scores by running around all four bases in order (first, second, third, and then home). Base runners can try to take bases whenever the ball is considered "alive." When there is a putout from catching a ball, the base runners must return to their respective bases before attempting to advance. Under certain circumstances, base runners can move forward a certain number of bases. When the ball is hit beyond the outfield fence (between the foul poles), it's a home run, and all base runners can advance to home plate (and score). When the ball bounces in fair territory and then out of the park, it's considered a ground rule double, and base runners are allowed to advance two bases. (Players can advance under some other circumstances; see the official rules for more information.)

If you want to know more, you can find the official rules of Major League Baseball on the Web at *http://mlb.mlb.com/NASApp/mlb/mlb/official_info/ official_rules/foreword.jsp*. Appendix B lists many of the common abbreviations for statistics.

Score a Baseball Game

H A C K #1 This book shows you a lot of neat things you can do with computers and databases, but it's important to remember that all of those numbers come from the same place: a person with a score sheet.

Many fans watch baseball passively, chatting with friends, sipping beer, and trying to make sense of the first base coach's signals. But at any ballpark, you'll find fans of all ages taking part in a ritual as old as baseball itself: keeping score.

Some people, like Yankees fan Nancy Smith, have kept score at every game for 40 years. "For some reason, the people I've met at the stadium over the years were fascinated by [my] keeping score," she said in a *New York Times* article published June 1, 2005. "But I'm fascinated when I don't see people keeping score; it's a part of the game."*

This hack describes a popular method for keeping score. It uses the score-books sold at ballparks and gives a good visual record of everything that happened in a game. Even if you never plan to score a game yourself, knowing how a game is scored helps you understand where statistics come from.

Traditional Scoring

At a ballpark, most programs come with a score sheet for the game that resembles the score sheet in Figure 1-1 (from *http://www.baseballscorecard. com/images/scorecard.gif*). I've kept the description here a little vague because there are many variations on scoring methods. You're welcome to include more or less information when you score a game or to record it differently.

The purpose of scoring a game is to record everything that happened during the game so that you can calculate player statistics. As you can see in Figure 1-1, the score sheet has spaces to record information about the game, to list all of the players' names, and to record a description of every play in the game.

This score sheet lets you record the results for one team. Note that you need two of these score sheets for a game: one for the home team and one for the opposing team. By switching score sheets after every half inning (three outs), you can record everything that happens during a game. Here's how to use a score sheet.

---

* For the full article, see the following URL: *http://www.nytimes.com/2005/06/01/nyregion/01fan. html?ex=1275278400&en=9e100af6de19a6ce&ei=5090&partner=rssuserland&emc=rss.*

Baseball score sheet

_____ at _____   Date: _____

Team: _____ Weather: _____   Team: _____

#	Player	Pos	1	2	3	4	5	6	7	8	9	10
		sub										
		sub										
		sub										
		sub										
		sub										
		sub										
		sub										
		sub										
		sub										
		sub										
		sub										
		sub										
		sub										
		sub										
		sub										
		sub										
		sub										
		sub										
		sub										
		sub										
Runs												
Hits												
Errors												
Passed balls												
Left on base												

#	Pitcher	W-L	IP	BF	K	BB	H	R	ER	WP	HBP	BALK

Figure 1-1. A sample score sheet

Record starting players' names. Each row in the table represents a batter. Each column represents an at bat. (You could also use a column to represent an inning, but this would become confusing every time the first player in the batting order came to the plate.)

At the beginning of the game, you'll want to write in the starting lineup in the rows on the left side of the table. Notice that there are three lines for players next to every row of diamonds; these extra lines are for substitutions (we'll get to this later). Write in the name, number, and position of each player.

You should also record the name of the opposing starting pitcher.

Record plays during the game. You use the diamonds in the score sheet for two purposes: to record the result of each at bat and to record the progress of each player around the base paths. Even after a player finishes an at bat, you can revisit the diamond chart to record putouts, stolen bases, advances on balks, advances on balls in play, and other events.

Table 1-1 lists some of the more common scorekeeping abbreviations for the things that can happen during a game.

Table 1-1. Common scorekeeping abbreviations

Event	Abbreviations
Single	S, 1B
Double	D, 2B
Triple	T, 3B
Home run	HR
Walk (base on balls)	W, BB
Intentional walk	IW, IBB
Strikeout (swinging)	K
Strikeout (called)	<backward K>
Balk	BK
Fielder's choice	FC
Hit by pitch	HP, HBP
Wild pitch	WP
Passed ball	PB
Stolen base	SB
Caught stealing	CS
Double play	DP
Triple play	TP
Error	E
Foul ball	F
Force out	FO
Line drive	L
Bunt	B
Unassisted	U
Fly ball	FL

A standard system is used for referring to defensive positions. Figure 1-2 illustrates the name and number associated with each position (from *http:// mlb.mlb.com/images/baseball_basics/basics_score_numbers.gif*).

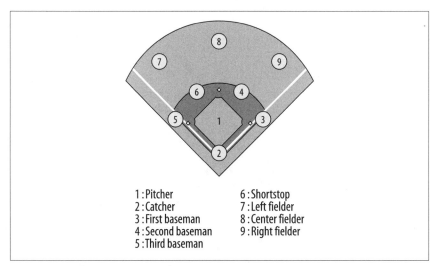

1 : Pitcher	6 : Shortstop
2 : Catcher	7 : Left fielder
3 : First baseman	8 : Center fielder
4 : Second baseman	9 : Right fielder
5 : Third baseman	

Figure 1-2. Defensive-position codes

These symbols are used to describe fielding. For example, suppose the short-stop fields a ball and throws it to the second baseman to get one out, and the second baseman throws it to the first baseman to get a second out. This is known as a 6-4-3 double play. If the third baseman commits an error, this is noted as E5.

After each at bat, you should record the base reached by that player and note how the player reached the base. (If the player was put out, you don't record the advancement.) Figures 1-3 through 1-8 show common notations for recording plays (singles, doubles, triples, home runs, walks, and strikeouts). Notice that the base paths are darkened to show where a player has run.

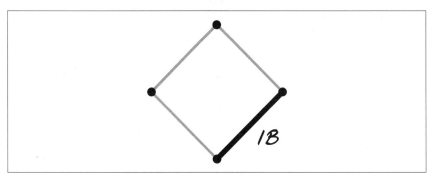

Figure 1-3. Single

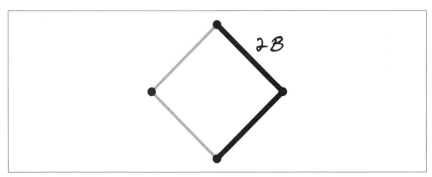

Figure 1-4. Double

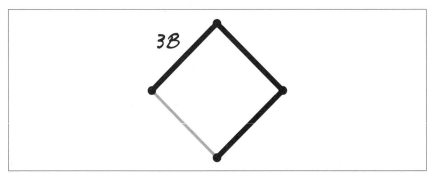

Figure 1-5. Triple

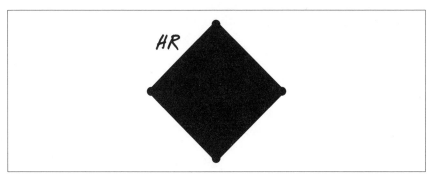

Figure 1-6. Home run

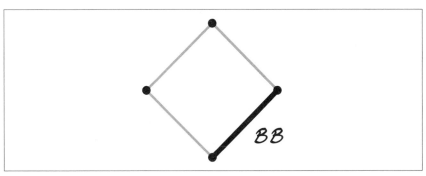

Figure 1-7. Walk

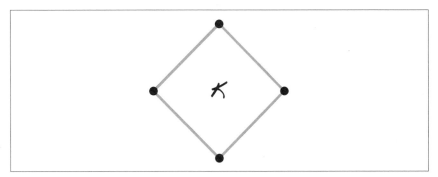

Figure 1-8. Strikeout

Optionally, you can include more information about each hit. For example, you can draw a line showing where the ball was hit, and you can include a notation showing whether it was a fly ball, line drive, or ground ball. See Figure 1-9 for an example of this.

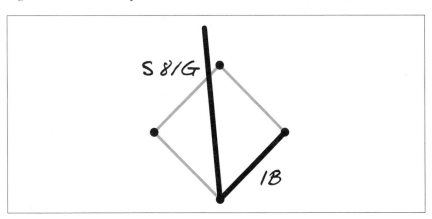

Figure 1-9. Single on a ground ball to center field

On outs, include a description of the defensive play and show the number of outs on the diagram. For example, Figure 1-10 shows a 6-4-3 double play.

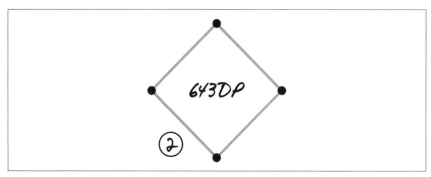

Figure 1-10. Double play

Finally, you indicate base-running moves by a base runner. If a player steals a base on a subsequent at bat, you can indicate this (see Figure 1-11). If a player is put out running from first to second on a later play (for example, if the next batter hits into a double play), you indicate this with a broken line on that base path. Figure 1-12 shows an example of this.

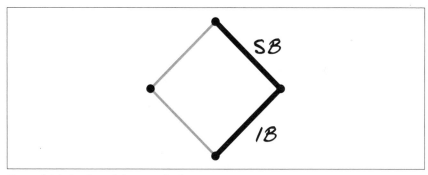

Figure 1-11. Single and then a stolen base

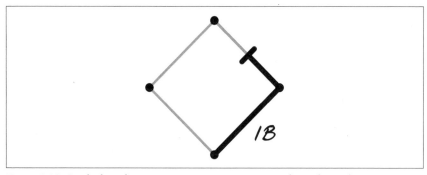

Figure 1-12. Single, but player was put out running to second on a later play

At the bottom of the score sheet, you'll notice the pitching lines. You can use these to keep track of pitching performance.

Record substitutions. Sometimes the same players who start a game finish it. But often, relief pitchers come in during the game to help the starting pitcher. Additionally, pinch hitters, pinch runners, and defensive substitutes are used during the game. Sometimes a player changes position.

When one of these things happens, note this on your score sheet. Write the name of the substitute player on the left. Next to the diamond representing the play, darken the outside of the box and note the substitution.

Record other information. It's helpful to include other notes about things that happen during the game. For example, to save you the trouble of counting outs, it's a good idea to write the number of outs in the diamond where the outs were made and to circle that number, as shown in Figure 1-10.

Some people like to include information about the direction of each ball put in play, noting how the ball traveled and where it was fielded. For example, here is a way to note that a player singled on a ground ball to center field: as the game progresses, track the number of batters faced by each pitcher, the number of outs pitched, and the number of runs scored against a pitcher (and the number of earned runs). The easiest way to do this is to add a tick mark beside the pitcher's name for each inning, out, run scored, error, or other statistic that you want to count. At the end of the game, calculate the total.

Hacking the Hack

Many software programs are available to help you keep score at a baseball game; some of them are available for handheld devices. Honestly, I have never used any of them, and I can't make any recommendations. One piece of software that looked neat to me is ScorePAD. This software is available for Palm OS devices (from *http://www.scorepad.com*) and is used by several major sports networks and professional baseball teams.

Using your notes, you're now ready to turn the score sheet into a box score, as discussed in "Make a Box Score from a Score Sheet" [Hack #2]. For a more modern method of scorekeeping that's better for computer processing, see "Keep Score, Project Scoresheet–Style" [Hack #3].

See Also

On the Web, you can find a number of sites devoted to scoring baseball, with a few different score sheets. Here are a couple of my favorites:

Alex Reisner's Baseball Data Graphics
Nicely formatted spreadsheets as Adobe Acrobat files, available at *http:// baseball.alexreisner.com.*

The Baseball Scorecard
A few more score sheets, created in Microsoft Excel, so they're easy to edit: *http://www.baseballscorecard.com/downloads.htm.*

Make a Box Score from a Score Sheet
Create a box score to summarize player performance.

Although a score sheet [Hack #1] describes everything that happened during a game, it doesn't tell you directly how each player performed. This hack explains how to use a score sheet to calculate a *box score*, a neat way to summarize how each player performed during a game.

Box scores are a traditional way to summarize baseball games, dating back to Chadwick in the 19th century. A box score captures a lot of information about the game. For each batter, it captures the number of at bats (AB), hits (H), runs (R), runs batted in (RBI), doubles (2B), home runs (HR), stolen bases (SB), and sacrifice hits (SH). For each pitcher, it includes the number of innings pitched, hits, runs, earned runs, walks, and strikeouts. It also includes notes on the number of players left on base; the winning, losing, and saving pitchers; and some other miscellaneous information.

As an example, here is the box score from the October 2, 1978 playoff game between the Yankees and the Red Sox:

```
Game of 10/2/1978 -- New York at Boston (D)
```

New York	AB	R	H	RBI	Boston	AB	R	H	RBI
Rivers M, cf	2	1	1	0	Burleson R, ss	4	1	1	0
Blair P, ph-cf	1	0	1	0	Remy J, 2b	4	1	2	0
Munson T, c	5	0	1	1	Rice J, rf	5	0	1	1
Piniella L, rf	4	0	1	0	Yastrzemski C, lf	5	2	2	2
Jackson R, dh	4	1	1	1	Fisk C, c	3	0	1	0
Nettles G, 3b	4	0	0	0	Lynn F, cf	4	0	1	1
Chambliss C, 1b	4	1	1	0	Hobson B, dh	4	0	1	0
White R, lf	3	1	1	0	Scott G, 1b	4	0	2	0
Thomasson G, lf	0	0	0	0	Brohamer J, 3b	1	0	0	0
Doyle B, 2b	2	0	0	0	Bailey B, ph	1	0	0	0
Spencer J, ph	1	0	0	0	Duffy F, 3b	0	0	0	0

Stanley F, 2b	1	0	0	0	Evans D, ph	1	0	0	0
Dent B, ss	4	1	1	3					
	--	--	--	--		--	--	--	--
	35	5	8	5		36	4	11	4

| New York | 000 | 000 | 410 | -- | 5 |
| Boston | 010 | 001 | 020 | -- | 4 |

New York	IP	H	R	ER	BB	SO
Guidry R (W)	6.1	6	2	2	1	5
Gossage R (S)	2.2	5	2	2	1	2

Boston	IP	H	R	ER	BB	SO
Torrez M (L)	6.2	5	4	4	3	4
Stanley B*	0.1	2	1	1	0	0
Hassler A	1.2	1	0	0	0	2
Drago D	0.1	0	0	0	0	0

```
   * Pitched to 1 batter in 8th

LOB -- New York 6, Boston 9
2B -- Rivers M, Scott G, Burleson R, Munson T, Remy J
HR -- Yastrzemski C, Dent B, Jackson R
SB -- Rivers M 2
SH -- Brohamer J, Remy J
PB -- Munson T
T -- 2:52
A -- 32925
```

To see how a box score is useful, let's focus on a specific player: Bucky Dent. From the table on top, we can see that Bucky Dent had four at bats, scored one run, had one hit, and batted in three runs. Looking at the notes at the bottom, we see that he had one home run. The box score tells you that Bucky had a pretty good game, scoring three of the Yankees' five runs. In fact, he did have a good game, breaking the heart of every Red Sox fan when he hit a home run over the Green Monster onto Lansdowne Street, sending the Yankees to the playoffs.

The Official Rules for Scoring

Major League Baseball has official rules on scoring the game and an official scorer for each game. The scorer sits in the press booth (near the radio announcers, the TV announcers, and the scoreboard operator) and writes a score sheet that is considered the official record of the game. It consists of player information, offensive statistics, fielding statistics, pitching statistics, and other miscellaneous information.

Player information

Player information is the most straightforward and consists of each player's name, uniform number, defensive position, and lineup position.

Here are the offensive statistics that the scorer must record for each player:

At bats (AB)
> The scorer needs to record the number of at bats for each player. Each time a player comes to the plate to bat, it is considered an official at bat if the ball is placed in play and results in a hit, out, error, or if the player strikes out. If the player reaches first base as a walk because a pitch hit him, because he hit a sacrifice fly, or because of the catcher's interference or obstruction, it's not considered an at bat.

Runs scored (R)
> This statistic refers to each time a player crosses home and scores a run.

Safe hits (H)
> This is the number of times the ball is put in play and the player successfully reaches a base without making any outs, and without the opponent committing any errors. (It's still possible for there to be an out on the play, if the batter or another base runner tries to run too far.)

Runs batted in (RBI)
> Each time a run is scored as the result of a player putting a ball in play (or reaching a base through a walk or by being hit by a pitch), the player is credited with an RBI.

Doubles (D), triples (T), home runs (HR), and total bases (TB)
> The scorer needs to count the number of bases safely reached on each hit, tabulating the number of doubles, triples, and home runs. The scorer is also required to count the number of total bases reached by a player: a single counts for one base, a double for two, a triple for three, and a home run for four.

Stolen bases (SB)
> Each time a player successfully steals a base, the scorer is required to note this. (The rules also require the scorer to note when a batter is caught stealing [CS], which is for defensive statistics. We'll get to that shortly.)

Sacrifice bunts (SAC), sacrifice flies (SF), and sacrifice hits (SH)
> The scorer also needs to note each time a player puts a ball in play that makes an out but advances at least one runner (possibly allowing the runner on third base to score).

Base on balls (BB), intentional base on balls (IBB), and hit by pitch (HBP)
> The scorer also needs to tabulate the number of times a batter reaches a base by walking.

Strikeouts (K)
> Finally, the scorer needs to count the number of strikeouts per batter.

The mandatory fielding statistics are as follows:

Putouts (PO)
> This refers to each time a defensive player catches a fly ball, beats a player to a base on a force while holding a ball, or tags a player out. (The catcher is awarded the putout when a batter strikes out.)

Assists (A)
> This refers to each time a player fields a ball and throws it to another defender who gets an out.

Errors (E)
> According to the official rules, "An error shall be charged for each misplay (fumble, muff, or wild throw), which prolongs the time at bat of a batter, or which prolongs the life of a runner, or which permits a runner to advance one or more bases." (In practice, errors are somewhat subjective.)

Double plays (DP) and triple plays (TP)
> The scorer is required to record each time a double or triple play is made, the player who hit into the play, and the fielders who made the play.

Passed balls (PB)
> When a ball gets away from the catcher and a base runner advances, the catcher can be charged with a passed ball. (If the scorer thinks it's the pitcher's fault, it might be called a wild pitch.)

Required pitching statistics include the following:

Innings pitched (IP)
> For each pitcher, the scorer is required to record the number of innings pitched, including parts of innings. Really, this is equivalent to the number of outs pitched.

Batters faced (BFP)
> The scorer needs to count the total number of batters faced by a pitcher.

At bats (ABA)
> The scorer also needs to record the number of official at bats against a pitcher (see the description of at bats earlier in this section).

Hits allowed (HA), runs allowed (RA), sacrifice hits allowed (SHA), sacrifice flies allowed (SFA), total bases allowed (TBA), base on balls allowed (BBA), intentional base on balls allowed (IBBA), batters hit by pitch (HBPA), and strikeouts allowed (KA)
> Each of these is pretty straightforward: every time a batter is credited with a statistic (such as a hit), the pitcher is credited with a statistic (such as a hit allowed).

Earned runs (ER)

The idea of earned runs is to separate a pitcher's performance from the fielders' performance. Here is how this works. First, a batter can earn a run only if the scoring runner reached base while the pitcher was pitching. (This means that relief pitchers can't get earned runs from inherited runners.) Second, the pitcher is not charged with runs scored due to passed balls, errors, or interferences. To determine the number of earned runs, the scorer tries to figure out what would have happened in an inning if there had been no errors, passed balls, or interference calls. Let's consider a simple example. Suppose a pitcher strikes out the first two batters in an inning, and the third batter hits a triple. Next, suppose the fourth batter hits a ground ball to the first base side and reaches first base on error, and the runner on third scores. Now, suppose the pitcher strikes out the fifth batter. Without the error, the runner on third would not have scored. Therefore, the pitcher is not credited with an earned run, but with one run. (The difference between the two is the number of unearned runs.)

Wild pitches (WP)

A pitcher is credited with a wild pitch when the pitcher throws a pitch very different from the pitch expected by the catcher, and the catcher fails to field the ball. (If the scorer thinks it's the catcher's fault, it's called a passed ball [PB].)

Balks (BK)

A balk is officially defined as "an illegal act by the pitcher with a runner or runners on base, entitling all runners to advance one base." Basically, a balk is a "fake" of some type. A pitcher is required to pitch from one of two positions (called "the windup" or "the set"), stand in the right spot on the pitcher's mound facing the batter, and throw the ball toward the catcher. If a pitcher pretends that he is going to do one thing but does something else, it counts as a balk.

The scorer also must record a variety of miscellaneous information:

Winning pitcher (W) and losing pitcher (L)

The scorer needs to credit the winning and losing pitcher for each team. At the end of the game, there is a winning team and a losing team. At some point in the game (maybe the first at bat in the first inning, maybe the second at bat in the fifth inning, maybe the last at bat in the game), the winning team took the lead and kept it through the end of the game. At that point in the game, the current pitcher for the winning team is credited with the win, and the current pitcher for the losing team is credited with the loss. (There is an exception to this rule. If the winning team takes and holds the lead at some time in the first five innings, but the starting pitcher leaves the game before the end of the first five innings, the starting pitcher might not be credited with the win. The scorer can give the win to the relieving pitcher whom he believes was most effective.)

Left on base (LOB)
This refers to the number of base runners left on base at the end of each inning by each team.

Line score
The scorer is required to record the number of runs scored in each inning by each team during the game.

Umpires
The scorer must record the name of the home plate umpire, first base umpire, second base umpire, and third base umpire.

Time
Finally, the scorer is required to note the start and end times of the game, deducting any weather (or other) delays.

Some decisions the scorer makes are not subjective, such as strikeouts and home runs. But sometimes the scorer needs to make a judgment call. For example, suppose a batter hits a ball hard to the third base side and runs hard for first base. The third baseman dives to get the ball and makes a low throw to the first baseman. The first baseman takes his foot off the base, stretching to catch the ball, just as the batter reaches the base. Is this play an error on the third baseman, or is it a single? This is the decision of the scorer; if he feels it was exceptionally difficult for the third baseman to make that play, he might score it as a single. But if he feels the third baseman just made a bad throw, he might score it as an error.

You can find a complete description of scorer rules on the official MLB web site, at *http://mlb.mlb.com/NASApp/mlb/ mlb/official_info/official_rules/official_scorer_10.jsp*.

We'll come back to a lot of these statistics later in this book. These are the basic counts in all the databases in this book, and they are the building blocks for all the formulas.

Calculating a Box Score from a Score Sheet

Once you've filled out a score sheet **[Hack #1]**, you've done most of the hard work and are ready to calculate the box score. Here are the steps to follow.

Step 1: Draw columns for names, at bats, runs, hits, and anything else. First, draw a set of columns for player names and any statistics you want to count. You should draw separate boxes for each team's batters (to capture batting statistics) and for each team's pitchers (to capture pitching statistics).

Step 2: Copy the batters' names. Start by copying the names of the batters from the score sheet onto another piece of paper. Copy all of the names from the left side of the score sheet, including players who were substituted out of the game.

Step 3: Count statistics for each batter. You'll notice that you can read the statistics for each player off of the diamond charts to the right of their names on the score sheet. For each player, count the number of times each statistic occurs. For example, to count the number of at bats, you should look at all the diagrams for a player's at bats. (Remember, when you took notes, you marked when substitutions occurred!) Each time a player came to the plate, and the plate appearance ended in a ball in play, a home run, or a strikeout, count that as an at bat. Write the total in the appropriate column.

Step 4: Count statistics for each pitcher. Just like you did with batters, count the statistics for each pitcher: innings pitched, batters faced, earned runs, strikeouts, etc. Copy these numbers into the appropriate column for each player.

Step 5: Prove the box score. Finally, it's a good idea to check your work. If you're familiar with double-entry accounting, you'll notice that baseball scoring uses the same method. Each hit is recorded in two places: it's credited to a batter and charged to a pitcher. At the end of a game, the scorer is required to "prove" the correctness of a score sheet by making sure all of these things add up.

To prove a box score using the official rules, make sure the following things are equal for each team:

- At bats (AB) + walks (BB) + hit batsmen (HBP) + sacrifice bunts (SAC) + sacrifice flies (SF) + batters awarded base on interference and obstruction
- Runs scored + players left on base + opposing team's putouts

You can also check that other statistics add up. For example, the total number of hits scored by a team should equal the total number of hits allowed by the opposing team.

Hacking the Hack

It takes a lot of work to calculate a box score by hand, and I'll admit that I don't do this very often. Instead, I usually use the codes shown in "Keep Score, Project Scoresheet–Style" [Hack #3], and then run the BGAME program described in "Make Box Scores or Database Tables from Play-by-Play Data with Retrosheet Tools" [Hack #15].

Keep Score, Project Scoresheet–Style

Use the Project Scoresheet system to record the plays during a baseball game.

About 20 years ago, a group of baseball fans started Project Scoresheet. This was a collaborative effort by baseball fans to record every play of every game. Bill James started this project out of frustration because the Elias Sports Bureau (the official statistics provider) refused to make this data available to fans. So, in true hacker tradition, the members of the project designed a neat, simple scoring method that was perfect for describing plays to computers. Today this system lives on as the preferred encoding method of Retrosheet. In fact, it's even used by STATS, Inc. and the Elias Sports Bureau.

With Project Scoresheet record keeping, you write down a code each time something happens during the game, in chronological order. You don't need two score sheets (one for each team) or special scoring paper. Even better, you don't need to use any weird symbols—you can just write codes using the letters of the alphabet. This makes Project Scoresheet descriptions ideal for computer use because they're easy to enter, email, and save to a database. The disadvantage of this system is that it's a little tough to compute a box score by hand or manually read a game description. After you get the hang of this system (and you learn all the codes, which admittedly is a big hurdle), you may find it faster and easier than traditional scoring.

Even if you never plan to use this system, you might find it helpful to read this hack because Retrosheet uses this system to describe play-by-play data. We'll revisit Project Scoresheet–style scoring throughout the book. For example, once you're familiar with the system, you can use it to understand historical play-by-play information [Hack #14].

The Contents of a Play Code

Each play code in this system captures several types of information:

Fielding of balls in play
When a ball is put in play, the pitching team will field the ball. Number codes are used to describe who fields the ball and to whom they throw the ball.

Type of play
Each at bat results in a walk, hit by pitch, single, double, triple, home run, or out. Codes are also used to describe any outs made during the play: normal outs, fielder's choice, sacrifices, double plays, triple plays, force-outs, strikeouts, pickoffs, and caught stealing.

Description
Codes are used to describe the type of hit: line drive, ground ball, fly ball, bunt, and lots of other things.

Base running
When a ball is put in play, base runners can advance, and they can be put out. Within an at bat, base runners can attempt to steal bases. Runs scored are a special case. (They are an advancement to home plate.)

Errors
The pitching team can make a number of mistakes captured in this code: passed balls, wild pitches, balks, interference calls, throwing errors, foul ball errors, and other errors. The batting team can make base running errors.

Substitutions
Play codes capture pinch runners.

Play code structure. Each play code follows a simple sequence:

```
[<type>] <fielding> [ / location] [/ <description>] [ .<base runner
advancement> ]
```

The first code represents the "type of play." This code is optional. The second code represents any players who fielded the ball. The third code represents how the ball moved (i.e., ground ball, fly ball, etc.). A period (.) precedes the base running description. The final code describes any base runners that advanced on the play; a semicolon separates descriptions.

Fielding. The fielding codes describe who fielded that ball and where he threw it. The letter E preceding a number indicates that the player made an error. On a play where more than one out is made, parenthetical notes describe which fielder put out which base runner. Let's give a few examples of fielding:

13
> Throw from pitcher to first baseman.

643
> Throw from shortstop to second baseman to first baseman.

24
> Throw from catcher to second baseman.

E3
> Error by first baseman.

6E5
> Throw from shortstop to third baseman. Error as ball is dropped by third baseman.

64(1)3
> Fielded by shortstop, thrown to second baseman. Second baseman puts out runner from first and then throws ball to first baseman, who puts out batter.

Type of play. Let's start with things that happen before or during an at bat, leaving the batter still batting:

Code	Meaning
PB	Passed ball
WP	Wild pitch
BK	Balk
SB	Stolen base
PH	Pinch hitter
PR	Pinch runner
FLE	Foul ball error

That's not too complicated, is it? Now, let's list the codes for hits:

Code	Meaning
S	Single
D	Double
T	Triple
HR	Home run
DGR	Ground rule double

Now, let's show the codes for at bats where there is no hit, but the runner reaches base:

Code	Meaning
W	Walk
IW	Intentional walk
HP	Hit by pitch
C	Catcher's interference (usually C/E2; I explain the "/E2" part shortly)
K+	Strikeout, but batter advances to first base on a wild pitch (this is kind of a weird, complicated one and is usually scored as "K+WP"; I provide more about the "WP" part shortly)

There are a few codes for outs during at bats. These are accompanied by codes in parentheses that describe how the ball was fielded. For example, CS2(26) means that a batter was caught stealing second on a throw from the catcher to the shortstop.

Code	Meaning
PO1(<fielding note>)	Pickoff at first base
PO2(<fielding note>)	Pickoff at second base
PO3(<fielding note>)	Pickoff at third base
CS2(<fielding note>)	Caught stealing second base
CS3(<fielding note>)	Caught stealing third base
CSH(<fielding note>)	Caught stealing home base

Finally, here are the codes for outs at the end of an at bat:

Code	Meaning
K	Strikeout
No code, just a number	An out (the numbers represent the player who fielded the ball; I explain these codes in the next section)

Description. The ball movement codes describe how the ball was hit, or they elaborate on the type of out. Note that a slash (/) character precedes each code.

Code	Meaning
/G	Ground ball
/L	Line drive
/FL	Foul
/B	Bunt
/FC	Fielder's choice

Code	Meaning
/FO	Force out
/GDP	Ground into double play
/DP	Other double play
/TP	Triple play
/SH	Sacrifice hit
/SF	Sacrifice fly
/P	Pop out
WP	Wild pitch
/FINT	Fan interference
/INT	Interference
/BINT	Batter interference
/G+	Ground out sharply
/G-	Ground out softly
/L+	Line out sharply
/L-	Line out softly
/F+	Fly out sharply
/BG	Bunt
/P2F	Pop out to catcher in foul territory
/P3F	Pop out to first baseman in foul territory
/P5F	Pop out to third baseman in foul territory
/SAC/BG	Sacrifice bunt
/F	Fielding error, if play was an error
/TH	Error on throw

Base running. Numbers represent base running. Don't confuse these codes with fielding codes! These codes refer to the base number the runner is on. These codes are also always in the form "number hyphen number" (e.g., 1-3 for first base to third base). Hyphens are not used for fielding codes, only for base running codes. A semicolon separates the description of each base runner. Here is the list of these codes:

Code	Meaning
B-1	Batter to first
B-2	Batter to second
B-3	Batter to third
B-H	Batter to home
1-2	Runner on first to second
1-3	Runner on first to third
1-H	Runner on first to home

Code	Meaning
2-3	Runner on second to third
2-H	Runner on second to home
3-H	Runner on third to home
1X1(<fielding note>)	Runner out at first
1X2(<fielding note>)	Runner out running from first to second
1X3(<fielding note>)	Runner out running from first to third
1XH(<fielding note>)	Runner out running from first to home
2X2(<fielding note>)	Runner out at second
2X3(<fielding note>)	Runner out running from second to third
2XH(<fielding note>)	Runner out running from second to home
3X3(<fielding note>)	Runner out at third
3XH(<fielding note>)	Runner out running from third to home
WP	Wild pitch; a description of base runner movement follows
PB	Passed ball; a description of base runner movement follows

Usually, the first four codes are omitted if a player ends up on the base corresponding to the type of hit (e.g., the player ends up on first base on a single). Only if the player advances beyond this base (on a throwing error, for example) are these usually listed.

Example play codes. Here are a few examples of play codes:

K
> Strikeout. Sorry, that's the simplest one.

D7/L
> Line ball double. Fielded by left fielder.

SB3;SB2
> Double steal.

HR/F8
> Home run to center field. (Note the "fly ball" part.)

HR7/L
> Inside-the-park home run to left field. Notice that "7" is immediately after "HR"; this indicates that it is an inside-the-park home run.

S9/L
> Line drive single to right field.

S9/L.2-H
> Line drive single to right field. Runner scores from second base.

HR7/L.1-H;2-H;3-H
> Grand slam home run to center field.

3/L
   Line out to first baseman.
8/F
   Fly out to center fielder.
9/SF.3-H
   Sacrifice fly to right fielder. Runner on third base scores.
54(1)3/GDP
   Ground into double play, third baseman to second baseman to first baseman.
54/SAC/BG.2-3;1-2
   Sacrifice bunt, fielded by third baseman to second baseman. Runners on first and third advance.
13/SAC/BG.3-H
   Suicide squeeze. (Sacrifice bunt ground ball, fielded by pitcher to first baseman. Runner on third scores.)
FC1/G.3XH(1); B-1
   Batter reaches on a fielder's choice. Runner on third out at home plate by pitcher, unassisted.
6/LTP.2X2(6);1X1(6)
   Unassisted triple play. Line drive to shortstop.

Pitch codes. With the Project Scoresheet system, there is also a system for recording a brief description of every pitch:

Symbol	Meaning
.	Play not involving the batter
1	Pickoff throw to first
2	Pickoff throw to second
3	Pickoff throw to third
>	Runner going on pitch
B	Ball
C	Called strike
F	Foul
H	Batter hit by pitch
I	Intentional ball
K	Strike (unknown type: called or swinging)
L	Foul bunt
M	Missed bunt attempt
N	No pitch (balk or interference)
0	Foul tip on bunt

Symbol	Meaning
P	Pitchout
Q	Swinging on pitchout
R	Foul ball on pitchout
S	Swinging strike
T	Foul tip
U	Unknown (scorer missed pitch)
V	Called ball because pitcher went to his mouth
X	Ball put in play by batter
Y	Ball put in play on pitchout

HACK #4 Follow Pitches During a Game

Baseball can be boring unless you understand what pitch is being thrown, and why.

People who don't watch baseball all the time think it's a boring game. They don't think much happens; every minute or so, the pitcher throws a ball and the batter swings, and that's it. Over time, fans realize that a lot is going on; there is a lot of strategy involved in pitching to each batter. This hack helps you follow this battle—the subtlest and most elegant part of the game.

In addition to making the game a lot more interesting, understanding and following pitching strategies raises a number of interesting questions to ponder as you watch. Is the pitcher throwing the ball where he should, or is he throwing it at the wrong spot? Is he having trouble with a certain pitch? Does it seem like the other team always knows a certain pitch is coming? Finally, watching the pitcher and catcher can also tell you about who is making the decisions. Usually, the catcher selects the pitches, but there are exceptions. You can learn a lot by watching.

Following the Pitching Strategy

The pitcher's primary goal is to try to fool the hitter into swinging in the wrong place at the wrong time. There are a lot of ways to do this. Sometimes the pitcher wants to throw strikes that look like balls (so the batter doesn't swing at a called strike) or balls that look like strikes (so the batter swings at the ball and misses). Other times, the pitcher wants to throw the ball where the batter can't hit it well (often, this means a high, inside fastball). At still other times, the pitcher throws the ball at different speeds to fool the hitter into swinging too early or too late. Pitching strategy can be subtle and complicated. Pitchers often throw one pitch (say, a slider on the outside corner) to set up another pitch (say, a slider outside).

Good pitchers (usually catchers, actually) remember what they threw to a batter in previous innings, games, or even seasons! Professional ball players and coaches spend hours studying videos before each game to try to forecast what a pitcher will throw to them, and when. Catchers spend hours reading notes and watching videos to figure out what pitches hitters expect pitchers to throw, and at what times, so they can adjust their strategies. And then ball players adjust their hitting strategies to what they think are the pitcher's new strategies.... You get the idea.

It's really tough to predict what each side will do unless you have a lot of time and a big video collection. (As a fan, this is practically impossible.) But if you watch a lot of baseball, you can start to pick up on a few patterns in pitching strategy.

Set up a pitch outside. A pitcher (with good location) will throw a couple of strikes on the outside corner. Many batters will assume they look like balls (maybe they're sliders or curveballs that move into the strike zone at the last second). After two called strikes in that spot, the batter is conditioned to think that balls in that spot are strikes. The pitcher will then follow with an unhittable ball just outside the strike zone to try to strike out the batter.

Follow breaking balls with a fastball. Many pitchers will throw a few consecutive breaking balls to get the batter used to seeing slow pitches. Then the pitcher will throw a fastball, trying to get the batter to swing at the ball after it crosses the plate.

Follow fastballs with a breaking ball. This is the opposite of the previous strategy! A power pitcher (usually a guy like Eric Gagne, who can throw a 95 mph fastball) follows a few fastballs with a really slow pitch. Often, you'll see the hitter swing at the pitch long before it crosses the plate.

Always throw the same impossible-to-hit pitch. This isn't really much of a strategy. The only pitcher who has done this successfully is Mariano Rivera (the Yankees ace reliever), who throws a *cut fastball*. His pitch is a high inside fastball that moves in on the hands of lefthanded batters and away from righthanders. He throws the ball in a way that makes it move at the last minute. Sometimes he gets strikeouts, but often a hitter will hit the ball weakly off the inside of the bat, grounding out. His pitches cause more bats to break than almost any other pitcher in baseball. Incidentally, the only team that seems to be able to hit this pitch is the Red Sox, probably because the Yankees and Red Sox play each other 19 times during the regular season.

Move the player off the plate. Many batters like to stand over the plate, to hit balls on the outside with the *sweet spot* of the bat. (If you hit the ball in the right spot, it travels a lot farther.) A common strategy for a pitcher is to throw an inside fastball at a batter to scare him and get him to move off the plate.

Identifying Pitches

It's not easy to tell pitches apart. It all happens so fast, and there are so many distractions: the pitcher's big windup, the umpire's hand waving, and the bat swinging. As described earlier, a large part of a pitcher's job is to make it hard to tell pitches apart until the last instant; a good pitcher throws several different pitches with almost identical arm angles to confuse hitters. If a professional baseball player (a guy who is paid millions of dollars a year to hit balls because he is one of the best people in the world at hitting balls) can't always tell pitches apart in person (from 60 feet away), how can you do it on TV? Well, it turns out that there are a few tricks for doing this.

Here are five simple tips for deciphering pitches, arranged from easiest (and most useful) to hardest (and least useful). Train yourself to do these one at a time, in order.

Step 1: Watch the umpire for location. If you're watching the game, the scoreboard will usually tell you if the last pitch was a ball or a strike. But if you want more detail, watch the umpire. At the simplest, an umpire will stick his arm up in the air to indicate a strike. An umpire will keep his arms down to indicate a ball. Most umpires will follow a ball by looking to their left or right to indicate whether the ball was to their left or right. An umpire will indicate a foul tip (meaning that the ball grazed the bat) by imitating a foul tip with his hands (holding one hand out, and, with the other hand, tracing the path of a ball bouncing off the bat).

Step 2: Watch the catcher for location. To figure out where the ball is supposed to go, watch the catcher. Look at where the catcher *sets up*, or holds his glove, while the pitcher is throwing the ball. A catcher will usually hold his glove where he wants the ball to go. He does this for two reasons: to have the glove in the right place to catch the ball, and to give the pitcher a target for the ball. Looking at the catcher can let you distinguish high balls from low balls, and inside from outside. You can usually tell if the pitcher is intentionally throwing balls outside the strike zone.

This method isn't completely reliable. Sometimes hitters sneak a peak at the catcher, fans, or the base coach's signal to find out where the catcher set up.

To combat this, a catcher might intentionally move his glove at the last moment. More often, the pitcher misses, and the catcher has to move his glove to catch a ball that slipped away. So, by just looking at where the catcher holds his glove before and after the pitch, you can usually figure out where the pitcher wanted to throw the ball, and where it ended up.

But catchers tell you something else: whether the pitcher missed. If the catcher moves his glove at the last second, it's a pretty good sign that the pitcher didn't throw the ball where he wanted it. And if the catcher loses the ball, it's clear that the pitcher didn't throw the ball where he intended to.

Step 3: Look at pitch speeds to determine pitch type. It's difficult to distinguish pitches on TV. A changeup is just a little slower than a fastball, for example. A curveball looks a little slower and follows a curved path, but it can look a lot like a slider. Good pitchers alternate between pitches by changing grips, and they use the same arm motion on each one. Most major league pitchers throw at least three different pitches. (It's hard to confuse batters if you don't throw a lot of different pitches.)

So, here's the third tip: if radar guns are reading for pitch speeds, they can tell you what type of pitch was thrown. Not all pitchers throw pitches at three different speeds, but the ones who do help you out a lot. Here are a few rules of thumb:

The fastest pitch (usually 90+ mph)
    This is usually a fastball.
The middle pitch (usually in the 80s)
    This is usually a slider or a changeup.
The slowest pitch (usually in the 70s)
    This is usually a curveball (knuckleballs are also in this category, but they are less common).

Step 4: Watch what the ball does at the plate. You'll notice that this is the first time I told you to watch the ball. Don't watch the ball as it leaves the pitcher's hand. Just look at it at the end. This can help you distinguish subtle differences between pitch types (say, two-seam versus four-seam fastballs). And don't start looking at how the ball moves until you've trained yourself to watch the catcher set up.

Also, you should watch how the ball moves as it reaches the plate. A pitch that ends up in the dirt at the end is probably a splitter or a slider. A pitch that dives in a graceful arc is a curveball. A pitch that moves in toward the hitter, or away from the hitter, is probably a cut fastball or a two-seam fastball. Oh yeah, and a pitch that moves around and makes the hitter look dumb is probably a knuckleball. (There really are only a couple of active knuckleball pitchers, and the announcers will talk on and on about them.)

Step 5: Watch the pitcher react to the catcher's signals. Normally, the catcher decides what pitch to throw to whom. A catcher probably has the hardest position in the game. First, the catcher needs to squat throughout the whole game to catch the ball. Second, the catcher needs to know every batter and select the right pitches to get him out. Finally, the catcher needs to block the plate from a runner, often resulting in an ugly collision.

You can tell a little about the relationship between the pitcher and catcher by watching the pitcher's reactions. TV cameras love this stuff. They focus on the pitcher's head, as he slightly nods yes or shakes no. Sometimes this is done just so the catcher knows that the pitcher got the signal. Other times, the pitcher is *shaking off* the catcher's signs, saying, "I don't agree with that pitch, I want to throw something else." And, of course, sometimes all of this is a decoy designed to throw off the other team.

There are a lot of reasons why a pitcher might shake off a batter. Sometimes the pitcher remembers something about the batter that the catcher doesn't remember, and he thinks he can get an out with a different pitch from what the catcher requested. Other times, the pitcher might know something the catcher doesn't know—for instance, that he can't throw his sliders in the strike zone that day. Whatever the reasons, you can learn a lot about what the players are thinking by watching the pitcher's reactions to the signals.

Step 6: Watch the catcher's signals. If no men are on base, most catchers will resort to a few simple signs:

One finger
Fastball
Two fingers
Curveball
Three fingers
Changeup or other breaking ball

From Little League games to World Series games, catchers usually use the same basic signs. You can catch these signs on TV if the camera is behind the pitcher, showing both the batter and catcher. It's tough to catch these signs at the game. (With a pair of binoculars and a seat in the bleachers, you might be able to catch the signals. Sometimes, on a sunny day, you might be able to pick up the signs by the shadows on home plate.) If men are on base, catchers usually switch to more complex systems because base runners can also read the catcher's signals and communicate them to the batter.

Follow the Game Online

#5

Find some cool statistics and charts about baseball players on the Internet.

If you have a quick question about baseball (such as, "What was Reggie Jackson's batting average in 1977?"), some great web sites out there can help you. Even if you have the data in other places (I have more than 2 GB worth of baseball databases on my computer and a dozen phonebook-size statistics books), you might still want to look up player statistics on the Web.

Player Statistics

There are many good web sites for finding statistics on current players. Here are a few of my favorites:

Major League Baseball
>The best place to start is MLB.com (*http://www.mlb.com*), the official web site of Major League Baseball. Here you'll find the "official" statistics (as tabulated by the Elias Sports Bureau) for all current and past players. MLB.com lets you look at *spray charts* (diagrams showing where every ball was hit by a player) for all major league players. If you're curious why the defensive players shift positions for certain players, this can help answer your question.

ESPN
>Like most web sites, ESPN.com (*http://www.espn.com*) has current statistics on every baseball player. But ESPN adds a unique twist: it includes a number of sabermetric stats, including park factors and DIPS. (I explain a lot of these statistics in Chapter 5.) If you subscribe to the web site, you'll get access to more content, including commentary from scouting agencies and a print subscription to *ESPN The Magazine*.

Baseball Reference
>The Baseball Reference web site (*http://www.baseballreference.com*) is one of my favorite sources for information. This web site is based on the data from the Baseball DataBank (see "Get a MySQL Database of Player and Team Statistics" [Hack #10]), so you will find that its statistics are consistent with the stats in this book. This site includes all the basic, familiar statistics, plus some sabermetric stats like ERA+, OPS+, RF, and similarity scores. I like the straightforward user interface and the simple, text-format results. (According to this site, Reggie's AVG was .286 in 1977, in case you were wondering.)

Retrosheet
The best source for information on baseball games is *http://www. retrosheet.org.* You'll find some statistics on players, but the best stuff here is the box scores going back 100 years, and play-by-play information going back almost 50 years.

Independent Commentary (Including Blogs)

It seems a little silly to list a set of blogs in a book, but many of these sites have been around for years and are very well produced. The best have evolved into subscription services, and they offer some pretty good content for the money.

Baseball Prospectus
This is the most entertaining source for forecasts and commentary on baseball, with good resources for the fantasy player. The web site, *http:// www.baseballprospectus.com,* has many good articles and statistics available free of charge and a lot more good stuff for subscribers.

Baseball Graphs
One of my favorite independent web sites is *http://www.baseballgraphs. com.* This site presents groups of statistics graphically, looking at statistics in ways that you've never seen them before.

Baseball Musings
Check out *http://www.baseballmusings.com,* the blog from David Pinto, the former lead researcher for ESPN's *Baseball Tonight.* This is a great source of commentary from a really knowledgeable fan. In particular, look at the "Defensive Charts, Probabilistic" analysis.

Thorn's Blog
John Thorn wrote or edited some of the best books ever written about baseball, and he has a terrific blog at *http://thornpricks.blogspot.com.*

Most Valuable Network
There is a great set of blogs at *http://mostvaluablenetwork.com,* including a few devoted to specific teams.

Baseball Think Factory
You can find a really good web site for discussing baseball statistics at *http://www.baseballthinkfactory.org.*

Tango on Baseball
Check out *http://www.tangotiger.net,* a site that provides a great collection of essays and analysis.

Hacking the Hack

Tons of great baseball sites and analyses are available, and here are a few ways to discover new places for insights. A lot of fans frequently read and post to Usenet newsgroups like *rec.sport.baseball* and present their own analysis. You should check out *http://groups.google.com* if you want to find some of this stuff. Posters will often mention interesting places to explore.

A number of mailing lists for baseball fans also are available. The most active mailing list is probably SABR-L, which is open to SABR members. You will also find several newsgroups on Yahoo! Groups. These newsgroups and mailing lists are an interesting source for information in itself, but readers often explain where they find data for analysis. Try following their tips for both this and later chapters.

Another neat trick is to search for sites that link to ones you know you like, by using the link: command in Google. For example, to search for sites that link to Retrosheet, search for *link: http://www.retrosheet.org.*

HACK #6 Add Baseball Searches to Firefox

Add a few baseball web sites to the default list of search engines and search instantly for information on baseball players.

Do you use Firefox? Do you like to look up information about baseball players? Start searching the easy way by adding a few baseball web sites to the Firefox search dialog box. As shown in Figure 1-13, you can pick different search engines to use in the dialog box. Even cooler, you can add other search engines to the list. This hack shows you how to add some baseball-specific search engines to the search bar.

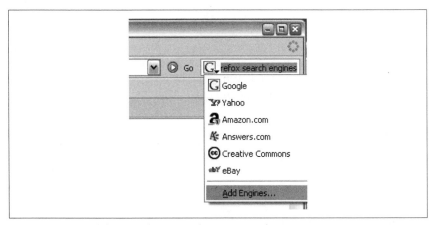

Figure 1-13. Search bar search engine selection in Firefox

Adding Search Engines to Firefox

You can find a list of search engine plug-ins at *http://mycroft.mozdev.org*. This web site lets you search for different search engine plug-ins. Searching for "baseball" in the "Find search plugins" section of the site produces results like the ones shown in Figure 1-14. If you click on one of the links shown, a dialog box will appear asking whether you want to add that particular search engine to the search bar. If you click OK, the search engine will be added to the list in Firefox.

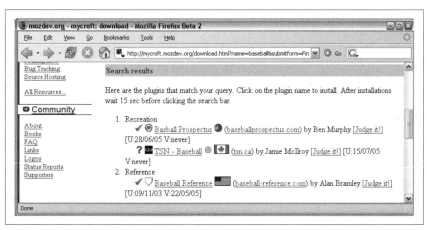

Figure 1-14. Baseball search engines

After adding the search engines you want, they will appear in the choices in the search bar, as shown in Figure 1-15.

Running the Hack

Now, you can quickly look up information about baseball players. For example, suppose you want statistics on a player named Rodriguez. Type Rodriguez into the search bar, pick a search engine (such as Baseball Prospectus), and press the Enter key to search. Firefox will quickly load the search results, like the ones shown in Figure 1-16.

Hacking the Hack

If you want to do even more, look at the tools available from Baseball Prospectus, at *http://www.baseballprospectus.com/plugins*. In addition to the search engines, you can add support for *contextual queries*. Contextual queries let you select a word on a web page, right-click, select "lookup player," and jump to a web page of statistics on that player.

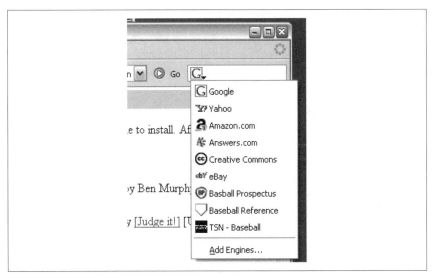

Figure 1-15. Search bar selections after adding baseball search engines

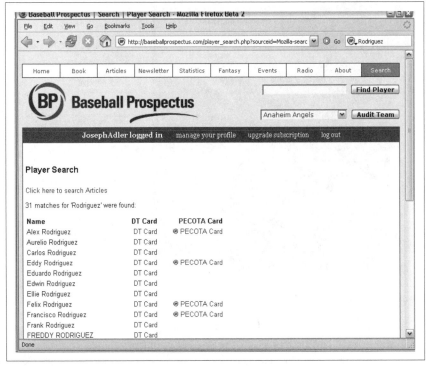

Figure 1-16. Searching for "Rodriguez" at Baseball Prospectus

Find Images of Stadiums

#7 Unlike most other sports, baseball fields are not uniform. Old parks like Fenway Park, Wrigley Field, and Yankee Stadium have short outfield walls and kinky corners where balls get lost. Here's an easy way to get an aerial view.

The easiest way to look at stadiums is through Google Maps (*http://maps. google.com*). To find a stadium, search by the name of the ballpark inside the city. For example, search for "SBC Park, San Francisco, CA" to find the ballpark where the San Francisco Giants play. Click the Satellite button in the top corner of the map and zoom in to take a closer look at the ballpark. Figure 1-17 shows the results.

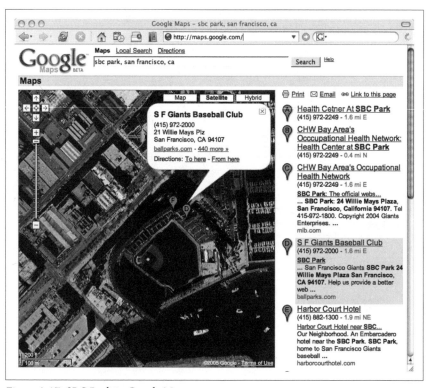

Figure 1-17. SBC Park in Google Maps

Google Maps will try to find the address and will return a list of possibilities. Sometimes the first link will be correct, but sometimes you'll have to check other items on the list. (For example, "Petco Park, San Diego, CA" doesn't return the right result at the top.)

Better Pictures and Distances with Google Earth

Google has released a cool new service called Google Earth that extends the
aerial views of Google Maps with better images and lots of additional features. You can download a free version from *http://earth.google.com*. My
favorite trick with Google Earth is to measure distances inside ballparks.
Curious how far a home run ball was hit? Check it out with Google Earth.

For example, at SBC Park in San Francisco, Barry Bonds often hit balls out
of the ballpark into McCovey Cove. How far did he actually have to hit the
balls for them to reach the water? Figure 1-18 illustrates how to calculate
this using Google Earth.

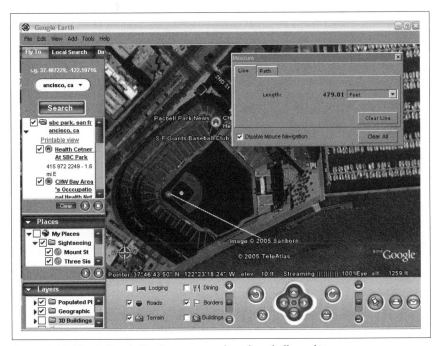

Figure 1-18. Using Google Earth to measure how far a ball was hit

Here's how to find out:

1. Search for the ballpark by typing sbc park, san francisco, ca into the
   search box and clicking the Search button.

2. On the results list, click SF Giants Baseball Club to zoom to this location.

3. Using the zoom controls under the image (the slider with the + and –
   buttons), zoom into the stadium until it fills the screen.

4. If you have 3D Buildings enabled, you'll probably want to turn them off. This feature is cool, but it will get in your way. Under the Layers list (in the bottom-left corner), make sure 3D Buildings is not selected.

5. Select Measure from the Tools menu. A window will pop up. Select "feet" as the measurement.

6. Click on home plate and drag a line out to the water. You'll see that the "measure" palette will record the distance as you move the line, allowing you to estimate distances. As shown in Figure 1-18, any fly ball hit more than 475 feet to right field will probably end up in McCovey Cove.

## CHAPTER TWO

Baseball Games from Past Years
Hacks 8–23

This chapter explains where to get information about baseball games and baseball players and tells you how to store this information for easy lookup. These hacks explain how to find or make box scores, player statistics, and even play-by-play data. You can get data about games from 1871 through last season. Several different groups of baseball fans have worked hard to compile and digitize this information, making it easy for any baseball fan to look up scores and stats, plan their fantasy team, or research baseball.

We use three primary types of data in this book. Here's a short explanation of each one, and how they all fit together:

Play-by-play
    The most detailed data we have is "play-by-play" or "event" data. The event files include information about every play in a game: every at bat, every stolen base, and sometimes every pitch.

Game logs
    Game logs include a summary of each game: playing conditions, scores, and starting players.

Player and team statistics
    Player statistics include statistics for each player on each team in each season. These files include offensive statistics like hits, home runs, and stolen bases; pitching statistics like batters faced, strikeouts, and earned runs; and fielding statistics like putouts, assists, and errors. Team statistics summarize this information for each team.

When you have detailed play-by-play descriptions for each game, you can derive game logs from those descriptions. (See "Make Box Scores or Database Tables from Play-by-Play Data with Retrosheet Tools" [Hack #15] for information on a tool that does this.)

Similarly, you can derive player and team statistics from play-by-play data. "Make a Box Score from a Score Sheet" [Hack #2] explains how to calculate player statistics for each game. Over the course of a season, you can just add up a player's hits, at bats, home runs, and other statistics to find his player statistics for a season.

If you want to research how teams fare in close games, compare ballparks, or study starting lineups, you will find game logs most convenient. If you want to compare individual players over seasons or careers, player and team statistics will be your best choice. If you want to research baseball strategy or look at how players fare in specific situations, play-by-play data is your best bet.

H A C K   Get and Install MySQL
#8   Get the free MySQL database and install it on your PC.

I hate to start this chapter with a hack about a piece of software instead of a hack about baseball statistics, but most of the hacks in this chapter require a database. This hack shows you how to install MySQL, a free database. If you already have a database (like Microsoft Access), you can skip ahead to the next hack.

A database organizes information into tables. Each table is organized into a set of columns that describe different attributes of the data, and a set of rows (called *records*) that contain different items of data. For example, a database of batting statistics might have columns representing player names, at bats, and hits, and rows representing players. Every value in a column is of the same type and can be referred to by the name of the column. In many respects, a table is similar to data in a spreadsheet.

In this book, we manipulate data with several pieces of software—Microsoft Excel, Perl, and R. You're probably wondering why I'm suggesting yet another way to manipulate data. Why do you need a database if you already have a spreadsheet? A database has several important advantages over a spreadsheet:

Strong types
    In a spreadsheet, you can enter any value anywhere at any time. (Or, you can use difficult procedures to restrict the contents of cells.) This can be convenient, but it can also lead to mistakes. In a database, you precisely define what is allowed in every column. Computer science types call this *strong typing*. The advantage of this approach is that it allows you to check for garbage data automatically. For example, if you're expecting a column of batting averages (a number) and, for some

reason, a player's name slips in because of a data entry error, the database can automatically warn you of the problem.

Transactions

In a spreadsheet, it is easy to accidentally delete or add data. (In the past, I've spent weeks searching for an incorrectly entered value.) In a database, values are added or deleted through insert, update, or delete queries. Moreover, all queries can be logged, providing a record of what changed. The main advantage of this is that if you accidentally change or delete some information, you can recover it automatically by rolling back to the previous values.

Queries

With a spreadsheet, it can be awkward to select a subset of rows or columns for analysis, particularly if you want to summarize the data by specific categories. This is the area in which a database truly shines. Using a straightforward language called SQL, you can select whatever part of the data you need and summarize it however you want, all while leaving the original data intact. For example, you can very easily pull out all AL batters with a batting average greater than .340 that struck out on a Thursday.

Joins

This is what truly sets a database apart from a spreadsheet: you can easily combine data from different tables to create new ways to look at the game. For example, if you have a table of astronomical data, you can easily combine this information with your other data to discover all teams that won the World Series during a full lunar eclipse.

Relationships

In a database, you can define the relationship between items in different tables. For example, you might have a baseball database that has two tables: a list of players and a list of batting averages. You might want to restrict entries in the batting average table so that every batter found in the batting average table can also be found in the player table. There is a lot more logic behind referential integrity constraints, but because the databases that we use in this book don't take advantage of this feature, I won't go into more depth.

Table sizes

If I still haven't convinced you that you sometimes need a database, there's another reason. In Excel, you're limited to 256 columns and 65,535 rows in a worksheet. Databases let you build much bigger tables. There have been more than 85,000 batter-seasons in major league history, and there are more than 100,000 plays every year. Spreadsheets aren't big enough to capture this much information.

Performance

Most spreadsheet programs, such as Microsoft Excel, hold spreadsheets in memory. These files can get very large, and, if you work with big files, you might find that your computer gets very slow.

This hack will show you how to download and install a very popular, robust, and easy-to-use database called MySQL. Once you've got the system installed, you can download and import data from the Internet (such as a file of statistics on every player and team in MLB history) and calculate statistics using this database.

> I used the release version of MySQL 4.1 and a beta version of MySQL 5.0 while writing this book. I recommend that you install a version of MySQL later than 4.1, but most SQL code in this book will work with other versions.

Installation on Windows

The following process will help you install the MySQL database server and configure a MySQL database. While the Installation wizard will present you with a number of options, I strongly recommend that you accept all the default values unless you know what you are doing. (Following the recommended options will install a working database, but you can accidentally break the database by incorrectly setting advanced options.) These options are Windows specific, but installers on other platforms are very similar.

> I have not tested the MySQL installer on all platforms, and I can't vouch for it. However, I have installed MySQL 4.1 and 5.0 from the packages for both Microsoft Windows XP and Mac OS X. If you stick with the standard installation options, the program should install cleanly with no problems. See the MySQL web site (*http://www.mysql.com*) for more information.

Step 0: Buy and install a software or hardware firewall. In my full-time job, I work on computer security (I write about baseball as a hobby). If you're like me, you probably access the Internet through a broadband connection (DSL, cable modem, T1, or something else) and keep your computer connected to the Internet at all times. If you connect your computer to the Internet without protection, your computer is very likely to become infected by viruses or worms, or be taken over by bot software. The risks become higher if you install server software like MySQL on your computer.

Luckily, it's easy to protect your computer: use a firewall. If you are running Mac OS X, Windows XP, or most Linux distributions, you already have a firewall. See the instruction manuals and help files with these systems to learn how to enable and properly configure the firewall. If you are running an older operating system, you might want to buy commercial firewall software. Companies like Zone Labs and Symantec offer good firewall software. Alternately, you can buy a cable/DSL router or a wireless router and enable network address translation (NAT) on the router. This simple precaution, which you should take even if you do not install MySQL, can significantly increase your computer's security.

Step 1: Download and unpack the installer. You can simply use the files we included, or you can get the latest version of MySQL from *http://dev.mysql.com/downloads/mysql/5.0.html*. You'll find versions for most popular operating systems; pick the appropriate version for your system. For Microsoft Windows users, I recommend getting the full version, called Windows (x86). The MySQL.com site directs you to several "mirror" sites from which you can download the file. Pick one close to you and download the file to your local hard drive.

This download is 36 MB. If you download this from a DSL line or cable modem, this should not be a problem, but if you are using a dial-up line, you might want to buy a copy on CD. You can get a copy of MySQL along, with an O'Reilly manual, from *http://order.mysql.com*.

Now, open the downloaded zip file. (Windows XP includes a program called Compressed Folders that can open this file. Alternately, you can use WinZip or PKUnzip to unpack the file.) Decompress the installer program in the archive, saving it to a location that you will remember.

Step 2: Run the Installation wizard. MySQL's Installation wizard makes the package a snap to install. To start the installer, double-click the installation file in the directory in which you unpacked the file. Once the wizard starts, click the Next button.

On the next panel, select Typical as the setup type and then click Next. On the third panel, click the Install button. The MySQL wizard will display the status while it installs the database to your computer. After it is finished, it will give you the option to sign up for a MySQL.com account. If you do not want to sign up, select Skip Sign-Up and proceed to the next page by clicking Next.

You should see a message telling you that the wizard has completed. Select "Configure the MySQL Server Now" box, and click the Finish button.

Step 3: Run the Configuration wizard. Now that MySQL is installed, the next step is to configure it. When the MySQL Server Instance Configuration wizard starts, you should select Standard Configuration unless you're comfortable working with databases.

On the next screen, if you are running Windows 2000 or Windows XP, you will be asked whether you want to Install As Windows Service. Select this option (it should be the default) and click Next.

Now, you need to configure a *root* account for your database. This account is used for database administration and is one of the most important screens in the entire installation. Select Modify Security Settings and pick a password for your database. For added security, do not check the "Enable root access from remote machines" box. Click the Next button. Finally, click Execute to finish the installation process.

XAMPP

Recently, a lot of people have written about the *LAMP stack*: Linux, Apache, MySQL, and Perl. With this package of free software, you can do everything you can do with commercial software packages from vendors like Microsoft, Oracle, and Sun.

A new project, XAMPP, packs the "AMP" part of the LAMP tools into a single, installable package for Linux, Windows, Mac OS, and Solaris. This package comprises a suite of tools including Apache, MySQL, PHP + PEAR, Perl, OpenSSL, and others. Many readers might find it easier to get and install this single package rather than all the individual components. See *http://www.apachefriends.org/en/xampp.html* for information on this project.

Testing the Installation

If you did not install MySQL as a service (or you are running an older version of Windows), you might need to start MySQL manually. You can check if MySQL is running through the `mysqladmin` command. Type `mysqladmin -u root -p status` at a command prompt to check the database status. If MySQL is running, you will see a message like this:

```
C:\Program Files\MySQL\MySQL Server 4.1\bin>mysqladmin -u root -p status
Enter password: ******
Uptime: 181682  Threads: 1  Questions: 1  Slow queries: 0  Opens: 11  Flush
tables: 1  Open tables: 0  Queries per second avg: 0.000
```

If you get an error indicating that the MySQL process is not running, you might need to start the database manually. To do this, open a command-line window and type mysqld to start the database server.

You can test the window from a command-line window. To open a command-line window, select Start → Run... and type cmd.exe. At the prompt, type cd "C:\Program Files\MySQL\MySQL Server 4.1\bin", as shown here:

```
Microsoft Windows XP [Version 5.1.2600]
(C) Copyright 1985-2001 Microsoft Corp.

C:> cd "C:\Program Files\MySQL\MySQL Server 4.1\bin"
```

Next, type mysql.exe –u root –p to start the MySQL query program. Use the password that you entered in the configuration process. If you see a mysql> prompt, the installation was successful and you can connect to the database. For now, quit this program by typing quit:

```
C:\Program Files\MySQL\MySQL Server 4.1\bin>
C:\Program Files\MySQL\MySQL Server 4.1\bin>mysql.exe -u root -p
Enter password: ******
Welcome to the MySQL monitor.  Commands end with ; or \g.
Your MySQL connection id is 4 to server version: 5.0.3-beta-nt

Type 'help;' or '\h' for help. Type '\c' to clear the buffer.

mysql> quit
Bye
```

Once you've successfully installed and tested the database, you're ready to import data, and slice and dice it however you want.

Hacking the Hack

Are you already familiar with databases? Here are a few suggestions on some other things you can try:

Change configuration options
> We stuck with a default installation, but you can optimize MySQL for different numbers of users, different patterns of usage (ad hoc queries versus transactions), or in other ways. If you know what you're doing, try changing the options.

Try a different open source database
> In this book, I use MySQL 4.1 and 5.0 for all my examples because they are popular, easy to install, and easy to use. Unfortunately, they're also missing a lot of features found in professional-strength databases (like query rewrite and optimization). If you're an advanced database user (for example, if you use Oracle at work), you might want to try PostgreSQL (see *http://www.postgresql.org*) or MySQL MaxDB (see *http://www.mysql.com/products/maxdb*).

See Also

If you're new to databases, you might not realize that many tools are available to help you configure, manage, and work with them. I introduce a few of my favorite tools in "Get a GUI for MySQL" [Hack #18].

HACK #9 Get an Access Database of Player and Team Statistics

Get a free database of historical baseball data from the Internet (covering every major league game from 1871 through today) in Microsoft Access format.

Suppose you want to know the average ERA for your fantasy league. Or maybe you want to settle a bet with a friend about which players got on base most often during the 1970s. Or perhaps you want to show that Jim Thome was a clutch hitter for the Phillies in 2004. To do this, you'll need to find some statistics.

Sometimes you can find the statistics you want from MLB.com, the Baseball Reference, or the Baseball Prospectus (see "Follow the Game Online" [Hack #5] for some suggestions), but other times you won't find exactly what you want. You might be able to find this information online by spending hours tediously searching for the raw data, cutting and pasting the data into a spreadsheet, and producing the stats you want in the form you want.

I think that it's often easier to find the stats you want if you have your own database. This hack shows you the easiest way I know to get a database of baseball players. These databases include the total statistics, by year, for each baseball player. Later in this book, I'll show how to find records by game and play-by-play information. I'll also show how to get data in two common database formats: Microsoft Access and MySQL, the popular (and free!) open source database.

The information in these databases is identical, so you can pick whichever format is easiest for you. (When I wrote this book, I used a MySQL database containing the Baseball DataBank information. If you want to follow along with all the hacks in this book, you'll probably find it easiest to use the MySQL version. However, I do include some tips for using Microsoft Access. The idea of this book is to do things the easy way: if Microsoft Access is the easiest tool for you, go ahead and use it.)

A Player and Team Statistics Database for Microsoft Access

If you are using Microsoft Windows and have Microsoft Access, you will probably find this the easiest place to start. You can download the file from the Baseball Archive web site at *http://www.baseball1.com*. (Notice the number 1 at the end of the word *baseball* in the URL.)

Step 1: Download the file. The Baseball Archive web site (*http://www.baseball1. com*) distributes a ready-to-use database in Microsoft Access format. You are free to use this database for noncommercial use, but the authors request a donation. (Again, notice the 1 in the domain name. If that doesn't work, just type the words "baseball archive" in Google and click the I'm Feeling Lucky button. I can't promise it will work by the time this book is published, but it gives me the right result now.)

Sean Lahman originally developed, and still maintains, this database. This is worth mentioning, because the database files have names like *lahman51.mdb* and because people sometimes refer to this as "the Lahman database."

You can download the current version of the database from *http://baseball1. com/statistics*. You should download the version for Access 2000 (if you are using Microsoft Access 2000 or later); otherwise, download the version for Access 97.

Step 2: Decompress and save the file. The file is distributed as a single zipped file. You need to decompress this file and copy the contents to a local drive to use the database. On a Windows machine, you can use whatever utility you like (as of Windows XP, a zipped folders application is included). I decompressed this to my desktop.

Step 3: Open the database file. You can now open the database file. Double-click the icon (for Version 5.1, it is called *lahman51.mdb*). You will see a screen like the one shown in Figure 2-1.

Step 4: Test the database. As a quick test, try opening the 500 HR Club query. You should see a table showing all players with 500 or more home runs over the course of their careers. If so, everything is fine and you're ready to start.

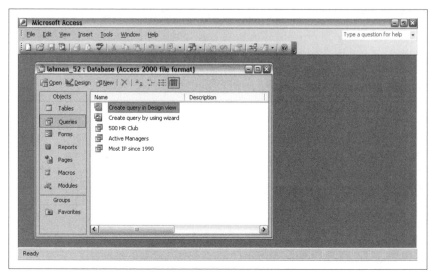

Figure 2-1. Lahman database

The Contents of the Database

Version 5.2 of the Baseball Archive database currently contains 21 tables and includes statistics through the 2004 season. Here is a short description of these tables:

Master

This table contains biographical information about each player, including their full name, birth date, country of origin, and batting and throwing hands. Each player has a unique ID (called playerID) that is referenced from other tables in the database.

Batting

This table contains batting statistics for each player, on each team, during each season. Rows are uniquely identified by playerID, teamID, yearID, and stint.

Fielding

This table contains fielding statistics for each player, on each team, during each season. Rows are uniquely identified by playerID, teamID, yearID, and stint.

FieldingOF

This table tells you how much time outfielders spent in each fielding position. Rows are uniquely identified by playerID, yearID, and stint.

Pitching

This table contains pitching statistics for each player, on each team, during each season. Rows are uniquely identified by playerID, teamID, yearID, and stint.

Teams

This table contains information on each team for each season, including aggregate batting statistics, pitching statistics, the team record, and postseason performance. Each line is uniquely referenced by yearID and teamID.

TeamsHalf

This table shows win-loss records for each team, midway through each season.

TeamsFranchises

This table includes the full name of each team, indexed by the franchID field.

Allstar, AwardsVotes, AwardsWinners, AwardsShareManager, AwardsSharePlayers, Managers, ManagersHalf, Salaries, Transactions, HallOfFame, BattingPost, PitchingPost, *and* FieldingPost

These tables contain what you would expect; I don't use any of these in this book, so I'm not going to describe them in depth.

HACK #10 Get a MySQL Database of Player and Team Statistics

Get a free database of historical baseball data from the Internet (covering every major league game from 1871 through today) in MySQL format.

If you don't have Microsoft Access (and you don't want to buy it), or if you are a more experienced database user, you might prefer to use MySQL. The web site *http://www.baseball-databank.org* offers the same database that the Baseball Archive web site offers, but as a MySQL dump file.

Even if you have Microsoft Access, I recommend that you try MySQL, because it's faster, more standards compliant, more flexible, and relatively painless once it's up and running. It's also easier to use with other software, which is important for many hacks in this book. For instructions on getting MySQL, see "Get and Install MySQL" [Hack #8]. For suggestions on how to make it easier to work with MySQL, see "Get a GUI for MySQL" [Hack #18]. Finally, see "Use SQL to Explore Game Data" [Hack #16] for more information about the SQL language.

After you have MySQL installed, here's how to get the files and load them into your database.

Step 1: Download the File

You can get the file you need from *http://www.Baseball-DataBank.org*. From the web site, just download the file labeled "Database in MySQL form" and save it to your local disk. (You can download the 2004 database file from *http://www.baseball-databank.org/files/BDB-sql-2005-08-02.sql.zip*. Or, you can check for a more current version and use it instead. Just be sure to change the filename in the instructions I'm outlining here.) This database is produced by a volunteer effort led by Sean Forman and Peter Kreutzer.

If you are using Mac OS X, Linux, or another system with standard Unix commands installed, download the file using the following command:

```
% curl http://www.baseball-databank.org/files/BDB-sql-2005-08-02.sql.zip\
> BDB-sql-2005-08-02.sql.zip
  % Total    % Received % Xferd  Average Speed   Time     Time     Time
Current
                               Dload  Upload   Total    Spent    Left
Speed
100 6495k  100 6495k    0      0   587k      0  0:00:11  0:00:11 --:--:--
623k
```

Step 2: Decompress the File

The file is distributed as a single zipped file. You need to decompress this file to use it, just like the Access version described earlier. On Windows, you can double-click the file and your compression program should allow you to open the archive and extract the files. On Mac OS X, I decompressed this to the folder using this command:

```
~ % unzip BDB-sql-2005-08-02.sql.zip
```

Step 3: Create the Database

You need to create a database in MySQL before you can import the files. You can do this in two steps. First, give yourself permission to access the database. Then run the command to create the database. Here are the commands I used to create this database and the responses from MySQL:

```
1  ~ % mysql -p -u root
2  Enter password:
3  Welcome to the MySQL monitor.  Commands end with ; or \g.
4  Your MySQL connection id is 22 to server version: 4.0.21-standard
5
6  Type 'help;' or '\h' for help. Type '\c' to clear the buffer.
7
8  mysql> GRANT ALL ON bbdatabank.* TO 'jadler'@'localhost' IDENTIFIED BY
   'P@ssw0rd';
9  Query OK, 0 rows affected (0.07 sec)
10
```

```
11  mysql> CREATE DATABASE bbdatabank;
12  Query OK, 1 row affected (0.00 sec)
13
14  mysql> quit
15  Bye
```

In line 8, notice that I created a database called *bbdatabank* and granted access to a user named jadler with the password P@ssw0rd. That's my username and an example password. You should change this to your username and pick a password that you like.

You're welcome to change the name of the database, but you will find that most hacks in this book refer to this database as *bbdatabank*. If you pick another name, make sure you modify my examples to reflect the name of your database.

You can also create a database using a GUI-driven tool like MySQL Administrator. See "Get a GUI for MySQL" [Hack #18] for instructions on where to get such programs.

Step 4: Import the Database

The file I unzipped was called *BDB-sql-2005-08-02.sql*. You can import this in a single step using this command (you will need to use the same username and password you used in the previous step):

```
~ % mysql -u jadler -p -s bbdatabank < BDB-sql-2004-12-02.sql
Enter password:P@ssw0rd
```

The < sign means "read the filename to the right and send it to the program to the left."

The -s option stops MySQL from providing feedback. (Trust me. You don't want feedback. The script manually inserts thousands and thousands of lines. If you omit this, MySQL prints "Query OK, 1 row affected (0.00 sec)" to the screen after each record is inserted, which means that MySQL prints this message a few hundred thousand times.) This command will finish within a couple of minutes on a typical computer.

Step 5: Check That Everything Is There

Now, let's check that the database has loaded. Start the MySQL program and type show tables;. You should see something like this:

```
mysql> show tables;
+----------------------+
| Tables_in_bbdatabank2 |
+----------------------+
```

```
| Allstar            |
| AwardsVotes        |
| AwardsWinners      |
| Batting            |
| Fielding           |
| FieldingOF         |
| Managers           |
| ManagersHalf       |
| Master             |
| Pitching           |
| Salaries           |
| Teams              |
| TeamsFranchises    |
| TeamsHalf          |
| Transactions       |
+--------------------+
15 rows in set (0.01 sec)
```

If you want to check more carefully that everything is there, you can count the number of rows in each table. The Baseball DataBank web site includes information on the number of rows in each table. You can find this at *http://www.baseball-databank.org/files/tables.txt*. To check the number of rows in each table, you can use a SQL query to count the number of rows:

```
mysql> select count(*) from batting;
+----------+
| count(*) |
+----------+
|    85978 |
+----------+
1 row in set (0.03 sec)
```

The Contents of the Database

The current version of the Baseball DataBank database contains data through 2005; you can download it from *http://www.baseball-databank.org/files/BDB-sql-2005-12-30.sql.zip*. Currently, the Baseball DataBank database contains over 20 tables. The structure of this database is almost identical to the structure of the Baseball Archive database (see "Get an Access Database of Player and Team Statistics" **[Hack #9]** for more information).

While I was writing this book, the structure of the database changed twice. For this book, I used the August 2005 version, which used a slightly different database structure than the current version. (The August 2005 database was normalized to remove duplicate keys and better utilize the features of a relational database.) You can download a SQL script to convert the current Baseball DataBank database to the correct format, plus a copy of the database that works with the code in this book, at *http://www.oreilly.com/catalog/baseballhks*.

Here is a short description of the database structure used in this book:

Master
: This table contains biographical information about each player, including their full name, birth date, country of origin, and batting and throwing hands. Each player has a unique ID (called idxLahman) that is referenced from other tables in the database.

Batting
: This table contains batting statistics for each player, on each team, during each season. Rows are uniquely identified by idxBatting, or by idxLahman, idxTeams, and stint.

Fielding
: This table contains fielding statistics for each player, on each team, during each season. Rows are uniquely identified by idxFielding, or by idxLahman, idxTeams, and stint.

FieldingOF
: This table tells you how much time outfielders spent in each fielding position. It is referenced by idxFielding.

Pitching
: This table contains pitching statistics for each player, on each team, during each season. Rows are uniquely identified by idxPitching, or by idxLahman, idxTeams, and stint.

Teams
: This table contains information on each team for each season, including aggregate batting statistics, pitching statistics, the team record, and postseason performance. Each line is uniquely referenced by a field called idxTeams. (You need to join the batting, fielding, or pitching tables with the Teams table to determine the year.)

TeamsHalf
: This table shows win–loss records for each team, midway through each season.

TeamsFranchises
: This table includes the full name of each team, indexed by the idxTeamsFranchises field.

Allstar, AwardsVotes, AwardsWinners, Managers, ManagersHalf, Salaries, *and* Transactions
: These tables contain what you would expect; I don't use any of these in this book, so I'm not going to describe them in depth.

The Baseball Archive database contains a similar set of tables but with slightly different indexes. Here are the key differences in how the tables are indexed:

Master
   The unique key is called playerID.

Batting, Pitching, *and* Fielding
   Rows are uniquely identified by playerID, teamID, yearID, and stint.

Teams
   Rows are uniquely identified by teamID and yearID.

Hacking the Hack

Here are a few tweaks to help you get the most from the career databases.

Annual updates. These databases are updated annually with new statistics. These web sites might offer files containing incremental updates (new players and annual statistics). If not, just create a new database with the year name (for example, *bbdatabank2004*), download the entire new version, and import it into this new database. (Replace bbdatabank in the previous commands with bbdatabank2004.) This way, you'll be able to keep any work you did with the old tables.

Getting baseball statistics as text files. Finally, you can download baseball statistics as (comma-separated) text files. This is a good choice if you plan to use another database or a statistical analysis program such as R [Hack #34]. You can download the current version of the text files from *http://baseball1.com/ statistics*.

HACK #11 Make Your Own Stats Book

Produce your own book of baseball statistics using Microsoft Access reports.

Every year, publishers release a set of new phonebook-size directories of baseball statistics. You can find the exact same statistics in free sources like the Baseball DataBank and Baseball Archive databases. (You can't get any accompanying insight, though, which is why it can still be worth buying these books.)

I usually find electronic databases more convenient than printed copies, but sometimes paper is better. For example, if your fantasy baseball league does a live draft, you might find a prioritized list of players. This hack tells you how to use Microsoft Access to print a professional-looking statistics report.

A History of the Player and Team Databases

The Baseball Archive and Baseball DataBank databases have a long history. As you might imagine, it took a lot of work to assemble a database of player statistics going back to 1871. The story of the free databases begins with Pete Palmer. During the 1970s and 1980s, Pete compiled paper records for baseball games into a computer database and used this database to produce the statistics in the book *Total Baseball* (Total Sports). CMC Corporation of Portland, Oregon, released a CD-ROM containing all the statistics from the 1993 edition of *Total Baseball*.

According to Pete Palmer, Sean Lahman took the data from this CD and used it to build the files available at *http://www.baseball1.com*. Over time, Sean and other people have worked to keep this database up-to-date, and they have supplemented the original database with tables describing awards, all-stars, and other information. Somewhat amazingly, Lahman does not allow his database to be redistributed by others. (If you intend to share data with others, I recommend that you use the Baseball DataBank data instead because there are restrictions on redistributing Lahman's information.)

The same files are used at *http://www.baseballreference.com*, *http://www.espn.com*, and even *http://www.mlb.com*. It's a shame that Pete Palmer is not more widely acknowledged for his work. However, these databases are a great resource for baseball fans, and I'm glad this information is freely available.

To use this hack, you will need Microsoft Access. For the example here, we'll only print batting statistics. We'll limit this further to show only:

- Players who played in the last year
- Players with more than 50 at bats (no batting stats are available on AL pitchers!)
- Most frequently played position

To create the book, you'll first need to download and install the Microsoft Access database from the Baseball Reference [Hack #9].

Write the Queries

We're going to use several queries to create this report, starting with the simplest. We need a list of all batters who played in the year prior to the year in which we are interested. For example, if you want to create a stats book to use at the start of the 2004 season (as in this example), use the statistics from the 2003 season. You will need to change the years accordingly.

Step 1: Create "batters who played in 2004" query. To create a new query, go to the Insert menu and select the Query item. A dialog box will pop up asking you how you would like to create a query. Click Design View. Now, two windows should pop up: a dialog box on top called Show Table and a window in back that we'll get to in a minute. In the Show Table list, select Batting, click Add, and then click Close. You will now see a window that looks something like the one in Figure 2-2.

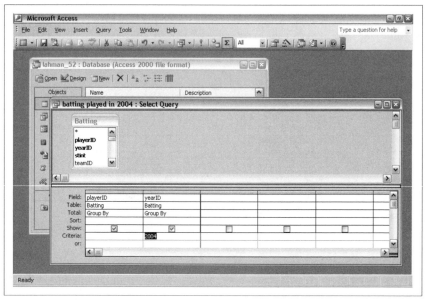

Figure 2-2. "batters who played in 2004" query

Complete the window as shown, with playerID in the first column, yearID in the second column, and the year "2004" in the Criteria row in the yearID column. You can select fields in several ways: from the Field list in the table at the bottom, by double-clicking the name in the little table in the top box, or by dragging and dropping the name from the top box.

When you're done selecting columns, save the query by clicking the disk icon in the toolbar or by selecting Save from the File menu. Name the query "batters who played in 2004" and close the query window. You can click the exclamation point (!) button or select Run from the Query menu if you are curious what this query returns.

Step 2: Create "fielding by games" query. Next, we need to figure out what position each player played most frequently each year. To do this, insert a new query into the database. This time, select the Fielding table and then select the playerID, yearID, stint, teamID, lgID, POS, and G fields. Under G (games) in the table, click in the Sort row and select Descending, as shown in Figure 2-3. Now, save this query as "fielding by games."

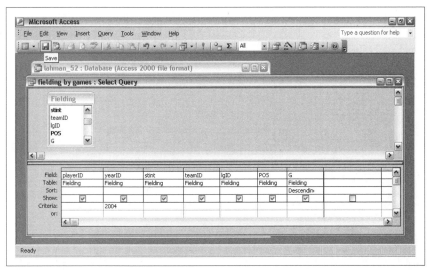

Figure 2-3. "fielding by games" query

Step 3: Create "fielding by most frequent position" query. Let's repeat the same process of inserting a new query. This time, we will select a *query* in the Add Table dialog box: "fielding by games." Now, we are going to do something a little different. We don't want every row in the Fielding by Games table, just the first row for each player/year/stint/team/league combination. We know the first row will have the position the player fielded most frequently, and that's what we want. So, we will use a summary query.

In the query design toolbar in Access, click the large sigma (Σ) button. A new row will appear in the query window, labeled Total. Add six fields: playerID, yearID, stint, teamID, lgID, and POS. For the first five columns, select Group By. For the POS field, select First. It should look something like Figure 2-4. Save the query as "fielding by most frequent position." If you're curious, go ahead and run the query to see what it does.

Step 4: Create "team names" query. This step creates a "helper" query that makes the next query a little less complicated.* Select the Teams table as the

---

* Specifically, it clears up a lot of ambiguity in offensive statistics. The Teams table has variables named AB, R, HR, etc., and so does the Batting table. We could have just been very specific every-where and written things like [Teams]![AB], but that would have been really painful to type. Trust me, the extra query here, trivial as it is, makes things nicer in the next step.

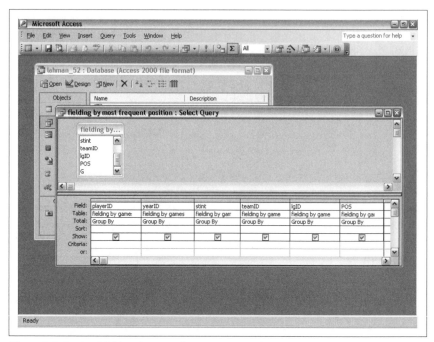

Figure 2-4. Saving "fielding by most frequent position" query

source, and pick the yearID, teamID, and lgID variables. In the fourth field column, type TeamName: name. This will just take the value of the name column, but the column in the query will be named TeamName. Save the query using the name "team names."

Step 5: Create "batting plus" query. We're almost done, but this last query is pretty complicated. It's long, but this is where all the work is done. Start by inserting another query. Next, add the following tables and queries:

- The Batting table
- The Master table
- The "batters who played in 2004" query
- The "fielding by most frequent position" query
- The "team names" query

We're going to want Access to *join*, or link, all of these tables by a common field that relates them to one another, so we need to tell Access how all of these tables are related. In the Master (or "From") table, click on "playerID" and drag-and-drop it to "playerID" in the Batting (or "To") table. You should see a line connecting the two fields. Follow the same procedure to join the other tables:

"From" table	Field	"To" table
Master	playerID	Batting
"fielding by most frequent position"	playerID	Batting
"fielding by most frequent position"	yearID	Batting
"fielding by most frequent position"	stint	Batting
"fielding by most frequent position"	teamID	Batting
"fielding by most frequent position"	lgID	Batting
"batters who played in 2004"	playerID	Batting
"team names"	yearID	Batting
"team names"	teamID	Batting
"team names"	lgID	Batting

Now that we've linked all the tables together, we need to specify the fields we'd like to include in the query's output. We're going to select each field that we want in the report and then add a few formulas for special fields that we also want to include. The next table shows the fields we want to add, including source tables; where there is a formula, you can just type the formula (as written!) into the Field box. (If it's tough to see the formula in the box, right-click on the box and select Zoom for a bigger view of the contents.)

Field	Table	Criteria
AB	Batting	> 50
Player name: [nameLast] & ", " & [NameFirst] & " (" & [birthMonth] & "/" & [birthDay] & "/" & [birthYear] & ")"	Master	
Team name	Team names	
yearID	Batting	
G	Batting	
R	Batting	
H	Batting	
2B	Batting	
3B	Batting	
HR	Batting	
RBI	Batting	
SB	Batting	
CS	Batting	
BB	Batting	
SO	Batting	
HBP	Batting	
SH	Batting	
SF	Batting	

Field	Table	Criteria
GIDP	Batting	
AVG: [R]/[AB]		
TB: [R]+[2B]+2*[3B]+3*[HR]		
SLG: [TB]/[AB]		
OBP: ([H]+[BB]+[HBP])/([AB]+[BB]+[HBP]+[SF])		
OPS: [SLG]+[OBP]		
Position: FirstOfPOS		

After you have linked together all the tables, the query will look like the one shown in Figure 2-5.

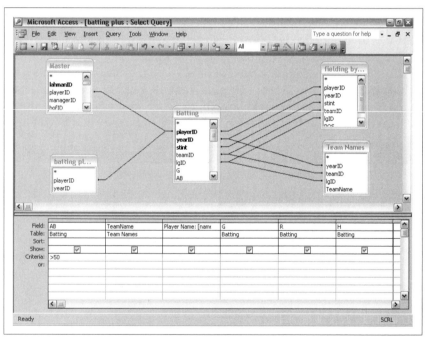

Figure 2-5. "batting plus" query

When you have this all set up, save the query as "batting plus." (By the way, this is one of the few places in the book where I explain how to calculate things in Microsoft Access. I hope you can see why; it's easy to use Access, but it's very difficult to describe how to set up a complex query in Access. Don't worry; the SQL code shown in other hacks will still work in Access. See "Use Microsoft Access to Run SQL Queries" [Hack #17] for instructions on how to run SQL queries in Access.)

Build the Report

This is the easy part because we can use a wizard. Go to the Database window and select Report from the Insert menu. A New Report dialog box will appear. Choose Report Wizard from the list and select Batting Plus as the source of the data. You will now see a dialog box labeled Report Wizard. We want all the fields, so just click the > > button to choose everything. When you're done, click Next.

The next panel will ask if you want to add any grouping levels. We want to group by team and player, so we will select Team Name first and Player Name second. If you mix up the order, you can use the Priority keys to change it. Click the Next button.

In the next panel, the wizard asks you what sort order and summary information you want for detail records. We want the results sorted by yearID, but nothing else. So select "yearID" in the box, and click the Ascending button to toggle this to Descending. Click Next when you're done.

The next screen gives you some formatting options. Whatever appeals to you is fine. (I like Outline 1.) Oh, but make sure you pick Landscape, or you won't see all the fields in the report.

For the style, pick whatever you want. I usually pick Compact because there is a lot of text on each page. Click Next when you're done. Now, give the report whatever name you want, select Preview the Report, and click Finish.

If you're lucky, you will have a nicely formatted document of baseball statistics, just like the giant books sold in stores. I found that I needed to edit the report slightly to make it readable. If you choose to edit the design, you will see a screen like the one shown in Figure 2-6.

To make the report readable, I changed two things. First, I selected all of the fields under Detail and changed the text size to 7 points. Then, I selected the average fields (AVG, OBP, SLG, and OPS) and changed the number format. To change a number format from the design view, right-click on the field and choose Properties. Under Format, choose Fixed; under Decimal Places, enter 3. Figure 2-7 illustrates the process. When you're done, save the query.

If all has gone well, running the report will produce a screen like the one shown in Figure 2-8.

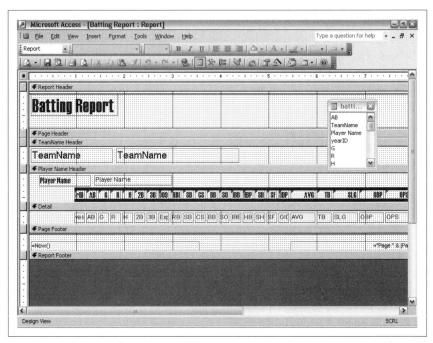

Figure 2-6. Edit report design

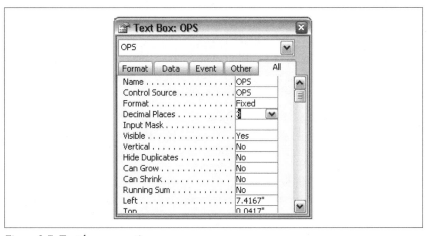

Figure 2-7. Text box properties

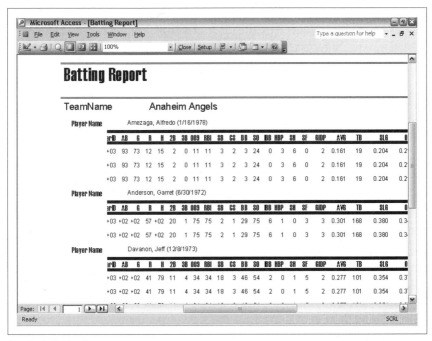

Figure 2-8. Final report

Hacking the Hack

That's it for the basics, but you can expand this in any way you like. Here are a few suggestions:

Pitching statistics
> Why not make a report of pitching statistics? Substitute a "Pitchers who pitched in 2004" table for the "Batters who played in 2004" table, drop the "fielding by most frequent position" table (pitchers are usually pitchers), and substitute the Pitching table for the Batting table. Change the statistics for more pitcher-friendly stats, and you're ready to go!

Add your own commentary
> You can add commentary to your report. Just create another table in your database with two fields: playerID and comments (as a text field), and join this to the Batting table. When you use the wizard, add another level to the report after Player Name. You may need to customize the format after you're done; see the help files in Access for more information on how to do that.

Add career stats
  Use a summary query to calculate career stats. Use a union query to
  merge this Summary table into the Batting table (changing yearID to a
  text field and calling it "career" for the career stats).

Get Perl

#12   Perl is a powerful tool for processing data. Here is how to get a free version
          for your PC.

Many hacks in this book require tedious, repetitive, and boring work: fetching files from the Internet, running programs to transform them, and saving
them to databases. I hate doing tedious work, so I get my computer to do it
for me. I usually use Perl for tasks like these, and I have chosen to use Perl in
many of the hacks provided in this book.

Perl is a very powerful scripting tool that we'll use to download files from
the Internet, parse files to extract information, and write output to a database. (You can use it for many other things, but we won't.)

If you want to run Perl scripts, this hack explains how to do that. If you're
interested in understanding how my scripts work and want to modify them
to do other things, see "Learn Perl" [Hack #13] for more information about the
Perl language.

Getting and Installing Perl

If you're using Linux or the Mac OS, you probably already have Perl
installed on your computer. (Just make sure you install all the modules we'll
need, which I'll describe shortly.) But if you use Windows, you'll need to
install Perl yourself. Since Perl is essential to running many of the hacks in
this book, here is how to get it and install it.

Installing Perl on Windows is fairly straightforward, and you can do it with
a minimum of fuss using ActiveState's ActivePerl, a free version of Perl for
Windows. The first step is to download the installation files from *http://
www.activestate.com/Products/ActivePerl*. Follow the download links and
download the installer program. (I recommend the MSI version because it
includes uninstall functionality.)

Once you've downloaded the file, you need to run the install program. The
first screen of the install program has no options; just click Next. The second one asks you to accept a license agreement to continue; if you don't
object to the agreement, click Next. The third screen presents custom setup
options. Just accept the defaults and click Next. The fourth screen asks if
you want to "Enable PPM3 to send profile info to ASPN." It's up to you

whether you want to select this option (I didn't select it); once you've made your choice, click Next. The next screen shows several options but doesn't allow you to check any, so just click Next to start the installation. Once the installation process completes, click the Finish button.

After you've installed the system, you need to add Perl to your default path to make it a little easier to run Perl. (You will need Administrator access for this step.) To do this, open the Control Panel on your computer, and then open the System control panel. Select the Advanced tab and click the Environment Variables button. Click on Path and select Edit. At the end of the string of stuff in the Variable Value box, add the following text: ;C:\Perl\ bin. Do not erase the stuff at the beginning! When you are done, click OK. You can now click OK to exit the Control Panel.

Finally, test that everything installed correctly. Open a command-line window (go to Run... under the Start menu), type cmd.exe, and click OK to run. Then type:

```
perl -e "print \"hello world!\n\";"
```

You should see something like this:

```
Microsoft Windows XP [Version 5.1.2600]
(C) Copyright 1985-2001 Microsoft Corp.

C:\>perl -e "print \"hello world!\n\";"
hello world!
```

If you see an error that says, "'perl' is not recognized as an internal or external command," double-check that you typed everything correctly when you set the path.

Install the Perl Modules Required in This Book

We are going to use several Perl modules in this book, so you might find it convenient to install all of them now. A Perl module is an extra feature that you can add to Perl. (Conceptually, it's a lot like a browser plug-in.) We're going to add modules to download web pages and extract tables from web pages. Luckily, the LWP package comes preinstalled with the ActivePerl distribution, but we still use the TableContentParser module. Here is how to install it.

To begin, go to the Start menu and open the Perl Package Manager under ActiveState ActivePerl 5.8. (On Windows XP, you might have to select this under the All Programs list.) This will open a new window with the PPM interface. At the prompt, type the following:

```
install HTML-TableContentParser
```

If you're using Linux, Mac OS, or Cygwin on a PC, you'll need to follow a different way to get the modules. The easiest way to do this is through the CPAN shell. To start this program, type:

```
perl -MCPAN -e "shell"
```

in a command-line window. You can then install each module by typing install <module name>. If this does not work for you, it's possible to install Perl modules manually from a command line. For instructions, see *http://www.cpan.org/modules/INSTALL.html*.

You should see output like this:

```
ppm> install HTML-TableContentParser
====================
Install 'HTML-TableContentParser' version 0.13 in ActivePerl 5.8.4.810.
====================
Downloaded 3016 bytes.
Extracting 5/5: blib/arch/auto/HTML/TableContentParser/.exists
Installing C:\Perl\html\site\lib\HTML\TableContentParser.html
Installing C:\Perl\site\lib\HTML\TableContentParser.pm
Successfully installed HTML-TableContentParser version 0.13 in ActivePerl 5.
8.4.810.
```

Once you've installed the table parser, repeat the process for the following modules:

- libwww-perl
- HTML-TableContentParser
- HTML-Parser
- XML::Simple

Hacking the Hack

Most readers of this book will find it easiest to use the ActivePerl version of Perl, but I often use a different version. I often use not only Perl but also many other computer languages and command-line tools. I like to use Unix-style commands, so I use a toolkit called Cygwin that includes a version of Perl. If you run a lot of scripts from the command line, or if you're a Unix person stuck using a Windows machine, you'll probably prefer this version. The version of Perl itself is not very different from the ActiveState version, but the Cygwin version of Perl works well with all the other Cygwin tools. Here is how to get it.

Step 1: Download the Cygwin installer. Open your browser and go to *http://www.cygwin.com*. Click the Install Cygwin Now link to download the

Cygwin Setup program. My browser does not let me run executables directly from web sites. If your browser is set like mine, download the file to where you can find it, like your desktop. If your browser lets you run the program directly from a web site, you can do that and skip step 3. (But man, think about updating your browser and changing your security settings! The Internet is not a safe place.)

Step 2: Run the Cygwin installer. If you are running Windows 2000 or Windows XP, you will probably need to have Administrator access to install this software. Find the Cygwin setup program (called *setup.exe* unless you renamed it; it has a funky green and black C icon) and run the program.

Step 3: Configure Cygwin. The Cygwin installer will now use a wizard-like interface to guide you through the installation. For most users, I recommend keeping most of the default values on the first six screens. (If installation fails, see the User's Guide for more information.)

You need to change the contents of only one screen. When you get to the seventh screen (called "Select packages"), you need to select the packages that you want to install. You should not remove any of the default packages, but you do need to add Perl. Under the list of categories, click on the Interpreters category. If this screen shows the word *Skip* in the New column next to the "perl" package, you need to add Perl. Click on Skip until it shows a version number (like 5.8.2-1) or says Keep or Source. Click the Next button at the bottom of the window to continue. Cygwin will now install the software you have selected. (If you receive any warnings, please consult the Cygwin User's Guide for an explanation.) Click Next or OK on the remaining screens until the program finishes.

And that's all you need to do: type about 20 characters and click about 20 buttons. You can always rerun the Cygwin installer to update all the Cygwin programs to the latest versions, and to get more programs.

HACK #13 Learn Perl
This is a short introduction to Perl.

Many of the hacks in this book use Perl to process text files. I'm sure that many of you have never used Perl (or any programming language, for that matter), so I want to give a short introduction. This introduction should be enough to let you write really simple programs, to understand the sample programs in this book, and to modify the sample programs to do different things. If you don't want to understand my scripts, modify my scripts, or write your own scripts, you can safely skip this hack.

erl programs are usually called Perl scripts because they are interpreted in real time by the Perl program. (Perl is an example of an *interpreted language*. Other languages you might have heard of, like C++ and Java, are *compiled languages*. Here's a quick analogy: suppose the computer is a baker. The Perl program is similar to a recipe to make cake from scratch, and the compiled C++ program is similar to a cake mix. You can bake a cake from either recipe, but the cake mix eliminates steps for you ahead of time.)

The Basics

This section introduces some basic concepts in Perl, showing constructs we'll use many times in this book.

Statements. Perl statements tell the computer to do something. As a simple example, let's write a short program to print something:

```
print "hello world\n";
```

(Notice the semicolon at the end of the statement. You need to put a semicolon after the end of every statement in Perl. Oh, and the \n means "start a new line.") If you save this to a file called *helloworld.pl*, you can run the program like this:

```
% perl helloworld.pl
hello world
```

We'll get back to statements soon, but first we need to introduce variables.

Variables. In Perl, you can give a convenient name to a value and then use it later. The named thing is called a variable. (If that statement bothers you, you know too much to be reading this chapter. This book is about saving time! Don't read this. Skip to another hack.) Here are a couple of examples:

```
$name = "Barry Bonds";
$OPS2004 = 1.422;
print "The OPS of $name in 2004 was $OPS2004\n";
```

Running this program will produce the following:

```
The OPS of Barry Bonds in 2004 was 1.422
```

Datatypes. As you might guess, it can be nice to keep lists of things, where you can refer to each item in the list by a name or position. These lists of things are called data structures. In this book, I use only four different datatypes in Perl.

The first one is scalar values. Scalar values include numbers and strings, like the ones I used in the earlier example for variables. Notice that there is a dollar sign ($) in front of scalar values.

The second one is arrays. An array is a simple list of items. Here's an example:

```
@positions = ("P", "C", "1B","2B","3B","SS","LF","CF","RF","DH")
print "The third position in the list is $positions[2]\n";
```

You might have read that and said, "Hey, you wrote a two, but said third." You're right about that. Array positions are numbered from zero, not one. (You'll also notice that I put an at sign [@] in front of the variable name when I defined a list, but a $ when I looked up a value from the list. This is a kind of funny feature of Perl; you put a sign in front of a variable to explain how to interpret the result in the current context.) Running this code will show the following:

```
The third position in the list is 1B
```

The third datatype is associative arrays (also called hashes). An associative array lets you keep a list of stuff, with a name associated with each item. Here's an example:

```
%AVG = ("Suzuki" => .372,
        "Bonds" => .362,
        "Helton" => .347,
        "Mora" => .340,
        "Guerrero" => .337);
print "Melvin Mora's batting average was ", $AVG{"Mora"}, "\n";
```

Notice the percent sign (%) in front of the variable name when I define the variable, but the $ when I look up a value. Oh, and notice the way I used print in this example. You can print a set of different things, separated by commas. Running this code produces the following:

```
Melvin Mora's batting average was .340
```

The last datatype we use in this book is file handles, which we use to reference files. Traditionally, you write file handles in uppercase. Also, they don't have any symbol in front of them. See the next section for an example of using a file handle.

Control structures. I hate using that term (it seems so technical), but I can't think of a better one. Sometimes you want to tell Perl to do one thing if something is true and something else if it's false. You can use the if {} else {} structure to do this. I'll build on the previous example here:

```
if ($AVG{"Bonds"} > .350) {
    print "Whoah!\n";
} else {
    print "Eh.\n";
}
```

Of course, this code will print the following:

```
Whoah!
```

You can also use loops to repeat things in Perl. There are many different types of loops, but here is a simple example of one:

```
$i = 0;
while ($i < scalar(@positions)) {
    print $positions[$i], " ";
    $i = $i + 1;
}
print "\n";
```

Running this program produces the following output:

```
P C 1B 2B 3B SS LF CF RF DH
```

Comments. You can put comments in Perl programs that Perl ignores. They start with a pound sign (#). It is good practice to write comments in your programs. Sometimes a piece of code is complicated and difficult to read. It is often hard to remember what a piece of code does and how it works. To avoid confusing yourself and other people later, you can include comments that explain what the code does.

An Example Program

Almost every Perl script in this book follows the same basic structure, which I show in this section. This program will open an input file specified by the user and write the output to an output file specified by the user. Just to make it (slightly) interesting, this program will print a line number at the beginning of each line.

```
16  # check to make sure that there are the right number of arguments
17  unless ($#ARGV == 1) {die "usage $0 <input file> <output file>\n";}
18
19  # open the input and output files
20  open INFILE,  "<$ARGV[0]" or die "couldn't open input file $ARGV[0]: $!\n";
21  open OUTFILE, ">$ARGV[1]" or die "couldn't open output file $ARGV[1]: $!\n";
22
23  $lineno = 1;
24  while(<INFILE>) {
25      # loop over each line in the input file
26      print OUTFILE "$lineno: ", $_;
27      $lineno++;
28  }
29
30  close INFILE;
31  close OUTFILE;
```

A couple of quick notes on this example: first, you'll notice the weird filename in brackets in line 24. The part inside the parentheses is Perl shorthand for "read each line in the *INFILE* file and assign it to the $_ variable." The while means "keep doing the following until the thing inside the parentheses equals false." The stuff inside the parentheses equals false when the file runs out. In lines 20 and 21, you'll notice the > and < signs added to the filenames. These tell Perl that the file is an input or output file. In lines 17, 20, and 21, you'll see a reference to a list called ARGV. This is automatically set to whatever is on the command line. Finally, the ++ in line 27 means "add one to the variable." Oh, and in line 26, print OUTFILE means write to the OUTFILE file rather than to the screen.

Some Not-so-Basic Basics

We'll use three other Perl features in this book: objects, subroutines, and patterns.

Pattern matching through regular expressions. When trying to understand files from the Internet, we want to match a lot of patterns. For example, consider the play-by-play calls "Roger Clemens intentionally walks Barry Bonds," "Keith Foulke intentionally walks Rafael Palmeiro," and "Jake Westbrook intentionally walks Doug Mientkiewicz." You probably noticed that each expression fits a pattern: the name of a pitcher followed by the expression "intentionally walks" followed by a batter's name. A regular expression gives you a concise way to express this relationship.

Let's start with an example that uses this pattern:

```
$playbyplay = "Jake Westbrook intentionally walks Doug Mientkiewicz.";
if ($playbyplay =~ /\w+\s\w+\ intentionally\ walks\ \w+\s\w+/) {
    print "found an intentional walk\n";
}
```

If you run this code fragment, Perl will print the words "found an intentional walk." Here is how this works. The expression =~ means "if the variable on the left matches the pattern on the right." The expression between the slashes—/\w+\s\w+\ intentionally\ walks\ \w+\s\w+/—is the pattern. You can interpret this pattern as "a bunch of characters, then a space, then some more characters, another space, the words 'intentionally walks,' another space, some characters, another space, and some more characters." More specifically, the \w means "any word character," the \s means "any space character," and the + means "at least one of the things to the left."

See "Use Regular Expressions to Identify Events" **[Hack #23]** for an overview of regular expressions.

One feature needs an explanation. If you place parentheses around part of an expression, Perl will set a variable to the thing that matched inside the parentheses. These variables are named $1, $2, $3, etc.

This can be useful for extracting things from patterns. Let's use this technique to extract the name of the pitcher and batter in the earlier example:

```
$playbyplay = "Jake Westbrook intentionally walks Doug Mientkiewicz.";
if ($playbyplay =~ /(\w+\s\w+)\ intentionally\ walks\ (\w+\s\w+)/) {
    print "pitcher: $1, batter: $2\n";
}
```

If you run this code fragment, Perl will print:

```
pitcher: Jake Westbrook, batter: Doug Mientkiewicz
```

Subroutines. Often, you will want to repeat the same Perl code inside a script. Instead of writing the same few lines over again, you can place them in a subroutine and give the subroutine a name. Here's a simple example of a subroutine that prints the name of a pitcher and batter when given a play-by-play expression matching the "intentional walk" pattern:

```
sub intentional_walk_message($) {
    # takes one argument: play by play string
    my ($playbyplay) = (@_);
    if ($playbyplay =~ /(\w+\s\w+)\ intentionally\ walks\ (\w+\s\w+)/) {
        print "pitcher: $1, batter: $2\n";
    }
}
```

In this subroutine, the ($) is called a *prototype*—it tells Perl that this expression takes one argument. The arguments are contained in the list (@_). Finally, the my qualifier tells the script "set the variable $playbyplay only inside this subroutine" so that if another part of the script uses this value and the subroutine changes it, there will be no surprises.

Modules and packages. Perl supports a system called *packages* for grouping together data structures, functions, and variables that are often used together. A *module* is just a package defined in a file of the same name; I use these terms interchangeably in this book. Modules are a method of grouping together commonly used datatypes and subroutines into a single package. (This is an example of *object-oriented programming*.) The datatypes are called objects and the subroutines are called methods.

You tell Perl that you want to use an object through the use command. You access a method (subroutine) associated with an object through an expression such as $object->method( ). Here is a specific example that opens a file for output using the FileHandle package:

```
use FileHandle;
$fh = new FileHandle;
$fh->open(">file");
```

The first line loads the package. The second line new returns a new FileHandle object. The third line opens a file for output, associating the file with the FileHandle object. (You can use the FileHandle object in Perl to refer to the file.)

In this book, we use Perl packages for parsing web pages and reading baseball data. For more information on packages, see the Perl documentation.

Editors

You might be wondering where I write and edit all of these Perl scripts. You *could* write them in Microsoft Word and save them as text files, but the spellchecking and grammar checks would quickly drive you crazy. There are many, many options for text editors, but I'll list just a few favorites:*

Notepad.exe
> The Microsoft Windows Notepad application is a perfectly acceptable text editor. It's small, fast, and works well for editing simple files.

UltraEdit
> I like UltraEdit for editing code on Windows. It has some nice features for syntax highlighting and macros, and some very convenient functions for editing columns of text.

Xcode
> If you're fortunate enough to be using Mac OS X, you probably have the option to use Xcode, Apple's development environment. It includes some nice Perl editing functionality, including syntax highlighting and automatic indentation.

Komodo
> ActiveState, the company that makes ActivePerl, sells a tool called Komodo for editing dynamic languages like Perl. Komodo is an example of an Integrated Development Environment (IDE), and it provides a very sophisticated environment for editing scripts. Versions are currently available for Windows, Linux, and Mac OS. You can learn more about this tool at *http://www.activestate.com/Products/Komodo/?tn=1*.

Hacking the Hack

The key part of this hack is the short program. All of the Perl programs in this book are variations on this theme. Here are some things you can do with this structure:

Read multiple files, maybe a whole directory of files
> I do this in "Make a Historical Play-by-Play Database" [Hack #22].

---

* I actually use Emacs instead of these programs.

Don't blindly copy input to output; do it only if a pattern matches
I show how to do this in "Use Regular Expressions to Identify Events" [Hack #23], and I use this technique in several other hacks.

Keep track of state while you're looping through a file
I show how to do this in "Load Baseball Data into MySQL" [Hack #20].

Download web pages directly into Perl
That makes Perl much more interesting, doesn't it? You can use it to automatically get web pages and then do whatever you want with them; read *Spidering Hacks* (O'Reilly) to learn how to do this. I use this technique in a few different places in this book.

In general, it's pretty easy to modify Perl scripts to do more stuff. Here are a few tips:

Add more variables in the middle of code
It's usually safer to add than it is to delete, so just try adding new variables in the middle of code. For example, suppose you have a program that reformats play-by-play data. While you're reading it, suppose you want to check if a double was scored in the play, and you want to set a variable called $double to 1 if a double was scored and to 0 if not.

Add more print statements for debugging
If you don't understand what a program is doing, just add some print statements. Print to the screen what the program is reading in, the value of each variable, and what the program is writing out. This will help you understand what's going on.

Learn to use the Perl help files
For simple stuff, you can type man perl at a command line. This will tell you other stuff that you can type at a command line to get more specific help, like man perlintro. You can also check out *http://www.perl.com* (a shameless O'Reilly plug; this comes from me, not my editors). Best of all, you can invest in a Perl book, like O'Reilly's *Programming Perl* (yet another shameless plug, but this book is the bible of Perl).

HACK #14 Get Historical Play-by-Play Data

Get data on every play in MLB games from Retrosheet.

Retrosheet is a nonprofit organization dedicated to collecting and computerizing statistics on Major League Baseball games. David W. Smith started Retrosheet in 1994, and it has become the best source for historical baseball information. (David W. Smith won the prestigious 2005 SABR Bob Davids Award for his work.) Retrosheet provides lots of information on its web site, including old box scores, play-by-play game descriptions, and game summaries. Best of all, you can download datafiles that you can use for your own analysis.

Retrosheet supplies some tools for reading these files (see "Make Box Scores or Database Tables from Play-by-Play Data with Retrosheet Tools" [Hack #15] for more information), but this hack explains how to read these files. This can be very useful if you find the tools hard to run, or if you want to look for information that's not available through the standard tools.

Retrosheet and Project Scoresheet

In this book, I mention both Retrosheet and Project Scoresheet. These two things sound similar, and they are related, but they are not the same thing. About 20 years ago, a group of baseball fans started Project Scoresheet as a collaborative effort to record every play of every game. Bill James was frustrated that the Elias Sports Bureau (the official statistics provider) refused to make play-by-play data available to fans, and he started this organization to compile and share this data. Project Scoresheet designed a neat, simple scoring method that was perfect for describing plays to computers. Today, this system lives on as the preferred encoding method of Retrosheet, STATS, Inc., and the Elias Sports Bureau.

The Retrosheet web site is the product of a nonprofit association devoted to collecting and digitizing information about old baseball games. Retrosheet uses the play-by-play description language from Project Scoresheet in its event files. Retrosheet was originally concerned with collecting information on games before 1984, but it has expanded to include all baseball games. Gary Gillette donated the play-by-play data for 1984–1990 (created by Project Scoresheet) to Retrosheet. STATS, Inc. gave data on the 1991–1992 seasons to Retrosheet in exchange for some other data. Recently, Retrosheet added data for the 2000–2004 seasons.

You might notice that Retrosheet does not have play-by-play information for the period between 1993 and 1999. Gary Gillette started a business called The Baseball Workshop in 1992 to collect play-by-play information and compile event files, and he has compiled play-by-play data for 1992–1999. Since 1999, Gary Gillette has been working with Pete Palmer to collect play-by-play data, and they have worked hard to ensure that the data is as accurate as possible. If you would like to get access to this play-by-play data, you can contact Gary at *GGillette@247Baseball.com* for information on licensing it.

Retrosheet Event Files

My favorite files available from Retrosheet are the detailed event files, which contain a computer-readable description of every play for every game. You can get updated Retrosheet event files at *http://www.retrosheet.org/game.htm*. Event files are available for games between 1960–1992 and 2000–2004. (Complete information is available for most games. See the web site for more information.)

Retrosheet event files follow a specific format. Each event file spans multiple lines. There is one file for each stadium (home team) in the league archive files, though a file for an individual team is also available.

ID
> A unique 12-character ID for each game.

Version
> Version for the game.

Info
> Information about the game played, such as temperature, attendance, umpire, etc.

Starters
> The next 18 fields (for NL) or 20 fields (for AL with a designated hitter) list the starters for the game.

Play-by-play
> The next set of records contain play-by-play data, including inning, team batting, Retrosheet ID code, count on the batter, pitches thrown, the play that occurred, substitutions, and comments on anything that happened that couldn't be described in the other files.

Data
> Information about earned runs by each pitcher who pitched in the game.

Roster files for each team are also included in the Retrosheet files. Each *roster* file contains information about one player on each line: a player ID code, last name, first name, batting hand, and throwing hand. A *teams* file contains the code for each team, league, city, and team name.

The Code

There are a lot of event files to fetch (69 of them), so I use a short script to automate the download process. If you'd like to do the same thing, create a file called *fetchretro.pl* with the following contents:

```
use FileHandle;

use LWP::UserAgent;
$ua = LWP::UserAgent->new;
$baseurl = "http://www.retrosheet.org/";

for ($year = 60; $year <= 92; $year++) {
    foreach $league ("al", "nl") {
        my $filename = '19' . $year . $league . '.zip';
        my $url = $baseurl . '19' . $year . '/19' . $year . $league . '.
zip';
        my $req = HTTP::Request->new(GET => $url);
        my $res = $ua->request($req);

        print STDERR "fetching $filename\n";

        if ($res->is_success) {
            my $fh = new FileHandle ">$filename";
            if (defined $fh) {
                print $fh $res->content;
                $fh->close;
            } else {
                print STDERR "could not open file $filename: $!\n";
            }
        }
        else {
            print STDERR $res->status_line, "\n";
        }
    }
}

$league = 'ml';
for ($year = 00; $year <= 04; $year++) {
    my $filename = '200' . $year . $league . '.zip';
    my $url = $baseurl . '200' . $year . '/200' . $year . $league . '.zip';
    my $req = HTTP::Request->new(GET => $url);
    my $res = $ua->request($req);

    print STDERR "fetching $filename\n";

    if ($res->is_success) {
        my $fh = new FileHandle ">$filename";
            if (defined $fh) {
                print $fh $res->content;
                $fh->close;
            } else {
                print STDERR "could not open file $filename: $!\n";
            }
    }
    else {
        print STDERR $res->status_line, "\n";
    }
}
```

This script iterates through each file available on the Retrosheet web site (as of the summer of 2005), saving all the files locally.

Running the Hack

This hack is straightforward to execute; just type `perl fetchretro.pl` on a command line to fetch all the files:

```
% perl fetchretro.pl
fetching 1960al.zip
fetching 1961al.zip
...
```

See Also

If you want to do research using play-by-play data, you'll probably want to import it into a database. See "Make a Historical Play-by-Play Database" [Hack #22] for directions on how to do this.

Retrosheet also shares Game Log files that contain a summary of every Major League Baseball game. I describe these files in "Load Retrosheet Game Logs" [Hack #21].

HACK #15   Make Box Scores or Database Tables from Play-by-Play Data with Retrosheet Tools

Turn historical event files into box scores, summary statistics, and events suitable for database import using Chadwick and the DiamondWare tools.

It's pretty tough to work directly with the Retrosheet event files. They contain a description of everything that happened, but they're dense and hard to read. Two sets of tools can make things easier. These tools turn the event files into box scores and tables suitable for databases. There's even a new GUI-driven tool that can help you explore these files.

These tools don't include any data, nor do they fetch it from the Internet. Before using them, you'll need to get some baseball data. See "Get Historical Play-by-Play Data" [Hack #14] for more information.

A company called DiamondWare developed a set of three tools for Microsoft Windows for processing Retrosheet–style event files. These are:

BGAME
> The BGAME tool will import an event file and output a CSV file with one line per game containing summary statistics about each game. These statistics include home team, visiting team, runs scored, starting pitchers, umpires, starting lineups, and other information about each game.

BOX

The BOX tool generates a set of box scores from a historical event file. Many users will find a one-page box score easier to understand than 200 lines of event codes.

BEVENT

The BEVENT tool will import an event file and output a CSV file with one event per line, suitable for import into a database. This program can output very detailed information about each event, including which player was at each base, which runners were on base, whether bases were stolen, flags for double plays, the result of the at bat, and many other fields.

You can get these Retrosheet tools from *http://www.retrosheet.org/tools.htm*. The tools are distributed in zip archives. You can unpack them with a program like WinZip (see *http://www.winzip.com*) or with the Compressed Folders application that is included with Windows XP. Unpack the tools and save them in a folder on your hard drive.

You might find it convenient to place them in the same folder as the event files (that's what I do). Better yet, you might place them in a folder within the *Program Files* directory and add the folder to your local path. See "Get Perl" [Hack #12] for an example of how to do this.

Running the Tools

The three Retrosheet tools are command-line programs. To open a command-line window, go to Run... under the Start menu, type cmd.exe, and click Run. If you're new to the command line, you can find help by searching for "Command Shell Overview" in Help and Support under the Start menu.

A couple of tips for running these tools: first, you have to specify the year of the file (even though this might seem unnecessary), or you'll get an error message saying that the program "Can't find teamfile (team)." Second, you need to include the *TEAM<year>* file in the same directory as the event file or the tools won't work. Third, it's easier to download an entire season's worth of data than a single game. You need a few other files (*.ROS* roster files and the *TEAM* file) to make the programs work, and it's easiest to get the whole package. Finally, I included results for a specific game by using the -i option to specify a specific game ID. You can omit this part and get the results for all the games during that season.

The first example shows how to use BGAME to extract a summary of every game from an event file so that you can load this information into a database or spreadsheet. This program will provide lots of information, including the starting lineups, umpires, date, teams, and lots of other facts about the game. If you want, you can select only some of the information in a file. To run BGAME, you must supply:

- The year through the -y option
- The name of the event file from which you are reading the data (or, you can use a wildcard [*] to process multiple event files at the same time)

Optionally, you can supply:

- An identifier for a specific game. Each game in the Retrosheet data is represented by a 12-digit code. The first three digits are the abbreviation for the home team. The next set corresponds to the date: four characters for the year, exactly two for the month (as a number, including zero), and exactly two for the day (as a number, including zero). A final character identifies the game if more than one game was played that day: 1 for the first game and 2 for the second. (There is a 0 if the team played only one game.)
- Start and end dates (in months) with the -s and -e flags, respectively.
- The -f flag and a set of field numbers (if you want to add optional fields, or not display included fields).
- The -d flag to show all possible fields.
- The -h flag to print a help message and list other options.

The BGAME program just prints the results to your screen. Use a redirect (> *filename*) to save the output to a file.

As an example, let's walk through how we would use these tools to download data for a famous game: Yankees versus Red Sox, October 2, 1978. The two teams were tied at the end of the season, and this was a single playoff game to decide the pennant:

```
$ ../BGAME.EXE -y 1978 -i BOS197810020 1978BOS.EVA
"BOS197810020",0,"Monday",230,"T","D","NYA","BOS","","guidr001","to
rrm001","Don Denkinger","Jim Evans","Al Clark","Steve
Palermo","","",32925,"NY","Vincent","Vincent","1994/07/02 11:
04PM","",1,0,68,0,1,4,1,0,172,9,5,4,8,11,0,0,6,9,"guidr001","torrm001","goss
r001","","rivem001",8,"munst101",2,"pinil001",9,"jackr001",10,"nettg001",5,"
chamc001",3,"whitr101",7,"doylb101",4,"dentb001",6,"burlr001",6,"remyj001",4
,"ricej001",9,"yastc101",7,"fiskc001",2,"lynnf001",8,"hobsb101",10,"scotg102
",3,"brohj101",5,"gossr001","dragd101"
...

Expanded game descriptor, version 109(173) of 09/12/2002.
  Type 'bgame -h' for help.
Copyright (c) 2001 by DiamondWare.
[Processing file 1978BOS.EVA.]
```

In the next example, we use BOX to print a box score for this game from the event file (just like the box scores printed in the newspaper each day). A box score shows a summary of what happened in a game: the at bats, runs, hits, and runs batted in for each batter; the line score (of runs scored per inning); and the innings pitched, hits, runs, earned runs, walks, and strikeouts for each pitcher. To run BOX, you must supply:

- A year through the -y option
- The name of the event file from which you are reading the data

Optionally, you can supply:

- The -i option to specify an identifier for a specific game
- Start and end dates (in months) with the -s and -e flags, respectively
- The -h flag to print a help message and list other options

The BOX program just prints the box scores [Hack #2] to your screen. Use a redirect (> *filename*) to save the output to a file. Here is an example run of the BOX program:

```
$ ../BOX.EXE -y 1978 -i BOS197810020 1978BOS.EVA
    Game of 10/2/1978 -- New York at Boston (D)

  New York        AB  R  H RBI    Boston          AB  R  H RBI
  Rivers M, cf     2  1  1  0    Burleson R, ss    4  1  1  0
  Blair P, ph-cf   1  0  1  0    Remy J, 2b        4  1  2  0
  ...
Box score generator, version 106(173) of 09/21/2002. Type 'box -h' for help.

Copyright 1989, 1990 Tom Tippett and David Nichols, 1992, 1993, 1994 by
David W. Smith. All rights reserved.
```

Finally, we can use BEVENT to extract the play-by-play information for the game (or games). This tool is especially cool because it can tell you who was playing each position during the play. It also outputs fields showing other information about the play: the handedness of the batter, the number of runs scored or outs made, whether it was a double play, and dozens of other pieces of information.

To run BEVENT, you must supply:

- The year through the -y option
- The name of the event file from which you are reading the data

Optionally, you can supply:

- An identifier for a specific game
- Start and end dates (in months) with the -s and -e flags, respectively

- The -f flag and a set of field numbers (if you want to add optional fields or not display included fields)
- The -d flag to show all possible fields
- The -h flag to print a help message and list other options

The BEVENT program just prints the results to your screen. Use a redirect (like > <filename>) to save the output to a file. Here is an example of the BGAME program:

```
$ ../BEVENT.EXE -y 1978 -i BOS197810020 1978BOS.EVA
"BOS197810020","NYA",1,0,0,0,0,0,0,"rivem001","L","torrm001","R","","","","W
","T","F",8,1,14,"T","F",0,"F","F",0,0,"F","F",0,1,0,0,0
"BOS197810020","NYA",1,0,0,0,0,0,0,"munst101","R","torrm001","R","rivem001",
"","","SB2","F","F",2,2,4,"F","F",0,"F","F",0,0,"F","F",0,0,2,0,0
"BOS197810020","NYA",1,0,0,0,0,0,0,"munst101","R","torrm001","R","","rivem00
1","","K","F","F",2,2,3,"T","T",0,"F","F",1,0,"F","F",0,0,0,2,0
...
"BOS197810020","NYA",7,0,2,0,0,0,2,"dentb001","R","torrm001","R","whitr101",
"chamc001","","HR/7.2-H;1-
H","F","F",6,9,23,"T","T",4,"F","F",0,3,"F","F",0,4,4,4,0
...
"BOS197810020","NYA",9,1,2,0,0,5,4,"yastc101","L","gossr001","R","remyj001",
"","burlr001","5/P","F","F",7,4,2,"T","T",0,"F","F",1,0,"F","F",0,0,1,0,3
...

Expanded event descriptor, version 1143(173) of 09/12/2002.
  Type 'bevent -h' for help.
Copyright 1989 Tom Tippett and David Nichols, 1993 David W. Smith.

[Processing file 1978BOS.EVA.]
```

You'll notice that I highlighted one line in this file: Bucky Dent's home run over the Green Monster in the seventh inning—the home run that broke Bostonians' hearts for a generation and sent the Yankees to the World Series.

Surprisingly, the World Series was named after *The New York World*, a now-defunct newspaper. Many people think that the MLB championship is called the World Series because Americans don't know that people throughout the world (mostly in Latin America and Asia) play major-league-quality baseball. Well, Americans might or might not know or care about baseball in other countries, but that has nothing to do with the name of the championship.

Preprocessing event files with BEVENT. You can use BEVENT to show play-by-play information for specific games and to choose to display only a few fields, but I almost always use it with full seasons, and I almost always dump everything (using -f 0-96 as a command-line option). If you are short on disk space or you know you need only certain fields, you can choose a subset of fields for your analysis.

Chadwick

Baseball fan (and economics professor) Theodore Turocy wrote a set of tools for processing Retrosheet files and released the applications and code under the GNU Public License (GPL). Chadwick includes a set of command-line tools that function similarly to the DiamondWare tools, and it now includes a GUI for manually inspecting these files and calculating statistics! You can get Chadwick from *http://chadwick.sourceforge.net*.

Chadwick is a good alternative to the DiamondWare tools for several reasons. First, it's an active project, and new enhancements are being added regularly. Second, the application is open source, so if you like, you can modify the code to do other things. (Chadwick is written in C and Python. If you're a real geek, you can run the program with a debugger to try to find problems with source files.) You can find more information about this project at *http://chadwick.sourceforge.net*. You can also download the tools from the same web site. Finally, Chadwick runs on multiple platforms. If you use Windows, you can download a prebuilt version that is ready to use. If you use Mac OS X, Linux, or other POSIX-like systems, you can build a working version of Chadwick.

You can use Chadwick directly with files downloaded from the Retrosheet web site. If you want to use this tool with your own files, you need to create input files for this tool. Use a tool like WinZip to create a new zip file. Place the event files (ending with *.EVA* for AL teams and *.EVN* for NL teams), the *TEAM** file (specifying the year), and the roster files directly into the archive. (Don't put in subfolders!) You can then open the file in the Chadwick GUI to inspect the contents.

I've found that Chadwick doesn't work as well as the DiamondWare tools. (I've found cases where the Chadwick tools exit without producing results.) For the hacks in this book, I used the DiamondWare tools exclusively. I mention Chadwick in this book because I think Chadwick will be the tool of the future, but the DiamondWare tools are the best choice today.

See Also

If you use the Project Scoresheet symbols to keep score of baseball games [Hack #3], you can use these tools on games you score yourself.

I show how to read play-by-play information from the Web and turn it into Retrosheet format in "Get Recent Play-by-Play Data" [Hack #28]. After transforming the data, you can easily process it with these tools.

HACK #16   Use SQL to Explore Game Data

Understand databases and learn to read and write SQL queries.

In this book, I use a SQL database to query and store data. Specifically, I use MySQL. MySQL is a relational database, not unlike Microsoft Access, Oracle, Microsoft SQL Server, and IBM DB2, or any number of other expensive products that companies run on big, back-room servers. This hack describes the basics of databases and introduces Simple Query Language (SQL), which is the way you communicate with a database.

I suggest that you use MySQL for three reasons. First, it's free. Second, a MySQL database of baseball data that you can easily download and install is available free of charge. And finally, MySQL is very stable and robust, so you are assured fast performance and few errors.

If you're using another database, the basic techniques described in this book will still work for you. However, other databases might use slightly different notations for tasks such as adding users, creating tables, and managing your database.

Talking to Your Database

To begin using MySQL, you need to run the `mysql` program from a command line. (The database server is called MySQL. It includes a command-line tool called `mysql` that you can use to query your MySQL database.) On Microsoft Windows, go to the Start menu, select Programs → MySQL → MySQL Server 4.1 → MySQL Command Line Client. A window will open prompting you for a password. Type in your password and press Enter. You should see a prompt like this:

```
Enter password: ******
Welcome to the MySQL monitor.  Commands end with ; or \g.
Your MySQL connection id is 8 to server version: 4.1.7-nt

Type 'help;' or '\h' for help. Type '\c' to clear the buffer.

mysql>
```

At the prompt, type use *<database name>* to select a database. For example, to use the Baseball DataBank database described in "Get a MySQL Database of Player and Team Statistics" **[Hack #10]**, your interaction with MySQL would look like this:

```
mysql> use bbdatabank;
Database changed
```

Notice the semicolon at the end of the command. (Each SQL command needs to end with a semicolon.)

Alternately, you can use a GUI to access the database. See "Get a GUI for MySQL" **[Hack #18]** for more information about this option.

Tables

In a database, the data is stored in tables. Each table is sort of like a spreadsheet but more rigidly structured. Here is an example of a table:

First_Name	Last_Name	Team	OBP	SLG	BAVG
Barry	Bonds	SF	0.609	0.812	0.362
Todd	Helton	CO	0.469	0.62	0.347
Lance	Berkman	HO	0.45	0.566	0.316
J.D.	Drew	AT	0.436	0.569	0.305
Bobby	Abreu	PH	0.428	0.544	0.301

In a database, each column of a table has a name. All cells within a column have the same datatype. Let's suppose this table is called batting_averages. Here is some code that creates this table and inserts the five rows from the previous table:

```
mysql> create table batting_averages (
    ->     First_Name VARCHAR(16),
    ->     Last_Name  VARCHAR(16),
    ->     Team       CHAR(2),
    ->     OBP        DECIMAL(3,3),
    ->     SLG        DECIMAL(3,3),
    ->     BAVG       DECIMAL(3,3));
Query OK, 0 rows affected (0.06 sec)

mysql> insert into batting_averages values
    -> ('Barry','Bonds','SF',0.609,0.812,0.362),
    -> ('Todd','Helton','COL',0.469,0.62,0.347),
    -> ('Lance','Berkman','HOU',0.45,0.566,0.316),
    -> ('J.D.','Drew','ATL',0.436,0.569,0.305),
    -> ('Bobby','Abreu','PHI',0.428,0.544,0.301);
Query OK, 5 rows affected (0.04 sec)
Records: 5  Duplicates: 0  Warnings: 4
```

The create table statement creates a table. The statement tells MySQL about the format of the table: the column names and the types of fields in each column. The insert into statement inserts five rows of data into the table.

Queries

You can examine the contents of a table through a query. As a simple example, let's select the last name and batting average for every row in the table:

```
mysql> select Last_Name, BAVG from batting_averages;
+-----------+-------+
| Last_Name | BAVG  |
+-----------+-------+
| Bonds     | 0.362 |
| Helton    | 0.347 |
| Berkman   | 0.316 |
| Drew      | 0.305 |
| Abreu     | 0.301 |
+-----------+-------+
5 rows in set (0.00 sec)
```

Let me explain the contents of the preceding statement. This statement essentially comprises four parts:

select
    The select statement tells MySQL that this is a query to return values.

Column names
    This part of the SQL statement contains the set of columns that you want MySQL to return. To return all columns in a table, select *.

from
    This keyword tells MySQL that the next item is a table to select from.

Source table
    This section tells MySQL where the data in the statement will come from.

You can create more-complicated queries that select only rows that meet a specific condition. For example, let's select all columns (*) from the batting_averages table where the batting average is greater than .340:

```
mysql> select * from batting_averages where BAVG > .340;
+------------+-----------+------+-------+-------+-------+
| First_Name | Last_Name | Team | OBP   | SLG   | BAVG  |
+------------+-----------+------+-------+-------+-------+
| Barry      | Bonds     | SF   | 0.609 | 0.812 | 0.362 |
| Todd       | Helton    | CO   | 0.469 | 0.620 | 0.347 |
+------------+-----------+------+-------+-------+-------+
2 rows in set (0.00 sec)
```

As you can see, we append a clause at the end of the statement (called a where clause, for obvious reasons) that specifies the condition.

As another example, let's look up only Bobby Abreu's statistics:

```
mysql> select * from batting_averages where last_name = 'Abreu';
+------------+-----------+------+-------+-------+-------+
| First_Name | Last_Name | Team | OBP   | SLG   | BAVG  |
+------------+-----------+------+-------+-------+-------+
| Bobby      | Abreu     | PH   | 0.428 | 0.544 | 0.301 |
+------------+-----------+------+-------+-------+-------+
1 row in set (0.00 sec)
```

You can also combine variables in select queries to make new values. Let's calculate the OPS for each hitter:

```
mysql> select First_Name, Last_Name, (OBP + SLG) AS OPS
    -> from batting_averages;
+------------+-----------+-------+
| First_Name | Last_Name | OPS   |
+------------+-----------+-------+
| Barry      | Bonds     | 1.421 |
| Todd       | Helton    | 1.089 |
| Lance      | Berkman   | 1.016 |
| J.D.       | Drew      | 1.005 |
| Bobby      | Abreu     | 0.972 |
+------------+-----------+-------+
5 rows in set (0.05 sec)
```

Notice that you can compute a function based on several columns instead of just listing single columns. The optional (but highly recommended) AS keyword assigns a meaningful name to the calculated column.

Joins. The true power of a database is to combine tables in new and interesting ways. MySQL is a relational database. This means tables can be related to each other through common fields. You can combine related tables using SQL queries. Let's create a table of long team names. (The table we defined earlier includes only short abbreviations.)

```
mysql> create table team_names (
    ->     Team CHAR(2),
    ->     TeamName Varchar(16)
    -> );
Query OK, 0 rows affected (0.01 sec)

mysql> insert into team_names values
    -> ('SF', 'Giants'),
    -> ('CO', 'Rockies'),
    -> ('PH', 'Phillies'),
    -> ('HO', 'Astros'),
    -> ('AT', 'Braves');
Query OK, 5 rows affected (0.01 sec)
Records: 5  Duplicates: 0  Warnings: 0
```

Now, let's print a list of players with the team names. To do this, we'll join the two tables:

```
mysql> select a.*, b.TeamName
    -> from batting_averages a inner join team_names b
    -> on a.Team=b.Team;
+------------+-----------+------+-------+-------+-------+----------+
| First_Name | Last_Name | Team | OBP   | SLG   | BAVG  | TeamName |
+------------+-----------+------+-------+-------+-------+----------+
| Barry      | Bonds     | SF   | 0.609 | 0.812 | 0.362 | Giants   |
| Todd       | Helton    | CO   | 0.469 | 0.620 | 0.347 | Rockies  |
| Bobby      | Abreu     | PH   | 0.428 | 0.544 | 0.301 | Phillies |
| Lance      | Berkman   | HO   | 0.450 | 0.566 | 0.316 | Astros   |
| J.D.       | Drew      | AT   | 0.436 | 0.569 | 0.305 | Braves   |
+------------+-----------+------+-------+-------+-------+----------+
5 rows in set (0.00 sec)
```

There are a few changes to notice here. Let's start at the FROM keyword and then work our way back to the beginning. Instead of specifying one table, we specify two tables (batting_averages and team_names) and give each table a short nickname (a and b, respectively).

We also include a connecting phrase, INNER JOIN, which tells MySQL what type of join we want. SQL supports several different ways to link tables:

Only matching rows
    This is an inner join.

All rows from both tables (set to null if there is no match)
    This is a full join.

All rows from one table and only those rows from the second table where there is a match
    We use the extra keywords left and right to specify from which side everything is included.

Notice the extra clause at the end with the ON keyword. This specifies which columns are related to each other. MySQL only returns rows where the value in both columns matches. (Be careful: it will return all rows where the values match. So if you had two tables, each with three values that were BOS, and you joined the tables on this column, you would get nine rows back.)

Going back to the beginning, notice how we have appended an *a.* and a *b.* to the column names. If multiple tables have columns with the same names, these labels help SQL tell them apart.

Aggregates. SQL doesn't just let you select a single row of data, it lets you combine rows in any way you want. As an example, we'll show how you sum all the rows in a table and compute averages based on these numbers.

Suppose you have a table of 2004 batting statistics for the Red Sox. Let's calculate the team batting average and SLG:

```
mysql> select count(*) batters, round(sum(H) / sum(AB),3) team_AVG,
    -> round((sum(H) + sum(Doubles) + 2 * sum(Triples) + 3 * sum(HR)) /
sum(AB)
    ->        ,3) team_SLG
    -> from redsoxbatting2004;
+---------+----------+----------+
| batters | team_AVG | team_SLG |
+---------+----------+----------+
|      29 |    0.277 |    0.466 |
+---------+----------+----------+
1 row in set (0.01 sec)
```

What if you want to know performance by position? You can use a GROUP BY expression at the end, to tell SQL how to group the data:

```
mysql> select POS, count(*) batters, round(sum(H) / sum(AB),3) team_AVG,
    -> round((sum(H) + sum(Doubles) + 2 * sum(Triples) + 3 * sum(HR)) /
sum(AB)
    ->        ,3) team_SLG
    -> from redsoxbatting2004
    -> group by POS;
+------+---------+----------+----------+
| POS  | batters | team_AVG | team_SLG |
+------+---------+----------+----------+
| 1B   |       4 |    0.240 |    0.368 |
| 2B   |       2 |    0.265 |    0.433 |
| 3B   |       3 |    0.275 |    0.434 |
| C    |       3 |    0.289 |    0.488 |
| DH   |       2 |    0.294 |    0.585 |
| OF   |       6 |    0.296 |    0.511 |
| P    |       5 |    0.095 |    0.143 |
| SS   |       4 |    0.260 |    0.389 |
+------+---------+----------+----------+
8 rows in set (0.00 sec)
```

We'll use SQL code in many places in this book. Usually, we'll use it when we have data in multiple tables and we want to aggregate or merge it in complicated ways.

Subqueries. Sometimes it's convenient to proceed in multiple stages when performing calculations. For example, to calculate slugging average (SLG = TB / AB), it's a little neater to first calculate total bases (TB) and then calculate slugging average (SLG).

An easy way to show this in MySQL is through subqueries. A *subquery* is a SQL query used inside another SQL query. You place a subquery inside parentheses. Here's a simple example of a subquery that calculates SLG

from a table called Teams that contains information on hits (H), doubles
(2B), triples (3B), home runs (HR), and at bats (AB). Then it selects teams in
the American League only and shows the team averages from the year 2000.

```
mysql> select name, round(TB / AB, 3) AS SLG
    > from (select (H + 2B + 2 * 3B + 3 * HR) AS TB,
    >       AB, yearID, franchID as teamID, AB, lgID, name
    >       from teams l inner join teamsFranchises r
    >       on l.idxTeamsFranchises=r.idxTeamsFranchises) t
    > where t.yearID=2000 and t.lgid="AL";
```

```
+----------------------+-------+
| name                 | SLG   |
+----------------------+-------+
| Anaheim Angels       | 0.472 |
| Baltimore Orioles    | 0.435 |
| Boston Red Sox       | 0.423 |
| Chicago White Sox    | 0.470 |
| Cleveland Indians    | 0.470 |
| Detroit Tigers       | 0.438 |
| Kansas City Royals   | 0.425 |
| Minnesota Twins      | 0.407 |
| New York Yankees     | 0.450 |
| Oakland Athletics    | 0.458 |
| Seattle Mariners     | 0.442 |
| Tampa Bay Devil Rays | 0.399 |
| Texas Rangers        | 0.446 |
| Toronto Blue Jays    | 0.469 |
+----------------------+-------+
14 rows in set (0.06 sec)
```

Saving results in tables. Earlier we saw one way to add rows to create tables
and to add rows to tables. A very convenient technique that I will use in this
book is to create a table from a query. As an example, let's create a table
called teams2003 from the earlier query:

```
mysql> create table teams2003 AS
    > select name, round(TB / AB, 3) AS SLG
    > from (select (H + 2B + 2 * 3B + 3 * HR) AS TB,
    >       AB, yearID, franchID as teamID, AB, lgID, name
    >       from teams l inner join teamsFranchises r
    >       on l.idxTeamsFranchises=r.idxTeamsFranchises) t
    > where t.yearID=2000 and t.lgid="AL";
Query OK, 14 rows affected (0.10 sec)
Records: 14   Duplicates: 0   Warnings: 0
```

The columns in this table show that it contains two fields, name and SLG, just
like the results of the earlier query:

```
mysql> desc teams2003;
+-------+--------------+------+-----+---------+-------+
| Field | Type         | Null | Key | Default | Extra |
+-------+--------------+------+-----+---------+-------+
| name  | varchar(50)  |      |     |         |       |
| SLG   | double(19,3) | YES  |     | NULL    |       |
+-------+--------------+------+-----+---------+-------+
2 rows in set (0.00 sec)
```

If you don't want to save the results permanently but just want to use them during your session, you can use the command create temporary table.

Deleting tables. Of course, you can delete tables in MySQL. The command for deleting tables is DROP TABLE *tablename*. As an example, let's delete the teams2003 table we just created:

```
mysql> drop table teams2003;
Query OK, 0 rows affected (0.00 sec)
```

 There is no confirmation for this command. So be careful! (Then again, you do have to type 10 characters to execute it, so it's not that easy to type accidentally.) Also, you can't delete every table; you need to have permission to do this. See the MySQL manuals for more information.

Running Scripts

As you can see, database commands quickly become very complicated. You do not have to run every SQL statement by typing it onto a command line. Instead, you can use SQL scripts to make it easier to edit and run a complicated querying task.

To use scripts, write your SQL code in a text editor (such as Notepad) and save the results to a file ending in *.sql*. Suppose you saved the commands shown earlier in a file called *example.sql*. You can run them all at once by typing the following in the MySQL client:

```
mysql> source "example.sql"
```

Getting More Information and Help

Inside the MySQL command-line client, you can type help or help contents to get information on how to run MySQL. MySQL also comes with an HTML manual. On Windows, the default installation adds a link to your Start menu at Start → Programs → MySQL → MySQL Server 4.1 → My SQL Manual → Table of Contents. On other platforms, this file will be inside the MySQL directory, in the *Docs* folder, as *manual_toc.html*.

HACK #17 Use Microsoft Access to Run SQL Queries

Write queries in Microsoft Access using the SQL language.

Most Microsoft Access users like to build queries graphically, and I must admit that I also like to do that. But it's very hard to explain how to build a query in print. (See "Make Your Own Stats Book" [Hack #11] for an example.) SQL is a very concise way to explain database queries, so that is the way I explain queries in this book.

Luckily, Microsoft Access lets you enter queries as SQL code. This hack explains how to enter SQL queries in Microsoft Access.

SQL Queries in Access

To begin, start Microsoft Access and open the database file you want to query. You can do this by double-clicking the file in Windows Explorer or by starting Microsoft Access and choosing Open Database.

As an example, I chose to show batting averages by player, using the Baseball Archive database. (See "Get an Access Database of Player and Team Statistics" [Hack #9] for instructions on how to get this database.)

To create a new query, select Query from the Insert menu. A dialog box will appear, asking you how you want to create a new query. Select Design View. This will open a query design window in the default format. To get a SQL dialog box, select SQL View from the View menu. You will see a window like the one shown in Figure 2-9. Running the query shown in Figure 2-9 generates the results shown in Figure 2-10.

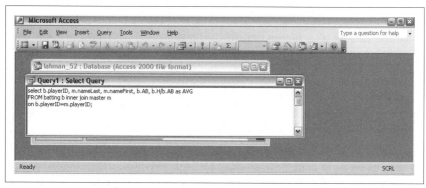

Figure 2-9. Access SQL edit window

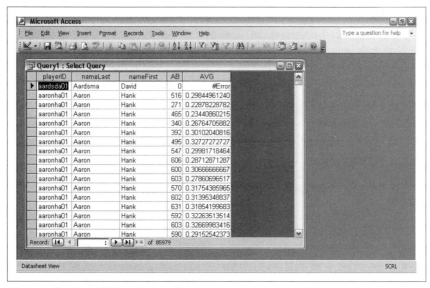

Figure 2-10. Access SQL query results

Changing SQL Queries to Graphical Queries

If you want, you can get Access to show the SQL query in the normal graphical edit window. To do this, choose Design View from the View menu.
Figure 2-11 shows the design view for the earlier query.

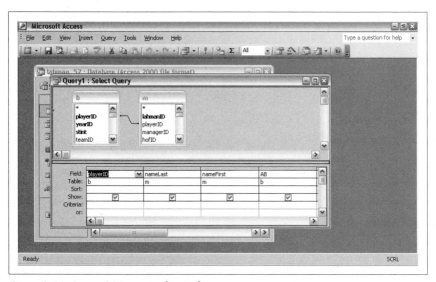

Figure 2-11. Access SQL query edit window

Subqueries in Access

Not all SQL features work in Microsoft Access, but if you want to use Microsoft Access, it is an alternative to MySQL. Specifically, if you are using Microsoft Access, you won't be able to use subqueries. Here is a way to work around this:

1. Create a query containing only the contents of the subquery. In the earlier example, this is:

    ```
    select (H + 2B + 2 * 3B + 3 * HR) AS TB, AB, yearID, teamID, AB, lgID,
    name from teams
    ```

2. Save this individual query. I like to use a name like slugging_inner_ query that corresponds to the name of the outside query.

3. Create another query that refers to the subquery. In the earlier example, this is:

    ```
    select name, round(TB / AB, 3) AS SLG from slugging_inner_query where t.
    yearID=2000 and t.lgid='AL';
    ```

Get a GUI for MySQL

HACK #18

Get a graphical database tool to make it easier to query a MySQL database.

If you are reluctant to use MySQL because its command-line interface is unfamiliar and nonintuitive, this hack is for you. MySQL (the company) makes an easy-to-use graphical query tool for MySQL (the database). This tool, called MySQL Query Browser, lets you explore a database through a point-and-click interface, edit queries, and save results to files that you can open in a spreadsheet.

You can get MySQL Query Browser from *http://dev.mysql.com/downloads/query-browser*. This web site includes easy-to-use installer programs for Windows, Linux, and Mac OS X. See the web site for download and installation instructions.

> Most users should probably download the standard installer program for Windows, the RPM packages for Linux, or the DMG files for Mac OS X. These versions will make installation easiest for most users. Unless you have unusual requirements and you know what you're doing, download and install the standard versions.

When you first open MySQL Query Browser, you will be prompted to enter information about your database connection. If you created a database using the instructions in "Get a MySQL Database of Player and Team Statistics" [Hack #10], you can follow along with this example.

Enter your username and the bbdatabank default schema. (Optionally, you can enter a name in the Stored Connection field to name these parameters. This lets you choose the connection from a menu the next time you run the program.) Figure 2-12 shows the connection screen.

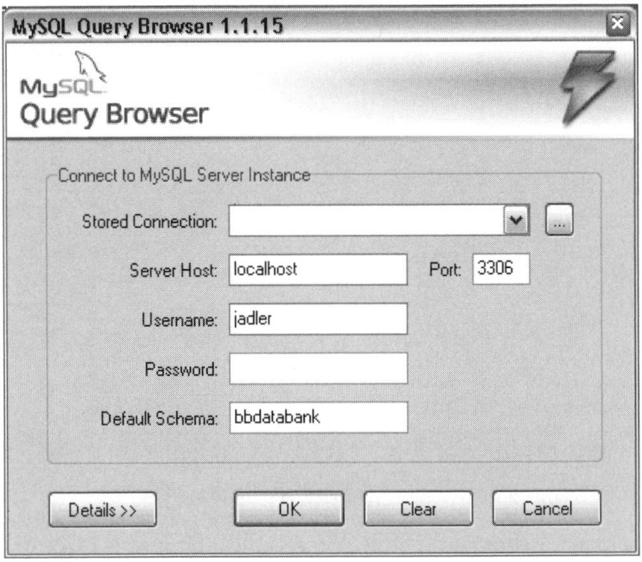

Figure 2-12. MySQL Query Browser login

Let's try a simple query to show off the query browser interface. Select "New query tab" from the File menu. A new tab will appear in the query browser window. As a simple example, let's look at the Batting table. Drag-and-drop the Batting table from the Schemata list to the query window at the top of the page. The SQL code SELECT * FROM 'batting' b will appear in this window. Click the Execute button, and the tool will show the contents of the table in the results window, as shown in Figure 2-13.

(As an alternative, you can also drag the table directly onto the results pane, and MySQL will write the query and show the results in a single step.) As you can see, this tool helps show SQL tables and queries in an easy-to-read, spreadsheet-like form.

Let's do something a little more interesting: make a list of players' seasons for players with more than 100 at bats per year, ranked by annual batting average since 2000. Type the following query into the query box:

```
select b.H/b.AB as AVG, m.nameLast, m.nameFirst, t.yearID
from batting b inner join master m inner join teams t
where b.idxLahman=m.idxLahman and b.idxTeams=t.idxTeams
and t.yearID>1999 and b.AB > 100 order by AVG DESC
```

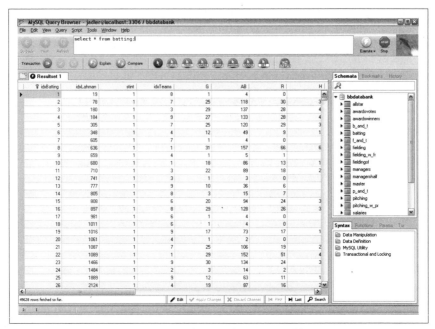

Figure 2-13. MySQL Query Browser, showing the Batting table

Click the Execute button. You'll see a table of players ranked by batting average, including their name and season.

MySQL Query Browser lets you do something very useful: export your results. Nothing beats a spreadsheet for scratch work and experimentation, and there is no more convenient way to transfer files to Excel. In the File menu, under the Export Resultset submenu, select "Export as Excel File...." Choose a filename in the dialog box and save the results, and you're ready to manipulate the results in Excel.

Other Tools

Dozens of similar tools are available from different vendors; the ones I cover here are just a few of my favorites. Any one of them should make your life easier if you work with databases. Try searching for "SQL query tool" on Google, or on CNET's Download.com, to see some other options. Here are a few of my favorites.

MySQL Administrator. In addition to MySQL Query Browser, MySQL makes a product called Administrator. This tool complements MySQL Query Browser. If you want to read data from or write data to a database, use MySQL Query Browser. If you want to create, delete, or modify database schema, tables, or users, use Administrator.

You can get more information about the MySQL Administrator and download executables and source code from *http://dev.mysql.com/downloads/administrator*.

Tora and Toad. Another popular GUI for MySQL is Tools for Oracle, or Tora. Versions of Tora for Linux and Windows are available from *http://tora.sourceforge.net*. You can use the Linux version free of charge (it's GPL licensed), but the Windows version is free for personal use only (and not commercial use). Like MySQL CC, Tora includes tools for database exploration and returning query results.

The maintainer of Tora, Globecom, was acquired by Quest Software. Quest Software makes Toad, a popular commercial tool for database access. Toad is a very good tool (I use it at work), but the full versions are too expensive for most home users.

Aqua Data Studio. Another popular query tool for databases is Aqua Data Studio from AquaFold, Inc. This tool is available for a wide selection of platforms (Windows, Linux, Mac OS, Solaris, and others) because it is a Java program. You can get it from *http://www.aquafold.com*. Like the other tools described in this section, Aqua Data Studio is available at no cost for personal use, but there is a fee for commercial use. While waiting for the Mac OS X version of MySQL Query Browser, I used this program as my primary SQL query tool.

HACK #19 Move Data from a Database to Excel

Get data out of your database and into Microsoft Excel for easy analysis.

In "Get and Install MySQL" [Hack #8], I listed a bunch of reasons why databases can be better than spreadsheets: database fields are strongly typed, database changes are transactional, database queries can be used to select data, database joins can be used to merge data, database relationships can be defined between data, and database file sizes can be very large. For storing and fetching data, I also think databases are better.

However, for analyzing and inspecting data, I prefer a spreadsheet. You can do a lot of things easily with spreadsheets that you can't do easily with a database—for instance, plot charts, create pivot tables, and do statistical calculations. In this hack, I'll show you a few ways to get data out of a database and into Microsoft Excel.

Select the Right Data for a Spreadsheet

Spreadsheets are very powerful, but they also have some limitations. Here are a few suggestions on how to select and format your data to make the most useful spreadsheet:

Table sizes
> Make sure there are fewer than 255 columns and 65,534 rows in the table. The limit is 65,535 rows, but you need to save one for column headers!

Counts versus ratios
> In general, I think it is better to export counts than averages. Here's an example that illustrates why this is.

> Suppose you want to calculate team batting averages from individual player statistics. Would it be better to export hits (H) and at bats (AB), or averages (AVG)? Team batting average usually means the total number of hits by a team, divided by the total number of at bats. The easiest way to do this is to sum H and AB for a team, and calculate the team AVG from there. If you have only the AVG for each player, you cannot calculate the team average correctly. (You can calculate this directly from the individual batting averages of individual players if you weight the results by AB, but that's ugly and complicated.)

Group in the database and use counts
> One of the most powerful things you can do with a database is to use functions like SUM and COUNT, and GROUP BY clauses, to aggregate data. For example, you might want to aggregate batting statistics by home versus away games, day versus night games, and month.

> When you group in the database, make sure you use counts and not ratios (i.e., include total H and AB, not AVG). This gives you maximum flexibility in your spreadsheet: you can easily calculate averages for the whole season, for home games only, for home night games only, etc.

> This is especially important if you plan to use pivot tables.

Merge in the database
> It is easier to merge tables in a database than it is in Excel. For example, suppose you want a spreadsheet that includes batting and fielding statistics for each player on the same line. Furthermore, let's assume the database has one table with batting statistics and another table with fielding statistics. (This is how the Baseball DataBank database is constructed.) You can export the two tables separately and combine them in Excel using functions like VLOOKUP, but it's much faster and easier to merge the data in the database.

Include as many columns as you can

If you want a small spreadsheet (say, to email to a friend) and you know exactly what data you need, it's fine to pick only a few columns. However, you might guess wrong. For example, you might initially decide you are interested only in players' first and last names but later change your mind and decide you want birth dates as well. Storage is cheap; if you get more data now, you might save yourself some work later.

Running the Hack

Now, let's get to some specific instructions on how to move data.

Moving data from Access to Excel. If you're using Microsoft Access, you can move a table into Microsoft Excel in two easy steps:

1. Open the table or query that you want to edit in Microsoft Excel.

2. From the Tools menu, under Office Links, select "Analyze It with Microsoft Office Excel." A few seconds later, Microsoft Excel will open with a new spreadsheet (see Figure 2-14) containing the contents of the table or query.

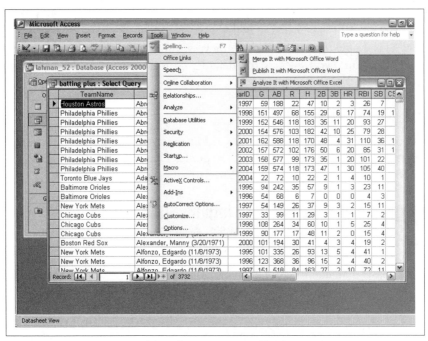

Figure 2-14. Creating a spreadsheet from an Access table

Moving data from MySQL Query Browser to Excel. If you have MySQL Query Browser installed, it's just as easy to move data from MySQL into Microsoft Excel:

1. Run a query to select the data that you want to move into Excel.
2. Select "Export as Excel File..." from the Export Resultset submenu in the File menu.
3. Choose a name and location for the exported file.

Moving data from MySQL to Excel. If you don't have MySQL Query Browser installed, here is a fast way to dump a table using the MySQL command-line tool:

1. Determine the query that you want to use. For example, to import the entire Allstar table in the Baseball DataBank files, you use the query SELECT * FROM Allstar.
2. On the command line, run the command mysql -e "<query>" > filename.txt". For example, to import the Allstar table, you can use the following statement:

    ```
    % mysql bbdatabank -e "SELECT * FROM allstar;" > allstar.txt
    ```

3. From Microsoft Excel, choose Open from the File dialog box and select the file. (It is a text file, so make sure you choose the right file type.)
4. This might open the Text Import wizard. Choose Finished because Microsoft Excel guesses the defaults correctly for a tab-delimited text file like this.

Hacking the Hack

If you move data between MySQL and Excel often, you might find it easier to use a mechanism called ODBC to transfer data. See "Access Databases Directly from Excel or R" [Hack #33] for instructions on how to do this.

HACK Load Baseball Data into MySQL
#20   Use a Perl script to generate MySQL statements automatically for loading baseball data into MySQL.

Most baseball data on the Web is available as flat files: text files where a tab, a comma, or another character separates each element. For example, here is the AwardsManagers table from the Baseball Archive data:

```
"managerID","awardID","yearID","lgID","tie","notes"
"larusto01m","Mgr of the year",1983,"AL",,
"lasorto01m","Mgr of the year",1983,"NL",,
"andersp01m","Mgr of the year",1984,"AL",,
...
```

The first line contains the *header* information (the name of each column). Each subsequent line represents a different manager award for a different league. Text fields are enclosed in quotes and are separated by commas. The fields are (from left to right): ID code, award name, year, league, a field that indicates ties, and notes.

As you can see, it is easy for a person to read these files. Often, it is convenient to create or edit files like these. For example, I show how to create formatted text files like these in "Make Box Scores or Database Tables from Play-by-Play Data with Retrosheet Tools" [Hack #15]. However, it's much easier to read these files using a database because it lets you search easily for specific lines or summarize the information in a file.

To load a text file like this into a database, you have to define an appropriate table type [Hack #16]. Writing a statement like this can be tedious, especially if you don't know the length of each field. If you guess field lengths incorrectly, you will either waste storage space or truncate some of the fields.

This hack presents a Perl script that will automatically read a text file and create SQL import code. This script works pretty simply. First, it reads the command-line options (specifying the delimiter, whether there is a header line, and the input filename). Next, the script reads each line of the file, measuring the length of each field and checking the type of each field. If it finds any nonnumerical values in a line, it sets the field type to `character`. Finally, it prints out some SQL code to define the table and load the text file. This script accepts three options:

Option	Meaning
-i <filename>	Specifies the input filename.
-s <separator>	Specifies the field that separates columns in the file. Usually, this will be a comma (,) or a tab (\t) character. You should place this in quotes on the command line.
-h	Tells the script to read variable names from the first line. (Otherwise, the script generates code with generic column names.)

The Code

Save the following code in a file named *check_field_sizes.pl*:

```
#!/usr/bin/perl

use Getopt::Std;
getopts('dhs:i:') or die "bad options: $!";
if ($opt_s) {
    $sep = $opt_s;
```

```perl
} else {
    $sep = "\t";
}
$useheader = $opt_h;
if ($opt_i) {
    open INFILE, "<$opt_i" or die "can't open input file: $!\n";
} else {
    die "must specify file name\n";
}

if ($useheader) {
    # read in the first line
    $headerline = <INFILE>;
    # split it into an array by commas
    $headerline =~ s/[\"\n\r\f]//g;
    @header = split /$sep/, $headerline;

    #read in the second line
    $second = <INFILE>;

    # split it into an array
    $second =~ s/[\"\r\n\f]//g;
    @types = split /$sep/, $second;
    @terms = split /$sep/, $second;

} else {
    # read in the first line
    $first = <INFILE>;
    # split it into an arry by commas
    $first =~ s/[\"\r\n\f]//g;
    @types = split /$sep/, $first;
    @terms = split /$sep/, $first;;
}

# count the number of fields
$fields = $#terms + 1;

# check if each element is numerical or character
for ($i = 0; $i < $fields; $i++) {
    # print $i, " ", $header[$i], "\n";
    if ($types[$i] =~ /^\s*\d*\s*$/) {
        $field_type[$i] = "I";
    } elsif ($types[$i] =~ /^\s*\d*\.(\d+)\s*$/) {
        $field_type[$i] = length($1);
    } else {
        $field_type[$i] = "V";
    }
}

# measure the length of each field
@maxlengths = map length, @terms;
```

```
# start looping through file:
while(<INFILE>) {
    $_ =~ s/B\,R\"/B\;R/g;
    $_ =~ s/[\"\r\n\f]//g;
    @terms = split /$sep/, $_;
    @lengths = map length, @terms;
    for ($i = 0; $i < $fields; $i++) {
        if ($lengths[$i] > $maxlengths[$i]) {
            if ($opt_d) {print "new max pos $i: $terms[$i]\n";}
            $maxlengths[$i] = $lengths[$i];
        }
        if ($terms[$i] !~ /^\s*[\d,\.]*\s*$/) {
            if (($opt_d) and ($field_type[$i] ne "V")) {
                print "changing field type for $header[$i]:"
                    . " \"$terms[$i]\"\n";
                print "\t$_\n\t";
                print join ",", @terms;
                print "\n";
            }
            $field_type[$i] = "V";
        }
    }
}
close(INFILE);

if ($opt_i =~ /([\w|\.]*)\.\w+$/) {
    $tablename = $1;
    $tablename =~ s/\.//;
} elsif ($opt_i =~ /.*\/([\w|\.]*)\.\w+$/) {
    $tablename = $1;
    $tablename =~ s/\.//;
} else {
    $tablename = "NONAMETABLE";
}

print "CREATE TABLE $tablename (\n";
for ($i = 0; $i < $fields; $i++) {
    if ($useheader) {
        $varname = $header[$i];
    } else {
        $varname = "variable$i";
    }
    if ($field_type[$i] =~ /I/ and $maxlengths[$i] < 6) {
        print "\t$varname SMALLINT($maxlengths[$i])";
    } elsif ($field_type[$i] =~ /I/) {
        print "\t$varname INTEGER($maxlengths[$i])";
    } elsif ($field_type[$i] =~ /V/ and $maxlengths[$i] > 255) {
        print "\t$varname TEXT";
    } elsif ($field_type[$i] =~ /V/) {
        print "\t$varname VARCHAR($maxlengths[$i])";
    } else {
        print "\t$varname DECIMAL($maxlengths[$i],$field_type[$i])";
    }
}
```

```
if ($i + 1 == $fields) {
    print "\n);\n";
} else {
    print ",\n";
}
}

print "LOAD DATA LOCAL INFILE '$opt_i'\n";
print "INTO TABLE $tablename\n";
if ($opt_s =~ /\t/) {$opt_s = "\\t";}
print "FIELDS TERMINATED BY '$opt_s'\n";
print "OPTIONALLY ENCLOSED BY '\"'";
print "LINES TERMINATED BY '\\n'";
if ($opt_h) {
    print "\nIGNORE 1 LINES;\n";
} else {
    print ";\n";
}
```

Running the Hack

Let's show the results of running this script on the *AwardsManagers.csv* file:

```
% perl check_field_sizes.pl -s "," -h -i AwardsManagers.csv
CREATE TABLE AwardsManagers (
        managerID VARCHAR(10),
        awardID VARCHAR(15),
        yearID SMALLINT(4),
        lgID VARCHAR(2)
);
LOAD DATA LOCAL INFILE 'AwardsManagers.csv'
INTO TABLE AwardsManagers
FIELDS TERMINATED BY ','
OPTIONALLY ENCLOSED BY '"'LINES TERMINATED BY '\n'
IGNORE 1 LINES;
```

We can use a trick to save this output as a script, making it easier to load this into a database. Here's how to use this script to load this table in two steps:

```
% perl check_field_sizes.pl -s "," -h -i AwardsManagers.csv\
> load_AwardsManagers.sql
% mysql test < load_AwardsManagers.sql ~/Desktop/book/code
```

MySQL won't return any output if this works. Let's take a look to make sure the table is there:

```
mysql> show tables;
+----------------+
| Tables_in_test |
+----------------+
| AwardsManagers |
+----------------+
1 row in set (0.00 sec)
```

```
mysql> desc AwardsManagers;
+-----------+-------------+------+-----+---------+-------+
| Field     | Type        | Null | Key | Default | Extra |
+-----------+-------------+------+-----+---------+-------+
| managerID | varchar(10) | YES  |     | NULL    |       |
| awardID   | varchar(15) | YES  |     | NULL    |       |
| yearID    | smallint(4) | YES  |     | NULL    |       |
| lgID      | char(2)     | YES  |     | NULL    |       |
+-----------+-------------+------+-----+---------+-------+
4 rows in set (0.00 sec)
```

Hacking the Hack

I kept this script simple, but you can modify it to do a lot more. Here are a few suggestions:

Output script results to a file
Suppose you want to save the results of running this script to a file called *code.sql*. To do this, add > code.sql at the end of the line.

Import directly into a database
Why save the SQL to a file? You can change this script to connect directly to a database and load the file using Perl's DBI interface.

Support a greater number of variable types
I included only a few very basic variable types in my example, but MySQL supports many other variable types. You can modify this script to identify these types as well.

See Also

While writing this book, I found a better script in Paul DuBois's *MySQL Cookbook* (O'Reilly). If you work with a lot of text files, you might prefer his version.

HACK #21 Load Retrosheet Game Logs

Load Retrosheet Game Log files to get a summary about every game played.

Sometimes you don't need information about every play, just how a team played. This hack shows you how to load the game files into MySQL for querying. For each game, the game log contains up to 161 different variables covering where the game was played, when the game was played, what teams played the game, what players started for each team, how each team scored, a variety of offensive and defensive statistics, the umpires for the game, and miscellaneous extra data. These files don't contain play-by-play data or stats on individual players.

Game log files are available for download from the Retrosheet web site, at *http://www.retrosheet.org/gamelogs/index.html*. The files are available for individual years or for multiple years as zip files. A second way to get these files is to generate them yourself from Retrosheet event files, using the BEVENT tool **[Hack #15]**.

You can use this data for any purpose where wins and losses are important, but individual events aren't. One example of this is in looking at park effects, as discussed in "Measure Park Effects" **[Hack #56]**, where we need to know wins and losses between teams in different ballparks.

The Code

You can probably type in all the variables, but it's a little tedious, so I'll save you the effort. (Check the book's web site to download the SQL code on this page.) I created a file with column names, called *game_log_header.csv*. The contents of this file look something like this:

```
Date,DoubleHeader DayOfWeek, VisitingTeam, VisitingTeamLeague,
VisitingTeamGameNumber HomeTeam, HomeTeamLeague, HomeTeamGameNumber,
VisitorRunsScored HomeRunsScore, LengthInOuts, DayNight, CompletionInfo,
...
HomeBatting7Name HomeBatting7Position, HomeBatting8PlayerID,
HomeBatting8Name HomeBatting8Position, HomeBatting9PlayerID,
HomeBatting9Name HomeBatting9Position, AdditionalInfo, AcquisitionInfo
```

(I omitted the middle part of the file because it's long and repetitive.) Note that there are no line breaks in this file.

Here are the steps to load this into the database:

1. Create a file containing only the field names, separated by commas (with no spaces or new lines), and call it *game_log_header.csv*.

2. Copy this file to a different name—say, *GL2003.HDR.TXT*—and append the *GL2003.TXT* file (the 2003 Game Log file from Retrosheet) onto the end of the file. Here are two commands to do this:
   ```
   % cp game_log_header.csv GL2003.HDR.TXT
   % cat GL2003.TXT >> GL2003.HDR.TXT
   ```

3. Now, run the script to create MySQL input code that we built in "Load Baseball Data into MySQL" **[Hack #20]**, using a command like this:
   ```
   % perl check_field_sizes.pl -h -s "," -i GL2003.HDR.TXT > GL2003.HDR.SQL
   ```

4. Finally, we have a statement we can use to create a game log table and then load it into the database. Assuming you want to load this file into a schema called gamelogs, you can use this command to load the file:
   ```
   % mysql gamelogs < GL2003.HDR.SQL
   ```

Incidentally, you can load all the files in a directory at once by substituting the name ALLGL.HDR.TXT for GL2003.HDR.TXT, cat *.TXT for cat GL2003.TXT, and ALLGL.HDR.SQL for GL2003.HDR.SQL. I loaded all the game logs into the gamelogs schema, and into a table called ALLGL.

#22 Make a Historical Play-by-Play Database

Turn the event files on the Retrosheet web site into an easy-to-query, play-by-play database.

The Retrosheet project includes play-by-play information on almost every game from 1960 through 1992, and every game from 2000 through the present. You can use these files in many ways: you can inspect them with Chadwick, turn them into box scores, or write your own scripts to read them. One of the easiest ways to use this data is to dump it into a MySQL database. This hack shows you a quick way to make a database of play-by-play information. I use this database in many hacks in this book.

The Code

There are a number of required steps:

1. Fetch the datafile from Retrosheet (*http://www.retrosheet.org*).
2. Transform the event file format into tabular flat files.
3. Import the CSV files into MySQL.

This hack uses a little Perl to fetch and move files. See "Get Perl" [Hack #12] and "Learn Perl" [Hack #13] for more information.

Fetching the data. The first step in building this database is to get the data. I show how to fetch the data in "Get Historical Play-by-Play Data" [Hack #14].

Transforming the data. The second step in making this data accessible is to process it with the BEVENT tool [Hack #15]. The purpose of this step is to create a column in the database for each thing that can happen on a play: base runner movement, player IDs, scoring, etc. Since storage is cheap, the easiest thing to do is to use the tool to dump every possible field. There are a lot of files to unpack and translate, so another script is in order.

> The BEVENT tools only run on a PC, but the Chadwick versions are available on other platforms.

First, I created a file called *all_hdr.txt* that contains names for all 97 variables output by the BEVENT tool. I created this file by first running BEVENT -d to produce a list of field names and then editing the output. This file contains each variable name separated by a comma. This line acts as a header for the output file, making it easy for a database program to load all of the fields:

```
game_id,visiting_team,inning,batting_team,outs,balls,strikes,pitch_
sequence,vis_score,home_score,batter,batter_hand,res_batter,res_batter_
hand,pitcher,pitcher_hand,res_pitcher,res_pitcher_hand,catcher,first_
base,second_base,third_base,sh
...
er_with_First_Putout,Fielder_with_Second_Putout,Fielder_with_Third_
Putout,Fielder_with_First_Assist,Fielder_with_Second_Assist,Fielder_with_
Third_Assist,Fielder_with_Fourth_Assist,Fielder_with_Fifth_Assist,event_num
```

(I omitted the middle part of this file because it's long and repetitive. See *http://www.oreilly.com/catalog/baseballhks* for the complete version.)

Next, save the following script in a file called *translate.pl*:

```perl
#!/usr/bin/perl
# print "opening .\n";


$outfile = "pbp1960-1992.csv";
$outfile2k = "pbp2000-2004.csv";
print `cat all_hdr.txt > $outfile`;
print `cat all_hdr.txt > $outfile2k`;

opendir INFDIR, "." or die "can't open directory .: $!\n";
@archives = readdir INFDIR;
close INFDIR;
 LOOP: foreach $archive (@archives) {
     unless ($archive =~ /(\d\d\d\d[anm]l)\.zip$/) {
         # print "skipping $file\n";
         next LOOP;}
     print STDERR "uncompressing $archive\n";
     print `unzip -qq -o $archive`;

     opendir INFDIR, "." or die "can't open directory .: $!\n";
     @files = readdir INFDIR;
 ILOOP: foreach $file (@files) {
       unless ($file =~ /(\d\d)(\d\d)(\w\w\w)\.EV[AN]$/) {
          print STDERR "not processing $file\n";
          next ILOOP;}
       $century = $1; $year = $2; $team = $3;
       print STDERR "processing $file\n";
       if ($century eq "19") {
           print `./BEVENT.EXE -y $century$year -f 0-96 $file >> $outfile`;
       } else {
           print `./BEVENT.EXE -y $century$year -f 0-96 $file >>
           $outfile2k`;
```

```
        }
    print `rm $file`;
    }
}
```

To run this script, place it in the same directory as the Retrosheet event files (as compressed archives) and run the following command:

```
% perl translate.pl > pbp.csv
```

This will print some information to the screen as it's running, and it will write the output to a file called *pbp.csv*. For convenience, these scripts and their output are also included on this book's web site.

Notice that this script unpacks and processes whatever files it finds in the current working directory. I separated *pbp* files from 1960–1992 and files from 2000–2004 when I ran this script, and I called the output files *pbp.csv* and *pbp2k.csv*, respectively.

I also wanted to turn the roster files into an easy-to-read form so that I could easily associate names, teams, and hands with players. You can do the same with a short script, called *rosters.pl*:

```
opendir DIR, ".";
@files = readdir DIR;
closedir DIR;

print "retroID,lastName,firstName,bats,throws,team,pos\n";

LOOP:
    foreach $file (@files) {
        unless ($file =~ /(\w{3})(\d{4})\.ROS/) {
            next LOOP;
        }
        $team = $1;
        $year = $2;

        open FILE, "<$file";
        while (<FILE>) {
            s/\n//;
            s/\cM//;
            s/\"//g;
            if (/[a-z]{5}\d{3}/) {
                if ($year >= 2002) {
                    # after 2002, these files included a team and position
                    print "$year,$_\n";
                } else {
                    # before 2002, no team or position
                    print "$year,$_,$team,\n";
                }
            }
        }
    }
}
```

You can run this script, after running the earlier script (all the roster files will be unpacked), with the following command:

```
% perl rosters.pl > rosters.csv
```

This will save the rosters into a single file called *rosters.csv*.

Creating a database import statement. The next step in building a database is to create a script for loading the file. To create this script, use the *check_field_sizes.pl* script from "Load Baseball Data into MySQL" **[Hack #20]**. Here is the command to process the *pbp2k.csv* file:

```
% perl check_field_sizes.pl -h -s "," -i pbp2k.csv > pbp2k.sql
```

The switches tell the script that there is a header on the file and that commas separate the fields. This command creates a file called *pbp2k.sql* that you can use to load the file into a database.

A similar command creates an import statement for the rosters file:

```
% perl check_field_sizes.pl -h -s "," -i rosters.csv > rosters.sql
```

Creating a play-by-play database and tables. Finally, use the following commands to create a database named *pbp* in MySQL and to load the file:

```
~ % mysql -p -u root
Enter password:
Welcome to the MySQL monitor.  Commands end with ; or \g.
Your MySQL connection id is 37 to server version: 5.0.11-beta-max

Type 'help;' or '\h' for help. Type '\c' to clear the buffer.

mysql> create database pbp;
Query OK, 1 row affected (0.12 sec)

mysql> -- let me grant myself permission to use the new db
mysql> GRANT ALL ON pbp.* to 'jadler'@'localhost';
Query OK, 0 rows affected (0.41 sec)

mysql> quit
Bye
~ % mysql -p pbp < pbp2k.sql
Enter password:
~ % mysql -p pbp < rosters.sql
Enter password:
```

And that's it! You now have a table with every play from the past five years and a table with each player's name.

Use Regular Expressions to Identify Events
#23 Use the regular expression tools in MySQL to find events that match a pattern.

Sometimes you want to parse every event and calculate every statistic; other times, it's only important to find the events that match a pattern. This hack shows you how to use regular expressions for pattern matching. You can use this technique to create smaller files that you can open in a spreadsheet.

If you've imported play-by-play data into a MySQL database like the one we built in "Make a Historical Play-by-Play Database" [Hack #22], you can select lines using regular expressions.

Let's start with an easy example. Suppose you want to find all plays where the batter struck out. We know the play code for a strikeout always starts with K (see "Keep Score, Project Scoresheet–Style" [Hack #3] for information on play codes). To do this, we use the REGEXP operator in MySQL. This operator returns true if the field matches the regular expression, and false otherwise.

First, let's select the right database in MySQL:

```
~/Desktop % mysql pbp
Reading table information for completion of table and column names
You can turn off this feature to get a quicker startup with -A

Welcome to the MySQL monitor.  Commands end with ; or \g.
Your MySQL connection id is 3 to server version: 5.0.11-beta-max

Type 'help;' or '\h' for help. Type '\c' to clear the buffer.
```

Now, let's select a few items:

```
mysql> select game_id, visiting_team as vis,
    ->     concat(case when batting_team=1 THEN "B" ELSE "T" END,
    ->        inning) as inning,
    ->     outs, event_num as num,batter,
    ->     event_text
    -> from pbp2k
    -> where event_text REGEXP '^K' limit 5;
+--------------+------+--------+------+------+----------+------------+
| game_id      | vis  | inning | outs | num  | batter   | event_text |
+--------------+------+--------+------+------+----------+------------+
| ANA200004030 | NYA  | B1     |    2 |    8 | vaugm001 | K          |
| ANA200004030 | NYA  | B3     |    2 |   25 | vaugm001 | K          |
| ANA200004030 | NYA  | T4     |    2 |   29 | martt002 | K          |
| ANA200004030 | NYA  | T5     |    1 |   34 | posaj001 | K/C        |
| ANA200004030 | NYA  | B5     |    2 |   43 | vaugm001 | K          |
+--------------+------+--------+------+------+----------+------------+
5 rows in set (0.00 sec)
```

The interesting part here is the fourth line, where event_text REGEXP '^K'. (The limit 5 part just means "return no more than five lines." Without this part, I wouldn't be able to fit the response into this book.) The fourth line means "select only records where the event_text field starts with the letter K." Specifically, the ^ means "match the beginning of the column."

Here's an overview of regular expressions. (I'm leaving out a lot of details because this is just an introduction.) In this book, I stick to some simple patterns, most of which I can explain on this page. Here are a few rules for writing them, and some examples:

Alphabetical characters and numbers represent themselves
   To look for the word *strike*, you can use the expression /strike/.

You can't write all characters directly
   Suppose you want to look for / characters. You can use the expression /\// to match all strings with / characters. Without the \, Perl would not be able to distinguish between the end of the regular expression (/) and the character for which you are searching (/).

Wildcards can represent many different characters
   If you want to search for all errors, you can look for /E\d/. This expression matches all strings where a number comes after the letter E.

Special characters indicate repeats
   If you want to search for sequences of numbers, look for /\d+/. This matches all strings with sequences of one or more numbers.

Here is a short list of special characters and wildcards:

Special character	Meaning
\/	A forward slash (/) character
.	A wildcard matching any character
\d	A wildcard matching any digit
\s	A wildcard matching any whitespace
\w	A wildcard matching any word character (numbers, letters, and _)
*	An asterisk (*) character
\t	A tab character
\n	A newline character
\+	A plus (+) character
\\	A backslash (\) character

Here is a short list of ways to indicate repeated characters:

Special character	Meaning
*	Repeated any number of times, even zero
+	Repeated at least once
?	Repeated zero or one time

Here are a couple of other special characters that indicate placement:

Special character	Meaning
^	Match the beginning of the string
$	Match the end of the string

Hacking the Hack

You can search for any type of play that you want using regular expressions.
Here are a few ideas:

pitch_sequence REGEXP '^BBB'
: All plays that start with three straight balls

event_text REGEXP '\/G'
: All ground balls

event_text REGEXP '^HR.*3\-H.*2\-H.*1\-H.*'
: All grand slam home runs

See Also

We show you how to read play codes and pitch codes in "Keep Score,
Project Scoresheet–Style" [Hack #3].

If you want to know more about regular expressions, check out the help files
or manpages for Perl and SQL. (How do you get the manpages for Perl? If
you're using a PC and you installed Perl with Cygwin, you'll need to install
the man application as well. Then, open a command-line window and type
man perl to see the list of manpage options for Perl. For example, type man
perlrequick to get a short introduction to regular expressions in Perl.)

Even better, you might want to invest in a book on Perl or MySQL. I like the
O'Reilly books (and I'll bet my editors do, too), especially *Programming Perl*
and *MySQL Cookbook*.

## CHAPTER THREE

Stats from the Current Season
Hacks 24–29

On most sports web sites, it's easier to get statistics on the current season than on past seasons. However, if you want your own stats database for analysis, the opposite is true. I don't know of any web site that regularly publishes a database of information on the season so far. However, I do know of a lot of web sites that publish data on individual players, games, and teams.

This chapter shows you a few simple ways to collect data on individual games, players, and teams from the current season and to put this data into a single database. You can use this data to look at a player or team's performance, to manage your fantasy team, or even to run your own fantasy server.

The hacks in this chapter explain where to find data (and how to find new places to get data), how to spider web sites to get data, and how to turn that data into a format you can use. These hacks are probably the most technical and programming-intensive hacks in the book.

Use Microsoft Excel Web Queries to Get Stats

Create a spreadsheet of baseball statistics in Microsoft Excel 2003 that takes statistics directly from web sites using web queries.

Over the past few years, Microsoft has been adding more Internet functionality to the Office suite of applications (such as the ability to directly save and load HTML-format files). In Office 2003, Microsoft added some great new features to enable Office to read parts of web pages directly. If you're a baseball fan and you like to use Microsoft Excel, you'll find this feature really cool.

Web Queries

Web queries let you pull data from a web page directly into Microsoft Excel. If the web site is updated over time, your spreadsheet can also be updated. Even better, you can do this without any fancy Visual Basic scripting. Here is how to create a web query:

1. Open a new workbook, or create a new worksheet in an existing workbook.

2. Select New Web Query... from the Import External Data submenu in the Data menu.

3. A dialog box will appear, resembling the one in Figure 3-1. Type into the Address box the URL for the web site from which you want to fetch the data, and then click the Go button. This dialog box uses Internet Explorer to fetch and render web pages; there is a full working web browser in this dialog box. This means you can fill out forms on web sites or navigate to different sites from within the dialog box (no need to remember ugly URLs like the one in this example).

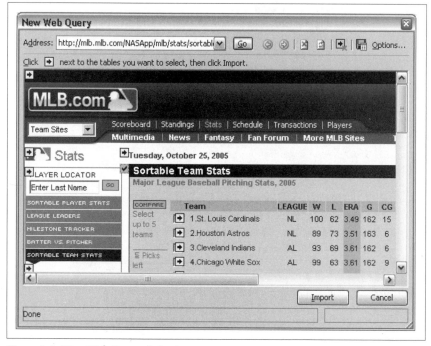

Figure 3-1. New Web Query dialog box

4. When the page containing the information you want has loaded, you need to select the table (or tables) you want to include in your web query. The dialog box places a small yellow box with an arrow in front of every table. You can click on these boxes to select individual tables. When you select a table, the box turns green and the arrow changes to a checkmark. In Figure 3-1, you will notice that I have selected the whole Sortable Team Stats table. When you are done, click the Import button.

5. The next dialog box asks you where you want the web query results. You can just choose the default. Additionally, a button labeled Properties… brings up the dialog box shown in Figure 3-2 and allows you to configure options for the query. If you want your spreadsheet to update daily, you can select the "Refresh every" checkbox and enter 1440 for the number of minutes. Click OK when you're done.

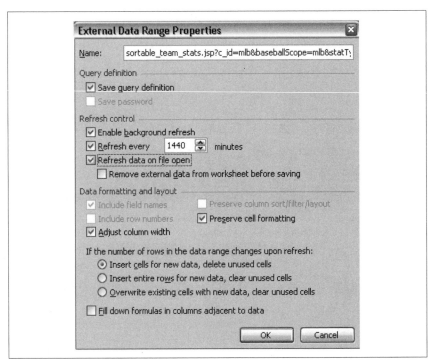

Figure 3-2. External Data Range Properties page

The results of your query will be imported into an Excel spreadsheet, like the one shown in Figure 3-3.

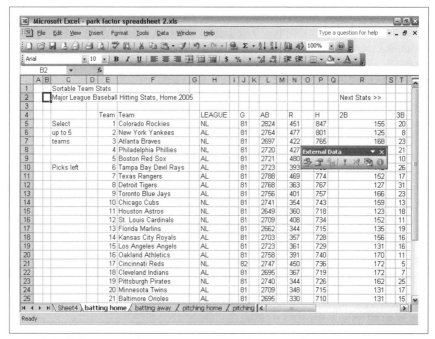

Figure 3-3. Web query results

Web Query Example: Up-to-Date Park Factors

Let's use web queries to do something useful: we'll use them to create a spreadsheet for calculating different park factors based on this year's time stats. (For more information on this formula, see "Measure Park Effects" [Hack #56].)

Step 1: Find the data. First, we need to pick a web site from which to retrieve the underlying data. MLB.com publishes team stats at *http://mlb.mlb.com/ NASApp/mlb/stats/sortable_team_stats.jsp*. This site includes key information on batters and pitchers, including games (G), at bats (AB), runs (R), strikeouts (SO), and home runs (HR). The web site also allows you to select only home or away games.

Step 2: Running the queries. We'll need to run four web queries: home batting stats, away batting stats, home pitching stats, and away pitching stats. I ran a query to select each of these tables from the MLB.com web site, saving each web query onto a different worksheet.

Step 3: Name stuff. I like to assign names to objects in Excel. It's a lot nicer to refer to the "batting home" worksheet than to "Sheet1." Double-click the name of each worksheet you created in step 2 and name them appropriately. I suggest using the names "batting home," "batting away," "pitching home," and "pitching away."

Next, you should name the data table within each worksheet. Let's start with the "batting home" table. As shown in Figure 3-3, the interesting part of the data began at cell F5 when I ran this query. Select the worksheet range containing all the home batting data. (I selected the range of cells F5:AN34 on the "batting home" worksheet. Unfortunately, web sites are often redesigned. If the underlying web page formatting changes, the data might move around. So, make sure you're selecting the right data on your spreadsheet.) Now, you need to name this range of data.

In the upper-left corner of the spreadsheet, at the left side of the formula bar, is a box you can use for naming cells. Right now, there is no name for this range, so F5 appears in this box. Click in this box, type batting_home, and click Enter. This will assign the name batting_home to this range of cells. (Alternately, you can choose Define... from the Name submenu in the Insert menu to name cells. You can also use these functions to manage named cells.) Repeat this process for the other worksheets, creating the batting_ away, pitching_home, and pitching_away ranges.

Additionally, we need to create two sets of names corresponding to the header names. Select the row headers in the "batting home" worksheet (range F4:AN4) and name this range batting_cols. Do the same thing on the "pitching home" worksheet and name this range pitching_cols.

Step 4: Create a results table. Now, let's create a menu from which you can select different types of park factor statistics. Insert a new worksheet and name it "results." In cell B3, type statistic. Name the C3 cell stat. Select the stat cell, and select Validation... from the Data menu. A dialog box like the one shown in Figure 3-4 appears. Select List from the Allow menu. In the Source field, enter =pitching_cols. (Alternately, you can save yourself some typing by clicking in the field and pressing the F3 function key to get a selectable list of named values.) Click OK when you're done. We'll refer to the stat cell in formulas described in this hack.

Name a set of cells in the spreadsheet Team, Home Batting, Away Batting, Home Pitching, Away Pitching, Home Games, Away Games, and Park Factor, as shown in Figure 3-5. (I changed the formatting of this spreadsheet to make it more readable, but this doesn't affect the functionality.) I placed these names on row 8 of the worksheet.

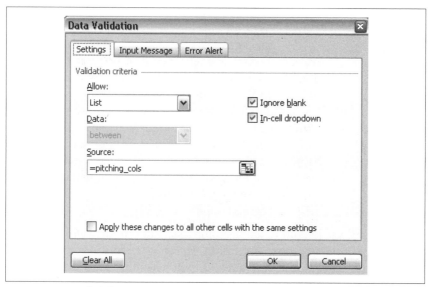

Figure 3-4. Data validation

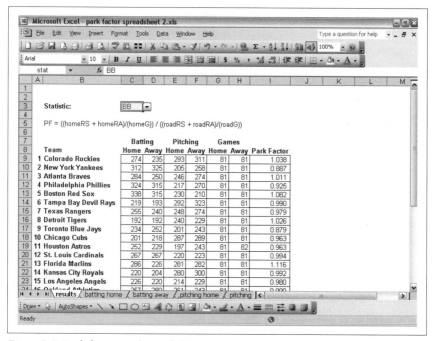

Figure 3-5. Park factor results worksheet

To prevent later errors if the data on the underlying web page moves, we're going to use cell references and formulas to create this table. First, we will create references for the team names. In the first cell of the Team column, below the label, we want to create a reference to a team name from the "batting home" worksheet. To do this, click this cell, type =, click on the "batting home" worksheet tab, and click on the first team name in the list (cell F5 for me). You should see a formula like ='batting home'!F5 in this cell, and the first team name should be displayed. You can copy and paste this formula 29 times underneath the first team, and the names of all the teams will appear. (Or, you can click on the first team name cell, click and hold on the small black box in the lower-right corner, drag the mouse down to select 30 cells, and release the mouse button. Excel will automatically fill the other cells with the next formulas in the sequence.)

Next, we will use lookup functions to find statistics. In the cell immediately to the right of the first team name (C9), we want to enter a formula to look up the batting statistic for the team to the left when they are at home. (In the specific illustration, this is strikeouts [SO] for the Colorado Rockies when they are at home.) I'll use two different formulas to do this.

The formula will figure out which column in the home_batting cell range contains the right information and will look up the result in this column for the appropriate team. To determine the correct column, we will use the MATCH Excel function. This function looks at a list of items and finds the index of the item that matches. The formula to return the right column is MATCH(stat,batting_cols,0). (Notice that this formula dynamically looks up the right column, depending on the value of the stat cell.) Assuming that the team name is in cell B9, the full formula for fetching the statistic is VLOOKUP(B9,batting_home,MATCH(stat,batting_cols,0),0). Enter this formula in cell C9 of the spreadsheet.

We can now enter similar formulas for away batting, home pitching, and away pitching. We can hardcode the G statistic to look up the number of games played. And, finally, we can calculate the team park factor, using the following formula:

```
PF = ((home batting stat + home pitching stat) / (home G)) /
     ((away batting stat + away pitching stat) / (away G))
```

This is a simple park factor formula like the one described in "Measure Park Effects" [Hack #56]. In this case, the formula is ((C9 + E9) / G9) / ((D9 + F9) / H9). Table 3-1 shows a complete set of formulas for the first row. You can copy this whole row and paste it 29 times, or click the corner and drag as described earlier. The final worksheet resembles the one shown in Figure 3-5.

Table 3-1. Formulas for row 9

Cell	Formula
B9	='batting home'!F5
C9	=VLOOKUP(B9,batting_home,MATCH(stat,batting_cols,0),0)
D9	=VLOOKUP(B9,batting_away,MATCH(stat,batting_cols,0),0)
E9	=VLOOKUP(B9,pitching_home,MATCH(stat,pitching_cols,0),0)
F9	=VLOOKUP(B9,pitching_away,MATCH(stat,pitching_cols,0),0)
G9	=VLOOKUP(B9,batting_home,MATCH("G",batting_cols,0),0)
H9	=VLOOKUP(B9,batting_away,MATCH("G",batting_cols,0),0)
I9	=((C9+E9)/G9)/((D9+F9)/H9)

That's all there is to it! You can select different statistics from the menu next to the stat box, and the worksheet will automatically calculate park factors. Even better, because MLB dynamically updates the data on the web site during the season, this worksheet will always contain up-to-date information!

Hacking the Hack

I hope you learned enough here to experiment on your own. Try querying different web sites or collecting raw statistics into other formats.

H A C K
#25 Spider Baseball Sites for Data
Sometimes the only way to get the data you want is to pull it directly from the source.

While I was writing this book, I came across the following request on the Retrosheet mailing list:

> I'm going to be doing the Fans' Scouting Report for a third
> year, but this time, I want to do it during the year.
>
> I'm looking to get the following information for 2005
> for all players, as of the all-star break:
> Team,playerID,player name,pos,innings
>
> Anyone who can help, please send me a note offlist.
>
> (playerid being whatever your data source is).
>
> Thanks, Tom

Basically, Tom needed to pull just a subset of data from the MLB.com site. Grabbing data from web pages so that you can reuse it for other purposes is a common task—so much so that it has its own name: *spidering*. Spidering allows you to write programs that read a web page and pull out just the parts you want, while throwing out the rest.

Web pages are written in a language called HyperText Markup Language (HTML). They contain different *tags* that explain to your computer how to format the page. Here is a short sample file that shows how this works:

```
<html>
<head>
<title>Baseball Sites</title>
</head>
<body>
<h1> Baseball Web Sites </h1>
This book describes many different baseball web sites. Here are a
few of my favorites:<br>
<a href="http://www.baseball1.com">The Baseball Archive</a><br>
<a href="http://www.retrosheet.org">Retrosheet</a><br>
<a href="http://www.mlb.com">MLB.com</a><br>
</body>
</html>
```

The <html> tags tell the computer that this document is in HTML. The <title> tags specify the title for the page. <h1> tells the computer to print a fancy header.
 tells the computer to insert a line break. The complicated <a href=...> tag tells the computer to put in a hyperlink to a web site. If we're just interested in the links (for example, suppose we want to compile a list of popular sites), most of the stuff on the page is junk. Our goal is to pull any useful stuff out of this pile of junk.

The first step in getting data from the Web is to find the data you want and understand how the URL that produces the page works. I found the data I wanted on the MLB.com web site, under Sortable Player Stats. A menu there lets you pick the exact statistics for which you are looking; I picked Major League, Fielding Stats, and 2005 to Date. For an illustration, see Figure 3-6.

This page was actually split into 32 different sections (the links to other sections are hidden in Figure 3-6). I needed to fetch all of these sections and put them into one file.

Many web sites use a similar URL for different pages in a sequence like this. I decided to see if I could figure out the pattern. The first page had this URL:

```
http://mlb.mlb.com/NASApp/mlb/stats/sortable_player_stats.jsp?c_
id=mlb&baseballScope=mlb&subScope=pos&teamPosCode=all&statType=3&timeSubFram
e=2005&sitSplit=&venueID=&Submit=Submit&timeFrame=1
```

The second page had this URL:

```
http://mlb.mlb.com/NASApp/mlb/stats/sortable_player_stats.jsp?c_
id=mlb&section3=2&statSet3=1&sortByStat=G&statType=3&timeFrame=1&timeSubFrame
=2005&baseballScope=mlb&prevPage3=1&readBoxes=true&sitSplit=&venueID=&subSco
pe=pos&teamPosCode=all
```

Figure 3-6. MLB.com fielding statistics

The third page had this URL:

```
http://mlb.mlb.com/NASApp/mlb/stats/sortable_player_stats.jsp?c_
id=mlb&section3=3&statSet3=1&sortByStat=G&statType=3&timeFrame=1&timeSubFrame
=2005&baseballScope=mlb&prevPage3=2&readBoxes=true&sitSplit=&venueID=&subSco
pe=pos&teamPosCode=all
```

Notice the highlighted parts. By changing just the *section3=* part of the URL, you can specify the page to fetch. Knowing this pattern allows you to write a spider to automate the process of grabbing all the fielding statistics.

Once you've figured out where the page is and how to call it, you have to do some detective work to figure out which sections you want to pull out. When spidering, you're interested in getting specific pieces of information; therefore, most HTML pages have a lot of extra "junk." So, basically, you need to throw away all of the stuff you don't need on that page: the menu bars at the front and sides, the "compare" buttons, etc. To do this, use the View Source option in your browser to look at the source code for the page.

Here was my detective work. Every one of the 35 pages was formatted identically. The different items on the page were embedded within different
HTML Table elements. All the stuff I wanted was inside one big table. I
decided to figure out a simple way to skip to the table I wanted and stop
after it was finished.

By inspecting the file, I discovered there were three <table> tags before the
one I wanted. I also discovered that the table I wanted always ended with a
tag containing <INPUT TYPE="IMAGE" NAME="compare">. This let me use a sim-
ple script to read each file: I simply threw out everything until the fourth
table and everything after the INPUT tag.

I needed to do a few other things to make the results readable: I put a header
at the top of the table; I added some code to join the HTML cleanly between
files; and I extracted the player ID from each player link and wrote it in a
new cell.

The Code

In the end, I came up with the following short script. This script fetches all
the data from the MLB.com web site and creates an HTML file containing a
table of all the fielding results. Type the following code into a file called *get_
fielding.pl*:

```perl
#!/usr/bin/perl

use LWP;
use Data::Dump;
use FileHandle;

$browser = LWP::UserAgent->new;

my $fh = new FileHandle ">fielding.html";
print $fh "<html><body>\n";
print $fh "<table><th>\n";
print $fh "    <td>checkbox</td>\n";
print $fh "    <td>Player</td>\n";
print $fh "    <td>ID</td>\n";
print $fh "    <td>TEAM</td>\n";
print $fh "    <td>POS</td>\n";
print $fh "    <td>G</td>\n";
print $fh "    <td>GS</td>\n";
print $fh "    <td>INN</td>\n";
print $fh "    <td>TC</td>\n";
print $fh "    <td>PO</td>\n";
print $fh "    <td>A</td>\n";
print $fh "    <td>E</td>\n";
print $fh "    <td>DP</td>\n";
print $fh "    <td>PB</td>\n";
```

```
print $fh "    <td>SB</td>\n";
print $fh "    <td>CS</td>\n";
print $fh "    <td>RF</td>\n";
print $fh "    <td>FPCT</td>\n";
print $fh "</th>\n";

for $i (1 .. 35) { # should go to 35
    print $fh "<tr><td><img src=\"/images/trans.gif\" width=\"1\" height=\
    "1\" b
order=\"0\" /></td><td><input type=\"checkbox\" name=\"box2\"
value=XXXX408307tb'aO onClick=\"countChoices3(this, 'box2');\"></td><td>\n";
    $url = "http://mlb.mlb.com/NASApp/mlb/stats/sortable_player_stats.jsp?c_
id=mlb&section3=$i&statSet3=1&sortByStat=G&statType=3&timeFrame=1&timeSubFra
me=2005&baseballScope=mlb&prevPage3=1&readBoxes=true&sitSplit=&venueID=&team
PosCode=all&print=true";
    $response = $browser->get($url);
        die "Couldn't get $url:", $response->status_line, "\n"
            unless $response->is_success;
        $html = $response->content;
        @lines = split "\n", $html;
        my $out = -2;
        foreach $line (@lines) {
            if ($line =~ /<table/) {$out++;}
            if ($line =~ /<INPUT TYPE="IMAGE" NAME="compare"/) {$out = 0;}
            if ($out > 0) { print $fh "$line\n";}
            if ($line =~ /playerID=(\d+)\8/) {
                print $fh "</tr></table></td><td><table><tr><td>$1</td>\n";
            }
        }
    }
}
$fh->close();
```

Running the Hack

To run the hack, you type `perl=get_fielding.pl` at a command prompt. The program will process this file and store the results in a file called *fielding.html*. Running this script produces the output shown in Figure 3-7. While it's impossible to show in the figure, this single table contains the complete 35 pages' worth of fielding stats.

With one short script, I could pull current statistics for every player into a single file. But we're not done yet. It's hard to work with files in an HTML table, but it's easy to turn HTML tables into spreadsheets that you can analyze in any way you want.

To do this with Microsoft Excel, just choose Open from the File menu in Excel. In the dialog box, select All Files (if you're working on a PC) or All Readable Files (if you're on a Mac), and pick the *fielding.html* file. Excel should open the table in a spreadsheet, ready for manipulation.

Spider Baseball Sites for Data

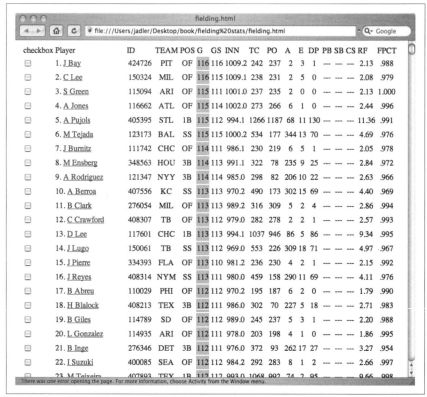

Figure 3-7. The fielding table generated by the script

Hacking the Hack

Here are a few ideas on where to go from here:

Different statistics

In this example, I looked at fielding statistics from this season. You can do exactly the same thing with pitching statistics, batting statistics, partial seasons, and past seasons. You'll need to modify the table headers, page counts, and URLs to make it work.

Other sources

I chose MLB.com because it included the statistics I wanted. But you can do the same thing with any web site that shares statistics.

More parsing

I chose to manipulate just the HTML to make a single table. As an alternative, you can use Perl to read the contents of the tables and dump the result into text files, a database, or any other form you like. A good way to do this is with the HTML::TableParser module for Perl. You can get information about this module by searching *http://search.cpan.org*.

See Also

If you want to learn more about HTML, a great place to start is the official World Wide Web Consortium (W3C) web site. You can find links to the HTML standards at *http://www.w3.org/MarkUp/#recommendations*. If you want some other ideas on how to get current data, see the other hacks in this chapter. For more information on spidering, see *Spidering Hacks* (O'Reilly).

Discover How Live Score Applications Work

#26

Practically any baseball site that presents live score data is probably accessing a hidden data source that you can use, too—provided you know where to look.

Many sports web sites include features for following along with games in real time. These features are usually implemented as either Java applet or Flash applications. In either case, they're miniature programs that your web browser downloads on the fly and runs on your local machine. These applications then request data (images, plays, and statistics) from the Internet and display this on your computer. If you just want to collect the data on a baseball game for analysis, but you don't want to follow along in real time, you need to figure out where the application gets its data.

Today, most live score applications simply get data through HTTP requests to web servers. This is the same way your web browser retrieves web pages from the Internet. This makes it very easy for the baseball hacker to get what he wants from those servers. In the future, these applications might get more sophisticated and start using web services mechanisms like SOAP, or they might start implementing digital rights management (DRM) features to make your life harder. For now, you can use a few simple tricks to figure out where live score applications get data.

Use Your Router's Content Filtering Feature

Many home cable/DSL routers or wireless routers have a URL filtering function to keep children from viewing certain content. (If you're a parent, I hope you're not using this feature to block your children from reading about baseball!) My $50 wireless router does this (I didn't even know it had this function when I bought it). Products from Linksys and D-Link also offer this functionality. Figure 3-8, for example, shows the log page for the content filtering function in my NETGEAR router.

As you can see, when I launched the MLB.com Gameday application, an entry appeared for *gd2.mlb.com*, indicating that this application was fetching data from this host.

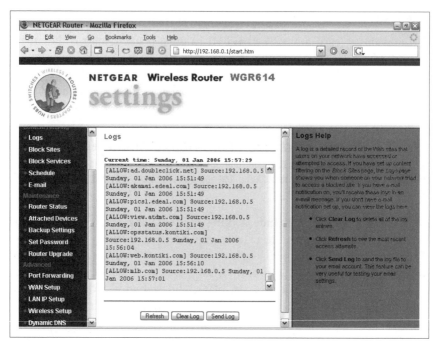

Figure 3-8. Log page from a wireless router

Use a Proxy Server

A better option is to install a proxy server on your Windows PC and to use this to look at what documents your browser gets from the Internet. I recommend Proxy Sniffer, available from *http://www.proxy-sniffer.com.* (I downloaded my copy from CNET's site, *http://www.downloadl.com.*) This software provides a log of every interaction between your web browser and other servers in a nice log format. Plus, a free edition is available that works perfectly for this application.

To use the proxy server, begin by downloading and installing the software. Next, start the Proxy Sniffer server by opening the program from your Start menu (select Start → Programs → Proxy Sniffer → Run Proxy Sniffer Server). By default, the server uses port 7999.

Next, configure the browser to use the proxy server. Open the Options... dialog box from the Tools menu in your browser (either Internet Explorer or Firefox). In Internet Explorer, click the Connections tab, click the LAN Settings button, and then enter localhost for the address and 7999 for the port. In Firefox, click the Connection Settings button under the Options tab; then select "Manual proxy configuration" and enter 7999 for the HTTP proxy port.

Open the management interface by selecting Start → Programs → Proxy
Sniffer → Proxy Sniffer Web Admin. Click the Start Record link in the upper-
left corner. Now, start running the baseball score application. Once the
application loads and is displaying data, return to the admin interface and
click Stop Record. As shown in Figure 3-9, you will see a record of every
document fetched from your web browser that you can use to decipher what
the baseball score application is doing.

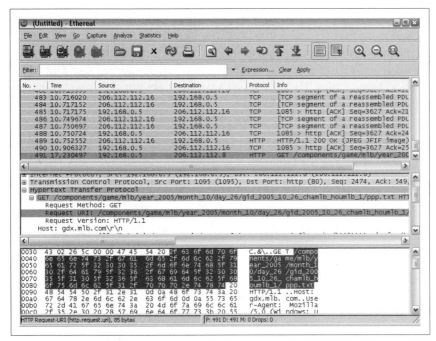

Figure 3-9. Proxy sniffer

Packet Filters

If you're really hardcore, you can try using a packet filter to snoop on your
network traffic. Packet filters monitor your network interfaces, showing all
traffic moving over the network. This technique guarantees that you will see
how an application communicates with other servers on the Internet. (However, it doesn't guarantee that you'll be able to understand what's going on.)

The easiest tool to use for this purpose is Ethereal. Ethereal is a GUI-driven
packet sniffer. It looks at every packet sent over a network interface, decom-
posing the network traffic into a nice, organized format. Ethereal is an open
source application, so you can download it free of charge. For more information about this application, see *http://www.ethereal.com*.

This hack is probably the most technical one in this book. I don't go through all the steps involved in using Ethereal or tcpdump—this is a book about baseball, not computer networking! If you know something about computer networks and network applications, you'll probably be comfortable reading the manpages and help files for these tools to figure out what they do.

When I did my investigations, I actually used a different tool, called tcpdump, which is another packet sniffer. This one is text driven (you run it from the command line) and is included with most Linux and BSD Unix distributions. It's not as user friendly as Ethereal, though you can use Ethereal to read its output files. Here's the call I used to monitor the traffic, dumping the results into the *packets.dmp* file:

```
root# tcpdump -A -s 0 -w packets.dump ip
```

As the Flash application loads, it requests information from several different web sites. Looking for GET requests (where an application was fetching a document from an HTTP server), I found that the application was fetching items in a *components* directory on host 216.74.142.22. (Further investigation revealed that this was *gd2.mlb.com*.)

Here is a sample of what it was showing:

```
10:17:32.992840 IP (tos 0x0, ttl  64, id 65008, offset 0, flags [DF],
length: 40)
192.168.0.2.52835 > 216.74.142.22.http: . [tcp sum ok] 1020:1020(0) ack 245
win 65
535
.       [S.P..$/[1..E..(..@.@........J...c.P[\N..v..P...k...
10:17:33.021167 IP (tos 0x0, ttl  64, id 65009, offset 0, flags [DF],
length: 1064
) 192.168.0.2.52837 > 216.74.142.22.http: P [bad tcp cksum 2b26 (->faef)!]
4284516
538:4284517562(1024) ack 1752587775 win 65535
.       [S.P..$/[1..E..(..@.@........J...e.P.`..hv].P...+&..GET /components/
game/y
ear_2004/month_07/day_01/gid_2004_07_01_bosmlb_nyamlb_1/players.txt HTTP/1.1
Host: gd2.mlb.com
User-Agent: Mozilla/5.0 (Macintosh; U; PPC Mac OS X Mach-O; en-US; rv:1.7.5)
Gecko
/20041107 Firefox/1.0
Accept: text/xml,application/xml,application/xhtml+xml,text/html;q=0.9,text/
plain;
q=0.8,image/png,*/*;q=0.5
```

```
Accept-Language: en-us,en;q=0.5
Accept-Encoding: gzip,deflate
Accept-Charset: ISO-8859-1,utf-8;q=0.7,*;q=0.7
Keep-Alive: 300
Connection: keep-alive
```

Notice the part in bold in the preceding code—this is where the application is fetching data from this server. If you want to use another data source or if this one changes in the future, you can use this method and a little detective work to find where to get the data.

HACK #27 Keep Your Stats Database Up-to-Date

Create your own database of player statistics and keep it up-to-date as the season progresses.

If you want to know how a player is doing this season, the easiest way to learn is by looking it up at a popular baseball web site [Hack #5]. Most of the time, this will be fine: for example, if you just want to know David Ortiz's slugging percentage for the year. However, suppose you want to ask a complicated question (say, how did David Ortiz do in the first two weeks of May?). Or suppose you want to use the data for something else, like managing your fantasy team (or league). In these cases, you might want to keep your own up-to-date database.

This hack shows a method for doing this.

The Code

Here's the code to fetch data from the Web and save it directly to a database. There are three parts to this code: a script to create a database, a script to fill the database initially, and a script to update the database.

Create the box score database. Let's start off by creating a simple database in MySQL. If you want to follow along, you can create a file called *create_boxes_db.sql* and enter all the code in this section into the file:

```
-- create a new database schema for the box score information,
-- and a user to access the database
GRANT ALL ON boxes.* to 'boxer'@'localhost'
          IDENTIFIED BY 'boxers password';
CREATE DATABASE boxes;
USE boxes;

-- Create three tables containing information about players:
-- batting, fielding, and pitching. Fields are sized to
-- minimize storage space for this database
```

```
CREATE TABLE batting (
        eliasID     INT(6),
        teamID      CHAR(3),
        gameID      VARCHAR(32),
        gameDate    DATE,
        h           SMALLINT(2), -- hits
        hr          SMALLINT(2), -- home runs
        bb          SMALLINT(2), -- walks
        so          SMALLINT(2), -- strikeouts
        rbi         SMALLINT(2), -- runs batted in
        ab          SMALLINT(2), -- at bats
        runs        SMALLINT(2), -- runs scored
        t           SMALLINT(2), -- triples
        d           SMALLINT(2), -- doubles
        lob         SMALLINT(2), -- left on base
        sb          SMALLINT(2), -- stolen bases
        cs          SMALLINT(2)  -- caught stealing
);

CREATE TABLE fielding (
        eliasID     INT(6),
        teamID      CHAR(3),
        gameID      VARCHAR(32),
        gameDate    DATE,
        pos         CHAR(2),     -- position
        po          SMALLINT(2), -- putouts
        da          SMALLINT(2), -- assists
        e           SMALLINT(2), -- errors
        pb          SMALLINT(2)  -- passed balls
);

CREATE TABLE pitching (
        eliasID     INT(6),
        teamID      VARCHAR(3),
        gameID      VARCHAR(32),
        gameDate    DATE,
        outs        SMALLINT(2),
        bf          SMALLINT(2), -- batters faced
        hr          SMALLINT(2), -- home runs
        bb          SMALLINT(2), -- walks
        so          SMALLINT(2), -- strikeouts
        er          SMALLINT(2), -- earned runs
        runs        SMALLINT(2), -- runs
        hits        SMALLINT(2), -- hits
        wins        SMALLINT(2), -- wins
        losses      SMALLINT(2), -- losses
        holds       SMALLINT(2), -- holds
        hopps       SMALLINT(2), -- hold opportunities
        saves       SMALLINT(2), -- saves
        sopps       SMALLINT(2)  -- save opportunities
);
```

```
-- Add a table to keep track of a little information
-- about each game, such as the opponents and date.

CREATE TABLE games (
        gameID      VARCHAR(32),
        gameDate    DATE,
        homeTeam    CHAR(3),
        awayTeam    CHAR(3)
);

-- Keep track of the complete daily rosters. This
-- table will include detailed information about
-- who played in each game.

CREATE TABLE rosters (
        gameID      VARCHAR(32),
        gameDate    DATE,
        teamID      CHAR(3),
        eliasID     INT(6),
        nameFirst   VARCHAR(32),
        nameLast    VARCHAR(32),
        nickName    VARCHAR(32),
        jersey      SMALLINT(2),
        throws      CHAR(1)
);

-- Show what we've created.
show tables;
```

The update script. Now we'll tackle the Perl code for populating the database. We want to update the tables in the previous code snippet daily, and we want to be careful that each game is finished before we update the database. To be sure that each game is finished, I decided that after 12:00 p.m., GMT (Greenwich Mean Time), all of the games from the previous day would be finished. (Note the use of 36 hours; date values have a time of midnight by default.)

The most important decision to make is where to get the data. You can get this information anywhere box scores are available, but in this section, I'm going to use a really simple one. MLB.com's Gameday servers include a copy of every box score in XML format. XML is a standard for sharing data in a computer-readable format. It looks a lot like HTML, the language used to make web pages; to learn more about XML, see *http://www.w3.org/XML*. This is great for us because some neat tools are available for reading XML files into Perl.

I used the same LWP library as before to download the files and a module called XML::Simple to make the downloaded file easy to read in Perl. (For more information on Perl modules, see "Get Perl" [Hack #12].)

To make this script readable, I placed the code for reading box scores and saving the contents into a Perl module, called save_to_db. I used four different subroutines to do this: save_batting_and_fielding, save_pitching, save_game, and save_roster. You can guess what each one does. Enter the code in this section into a file called *update_db.pl*:

```perl
#!/usr/bin/perl

# updates database with latest information from box scores
# To keep DB up to date, run with scheduled tasks or chron daily

# we'll use some of the same subroutines for booootstrapping and updating
use save_to_db;
use Mysql;
my $dbh = Mysql->connect('localhost', 'boxes', 'boxer', 'boxers password');
$dbh->{'dbh'}->{'PrintError'} = 1;
use XML::Simple;
my $xs = new XML::Simple(ForceArray => 1, KeepRoot => 1, KeyAttr =>
'boxscore');
use LWP;
my $browser = LWP::UserAgent->new;

# to prevent partial loading of games in progress, only load a day's games
# after 12:00 PM GMT

my ($sec,$min,$hour,$mday,$mon,$year,$wday,$yday,$isdst)
    = gmtime(time() - 60*60*36);
my $fmon = length($mon + 1) == 1 ? '0' . ($mon + 1) : ($mon + 1);
my $fday = length($mday) == 1 ?  '0' . $mon : $mday;

# build base url for fetching box scores and start fetching
my $baseurl = 'http://gd2.mlb.com/components/game/year_' . (1900 + $year) .
    '/month_' . $fmon .
    '/day_' . $fday . '/';

# fetch names of all games played
my $response = $browser->get($baseurl);
die "Couldn't get $baseurl: ", $response->status_line, "\n"
    unless $response->is_success;
my $dirhtml = $response->content;

# now, load the box score for each game played that day
while($dirhtml =~ m/<a href=\"(gid_.+)\/\"/g ) {
    my $game = $1;
    print "fetching box score for game $game\n";
    my $boxurl = $baseurl . $game . "/boxscore.xml";
    my $response = $browser->get($boxurl);
```

```
        die "Couldn't get $boxurl: ", $response->status_line, "\n"
            unless $response->is_success;
        my $box = $xs->XMLin($response->content);
        save_batting_and_fielding($dbh, $box);
        save_pitching($dbh, $box);
        save_game($dbh, $box);

        my $playersurl = $baseurl . $game . "/players.txt";
        my $response = $browser->get($playersurl);
        die "Couldn't get $playersurl: ", $response->status_line, "\n"
            unless $response->is_success;
        save_roster($dbh, $box, $response->content);
    }
```

The bootstrapping script. If you start building this database in the middle of
the season (as I did), you'll probably want to preload the database with
information on everything that has happened so far. Here's a simple script
to do this. By design, the bootstrapping script is very similar to the update
script. (I omitted redundant parts that are the same as the update script.
Actually, I kept all the tricky code in the save_to_db module.) Create a file
called *load_db.pl* and add the following code into the file as listed here:

```perl
#!/usr/bin/perl

# loads a database with this season's box scores up through yesterday's
games

use save_to_db;

use Mysql;
my $dbh = Mysql->connect('localhost', 'boxes', 'boxer', 'boxers password');
$dbh->{'dbh'}->{'PrintError'} = 1;
use XML::Simple;
my $xs = new XML::Simple(ForceArray => 1, KeepRoot => 1, KeyAttr =>
'boxscore');
use LWP;
my $browser = LWP::UserAgent->new;

# to prevent partial loading of games in progress, only load a day's games
# after 12:00 PM GMT
use Time::Local;
my $mintime = timegm(0,0,0,3,3,105);
my $maxtime = time() - 60*60*36;
my $mintimestr = gmtime(timegm(0,0,0,3,3,105));
my $maxtimestr = gmtime(time() - 60*60*36);

print "iterating from $mintimestr to $maxtimestr\n";
for ($i = $mintime; $i <= $maxtime; $i += 86400) {
    ($sec,$min,$hour,$mday,$mon,$year,$wday,$yday,$isdst) = gmtime($i);
    $fmon = length($mon + 1) == 1 ? '0' . ($mon + 1) : ($mon + 1);
    $fday = length($mday) == 1 ?  '0' . $mday : $mday;
```

```
# build base url for fetching box scores and start fetching
$baseurl = 'http://gd2.mlb.com/components/game/mlb/year_' . (1900 +
    $year) .
    '/month_' . $fmon .
    '/day_' . $fday . '/';

my $response = $browser->get($baseurl);
die "Couldn't get $baseurl: ", $response->status_line, "\n"
    unless $response->is_success;
my $dirhtml = $response->content;

while($dirhtml =~ m/<a href=\"(gid_.+)\/\"/g ) {
    my $game = $1;
    print "fetching box score for game $game\n";
    my $boxurl = $baseurl . $game . "/boxscore.xml";
    my $response = $browser->get($boxurl);
    # die "Couldn't get $boxurl: ", $response->status_line, "\n"
    unless ($response->is_success) {
        print "Couldn't get $boxurl: ", $response->status_line, "\n";
        next;
    }
    my $box = $xs->XMLin($response->content);
    save_batting_and_fielding($dbh, $box);
    save_pitching($dbh, $box);
    save_game($dbh, $box);

    my $playersurl = $baseurl . $game . "/players.txt";
    my $response = $browser->get($playersurl);
    unless ($response->is_success) {
        print "Couldn't get $playersurl: ", $response->status_line,
        "\ n";
        next;
    }
    save_roster($dbh, $box, $response->content);
}
# be a good spider and don't take up too much bandwidth
sleep(1);
}
```

The helping code. Create a file called *save_to_db.pm* for the helping code; make sure you save it in the same directory as the other Perl scripts for this hack. Then add all the following code snippets into the file.

First, we need some header information for the package, to give it a name and define what subroutines it exports:

```
package save_to_db;
require Exporter;
@ISA = qw(Exporter);
@EXPORT = qw (save_batting_and_fielding save_pitching save_game save_
roster);
```

Next, we'll define a couple of internal subroutines to simplify the code. The extract_date subroutine pulls a date out of a game identifier and formats it properly for MySQL. The extract_info subroutine pulls a few values out of the box score and assigns them to variables. These two subroutines contain code that repeats in each exported method.

```perl
sub extract_date($) {
    my($in) = @_;
    my $gmyr = substr($in,0,4);
    my $gmmn = substr($in,5,2);
    my $gmdy = substr($in,8,2);
    my $gamedate = '\'' . $gmyr . '-' . $gmmn . '-' . $gmdy . '\'';
    return $gamedate;
}


sub extract_info($) {
    my ($box) = @_;
    my $home = $box->{boxscore}->[0]->{home_team_code};
    my $away = $box->{boxscore}->[0]->{away_team_code};
    my $gameid = "'" . $box->{boxscore}->[0]->{game_id} . "'";
    my $gamedate = extract_date($box->{boxscore}->[0]->{game_id});
    return ($home, $away, $gameid, $gamedate);
}
```

Let's start with pitching. The following subroutine iterates over each pitcher on each team, generates a database record for each performance, and writes this query to the database:

```perl
sub save_pitching($$) {
    my ($dbh, $box) = @_;
    my ($home, $away, $gameid, $gamedate) = extract_info($box);
    foreach $team (@{$box->{boxscore}->[0]->{pitching}}) {
        foreach $pitcher (@{$team->{pitcher}}) {
            $win=0; $loss=0; $hold=0; $holdopp=0; $save=0; $saveopp=0;
            if    ($pitcher->{note} =~ /\(W/) { $win = 1; }
            elsif ($pitcher->{note} =~ /\(L/) {$loss = 1; }
            elsif ($pitcher->{note} =~ /\(S/) {$save = 1; $saveopp = 1;}
            elsif ($pitcher->{note} =~ /\(BS/) {$saveopp = 1;}
            elsif ($pitcher->{note} =~ /\(H/) {$hold = 1; $holdopp = 1;}
            elsif ($pitcher->{note} =~ /\(BH/) {$holdopp = 1;}
            $ptchr_query = 'INSERT INTO pitching VALUES ('
            . join(',', (
                $pitcher->{id},
                "'" . ($team->{team_flag}=="home" ?
                    $home : $away) . "'",
                $gameid,
                $gamedate,
                $pitcher->{out},
                $pitcher->{bf},
                $pitcher->{hr},
                $pitcher->{bb},
                $pitcher->{so},
```

```
                  $pitcher->{er},
                  $pitcher->{r},
                  $pitcher->{h},
                  $win,
                  $loss,
                  $hold,
                  $holdopp,
                  $save,
                  $saveopp
                  )) . ")";
          $sth = $dbh->query($ptchr_query);
          die ("MySQL Error: $dbh->$errmsg\n") unless defined($sth);
      }
      }
  }
```

The subroutine to extract batting and fielding information is similar, but I
defined an extra helper routine to make them work better. The XML box
scores, unfortunately, don't include line items for every important measurement. However, this information is included in HTML-formatted notes. To
extract the missing stuff (like stolen bases and errors), I used the following
subroutine. This procedure pulls out the information for each field and
returns an anonymous hash with information about what each player did.
For example, here is how to use this procedure to extract information on
steals:

```
  my %steals      = %{extractvars('SB', $team->{text_data}->[0])};
```

The process for pulling out the data is a little complicated and repetitive, so
I defined it once in a subroutine to keep the code clean. Here is the subroutine itself:

```
  sub extractvars($$) {
      # a procedure for extracting information from
      # the text data field (like stolen bases, errors, etc.)
      my ($type, $text) = @_;
      my $stuff = {};

      if ($text =~ m{ <b> $type <\/b>\:\s* (.*) \.<br\/> }x) {
      my @players = split /\),/, $1;
          foreach $player (@players) {
              # important: player names may include commas, spaces,
              #        apostrophes, and periods, but no numbers
              #        or parentheses
              $player =~ /([\w\s\,\.\']+)\s(\d?)\s?\(.*/;
              $name = $1;
              if ($2) {$num = $2;} else {$num = 1;}
              $stuff->{$name} = $num;
          }
      }
      return $stuff;
  }
```

Putting this together, here is the code for saving batting and fielding information:

```
sub save_batting_and_fielding($$) {
    my ($dbh, $box) = @_;
    my ($home, $away, $gameid, $gamedate) = extract_info($box);
    foreach $team (@{$box->{boxscore}->[0]->{batting}}) {
        my %steals        = %{extractvars('SB', $team->{text_data}->[0])};
        my %caughtstealing = %{extractvars('CS', $team->{text_data}->[0])};
        my %errors        = %{extractvars('E',  $team->{text_data}->[0])};
        my %passedballs   = %{extractvars('PB', $team->{text_data}->[0])};

        foreach $batter (@{$team->{batter}}) {
            my $sb = $steals{$batter->{name}};
            $sb = 0 unless defined($sb);
            my $cs = $caughtstealing{$batter->{name}};
            $cs = 0 unless defined($cs);
            my $e = $errors{$batter->{name}};
            $e = 0 unless defined($e);
            my $pb = $passedballs{$batter->{name}};
            $pb = 0 unless defined($pb);

            $batr_query = 'INSERT INTO batting VALUES ('
            . join(',', (
                $batter->{id},
                "'" . ($team->{team_flag}=="home" ?
                    $home : $away) . "'",
                $gameid,
                $gamedate,
                $batter->{h},
                $batter->{hr},
                $batter->{bb},
                $batter->{so},
                $batter->{rbi},
                $batter->{ab},
                $batter->{r},
                $batter->{t},
                $batter->{d},
                $batter->{lob},
                $sb,
                $cs
            )) . ")";
            $sth = $dbh->query($batr_query);
            die ("MySQL Error: $dbh->$errmsg\n") unless defined($sth);

            $fldr_query = 'INSERT INTO fielding VALUES ('
            . join(',', (
                $batter->{id},
                "'" . ($team->{team_flag}=="home" ?
                    $home : $away) ."'",
                $gameid,
                $gamedate,
                "'" . $batter->{pos} . "'",
```

```
                    $batter->{po},
                    $batter->{da},
                    $e,
                    $pb
                )) . ")";
            $sth = $dbh->query($fldr_query);
            die ("MySQL Error: $dbh->$errmsg\n") unless defined($sth);
        }
    }
}
```

And, finally, here are the subroutines for writing game and roster information to the database:

```
sub save_game($$) {
    my ($dbh, $box) = @_;
    my ($home, $away, $gameid, $gamedate) = extract_info($box);
    foreach $team (@{$box->{boxscore}->[0]->{pitching}}) {
        $game_query = 'INSERT INTO games VALUES ('
            . join(',', (
                    $gameid,
                    $gamedate,
                    "'" . $home . "'",
                    "'" . $away . "'"
                )) . ")";
        $sth = $dbh->query($game_query);
        die ("MySQL Error: $dbh->$errmsg\n") unless defined($sth);
    }
}

sub save_roster($$$) {
    my ($dbh, $box, $file) = @_;
    my ($home, $away, $gameid, $gamedate) = extract_info($box);
    @players = split /\&/, $file;
    foreach $player (@players) {
    ($playeridstr, $first, $last, $jersey, $nickname, $throws) =
        split /\|/, $player;
    if ($playeridstr =~ /([ha])\d\d?\=(\d+)/) {
        $homeaway = $1;
        $playerid = $2;
        if ($jersey == "--") {$jersey = "null";}
        $roster_query = 'INSERT INTO rosters VALUE ('
            . join(',', (
                    $gameid,
                    $gamedate,
                    "'" . ($homeaway=="h" ?
                        $home : $away) . "'",
                    $playerid,
                    '"' . $first . '"',
                    '"' . $last . '"',
                    '"' . $nickname . '"',
                    $jersey,
                    "'" . $throws . "'"
                )) . ")";
```

```
    $sth = $dbh->query($roster_query);
    die ("MySQL Error: $dbh->$errmsg\n") unless defined($sth);
    }
    }
}
# make sure to return a true value for the module
1;
```

Running the Hack

You can run the *create_boxes_db.sql* script with the following command:

```
% mysql -u root < create_boxes_db.sql
```

Barring any errors, this will show a list of the tables created:

```
mysql> use boxes;
Database changed
mysql> show tables;
+-----------------+
| Tables_in_boxes |
+-----------------+
| batting         |
| fielding        |
| games           |
| pitching        |
| rosters         |
+-----------------+
```

 You need to execute *create_boxes_db.sql* only once to create
the initial data structures!

You can run the bootstrap code manually with the following command:

```
% perl load_db.pl
```

This will display the name of each box score as it loads and show you alerts
if there are any problems:

```
iterating from Sun Apr  3 00:00:00 2005 to Sun May 29 07:27:41 2005
fetching box score for game gid_2005_04_03_anamlb_lanmlb_1
fetching box score for game gid_2005_04_03_balmlb_phimlb_1
fetching box score for game gid_2005_04_03_bosmlb_nyamlb_1
...
```

You should run this script exactly once per day to add new game data into
your database. I recommend using a utility like cron (on Unix-based platforms) or Scheduled Tasks (on Windows platforms) to execute this script
exactly once per day.

Hacking the Hack

I showed how to extract information for MLB games and save it to a database. Here are a few tips on where to go from here:

Use a different data source
Although the MLB.com XML files are the easiest place to start, any electronically available box score will work. For example, you can use the `HTML::TableContentParser` module to extract data from web pages.

Fetch data from other leagues
International and minor league game data is available online, and you can build a database of this data (helpful for sophisticated fantasy players). For example, MLB.com Gameday has AAA league information at *http://gd2.mlb.com/components/game/aaa* and AA information at *http://gd2.mlb.com/components/game/aax*.

Save more data
I skipped a lot of fields in this hack (like game temperatures and double plays), but you can easily modify this hack to track this stuff.

Get Recent Play-by-Play Data

HACK #28

Sometimes total statistics like hits, runs, and strikeouts aren't good enough for your analysis. This hack explains how to build a database of data on every play.

Many baseball books and baseball databases contain only seasonal statistics: the average or total performance of a team or player during the season. But sometimes these statistics aren't enough. You might want to know what tends to happen in certain situations (like with one man on first and no outs), or you might want a count of events (like the number of at bats with more than five pitchers) that aren't measured in standard statistics. If you knew everything that happened in a game, you could calculate these statistics. This hack shows you how to get data on every play of every game.

Many sports-oriented web sites give detailed play-by-play descriptions of individual games, including Yahoo! Sports, ESPN.com, CBS SportsLine, and MLB.com. Most of these web sites include detailed test descriptions of each play that you can easily encode and save in a database. We're going to use more spidering techniques [Hack #25] to find all files on a web site and save copies of them for later analysis. This hack shows you how to use the play-by-play descriptions on MLB.com because that site provides the data in XML format. While you can get the same data from other web sites in HTML format, it's a little easier to work with the XML files.

The best source of play-by-play data is to buy it from one of the commercial scoring bureaus: the Elias Sports Bureau, 24-7 Baseball, or STATS, Inc. They include the most detailed descriptions of every play that you can get: which players were on the field, what type of pitch was thrown, where the ball landed, etc.

MLB allows fans to use a Flash application called Gameday to follow games in progress or review every play in past games. These events are stored on a set of servers, such as *gd.mlb.com* and *gdx.mlb.com*. I discovered how this worked using some of the techniques described in "Discover How Live Score Applications Work" **[Hack #26]**.

The MLB.com Gameday web server is very well structured. At the top level are directories corresponding to different types of data. At the next level are directories for different years, then for different months, then for different days, and then for individual games. Inside each individual game directory is a set of files that describe what happened in that game.

For each game, this site contains a number of files corresponding to different data presented by the Flash application. Here is a list of the most interesting components:

boxscore.xml
An XML document that contains the box score for the game.

players.txt
A file that lists each player on each team. This file is very useful for mapping player ID numbers to player names.

Inning files
A directory containing an XML file describing what happened in each inning.

PBP files
A directory containing information on how each batter fared, down to the location of each pitch thrown and each ball hit.

You'll find lots of other stuff on this site (situational statistics for batters and pitchers, line scores, etc.), but most of these documents are redundant, and we'll ignore them. Let's start by fetching recent play-by-play information.

The Code

I used Perl to fetch, process, and create event files from the MLB.com web site. To make this hack easier to understand, I split it into two scripts:

spider.pl
    This script fetches all the relevant files from the MLB web site.

parser.pl
    This script reads all the fetched files, translating them into a Retrosheet–style event file.

I used the following different Perl modules to simplify my code; you will need to install them [Hack #12] before you can run these hacks:

LWP
    The LWP module provides a simple interface for fetching documents from URLs. I use LWP::UserAgent objects in the spider.

XML::Simple
    The XML::Simple module provides a simple interface for reading XML files. Specifically, it turns an XML file into a Perl data hash object.

Data::Dumper
    The final scripts don't use this module directly, but I found this module essential for debugging. It prints out the data objects returned by XML:: Simple.

The spider script. This script takes advantage of the structure of this web site and the directory listings, and it grabs all the files listed earlier for every game on the MLB.com Gameday web site. It saves the file on your computer under a unique name and then builds an HTML logfile that lets you inspect all the play-by-play files with your web browser.

 This script will pull down approximately 250 MB of data from the MLB.com web site if you run it as is. If you don't need all this data, delete the parts you don't care about. I could have done something less hack-like, allowing you to fetch individual games and/or select which files you want, but the title of this book isn't *Elegant Software Engineering for Baseball*.

Here is a Perl script for fetching play-by-play information from the Gameday web site. I omitted a little bit of redundant code for fetching the contents of the batters, pitchers, and PBP directories. Type the following listing into a file named *spider.pl*:

```perl
#! /usr/bin/perl

use LWP;
my $browser = LWP::UserAgent->new;
$baseurl = "http://gd2.mlb.com/components/game/mlb";
$outputdir = "./games";

use Time::Local;

sub extractDate($) {
    # extracts and formats date from a time stamp
    ($t) = @_;
    my ($sec,$min,$hour,$mday,$mon,$year,$wday,$yday,$isdst)
        = localtime($t);
    $mon  += 1;
    $year += 1900;
    $mon = (length($mon) == 1) ? "0$mon" : $mon;
    $mday = (length($mday) == 1) ? "0$mday" : $mday;
    return ($mon, $mday, $year);
}

sub verifyDir($) {
    # verifies that a directory exists,
    # creates the directory if the directory doesn't
    my ($d) = @_;
    if (-e $d) {
        die "$d not a directory\n" unless (-d $outputdir);
    } else {
        die "could not create $d: $!\n" unless (mkdir $d);
    }
}

# get all important files from MLB.com, 4/3/05 through yesterday
$start = timelocal(0,0,0,3,3,105);
($mon, $mday, $year) = extractDate($start);
print "starting at $mon/$mday/$year\n";

($sec,$min,$hour,$mday,$mon,$year,$wday,$yday,$isdst) = localtime(time);
$now = timelocal(0,0,0,$mday - 1,$mon,$year);
($mon, $mday, $year) = extractDate($now);
print "ending at $mon/$mday/$year\n";

verifyDir($outputdir);

for ($t = $start; $t < $now; $t += 60*60*24) {
    ($mon, $mday, $year) = extractDate($t);
    print "processing $mon/$mday/$year\n";

    verifyDir("$outputdir/year_$year");
    verifyDir("$outputdir/year_$year/month_$mon");
    verifyDir("$outputdir/year_$year/month_$mon/day_$mday");
```

```
$dayurl = "$baseurl/year_$year/month_$mon/day_$mday/";
print "\t$dayurl\n";

$response = $browser->get($dayurl);
die "Couldn't get $dayurl: ", $response->status_line, "\n"
    unless $response->is_success;
$html = $response->content;
my @games = ();
while($html =~ m/<a href=\"(gid_\w+\/)\"/g ) {
    push @games, $1;
}

foreach $game (@games) {
    $gamedir = "$outputdir/year_$year/month_$mon/day_$mday/$game";
    if (-e $gamedir) {
        # already fetched info on this game
        print "\t\tskipping game: $game\n";
    } else {
        print "\t\tfetchinggame: $game\n";
        verifyDir($gamedir);
        $gameurl = "$dayurl/$game";
        $response = $browser->get($gameurl);
        die "Couldn't get $gameurl: ", $response->status_line, "\n"
            unless $response->is_success;
        $gamehtml = $response->content;

if($gamehtml =~ m/<a href=\"boxscore\.xml\"/ ) {
            $boxurl = "$dayurl/$game/boxscore.xml";
            $response = $browser->get($boxurl);
            die "Couldn't get $boxurl: ", $response->status_line, "\n"
                unless $response->is_success;
            $boxhtml = $response->content;
            open BOX, ">$gamedir/boxscore.xml"
                or die "could not open file $gamedir/boxscore.xml: $|\n";
            print BOX $boxhtml;
            close BOX;
        } else {
            print "warning: no xml box score for $game\n";
        }

        if($gamehtml =~ m/<a href=\"players\.txt\"/ ) {
            $plyrurl = "$dayurl/$game/players.txt";
            $response = $browser->get($plyrurl);
            die "Couldn't get $plyrurl: ", $response->status_line, "\n"
                unless $response->is_success;
        $plyrhtml = $response->content;
            open PLYRS, ">$gamedir/players.txt"
                or die "could not open file $gamedir/players.txt: $|\n";
            print PLYRS $plyrhtml;
            close PLYRS;
        } else {
            print "warning: no player list for $game\n";
        }
```

```
          if($gamehtml =~ m/<a href=\"inning\/\"/ ) {
              $inningdir = "$gamedir/inning";
              verifyDir($inningdir);
              $inningurl = "$dayurl/$game/inning/";
              $response = $browser->get($inningurl);
              die "Couldn't get $gameurl: ", $response->status_line, "\n"
                  unless $response->is_success;
              $inninghtml = $response->content;

              my @files = ( );
       while($inninghtml =~ m/<a href=\"(inning_.*)\"/g ) {
                  push @files, $1;
              }

              foreach $file (@files) {
                  print "\t\t\tinning file: $file\n";
                  $fileurl = "$inningurl/$file";
                  $response = $browser->get($fileurl);
                  die "Couldn't get $fileurl: ", $response->status_line,
"\n"
                      unless $response->is_success;
                  $filehtml = $response->content;
                  open FILE, ">$inningdir/$file"
                      or die "could not open file $inningdir/$file: $|\n";
                  print FILE $filehtml;
                  close FILE;
              }
          }

          # some redundant code to fetch the contents of the pbp,
          # batters, and pitchers directories is omitted here

          sleep(1); # be at least somewhat polite; one game per second
      }
    }
}
```

The parser script. Fetching the data from the Web is the easy part. Turning it into a readable form is the hard part. I wrote a parser script to interpret the XML files and translate them into Retrosheet event file format. Because the script is about 1,200 lines long, it's not printed in full in this book. You can get a copy of the script from *http://www.oreilly.com/catalog/baseballhks*.

I divided the parser script into a set of subroutines to make it easier to understand, maintain, and modify. If you want to try reading play-by-play data from other web sites, you'll need to modify this script, but you can probably recycle many different pieces. For example, you might want to look at the subroutine that encodes English language pitch descriptions (e.g., called strike) into their Project Scoresheet equivalent (e.g., C).

Here is an explanation of the key subroutines in this script:

verifyDir($)

Takes a directory name as input. This subroutine verifies that a directory exists, creating the directory if it does not. This is a nice helper routine for saving files.

nameFixes($)

Takes a play string as input and returns a play string. Player names aren't always spelled identically. In particular, I found that names ending in Jr. or names with initials caused problems. This utility routine helps make names consistent.

namesToNumbers($$)

Takes a play string and a player hash as input and returns a play string. This procedure transforms names in play descriptions (e.g., "David Ortiz strikes out swinging") to player ID codes (e.g., "120074 strikes out swinging"). I think it is a lot easier to parse play descriptions if player identifiers are always coded as numbers. This isn't the most efficient way to process files, but the script still takes less than 15 minutes for a season.

decodeBase($), decodeLocations($), decodePos($), and decodeLongPos($)

These helper routines turn descriptions of base names and locations into Project Scoresheet–style descriptions. For example, decodeBase("home") returns H and decodeLocation("left field") returns 7.

decipherPitches($)

Takes a play object, turning an array of pitch descriptions into a Project Scoresheet–style pitch description string.

removeAdjectives($)

Removes "adjectives" from a play description, returning a cleaner description and a list of adjectives. removeAdjectives("120074 grounds out sharply"), for example, translates to 120074 out and includes flags for grounds and sharply.

extractFielding($)

Deciphers the fielding description in a play. For example, 120074 grounds into double play, 116539 to 429664 to 114739 translates to 643.

identifyPlay($)

Returns the Project Scoresheet code for the play. For example, 120074 strikes out on a foul tip translates to K.

decipherBaseRunning($$$)

Takes a play description, hash of players on base, and batter ID and returns a description of base running. (As a side effect, this subroutine modifies the hash of players on base to reflect changes.)

decipherSubstitution($$$$$)
> Deciphers a description of a substitution. (As a side effect, this subroutine modifies the hash of players on base to reflect changes.)

decipherDescription($$$$$$)
> This subroutine turns a play description into a line in a Retrosheet event file. It calls many of the procedures described earlier in the list.

decodeBatterAdj($$)
> When a play-by-play description notes that a player has turned around to bat from the other side, this subroutine can turn that description into a Retrosheet event description.

decodeEvents($$$$)
> This procedure parses a game's play-by-play description, turning it into Retrosheet–style event descriptions.

write_rosters( )
> This is a helper routine that writes roster files.

The main part of this script iterates through all the files fetched by the spider, interpreting each file and writing Retrosheet-style event descriptions for each play.

Running the Hack

Here's a sample run of the spider program. You might get different results, depending on when you run the script. The steps to running the script are as follows:

1. Create a directory for the files
2. Change into the directory
3. Run the script

The Perl script will print messages to the screen explaining what it's doing (what game it's fetching, what files). I chose to run the job in the background, logging the output to a file called *spider.log*, and using the tail command to view the log:

```
% mkdir games
% perl spiderl.pl > spider.log &
% tail -f spider.log
starting at 04/03/2005
ending at 07/21/2005
processing 04/03/2005
        http://gd2.mlb.com/components/game/mlb/year_2005/month_04/day_03/
                fetcing game: gid_2005_04_03_anamlb_lanmlb_1/
                        inning file: inning_1.xml
                        inning file: inning_2.xml
                        inning file: inning_3.xml
```

```
inning file: inning_4.xml
inning file: inning_5.xml
inning file: inning_6.xml
inning file: inning_7.xml
inning file: inning_8.xml
inning file: inning_9.xml
inning file: inning_Scores.xml
inning file: inning_hit.xml
batter file: 110209.xml
batter file: 110236.xml
batter file: 111838.xml
```

...

The *parser.pl* script produces very verbose output by default to make debugging easier. Running this script the same way as the earlier script will generate output like this:

```
% perl parser.pl > parser.log
% tail -f parser.log
GAME> '2005/04/03/anamlb-lanmlb-1'
FROM> Darin Erstad flies out to left fielder Ricky Ledee.
TO> play,1,0,113889,21,BCBX,7/F

GAME> '2005/04/03/anamlb-lanmlb-1'
FROM> Jeff DaVanon grounds out to first baseman Hee Seop Choi.
TO> play,1,0,237800,12,CSBX,3/G

GAME> '2005/04/03/anamlb-lanmlb-1'
FROM> Chone Figgins strikes out swinging.
TO> play,1,0,408210,03,CSS,K
...
```

I don't recommend running this script without redirecting the output to a file because it will run painfully slow. (If you don't plan to look at the file, you should try running it as `perl parser.pl > /dev/null`.) Once the script completes, you can use the `ls` command to get a list of the generated files:

```
% ls events/year_2005
2005AAS.EVA    2005HOU.EVA    2005SFN.EVA    CHN2005.ROS    NYN2005.ROS
2005ANA.EVA    2005KCA.EVA    2005SLN.EVA    CIN2005.ROS    OAK2005.ROS
2005ARI.EVA    2005LAN.EVA    2005TBA.EVA    CLE2005.ROS    PHI2005.ROS
2005ATL.EVA    2005MIL.EVA    2005TEX.EVA    COL2005.ROS    PIT2005.ROS
2005BAL.EVA    2005MIN.EVA    2005TOR.EVA    DET2005.ROS    SDN2005.ROS
2005BOS.EVA    2005NAS.EVA    2005WAS.EVA    FLO2005.ROS    SEA2005.ROS
2005CHA.EVA    2005NYA.EVA    AAS2005.ROS    HOU2005.ROS    SFN2005.ROS
2005CHN.EVA    2005NYN.EVA    ANA2005.ROS    KCA2005.ROS    SLN2005.ROS
2005CIN.EVA    2005OAK.EVA    ARI2005.ROS    LAN2005.ROS    TBA2005.ROS
2005CLE.EVA    2005PHI.EVA    ATL2005.ROS    MIL2005.ROS    TEAM2005
2005COL.EVA    2005PIT.EVA    BAL2005.ROS    MIN2005.ROS    TEX2005.ROS
2005DET.EVA    2005SDN.EVA    BOS2005.ROS    NAS2005.ROS    TOR2005.ROS
2005FLO.EVA    2005SEA.EVA    CHA2005.ROS    NYA2005.ROS    WAS2005.ROS
```

Hacking the Hack

If you want, you can modify this script in many ways:

Pull data off different sites
  If you know a site that publishes other statistics (like box scores), you can use a similar script to download all the content.

Calculate stats as you go
  If you don't need all the data but are just looking for something specific (like pitch counts), you can modify this script to save only the data you need.

Save to a database as you download
  Instead of saving to files on your local drive, you can parse the files as you download them off the Web and insert the results into a database.

See Also

If spidering in general intrigues you, O'Reilly has a book for you! Check out *Spidering Hacks*. (Author's note: this is my endorsement, not O'Reilly's. I'm recommending this book because I liked it, not because O'Reilly asked me to do so!)

This script shows you how to download a lot of historical information to your local computer to provide a valuable reference source. But this data would be much more useful if you could interpret it electronically.

Several other hacks in this book show you some cool stuff you can do with your complete play-by-play files, box scores, and hit charts. Here's a short list that explains how to process these files for analysis:

- To read the hit charts, see "Find Data on Hit Locations" [Hack #29].
- For some interesting ideas on what to do with play-by-play files, see Chapters 4, 5, and 6.

Find Data on Hit Locations

HACK #29

Read the hit location files from MLB.com.

Starting in 2004, MLB.com began to share information on Gameday about every ball put into play: the batter, the pitcher, the spot from which the ball was fielded, the type of hit or out (single, double, triple, home run, ground-out, fly out), the inning, and the coordinates where the ball landed. You can learn how to get files from MLB.com Gameday in "Get Recent Play-by-Play Data" [Hack #28].

This isn't complete data about matchups between batters and pitchers (it doesn't tell you about strikeouts or walks), but the information it includes is very cool. It tells you where hitters tend to hit balls and where balls are hit against pitchers, and it can tell you the ground ball/fly ball ratio. Basically, it's a big list of the (X,Y) coordinates of where the ball landed inside a grid, with the top-left corner of the field having the coordinates (0,0) and the lower right having the coordinates (250,250), as shown in Figure 3-10. You might want to use these to create a spray chart [Hack #37] that shows where players tend to hit against a pitcher, or to develop your own statistics.

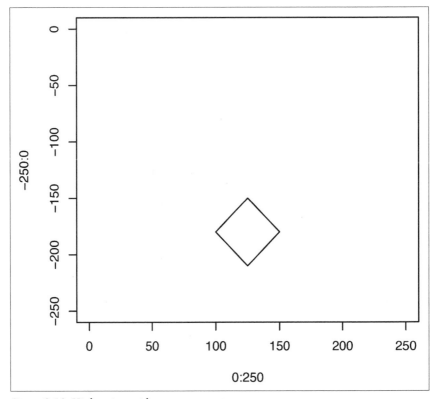

Figure 3-10. Hit location grid

This hack explains the file format and shows you a simple script to import this data into a database.

The Code

Like most of the other scripts in this book, this script loops through a directory of files, loading each one individually, reformatting the contents, and saving the output to a comma-delimited text file. Because this is a short example, it's a great way to explain the methodology I use to write these scripts and to give you an overview of how you can use your powers of observation to write your own scripts.

Let's look at an example, the April 20, 2005 game between the Chicago Cubs and St. Louis Cardinals. Figure 3-11 shows what this file looks like when you open it in the Firefox browser. (You can open XML files in most modern web browsers, and the browser will format the file, making it easy to read.)

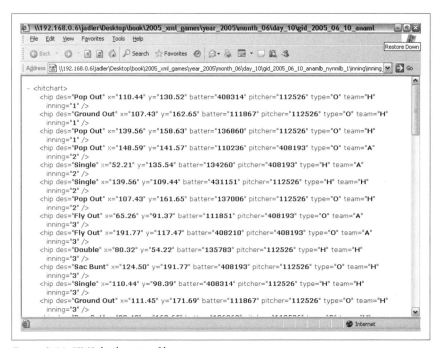

Figure 3-11. XML hit location file

Now, let's look at the contents of this file and figure out how to read it. First, it looks like this file contains one element called hitchart that contains a hip element for each hit made during the game. Next, it looks like the hip element contains a number of different fields. Des looks like a play description, and x and y look like coordinates. The pitcher and batter fields are probably identifiers for each of those players. The type field looks like it takes on two values: H and O. I'll guess that those are hits and outs. team takes on two values, H and A, which I'll guess are home and away. Finally, there is an inning field.

So, here is our plan for reading these files. We'll read them into Perl using the XML::Simple module. Let's do a quick test to see how this will work,

writing a short script that takes an XML-formatted hit location file into a
Perl data structure and prints out a description of the Perl data structure. I
created the following short script and saved it in a file called *test.pl*:

```perl
#!/usr/bin/perl

use XML::Simple;
use Data::Dumper;

while (<>) {
    # read from standard input
    $xml .= $_;
}

my $ref = XMLin($xml, ContentKey => 'hitchart');

print Dumper($ref);
```

You can run this script with a command like this:

```
% cat inning_hit.xml | perl test.pl > dump.txt
```

Looking at the output file (called *dump.txt*) shows a data structure like this:

```
$VAR1 = {
            'hip' => [
                    {
                        'x' => '124.50',
                        'y' => '76.31',
                        'inning' => '1',
                        'batter' => '279913',
                        'type' => '0',
                        'pitcher' => '122987',
                        'des' => 'Fly Out',
                        'team' => 'A'
                    },
                    {
                        'x' => '137.55',
                        'y' => '149.60',
                        'inning' => '1',
                        'batter' => '117601',
                        'type' => '0',
                        'pitcher' => '122987',
                        'des' => 'Force Out',
                        'team' => 'A'
                    },
                    {
                        'x' => '176.71',
                        'y' => '106.43',
                        'inning' => '1',
                        'batter' => '111742',
                        'type' => 'H',
                        'pitcher' => '122987',
                        'des' => 'Single',
```

```
                         'team' => 'A'
                    },
    ...
```

Here's our plan. (I assume you've already downloaded all the *inning_hit.xml* files using a script like the one described in "Get Recent Play-by-Play Data" [Hack #28].) We'll iterate through the files in each directory (by month, day, and game), reading each XML file into memory. Then we'll print each field to standard output.

Type the following listing into a file called *matchups.pl*:

```perl
#! /usr/bin/perl

use XML::Simple;

unless (scalar(@ARGV) == 1) {die "usage: $0 <directory>";}
my $basedir = $ARGV[0];

# list the fields in the xml
# we will use this array to print the header line, then to query the data
my @fields = ("batter","pitcher","inning","type","team","des","x","y");

print "game,";
print join ",", @fields;
print "\n";

opendir BD, $basedir;
my @monthdirs = grep /^month/, readdir BD;
closedir BD;
foreach $monthdir (@monthdirs) {
    opendir DD, "$basedir/$monthdir";
    my @daydirs = grep /^day/, readdir DD;
    closedir DD;
    foreach $daydir (@daydirs) {
    opendir GD, "$basedir/$monthdir/$daydir";
    my @gamedirs = grep /^gid/, readdir GD;
    closedir GD;
    foreach $gamedir (@gamedirs) {
        my $file = "$basedir/$monthdir/$daydir/$gamedir/inning/inning_hit.
                xml";
        # skip the file if it does not exist; game probably rained out
        if (-e $file) {
        my $ref = XMLin($file, ContentKey => 'hitchart');
        foreach $hip (@{$ref->{'hip'}}) {
            print "$gamedir";
            foreach $field (@fields) {print "," . $hip->{$field};}
            print "\n";
        }
        }
    }
    }
}
```

Running the Hack

The script requires one argument: a directory containing hit files. Here, I stored the files in the directory *Desktop/book/code/xmlpbp/games/year_2005/* and redirected the output to a file called *matchups.csv*. You can run this script with a statement like this:

```
% perl matchups.pl Desktop/book/code/xmlpbp/games/year_2005/ > matchups.csv
```

The generated file looks like this:

```
game,batter,pitcher,inning,type,team,des,x,ygame,8
gid_2005_04_03_bosmlb_nyamlb_1,113028,116615,1,O,A,Ground Out,140.56,152.61
gid_2005_04_03_bosmlb_nyamlb_1,116539,124071,1,H,H,Single,123.49,112.45
gid_2005_04_03_bosmlb_nyamlb_1,121347,124071,1,O,H,Fly Out,125.50,54.22
gid_2005_04_03_bosmlb_nyamlb_1,122111,124071,1,O,H,Ground Out,108.43,164.66
gid_2005_04_03_bosmlb_nyamlb_1,120074,116615,2,H,A,Double,150.60,168.67
...
```

You can open this file in a spreadsheet program for inspection, but there are too many (more than 65,535) at bats in a season to fit everything into a spreadsheet, so you're better off with a database.

As a final step in working with this file, we will use check_field_sizes.pl to measure the field lengths and to create the SQL code we need to import this file into a database table [Hack #20]. Here is what happened when I generated the SQL code and loaded the file into MySQL. (You might get a different row count; I ran this in August 2005, based on data from April through July 2005.)

```
% perl check_field_sizes.pl -s "," -h -i matchups.csv > matchups.sql
% mysql pbp
Reading table information for completion of table and column names
You can turn off this feature to get a quicker startup with -A

Welcome to the MySQL monitor.  Commands end with ; or \g.
Your MySQL connection id is 4 to server version: 5.0.11-beta-max

Type 'help;' or '\h' for help. Type '\c' to clear the buffer.

mysql> source matchups.sql
Query OK, 0 rows affected (0.09 sec)

Query OK, 79648 rows affected (1.29 sec)
Records: 79648  Deleted: 0  Skipped: 0  Warnings: 0
```

```
mysql> desc matchups;
+---------+--------------+------+-----+---------+-------+
| Field   | Type         | Null | Key | Default | Extra |
+---------+--------------+------+-----+---------+-------+
| game    | varchar(30)  | YES  |     | NULL    |       |
| batter  | int(6)       | YES  |     | NULL    |       |
| pitcher | int(6)       | YES  |     | NULL    |       |
| inning  | smallint(2)  | YES  |     | NULL    |       |
| type    | varchar(1)   | YES  |     | NULL    |       |
| team    | varchar(1)   | YES  |     | NULL    |       |
| des     | varchar(25)  | YES  |     | NULL    |       |
| x       | decimal(6,2) | YES  |     | NULL    |       |
| y       | decimal(6,2) | YES  |     | NULL    |       |
+---------+--------------+------+-----+---------+-------+
9 rows in set (0.03 sec)
```

If you get any warning messages, try typing the command SHOW WARNINGS in MySQL. You probably need to check the raw files to make sure all of them contain valid observations.

Hacking the Hack

Here are a few tips to do more with this hack:

Calculate batting average on balls in play (BABIP) for pitchers
You might be interested in how well different pitchers fare on balls hit into play. These files provide an easy way to check this. Just count the number of hits and outs.

Determine location of balls put in play
See whether balls hit against certain pitchers or hitters tend to cluster in the same place.

You can use this data to help answer these questions.

CHAPTER FOUR

Visualize Baseball Statistics
Hacks 30–39

In the past few chapters, I told you where to get information about baseball games. In the next few chapters, I give you a better understanding of the game of baseball. In this chapter, I present a set of hacks to help you explore baseball visually.

I'm a big fan of R, an open source application for working with data. It's very popular among statisticians for modeling and plotting data, and it's very popular among biologists. I think R is just as easy to use as a spreadsheet, and it's a lot easier to explain how to do something with R than with a spreadsheet. Most of the hacks in this chapter are about R.

But R isn't for everyone. You can do plenty of things with Microsoft Excel, so I'll also show you a few tricks for using Microsoft Excel to look at data.

 HACK **#30** **Plot Histograms in Excel**

Use Microsoft Excel to plot data distributions so that you can have a better understanding of statistics.

There is some truth to the cliché "a picture is worth a thousand words." A picture is often the best way to understand 1,000 numbers. People are visually oriented. We're good at looking at a picture and observing different characteristics; we're bad at looking at a list of 1,000 numbers.

One of the most powerful tools available for understanding data is the *histogram*, a picture of the distribution of values. Here is the idea of a histogram. Suppose you have a lot of data—say, the batting averages for all 6,032 baseball players between 1955 and 2004 who averaged 3.1 or more plate appearances per game. Let's also assume you want to know how these values are distributed. What are the lowest and highest values? Are there more low values than high values? Were batting averages totally random numbers between 0 and .400, or was there some pattern?

Batting average can take many different values. Between 1955 and 2004, 6,032 players had qualifying batting averages, and there were 1,229 unique values for batting average. You can plot the number of players with each unique batting average (though I can't imagine what this graph would look like). But we don't really care about each unique value; for example, the fact that 13 players had a batting average of .2862 is not that interesting. Instead, we might want to know the number of players with very similar batting averages—say, between .285 and .290.

Let's think of each range as a bucket. Every player-season goes into a bucket. For example, in 1959, Hank Aaron had a .354 average, so we'll put that season in the .350–.355 bucket. So, here's our plan: we'll put each player-season into a bucket, count the number of player-seasons in each bucket, and draw a graph showing (in ascending order) the number of players in each bucket. This single diagram is a histogram.

The Code

In this example, I wanted to look at the distribution of batting average. I used a table containing the total batting statistics for each player in each year (and the list of all teams for which each player played), and I called the table b_and_t. You can find complete instructions on how to create this table in "Measure Batting with Batting Average" [Hack #40]. I selected only batters with enough plate appearances to qualify for a league title, and only those players who played between 1955 and 2004:

```
SELECT b.playerID, M.nameLast, M.nameFirst, b.yearID, b.teamG,
b.teamIDs, b.AB, b.H,
b.H/b.AB AS AVG,
b.AB + b.BB + b.HBP + b.SF as PA
FROM b_and_t b inner join Master M
on b.playerID=m.playerID
WHERE yearID > 1954
AND  b.AB + b.BB + b.HBP + b.SF > b.teamG * 3.1;
```

After running this query, I saved the results to an Excel file named *batting_averages.xls*. For instructions on how to save query results as Excel files, see "Move Data from a Database to Excel" [Hack #19].

One way to draw histograms in Excel is to use the Analysis ToolPak add-in. You can add this by selecting Add-Ins... from the Tools menu, and then selecting Analysis ToolPak. This adds a new menu item to the Tools menu, called Data Analysis, which introduces several new functions, including a Histogram function. But I find this interface confusing and inflexible, so I do something else.

Here is my method for creating a histogram:

1. In the data worksheet, create a new column called Range.

2. In the first cell of this column, use a function to round the value for which you would like to plot the distribution. The simple way to do this is to use the Significant Figures option of the ROUND function. In my worksheet, column I contained the value for which I wanted to calculate the distribution (batting average), so I could use a formula such as ROUND(I2,2) to round to the nearest .010. Personally, I find a bucket size of .005 to be more descriptive, so I use a trick. You can multiply a value inside the ROUND function and then divide outside the function to get buckets of almost any size. Inside the ROUND function, I multiply by the reciprocal of the bucket size—in this case, 1 / .005 = 200. Outside the function, I multiply by the bucket size. In my worksheet, column I contained the average values. So, I used ROUND(I2 * 200,0) / 200 as my formula. Copy and paste this formula into every row of the worksheet. (You can double-click the bottom-right corner of the cell to do this quickly.)

3. Now, we're ready to count the number of players in each bucket. Select all of the data in the worksheet, including the new Range column. From the Data menu, select Pivot Table and Pivot Chart Report. Select Pivot Chart Report and click Finish (we'll use all the defaults). We will select two fields for our pivot table. From the Pivot Table Field List palette, select Range. Drag-and-drop this onto the Drop Row Fields Here part of the pivot table. Next, drag-and-drop "playerID" onto the Drop Data Item Here part of the pivot table. By default, Excel will count the number of player IDs in the underlying data that match each range value. The pivot table is now showing the number of items in each bucket. You should see a (very ugly) graph with the number of players in each bucket.

4. Clean up the graph. (I like to erase the background fill and lines and change the width of the columns.) Figure 4-1 shows an example of a cleaned-up graph.

Looking at the histogram, we see that the distribution looks similar to a bell curve; it skews toward the right and is centered at around .275.

Hacking the Hack

One of the nice things about calculating bins with formulas is that you can easily change the formula for binning. Here are a few suggestions for other formulas:

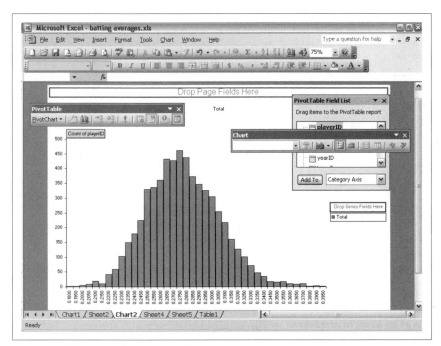

Figure 4-1. Histogram from a pivot chart report

ROUNDDOWN(*<value>*, *<significance>*) *and* ROUNDUP(*<value>*, *<significance>*)
  This ROUNDDOWN function rounds down to the nearest significant figure. For example, ROUNDDOWN(3.59,0) equals 3, and ROUNDDOWN(3.59,1) equals 3.5. Similarly, ROUNDUP rounds up to the nearest significant figure. ROUNDUP(3.59, 0) equals 4, and ROUNDUP(3.59,1) equals 3.6.

LOG(*<value>*, *<base>*)
  Sometimes it's useful to plot a value on a logarithmic scale, and to use logarithmic-size bins. You can combine LOG functions with ROUND functions to create variable-size bins.

CONCATENATE(...)
  The CONCATENATE function doesn't compute numbers, it puts text together. If you want to explicitly list ranges (such as 3.500–3.599), you can use the CONCATENATE function to create these; for example, CONCATENATE(ROUNDDOWN(3.59,1)," to ",ROUNDUP(3.59,1)-0.01) returns 3.5 to 3.59.

If you want to take this to the next level, you can replace the bin size with a named value. (For example, name cell A1 *bin_size*.) This makes it easy to change the bin size dynamically and experiment with different numbers of bins.

HACK #31 Get R and R Packages

How to get and install R, and add extra features through R packages.

R is a language and environment for statistical computing and graphics, but it's even more than that. R is a mature open source software project with support from many developers, an interpreted functional language, and an extensible system for data analysis. A large community of contributors has written libraries of functions for R, called *packages*.

I like to use R to examine baseball statistics because R is very intuitive. A fan can easily calculate formulas without doing any programming. For example, calculating the earned run average (ERA) for a few hundred pitchers is as easy as typing ERA <- ER/IP.

We will use R for a few tasks that are difficult (almost impossible) to perform with just a relational database or a spreadsheet, such as building statistical models and creating sophisticated plots and graphs (one of R's key strengths).

You can download R executables from the project's main web site, *http://www.r-project.org*. You probably should pick a web site that's kind of close to you, but it doesn't actually matter all that much.

The mirror sites offer precompiled binaries for Windows, Mac OS X, and Linux, and they include source code. I recommend downloading the precompiled binaries if you can; modifying the R source code is beyond the scope of this book. There's really no point in walking you through the installation on Windows. As with MySQL, R has a very slick installation wizard that will walk you through each step.

The binaries come in a standard install program (for Windows), a disk image (for Mac OS X), an RPM file (for Red Hat Linux), and forms for other versions of Linux. I haven't tested the Linux installations and can't vouch for them, but I bet they work just as well, given how slick the Windows and Mac versions are.

Once the installation is complete, start R. You'll see a command-line window with a > prompt, similar to a shell. (See Figure 4-2 for an illustration.) Try typing demo(graphics) and pressing Return to start a quick demonstration. R will prompt you to "Hit <Return> to see the next plot," so press your Enter/Return key to cycle through the demo.

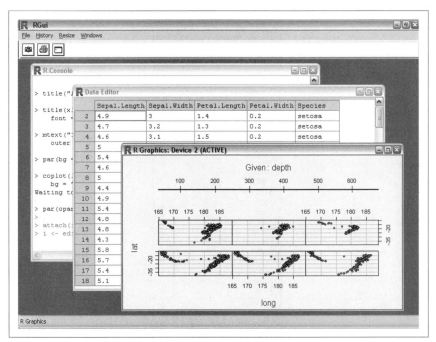

Figure 4-2. The R environment

In addition to the base program, R has a number of other packages that we'll use throughout this book. Similar to the modules in Perl, these packages provide enhanced functionality. For example, the lattice package [Hack #35] allows you to plot multiple graphs on the same plot area easily. Other more specialized packages are available for scientific, financial, and economics applications.

R makes it really easy to find and use these packages. Go to the Package menu in R and select "Install package(s) from CRAN..." (on Mac OS X, the menu name is R Package Installer). You will see a dialog box like the one shown in Figure 4-3. Select the items that you want from the list and click the OK button.

Sometimes you might that find it's easier to type a command to install a package. To do this in R, use the install.packages( ) command, which requires a vector with the package names that you want to install. Here is an example that installs the R Commander package (see "Analyze Baseball with R" [Hack #32] for more on this package):

```
install.packages(pkgs=list("Rcmdr")
```

Before using packages in R, you need to load them. You can do this through the GUI or by using command-line options. To load packages into R, use

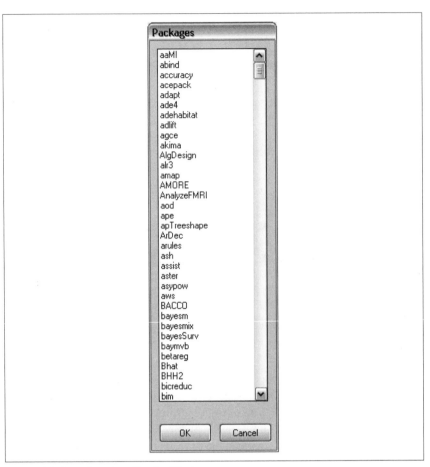

Figure 4-3. R package installer for Windows

the library( ) command with the package name as an argument. For example, the following command loads the Lattice graphics library:

```
> library("lattice")
```

HACK #32   Analyze Baseball with R

A short introduction to the R language and environment.

R is a terrific piece of software because it's stable, powerful, and easy to use. It's a great tool for doing many different things, including creating simple calculations and charts, building complex visualizations, and even building statistical models. This hack will give you enough of an overview to enable you to do really sophisticated studies that would be difficult or impossible to do in a tool like Excel.

Let's start by taking a look at the R environment. R includes a toolbar with some commonly used operations; a console window; and windows showing graphical output, help, edit windows, and other results. See Figure 4-2 for an illustration. The R environment looks a little different on Mac OS, Linux, and other Unix variants, but the language and tools are the same.

Notice the window with the > prompts and the messages. This is the *console* window. This is the primary way you communicate with R. Just type an expression in the window and press Return; R responds with results and errors when appropriate.

The GUI includes a lot of familiar operations: you can save and load files; cut, copy, and paste things; and get help. The most interesting feature is the packages menu. R packages are similar to browser plug-ins because they extend the functionality of R. The GUI lets you load packages that are stored locally, or install and update packages from the Internet.

Calculations in R

Let's start with a few simple examples. You can type mathematical expressions in R, and R will return the results.

```
> 5
[1] 5
> 5/6
[1] 0.8333333
> 1 == 2
[1] FALSE
> 2^3 + (4 * 5)
[1] 28
```

(Notice the two equals [=] signs in the third line. That expression just means "1 equals 2," which is, of course, false.)

Assignment in R

Everything you type in R returns a result of some sort. You can give the answer a name and refer to it later. This process is called *assignment*. The named object is called a *variable*. To do this, type *some_name <- some_value*. To see the value a variable is assigned, just type its name. Here is an example of assigning and using variables:

```
> earned_runs <- 5
> innings <- 7
> ERA <- earned_runs / innings * 9
> ERA
[1] 6.428571
```

Arrays

Often, you want to do a calculation with several values at once. You can group together a set of values into an ordered set of values (called an *array*, *vector*, or *column*) and use this just as you would use a single value:

```
> strikeouts <- c(290, 265, 264, 251, 239)
> inningspitched <- c(245.6666, 228, 237, 225, 196)
> strikeouts_perinning <- strikeouts / inningspitched
> strikeouts_perinning
[1] 1.180462 1.162281 1.113924 1.115556 1.219388
```

You can also mix arrays with single values:

```
> strikeouts_per_nine <- strikeouts_perinning * 9
> strikeouts_per_nine
[1] 10.62415 10.46053 10.02532 10.04000 10.97449
```

Oh, by the way, R also supports *strings* (an expression with characters, such as a name), not just numbers:

```
> players <- c("R Johnson", "J Santana", "B Sheets", "J Schmidt", "O Perez")
> players
[1] "R Johnson" "J Santana" "B Sheets"  "J Schmidt" "O Perez"
```

Data Frames

Suppose that you have several columns of associated information—say, a table of data. R includes a *data frame* that lets you store and manipulate a table of values. Data frames are similar to spreadsheets (though more like database tables) because they let you organize and group information into tables. Here is how you define a data frame from a set of columns:

```
> earned_runs <- c(71, 66, 71, 80, 65)
> strikeout_leaders <- data.frame(players, earned_runs, strikeouts,
inningspitched)
> strikeout_leaders
    players earned_runs strikeouts inningspitched
1 R Johnson          71        290       245.6666
2 J Santana          66        265       228.0000
3  B Sheets          71        264       237.0000
4 J Schmidt          80        251       225.0000
5   O Perez          65        239       196.0000
```

You can refer to specific vectors within a data frame by name:

```
> strikeout_leaders$players
[1] R Johnson J Santana B Sheets  J Schmidt O Perez
Levels: B Sheets J Santana J Schmidt O Perez R Johnson
```

Comments

Comments allow you to leave notes for yourself and others about what the program is doing. Comments start with a hash (#) sign and run to the end of the line:

```
> # copy strikeout leaders to so_leaders and change names
> # of columns to abbreviations
> so_leaders <- strikeout_leaders
> names(so_leaders) <- c('NAME', 'ER', 'SO', 'IP')
```

Functions

R contains many functions that extend its functionality. Each function is an expression of the form f(*a, b, c,...*). The list of stuff between the parentheses (*a, b, c,...*) comprises the *arguments* to the function. Here are some simple examples:

```
> # the cosine function
> cos(0)
[1] 1
> # the exp(x) functions, which returns e ^ x
> exp(1)
[1] 2.718282
> # the (natural)log function
> log(exp(7))
[1] 7
```

Some functions in R can take different numbers of arguments at different times, and let you explain what each argument means:

```
> log(x=1000, base=10)
[1] 3
```

Other functions in R can open windows showing graphics or other information. For example, a convenient tool for editing the contents of a data frame (or just looking at what it contains) is the edit( ) function. Here is an example of how to use this function:

```
> strikeout_leaders_edited <- edit(strikeout_leaders)
```

Notice that this function does not change the original strikeout_leaders data frame but returns a result assigned to strikeout_leaders_edited.

Some functions do different things with different types of arguments. One example is the summary( ) function, which returns statistical summary information about an object. It returns different results for columns and data frames.

```
> summary(earned_runs)
  Min. 1st Qu.  Median    Mean 3rd Qu.    Max.
  65.0   66.0    71.0    70.6    71.0    80.0
> summary(strikeout_leaders)
      players    earned_runs       strikeouts     inningspitched
 B Sheets :1   Min.   :65.0   Min.   :239.0   Min.   :196.0
 J Santana:1   1st Qu.:66.0   1st Qu.:251.0   1st Qu.:225.0
 J Schmidt:1   Median :71.0   Median :264.0   Median :228.0
 O Perez  :1   Mean   :70.6   Mean   :261.8   Mean   :226.3
 R Johnson:1   3rd Qu.:71.0   3rd Qu.:265.0   3rd Qu.:237.0
               Max.   :80.0   Max.   :290.0   Max.   :245.7
```

Moreover, some functions have side effects (that is, they do more than just return a value). For example, the edit( ) function opens a window that allows a value (such as a data frame) to be edited. The plot( ) function prints a graph to a separate window.

We will use only a few functions in this book. Here is a short table of the most useful functions and the most common arguments:

Function	Arguments	Description	Example
help( )	Topic	Returns a description of the function.	help(summary)
summary( )	Object, [optional args]	Returns statistical summary information about an object. (See help(summary) for more details.)	summary(earned_runs)
subset( )	X, subset, select	Returns a subset of an object, such as a data frame. X is the object to subset, subset is the description of which rows to keep, and select is an (optional) list of columns to keep.	subset(earned_runs, inningspitched > 200)
read.table( )	File, header, sep, col. names, [more args]	Reads values from a text file into a data frame. Values are separated by the value sep. col.names contains a list of column names.	Batting <- read. table("batting.csv")
merge( )	X, y, by	Merges rows from two data frames (x and y) into a single data frame when the variable specified by by matches.	Plyrstats <- merge(batting, fielding, by=playerID)

Graphics in R

One of R's best features is its support for many different types of plots. Here is a simple example of a plot, using the data we defined earlier:

```
> barplot(strikeouts, names.arg=players)
```

For some cool demonstrations of the graphics functions in R, try typing this:

```
> demo(graphics)
```

Hacking the Hack

If you're new to R, you might find the default environment a bit daunting. John Fox, a statistics professor at McMaster University, developed a tool called R Commander to help his students use R without too much of a programming background. I recommend this tool for learning R because it shows you the R commands that it generates in one window and the output in other windows. For an illustration, see Figure 4-4.

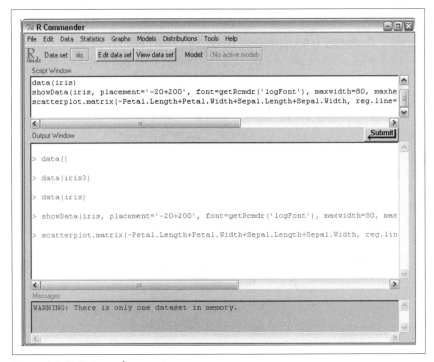

Figure 4-4. R Commander

You can get more information about the R Commander package from *http://socserv.mcmaster.ca/jfox/Misc/Rcmdr*. This tool is available as an R package called Rcmdr. For instructions on installing and loading R packages, see "Get R and R Packages" **[Hack #31]**. R Commander works on Windows, but it might not run on other platforms. (While I was writing this book, I tried testing it on Mac OS X and could not get it to run.)

See Also

R includes lots of other features and functions. For more information about the R language and system, see *http://cran.r-project.org/manuals.html*.

R is based on the S language, which was was developed at Bell Labs in the 1980s and has since been purchased by Insightful Corporation. Insightful offers a commercial version of the S language, called S-Plus, that includes many more modeling, graphing, and analysis features. It also includes a very easy-to-navigate GUI. The only bad thing about S-Plus: the cost. It's a very expensive piece of software, unless you are a student or educator.

Access Databases Directly from Excel or R
#33   If you store your data in a database, this hack shows you how to fetch it from R or Excel.

In "Move Data from a Database to Excel" **[Hack #19]**, I show several ways to export data from a database program into an Excel spreadsheet. This hack shows you another way to access data using ODBC (which stands for Open Database Connectivity). ODBC provides a standard interface for different programs to connect to databases, and it allows you to use the right tool for each job. As shown in Figure 4-5, you can do data selection and manipulation using SQL and then analyze the data in a tool such as R or Excel.

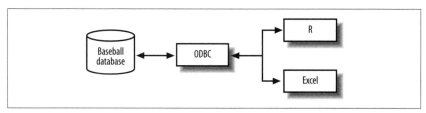

Figure 4-5. ODBC

To use ODBC for MySQL, first you must install the MySQL ODBC drivers on your computer. (MyODBC is available for Windows, Mac OS X, Linux, and other platforms.) You can download the files from *http://dev.mysql.com/downloads/connector/odbc/3.51.html*. The simplest way to install MyODBC is to download the precompiled binaries and then run the install program to install the drivers.

If you don't want to use MySQL at all, you might not have to. If you have Microsoft Access installed on your Windows XP machine, you should already have the Microsoft Access ODBC drivers installed. Plus, the Baseball Archive database is available as a Microsoft Access database.

If you're using Mac OS X, you might have some problems with the MyODBC drivers, depending on the versions of MySQL, MyODBC, and Mac OS X that you are using. I found that the drivers from Actual Technologies worked somewhat better, but you have to pay for the software. See *http://www.actualtechnologies.com* for more information.

Now, you need to configure an ODBC connection for your database. Under the Start menu, go to Programs → Administrative Tools → Data Sources (ODBC); you will also find this in the Administrative Tools section of the Control Panel. Once you've opened the configuration manager, you will see a list of user data sources. If you are using MySQL, you need to add a MySQL ODBC connection. Click the Add... button. Select MySQL ODBC 3.51 Driver from the list in the New Dialog box, and then click Finish.

Here's an example of what you would enter to access a MySQL database of player and team statistics from the Baseball DataBank database **[Hack #10]**:

Data source name
   This is the name you will use to refer to the database—a completely separate name from the underlying database itself. I used `bballdata`.

Description
   The description of the data source, which can be whatever you like.

Server
   The name of the machine on which the MySQL server resides. In most cases, this will be your local machine, referred to as `localhost`.

User
   The username of the account that you use to log in. Use the name you created when you set up the database. (In "Get a MySQL Database of Player and Team Statistics" **[Hack #10]**, I chose `jadler`.)

Password
   The password for the account. (In "Get a MySQL Database of Player and Team Statistics" **[Hack #10]**, I chose `P@ssw0rd`.)

Database
   The name of the database to which you would like to connect. This is the name of the database in MySQL. (In "Get a MySQL Database of Player and Team Statistics" **[Hack #10]**, I used `bbdatabank`.)

Figure 4-6 shows the configuration screen.

Figure 4-6. Configuring an ODBC connection

If you are using Microsoft Access, you need to add an Access ODBC connection. This is just as simple. Click the Add... button, select Microsoft Access Driver from the list, and choose the Access database file.

Use ODBC in R

R is a terrific language for calculations, models, and visualization, but SQL [Hack #8] is a better choice for data storage and retrieval. Once you've installed the ODBC drivers and configured a data source, you're almost ready to use R. The last preparatory step is to install RODBC, the package [Hack #31] that "ODBC-enables" R. Start R, select Packages → Load Package..., and then select RODBC from the list of options. Once you've installed the package, you must load it using the command library(RODBC) each time you use R.

With the package installed, you're ready to crunch data with R. The
RODBC package includes many commands; for more information, see the
RODBC manual or type help(RODBC). Here are a few key functions (and
arguments to those functions; I'm omitting a few to keep this easy) that you
may find useful:

Function name	Arguments	Description
odbcConnect	<ODBC data source>, [uid=<username>], [pwd=<password>], etc.	Connects to the ODBC data source named in the first argument (using the name you assigned to it in the Data Sources administrative tool). User ID and password are optional. Returns an object that you can use with other ODBC functions.
odbcGetInfo	<channel>	Returns information about the ODBC connection.
sqlTables	<channel>	Lists the tables available from the ODBC data source.
sqlFetch	<channel>, <table name>, [max=<max rows>]	Returns a data frame containing the data from the specified table name. Optionally, you can specify a limited number of rows.
sqlQuery	<channel>, <query>	Returns a data frame containing the results of the SQL query.

Here's a sample run of this program, using the commands that we described
earlier. In this example, we start by opening a "channel" in R for accessing
the database using the odbcConnect function. Next, we look at some information about the database (using the odbcGetInfo function), and we get a set
of tables available on the database. Finally, we copy a few observations into
R using the sqlFetch function and display the results to make sure everything worked:

```
> library(RODBC)
> channel <- odbcConnect('bballdata')
> odbcGetInfo(channel)
            DBMS_Name              DBMS_Ver         Driver_ODBC_Ver
              "MySQL"      "4.0.21-standard"                "03.51"
      Data_Source_Name           Driver_Name              Driver_Ver
            "bballdata"          "myodbc3.dll"             "03.51.09"
              ODBC_Ver           Server_Name
         "03.52.0000" "192.168.0.3 via TCP/IP"
> sqlTables(channel)
    TABLE_CAT TABLE_SCHEM TABLE_NAME TABLE_TYPE      REMARKS
1 bballdata                  events        TABLE MySQL table
> events <- sqlFetch(channel, "events", max=9)
> events
```

```
                              gid AB Pitches      Play
1 gid_2004_01_15_aasmlb_nasmlb_1  0
2 gid_2004_01_15_aasmlb_nasmlb_1  0
3 gid_2004_01_15_aasmlb_nasmlb_1  1    .BFE    HR/7/L
4 gid_2004_01_15_aasmlb_nasmlb_1  2    .CFX      63/G
5 gid_2004_01_15_aasmlb_nasmlb_1  3    .SBX       8/F
6 gid_2004_01_15_aasmlb_nasmlb_1  4
7 gid_2004_01_15_aasmlb_nasmlb_1  4    ..BD      S9/G
8 gid_2004_01_15_aasmlb_nasmlb_1  5
9 gid_2004_01_15_aasmlb_nasmlb_1  5    .B1.D D8/F.1-3
```

```
PlayByPlay
1
2
3  Carlos Febles homers (1) on a line drive to left field.
4  Kimera Bartee grounds out, shortstop Kevin Polcovich to first baseman
   Kevin Young.
5  Geronimo Berroa flies out to center fielder Rich Becker.
6  National Manager Walter Alston ejected by HP umpire Mark Carlson.
7  Mark Whiten singles on a ground ball to right fielder Rob Ducey.
8  American first baseman Larry Barnes left the game due to an injured
   chest.
9  Larry Barnes doubles (1) on a fly ball to center fielder Rich Becker.
   Mark Whiten to 3rd.
```

Use ODBC in Excel

The cool thing about ODBC is that it gives you lots of options for how to
work with the data. Here's how to use the Baseball DataBank database in
Excel. Open Excel and click Data → Import External Data → New Database
Query. Select the bballdata ODBC source in the Choose Data Source window (Figure 4-7).

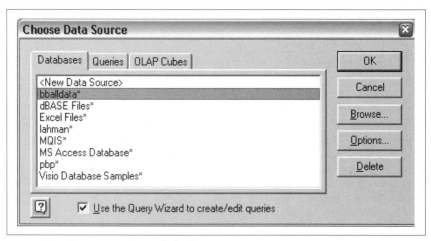

Figure 4-7. Choose Data Source dialog box

If you deselect the "Use the Query Wizard to create/edit queries" box, you can skip directly to the Microsoft Query application.

The first step of the Query Wizard allows you to select columns, as shown in Figure 4-8. I chose to select all columns from the Batting table and a few columns from the Master table (nameFirst, nameLast, birthYear, birthMonth, and birthDay). Next, the wizard allows you to choose to filter data, as shown in Figure 4-9. I chose to select player-seasons after the year 2000. After that, you can choose how you would like to sort columns (this is not pictured here). I chose not to sort the results. Finally, you can choose to save the query, return the results in Excel, create an OLAP cube, or edit the query using Microsoft Query (this step is also not shown). I chose to open the results in the Microsoft Query application.

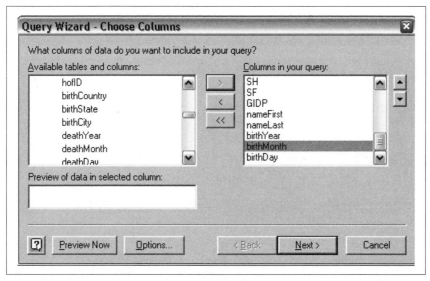

Figure 4-8. Choosing columns in the Query wizard

Figure 4-10 shows a screenshot of the Microsoft Query application. If you are familiar with Microsoft Access, you'll notice that Microsoft Query looks very similar. (See "Make Your Own Stats Book" [Hack #11] for more about Microsoft Access.) You can move around the order of the columns, add and subtract columns, join columns, add more tables, sort the results, filter the results, and do dozens of other things with this program. (Alternatively, you can click the SQL button and enter your SQL directly [Hack #16].)

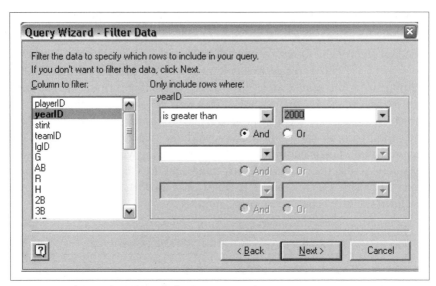

Figure 4-9. Filtering data through the Query Wizard

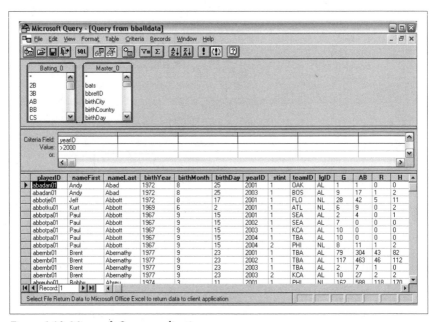

Figure 4-10. Microsoft Query application

Once you're satisfied with the query, go to the File menu in Microsoft Query and select Return Data to Microsoft Office Excel. Excel will then ask where you'd like to store the results (e.g., the current worksheet, a new worksheet, etc.). Once you've inserted the data, you can use Excel to slice, dice, or sort it in any way you want. Figure 4-11 shows the resulting spreadsheet.

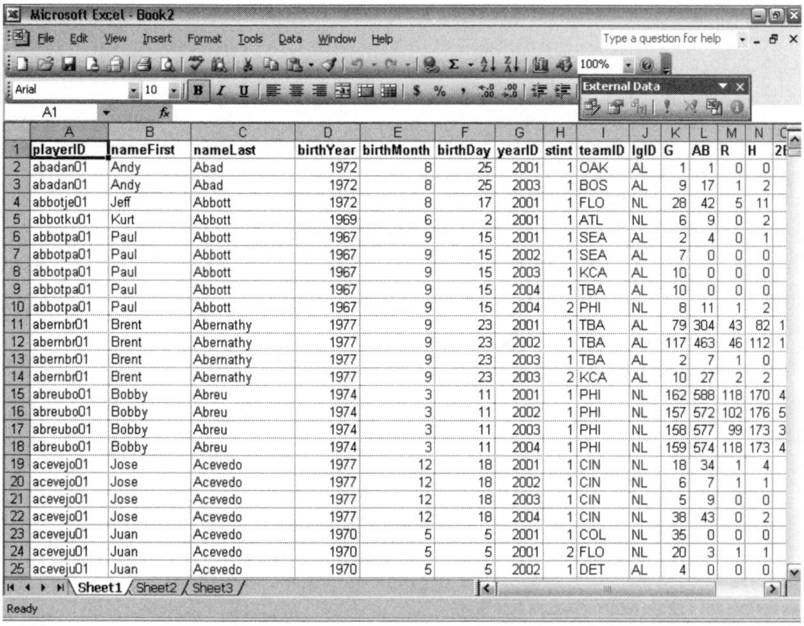

	playerID	nameFirst	nameLast	birthYear	birthMonth	birthDay	yearID	stint	teamID	lgID	G	AB	R	H	2B
2	abadan01	Andy	Abad	1972	8	25	2001	1	OAK	AL	1	1	0	0	
3	abadan01	Andy	Abad	1972	8	25	2003	1	BOS	AL	9	17	1	2	
4	abbotje01	Jeff	Abbott	1972	8	17	2001	1	FLO	NL	28	42	5	11	
5	abbotku01	Kurt	Abbott	1969	6	2	2001	1	ATL	NL	6	9	0	2	
6	abbotpa01	Paul	Abbott	1967	9	15	2001	1	SEA	AL	2	4	0	1	
7	abbotpa01	Paul	Abbott	1967	9	15	2002	1	SEA	AL	7	0	0	0	
8	abbotpa01	Paul	Abbott	1967	9	15	2003	1	KCA	AL	10	0	0	0	
9	abbotpa01	Paul	Abbott	1967	9	15	2004	1	TBA	AL	10	0	0	0	
10	abbotpa01	Paul	Abbott	1967	9	15	2004	2	PHI	NL	8	11	1	2	
11	abernbr01	Brent	Abernathy	1977	9	23	2001	1	TBA	AL	79	304	43	82	1
12	abernbr01	Brent	Abernathy	1977	9	23	2002	1	TBA	AL	117	463	46	112	1
13	abernbr01	Brent	Abernathy	1977	9	23	2003	1	TBA	AL	2	7	1	0	
14	abernbr01	Brent	Abernathy	1977	9	23	2003	2	KCA	AL	10	27	2	2	
15	abreubo01	Bobby	Abreu	1974	3	11	2001	1	PHI	NL	162	588	118	170	4
16	abreubo01	Bobby	Abreu	1974	3	11	2002	1	PHI	NL	157	572	102	176	5
17	abreubo01	Bobby	Abreu	1974	3	11	2003	1	PHI	NL	158	577	99	173	3
18	abreubo01	Bobby	Abreu	1974	3	11	2004	1	PHI	NL	159	574	118	173	4
19	acevejo01	Jose	Acevedo	1977	12	18	2001	1	CIN	NL	18	34	1	4	
20	acevejo01	Jose	Acevedo	1977	12	18	2002	1	CIN	NL	6	7	1	1	
21	acevejo01	Jose	Acevedo	1977	12	18	2003	1	CIN	NL	5	9	0	0	
22	acevejo01	Jose	Acevedo	1977	12	18	2004	1	CIN	NL	38	43	0	2	
23	aceveju01	Juan	Acevedo	1970	5	5	2001	1	COL	NL	35	0	0	0	
24	aceveju01	Juan	Acevedo	1970	5	5	2001	2	FLO	NL	20	3	1	1	
25	aceveju01	Juan	Acevedo	1970	5	5	2002	1	DET	AL	4	0	0	0	

Figure 4-11. ODBC Query results in Excel

Hacking the Hack

If you're not on Windows, RODBC can be tough to work with sometimes. (For example, I could not get RODBC to work at all on a Mac.) RMySQL, an alternative package, might be a better solution.

To install RMySQL from source, on Mac OS X, you can use the following set of R commands. You will need to have MySQL installed locally in */usr/local/mysql*. The first command sets two environment variables so that the package builds correctly. The next two commands install the DBI package and the RMySQL package, respectively.

```
> print(Sys.putenv("PKG_CPPFLAGS"="-I/usr/local/mysql/include",
+ "PKG_LIBS"="-L/usr/local/mysql/lib -L/usr/lib -lmysqlclient"))
> install.packages('DBI')
> install.packages('RMySQL')
```

You can also use RMySQL on Windows. To do this, download the package from *http://stat.bell-labs.com/RS-DBI/download/index.html* and use the Packages → "Install Package(s) from Local Zip Files" menu item in R to load it.

To use this package in your R programs, you can use a set of commands, as shown here:

```
> # load libraries
> library(DBI)
> library(RMySQL)
> # load MySQL driver into R and start connection
> drv <-dbDriver("MySQL")
> con <- dbConnect(drv, username="jadler", password="P@ssw0rd",
+   dbname="bbdatabank", host="localhost")
```

Then, you can submit queries to a MySQL database directly from R and fetch the results into R tables. Here's an example:

```
> res<-dbSendQuery(con, "select * from teams");
> teams<-fetch(res,n=-1);
> summary(teams);
```

```
    idxTeams          yearID          lgID
 Min.   :   1.0   Min.   :1871   Length:2475
 1st Qu.: 619.5   1st Qu.:1915   Class :character
 Median :1238.0   Median :1953   Mode  :character
 Mean   :1238.0   Mean   :1948
 3rd Qu.:1856.5   3rd Qu.:1982
 Max.   :2475.0   Max.   :2004

 idxTeamsFranchises     divID             Rank
 Min.   :   1.00   Length:2475       Min.   : 1.000
 1st Qu.: 29.00    Class :character  1st Qu.: 2.000
 Median : 57.00    Mode  :character  Median : 4.000
 Mean   : 54.63                      Mean   : 4.273
 3rd Qu.: 82.00                      3rd Qu.: 6.000
 Max.   :120.00                      Max.   :13.000

       G               Ghome              W
 Min.   :   6.0   Min.   : 44.00   Min.   :  0.00
 1st Qu.:153.0    1st Qu.: 77.00   1st Qu.: 64.50
 Median :155.0    Median : 79.00   Median : 76.00
 Mean   :148.8    Mean   : 78.06   Mean   : 73.92
 3rd Qu.:162.0    3rd Qu.: 81.00   3rd Qu.: 87.00
 Max.   :165.0    Max.   : 84.00   Max.   :116.00
                  NA's   :399.00
```

```
        L              DivWin            WCWin
Min.   :   4.00   Length:2475       Length:2475
1st Qu.:  64.00   Class :character  Class :character
Median :  75.00   Mode  :character  Mode  :character
Mean   :  73.92
3rd Qu.:  86.00
Max.   : 134.00


      LgWin            WSWin               R
Length:2475       Length:2475       Min.   :  24.0
Class :character  Class :character  1st Qu.: 600.5
Mode  :character  Mode  :character  Median : 684.0
                                    Mean   : 676.7
                                    3rd Qu.: 760.0
                                    Max.   :1220.0


       AB               H                2B               3B
Min.   : 211     Min.   :  33     Min.   :  3.0    Min.   :  0.0
1st Qu.:5074     1st Qu.:1279     1st Qu.:187.0    1st Qu.: 32.0
Median :5339     Median :1384     Median :223.0    Median : 45.0
Mean   :5090     Mean   :1334     Mean   :219.7    Mean   : 49.4
3rd Qu.:5496     3rd Qu.:1463     3rd Qu.:259.0    3rd Qu.: 63.0
Max.   :5781     Max.   :1783     Max.   :373.0    Max.   :150.0


      HR               BB                SO
Min.   :  0.00   Min.   :  0.0    Min.   :   0.0
1st Qu.: 35.00   1st Qu.:416.5    1st Qu.: 482.0
Median : 96.00   Median :490.0    Median : 674.0
Mean   : 93.15   Mean   :468.8    Mean   : 680.9
3rd Qu.:139.00   3rd Qu.:554.0    3rd Qu.: 906.5
Max.   :264.00   Max.   :835.0    Max.   :1399.0
                                  NA's   : 120.0


      SB               CS               HBP
Min.   :  0.0    Min.   :  0.00   Min.   : 29.00
1st Qu.: 62.0    1st Qu.: 37.00   1st Qu.: 51.00
Median : 97.0    Median : 48.00   Median : 58.00
Mean   :114.7    Mean   : 51.31   Mean   : 59.37
3rd Qu.:149.0    3rd Qu.: 61.00   3rd Qu.: 67.00
Max.   :581.0    Max.   :191.00   Max.   : 95.00
NA's   :144.0    NA's   :859.00   NA's   :2325.00


      SF               RA               ER
Min.   : 25.00   Min.   :  34.0   Min.   :  25.0
1st Qu.: 40.00   1st Qu.: 599.0   1st Qu.: 484.0
Median : 46.50   Median : 680.0   Median : 579.0
Mean   : 46.91   Mean   : 676.7   Mean   : 558.5
3rd Qu.: 52.00   3rd Qu.: 761.0   3rd Qu.: 655.0
Max.   : 75.00   Max.   :1252.0   Max.   :1023.0
NA's   :2325.00
```

```
        ERA                  CG                   SHO
Length:2475        Min.   :  1.00       Min.   : 0.000
Class :character   1st Qu.: 25.00       1st Qu.: 6.000
Mode  :character   Median : 53.00       Median : 9.000
                   Mean   : 56.59       Mean   : 9.622
                   3rd Qu.: 82.00       3rd Qu.:13.000
                   Max.   :148.00       Max.   :32.000

        SV                 IPouts                HA                   HRA
Min.   : 0.00      Min.   :  162       Min.   :  49       Min.   :  0.00
1st Qu.: 7.00      1st Qu.:4050        1st Qu.:1277       1st Qu.: 38.00
Median :20.00      Median :4182        Median :1384       Median : 98.00
Mean   :21.34      Mean   :3980        Mean   :1334       Mean   : 93.15
3rd Qu.:34.00      3rd Qu.:4332        3rd Qu.:1467       3rd Qu.:136.00
Max.   :68.00      Max.   :4518        Max.   :1993       Max.   :241.00

        BBA                 SOA                  E                    DP
Min.   :  0.0      Min.   :   0.0      Min.   : 47.0      Min.   : 18.0
1st Qu.:418.0      1st Qu.: 481.0      1st Qu.:126.0      1st Qu.:124.0
Median :491.0      Median : 664.0      Median :155.0      Median :144.0
Mean   :469.2      Mean   : 676.1      Mean   :198.0      Mean   :139.0
3rd Qu.:556.0      3rd Qu.: 895.0      3rd Qu.:231.0      3rd Qu.:160.0
Max.   :827.0      Max.   :1404.0      Max.   :639.0      Max.   :217.0
                                                          NA's   :317.0

        FP                  name                 park
Length:2475        Length:2475         Length:2475
Class :character   Class :character    Class :character
Mode  :character   Mode  :character    Mode  :character

    attendance              BPF                  PPF
Min.   :   6088    Min.   : 54.0       Min.   : 54.0
1st Qu.: 468365    1st Qu.: 97.0       1st Qu.: 97.0
Median : 963895    Median :100.0       Median :100.0
Mean   :1170516    Mean   :100.2       Mean   :100.2
3rd Qu.:1705375    3rd Qu.:103.0       3rd Qu.:103.0
Max.   :4483350    Max.   :131.0       Max.   :129.0
NA's   :    279
```

Load Text Files into R

HACK #34

Load text files, such as Baseball Archive data or Retrosheet data, into R and save it as an R datafile for later access.

In the previous hack, I explain how to load data into R by connecting to a database. If you don't want to install a database, you don't have to. This hack explains how to load text files directly into R. Loading the data into R is pretty straightforward, but there are a few tricks. We'll use the read.csv( ) command in R to load the data, which loads a comma-delimited text file into an R data frame. (For more information about functions and data frames in R, see "Analyze Baseball with R" [Hack #32].)

R includes several functions for loading text files. Each is similar, but there are differences in the default separators for each one. You must specify a file location and then a field separator, a line separator, a decimal separator, column names, and several other options. They all return a data frame corresponding to the contents of the file, as shown in the following table:

Function	Header	Field separator	Decimal separator
read.table	FALSE	None	Period
read.csv	TRUE	Comma	Period
read.csv2	TRUE	Semicolon	Comma
read.delim	TRUE	Tab	Period
read.delim2	TRUE	Tab	Comma

The Baseball Archive files include a header, are separated by commas, and use periods to indicate decimal points. I use the following read.csv( ) function. In this example, I assume that the files are in a directory called *lahman52-csv*. Make sure to use the correct location for the file if you run this code. (And remember, R uses forward slashes to separate directory names, even on Windows.)

```
> batting <- read.csv(file="lahman52-csv/Batting.csv")
> names(batting)
 [1] "playerID" "yearID"  "stint"   "teamID"  "lgID"
 [6] "G"        "AB"      "R"       "H"       "X2B"
[11] "X3B"      "HR"      "RBI"     "SB"      "CS"
[16] "BB"       "SO"      "IBB"     "HBP"     "SH"
[21] "SF"       "GIDP"
```

Finally, I use the R save( ) function to save the data frame to an external file:

```
save(batting, file="~/lahman52-csv/batting.RData")
```

This makes it easy to use this data any time you start R. Just use the load( ) command to load the files:

```
load("~/lahman52-csv/batting.RData")
```

The Code

This code will load each file into a data frame in R and then save all of the files as an R datafile for later retrieval using the data( ) command. The code for loading Baseball Archive datafiles into R is included on the web site for this book (just download it and save yourself a lot of typing!). For reference, here is the complete code that I use to load the Baseball Archive files:

```
teams <- read.csv(file="~/Desktop/book/data/lahman52/Teams.csv")
master <- read.csv(file="~/Desktop/book/data/lahman52/Master.csv")
batting <- read.csv(file="~/Desktop/book/data/lahman52/Batting.csv")
pitching <- read.csv(file="~/Desktop/book/data/lahman52/Pitching.csv")
```

```
fielding <- read.csv(file="~/Desktop/book/data/lahman52/Fielding.csv")
allstars <- read.csv(file="~/Desktop/book/data/lahman52/allstar.csv")
hof <- read.csv(file="~/Desktop/book/data/lahman52/halloffame.csv")
managers <- read.csv(file="~/Desktop/book/data/lahman52/managers.csv")
battingpost <- read.csv(file="~/Desktop/book/data/lahman52/battingpost.csv")
pitchingpost <- read.csv(file="~/Desktop/book/data/lahman52/pitchingpost.
csv")
teamsfranchises <-
    read.csv(file="~/Desktop/book/data/lahman52/teamsfranchises.csv")
fieldingOF <- read.csv(file="~/Desktop/book/data/lahman52/fieldingOF.csv")
managershalf <- read.csv(file="~/Desktop/book/data/lahman52/managershalf.
csv")
teamshalf <- read.csv(file="~/Desktop/book/data/lahman52/Teamshalf.csv")
seriespost <- read.csv(file="~/Desktop/book/data/lahman52/seriespost.csv")
awardsmanagers <- read.csv(file="~/Desktop/book/data/lahman52/
awardsmanagers.csv")
awardsplayers <- read.csv(file="~/Desktop/book/data/lahman52/awardsplayers.
csv")
save(allstars, awardsmanagers, awardsplayers, batting, battingpost,
    fielding, fieldingOF, hof, managershalf, master, pitching,
    pitchingpost, seriespost, teams, teamsfranchises, teamshalf,
    file="~/Desktop/book/data/lahman52.RData")
```

Under file, make sure that you include the complete pathname of the location where you want to save the file. Many other hacks in this book will use this same data, so you'll probably find it useful to load this data into R again (and not start with the text files each time!). To do that, use the following R command:

```
>  load("lahman52.RData")
```

(Of course, you should include the full pathname of the datafile.)

See Also

If you have MySQL installed, you might find it easier to load the data into R from the Baseball DataBank database. See "Access Databases Directly from Excel or R" [Hack #33] for instructions.

 HACK
#35 Compare Teams and Players with Lattices
Plot histograms of batting averages for each team in just a few lines of code.

Lattices are a powerful technique for plotting lots of different graphs at once. With the Lattice package, you can divide observations into multiple groups (for example, teams, positions, and stadiums) and draw a different plot for each group. You can also use the package to plot any combination of graphs in one shot—say, a scatter plot, histogram, pie chart, and bar chart—but I think that's a lot less interesting. Lattices are incredibly useful for comparing groups of teams or players. At a glance, you can quickly see how one group is different from another. You can do this in Excel (plot lots of little diagrams for different subsets of players), but it would take you quite a while.

For these examples, I looked at 2003 batting averages by team. I was curious how the distribution of batting averages differed between teams. Were some teams spread wide apart, with a large difference between best and worst teams? Were other teams packed closely together, with a large number of similarly performing players? Let's see if there is anything interesting in the data.

In this hack, I examine statistics from 2004, taking only players with more than 250 at bats. (Normally, I like to use 502 plate appearances, which is the number a player needs to qualify for MLB awards. However, there weren't enough players with qualifying at bats to make these charts interesting, so I reduced the threshold to 250. See "Significant Number of At Bats" [Hack #63] for a more thorough discussion of this subject.)

With the data in hand, you can plot the batting average (AVG = H / AB) for players on each team. First, the code uses R's histogram( ) command to plot a histogram for each team, splitting each plot into 10 columns so that we can see some detail. The next example shows how to use densityplot( ) to produce a continuous curve that you can use to estimate the density of players close to each average. (That's a fancy way of saying that R is going to draw a line that follows the shape of the histogram.)

As with most Lattice package functions, the commands have dozens of possible options, but you need almost none of them. The key argument to this function is the formula. Most Lattice package plotting tools use formulas to express the input. A formula takes this form:

```
<dependent variable> ~ <independent variables> | <conditioning variables>
```

The dependent variable corresponds to the y axis. (If you plan to build a model from your data, this is what you are trying to predict.) This part is not required for univariate (single-variable) functions, such as histograms. The independent variables are the x variables (the predictors in a model). The conditioning variable is the term that you are using to specify which observations go in which graphs. In our example cases, we want to produce histogram and density plots of the batting average, so we use the ~ AVG | teamID formula.

The Code

We'll use RMySQL [Hack #33] to connect to the Baseball DataBank database [Hack #10] and generate a lattice. The code is remarkably short:

```
#Load the appropriate libraries
library(DBI);
library (RMySQL);
library (lattice);

#Establish the connection to the database
drv<-dbDriver("MySQL");
con<-dbConnect( drv, username="jadler", password="P@ssw0rd",
    dbname="bbdatabank",host="localhost");

#Build the data set
res<-dbSendQuery(con,
    "select * from batting where yearID=2003 and AB > 250");
batting2003<-fetch(res, n=-1);
attach(batting2003);

#Compute batting averages
AVG<-H/AB;

#Plot the charts
histogram(~ AVG | teamID), nint=10)
densityplot(~ AVG | teamID), plot.points=FALSE
```

Running the Hack

The last two lines in the code listing actually produce the plots. The histogram(~ AVG | teamID, nint=10) command produces a diagram like the one shown in Figure 4-12.

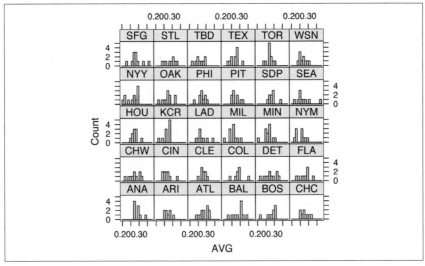

Figure 4-12. Histogram lattice

The densityplot(~ AVG | teamID, plot.points=FALSE) line produces a diagram similar to the one shown in Figure 4-13.

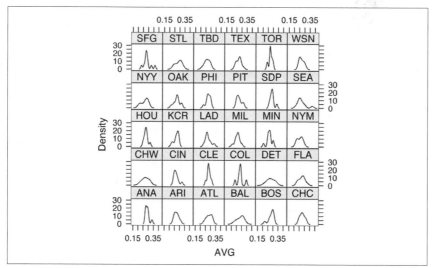

Figure 4-13. Density plot lattice

A quick look at this plot shows some surprising results. Some teams are much more concentrated than others are (e.g., Boston, all of whose players hit well). Others, like Philadelphia, are spread out. And more surprisingly, a few teams, including the Cubs (CHN), have two pronounced peaks.

Some of these effects are probably due to stadiums. For example, Boston's high average is probably caused by Fenway Park's Green Monster in left field, and the Dodgers' (LAN) low average is probably the result of playing in Dodger Stadium (famously a pitcher's park).

HACK #36 Compare Teams Using Chernoff Faces

Use your innate ability to recognize facial features to compare teams.

People are naturally very good at recognizing visual patterns, particularly similarities and differences in human faces. In 1973, statistician Herman Chernoff developed a novel technique for comparing data points: plot data points as human faces, where each facial characteristic (mouth size, mouth expression, face shape, eye shape, etc.) represents a different variable in the data. This hack shows you how to apply this idea to baseball teams (or to anything else that you want to compare).

I found two sources of free code for plotting Chernoff faces. The first is from Dr. Hans Peter Wolf. You can find the code on his home page at *http://www.wiwi.uni-bielefeld.de/~wolf*. The second source is from Shigenobu AOKI, available at *http://aoki2.si.gunma-u.ac.jp/R/face.html*. In this book, I use Dr. Wolf's code. (It doesn't implement the original algorithm exactly, but it's a lot easier to use.) Just copy all the code from *http://www.wiwi.uni-bielefeld.de/~wolf/software/R-wtools/faces/faces.R*, paste it into your R window, and hit Return. Or, easier yet, you can just use R's source( ) command to load the code in one step. (I show this in the next section.)

Dr. Wolf's faces( ) code requires a matrix of values to run. The data in the first column controls the height of the face, the data in the second controls the width, and so on. (See his site for the complete details.) Here are mappings you can use to find teams that are similar offensively:

Column	Facial characteristics	Variable
1	Height of face	HR
2	Width of face	H
3	Shape of face	HA
4	Height of mouth	HRA
5	Width of mouth	SOA
6	Curve of smile	BB
7	Height of eyes	BBA

As a small wrinkle, the faces( ) function uses the row names to label the diagram. Because it's a lot nicer to know which face corresponds to which team than it is to associate row numbers such as "2416," there's an extra step to grab the team names. You'll see this in the code.

The Code

We'll use an ODBC connection **[Hack #33]** to the Baseball DataBank database **[Hack #10]**. Because the SQL statement to select the data spans several lines, the code uses R's paste( ) function to concatenate the multiple lines into a single string. Type the following code into R:

```
#Load the required libraries
library(RODBC);

#Load the faces code
source("http://www.wiwi.uni-bielefeld.de/~wolf/software/R-wtools/faces/
faces.R");
```

```
#Fetch the data that will be used for the faces
channel<-odbcConnect('bballdata');
al2003<-sqlQuery(channel, paste (
  "SELECT HR, H,HA,HRA,SOA,BB, BBA ",
  "FROM teams WHERE ",
  "lgID = 'AL' AND ",
  "yearID = 2003"));
#Fetch the team names and save as the row names
row.names(al2003)<- sqlQuery(channel, paste (
  "SELECT teamID FROM teams WHERE lgID = 'AL' AND yearID = 2003"))$teamID;

# Run the faces program
faces(as.matrix(al2003));
```

Run the Hack

Here's the al2003 data set that I got when I ran the preceding code:

```
> al2003
      HR    H   HA HRA  SOA  BB BBA
ANA  150 1473 1444 190  980 476 486
BAL  152 1516 1579 198  981 431 526
BOS  238 1667 1503 153 1141 620 488
CHA  220 1445 1364 162 1056 519 518
CLE  158 1413 1477 179  943 466 501
DET  153 1312 1616 195  764 443 557
KCA  162 1526 1569 190  865 476 566
MIN  155 1567 1526 187  997 512 402
NYA  230 1518 1512 145 1119 684 375
OAK  176 1398 1336 140 1018 556 499
SEA  139 1509 1340 173 1001 586 466
TBA  137 1501 1454 196  877 420 639
TEX  239 1506 1625 208 1009 488 603
TOR  190 1580 1560 184  984 546 485
```

Figure 4-14 shows the output of the faces( ) plot for this data. As you can see, Boston scored many more runs than Baltimore did, so its face is much taller; Texas allowed a lot more home runs than Oakland did, so its mouth is larger.

What I find most remarkable about this diagram is that it's not total nonsense. For example, the Yankees and the Red Sox are fairly similar offensive teams in many ways, and their "faces" bear out this resemblance.

Hacking the Hack

Here are some ideas for different things to compare with faces( ):

Compare groups of players
   You can easily run this code on other groups of players to try to find similarities. I suggest trying groups of batters and pitchers.

Find players similar in some characteristics
If, for example, you want to look at pitcher injuries and compare similar players, you can use Chernoff faces to find pitchers who are most similar to one another.

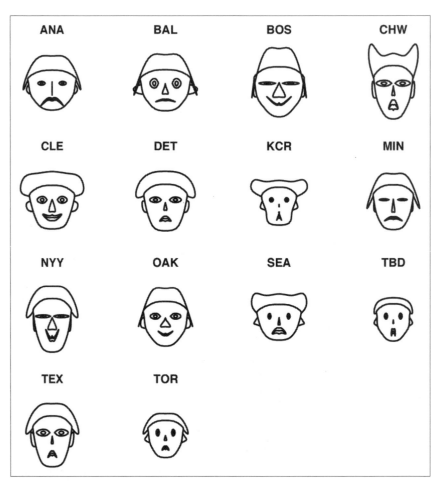

Figure 4-14. Chernoff faces

Plot Spray Charts
Plot charts showing where players hit the most baseballs.

Many baseball players tend to hit balls to some parts of the field more often than to others. Perhaps the best illustrations are sluggers Jason Giambi and Barry Bonds. Each player hits the most balls to the right side of the field.

When these guys are batting, the opposing defense will shift toward the right side of the field.

Managers use a tool called *spray charts* to decide where to position defensive players because it shows where baseballs are most likely to be hit. This hack teaches you how to plot spray charts, using data from MLB Gameday. You can find similar charts on the Internet (for example, try the Hitting Chart links for individual players at MLB.com), but there are some advantages in plotting these yourself. First, you can choose any set of players to plot. Second, you can focus on certain situations and matchups. Finally, you can draw some easier-to-read charts, such as hexagonal bins.

For this hack, we're going to use the matchup data we derived in "Find Data on Hit Locations" **[Hack #29]**. This file includes game IDs, game dates, teams, a hit indicator, x and y coordinates of each ball in play, the name of the pitcher and batter, and the way the play was scored (i.e., single, groundout, or home run). We'll load this data into R, set up axes to show the field, and then plot hits and outs.

In "Find Data on Hit Locations" **[Hack #29]**, we created a file containing the results of each hitter-pitcher matchup.

Step 1: Load the file into a data frame. The file was just a comma-separated value file with a header, so we can load this file into a data frame with R's read.csv( ) procedure:

```
> matchups <- read.csv("~/Desktop/book/matchups.txt")
> names(matchups)
 [1] "gid"    "year"   "month"  "day"    "away"   "home"   "game"
"hit"    "x"
[10] "y"      "inning" "batter" "pitcher" "type"   "batting"
```

Step 2: Set up the axes and the diamond. We need to set the right window size (to show the whole field) and plot the diamond. We will do this with two plotting commands in R. We use the plot( ) command to draw the window and set the appropriate axes. We then use the lines( ) command to draw the diamond.

```
> plot (0:250, -250:0, type="n", bg="white")
> lines(c(125,150,125,100,125),c(-210,-180,-150,-180,-210), col=c("black"))
```

Step 3: Plot matchups. Now, let's plot some hits and outs! To do this, we will use the points( ) function to add points to the diagram. As arguments, this function requires a set of x and y coordinates (as two separate vectors). Optionally, you can choose colors and shapes for points. For details, see the help file.

In this example, we'll look at where Jorge Posada (NY Yankees catcher) hit off Pedro Martinez (Red Sox pitcher) in 2003. We'll start by extracting a subset of the match-up data to include only these players:

```
> jorge.vs.pedro <- subset(matchups, pitcher=="Martinez" & batter ==
"Posada")
```

Next, we'll use blue to show hits (through the col=c("blue") option) and red to show outs (through the col=c("red") option). We'll plot a small, solid dot at each location (using the pch=20 option).

```
> points(subset(jorge.vs.pedro$x, jorge.vs.pedro$hit==0), subset(-jorge.vs.
pedro$y, jorge.vs.pedro$hit==0), pch=20, col=c("red"))
> points(subset(jorge.vs.pedro$x, jorge.vs.pedro$hit==1), subset(-jorge.vs.
pedro$y, jorge.vs.pedro$hit==1), pch=20, col=c("blue"))
```

This produces a simple diagram like the one shown in Figure 4-15.

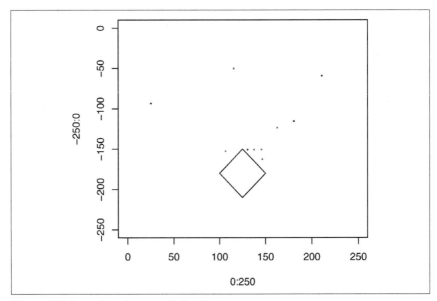

Figure 4-15. Jorge Posada versus Pedro Martinez

Batter Spray Diagrams

You can also look at where all the balls by a player landed. Let's look at where all the balls that David Ortiz hit in play in 2003 landed. We'll use the same code as we did earlier, but we'll define a subset containing all the places where David Ortiz was the batter:

```
> plot (0:250, -250:0, type="n",bg="white")
> lines(c(125,150,125,100,125),c(-210,-180,-150,-180,-210), col=c("black"))
> ortiz <- subset(matchups, batter == "Ortiz")
```

```
> points(subset(ortiz$x, ortiz$hit==0), subset(-ortiz$y, ortiz$hit==0),
pch=20, col=c("red"))
> points(subset(ortiz$x, ortiz$hit==1), subset(-ortiz$y, ortiz$hit==1),
pch=20, col=c("blue"))
```

This produces a diagram like the one shown in Figure 4-16.

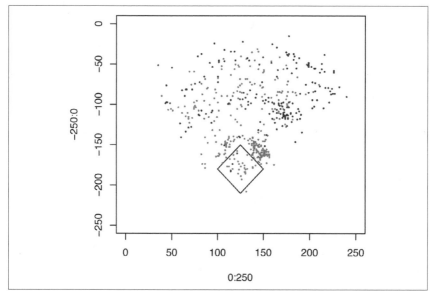

Figure 4-16. David Ortiz spray chart

Hexagonal Binning

Clearly, you can see that David Ortiz tends to hit balls more often to right field. Wouldn't it be nice to have a cleaner way to see this density? We'll use another visualization technique, called hexagonal binning, to get a clearer picture of where Ortiz's hits land.

The idea of hexagonal binning is to break a two-dimensional plane into different bins. First, the bins make interlocking hexagons. It is possible to use squares (or interlocking triangles or another shape), but hexagons look "rounder" than squares. Next, the algorithm counts the number of points inside each bin. Finally, a plotting tool colors hexagons according to the density of points.

Step 1: Get the hexbin package. To use this tool, you need to download the hexbin package. In the Windows version of R, go to the Packages menu and select "Install Packages from Bioconductor." (This package is available from Bioconductor, not CRAN.) Select "hexbin" from the list and click OK. R will install the package on your local machine.

In the Mac OS X version of R, select Package Installer from the Packages & Data menu. Select "Bioconductor (binaries)" from the Packages Repository menu. Click the Get List button to see a list of the available packages. Select "hexbin" and click the Install/Update button to install.

Step 2: Load the hexbin package. After installing the package, you need to load it. You can do this from the Packages menu, or you can issue the following command:

```
> library(hexbin)
```

Step 3: Plot the graph. There are two steps to doing a hexagonal bin plot. First, you create the R hexagonal bin object. Then, you plot the object to view it. Here is a hexagonal bin plot for the David Ortiz batting data set:

```
> ortiz.hexbins <- hexbin(ortiz$x, -ortiz$y)
> plot(ortiz.hexbins)
```

And that's it! This produces a graph like the one shown in Figure 4-17. Darker areas indicate a greater number of balls.

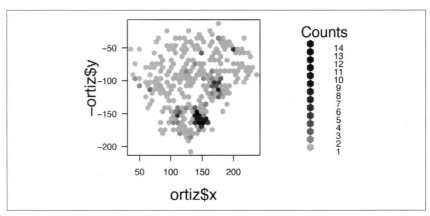

Figure 4-17. David Ortiz hexbin plot

Hacking the Hack

You can do many additional things with this information. Here are a few suggestions:

Show edges of specific ballparks
   In this example, I just showed how to plot a diamond in roughly the right spot, but you can use information about each ballpark to show the exact borders of a particular stadium.

Use more colors to differentiate types of hits
> You can use different colors for line drives, ground balls, and fly balls. Or maybe for singles, doubles, triples, home runs, and outs.

Show lefty-righty matchups
> Curious how a batter fares against lefties or righties? Or how well a pitcher fares against each? Join the matchup information with a table showing which players are lefties and righties and plot these matchups in different colors to look for patterns.

Find outfield borders from HR data
> If you look at where home runs land, you can determine where the outfield borders are.

HACK #38 Chart Team Stats in Real Time

Use Perl to dynamically fetch data from the Web, and then use R to create scatter plots.

ESPN's stats page has lots of good data about team performance. As you can see in Figure 4-18, the data is comprehensive and useful, but it appears in long, boring tables. This hack shows how to use Perl to extract this data, directly from the Web and from R, to create nice charts and graphs.

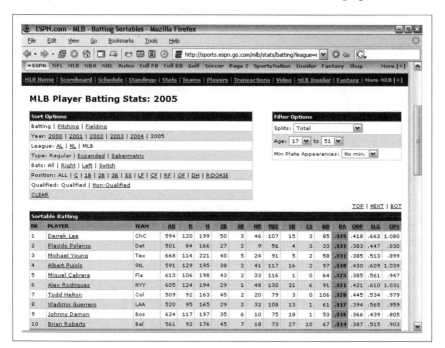

Figure 4-18. ESPN's team stats page

You access the data using a URL that looks like this: *http://sports.espn.go.com/mlb/teams/batting?team=TeamID*. **TeamID** is a three-letter abbreviation. For example, if you're looking for data on the Red Sox, replace **TeamID** with BOS; if you're looking for data on the Tigers, replace **TeamID** with DET; and so on. (If you're in doubt about a team's ID, go to the ESPN web site, select the stats for the team you want, and then read the URL.)

The Code

This hack is comprised of two parts: one part extracts the data from the ESPN site, and the other creates the display. This first script queries *http://www.espn.com* for the TeamID value you pass it and then writes a pipe (|) delimited text file that you can easily import into R. Save the following listing into a file called *get_data.pl*:

```perl
#!/usr/bin/perl

# PERL MODULES TO USE
use LWP::Simple;
use HTML::TableExtract;

# WHAT TEAM TO PULL?
$TeamID = $ARGV[0];

# CREATE FILE TO PLACE OUTPUT INTO
$outfile = 'data.txt';
open OUT,">$outfile" or die "can't open file $outfile for output!\n";

# GRAB HTML OF ESPN WEBPAGE FOR GIVEN TEAM
$URL  = "http://sports.espn.go.com/mlb/teams/batting?team=" . $TeamID;
$html = get($URL);

# PARSE HTML INTO NEW TABLEEXTRACT OBJECT
$te = new HTML::TableExtract();
$te->parse($html);

# WE'RE INTERESTED IN THE 5TH HTML TABLE IN THE PAGE
$ts = $te->table_state(0,5);
@rows = $ts->rows;

# HOW MANY HTML TABLE ROWS?
$N = scalar(@rows);

# NOTE: WE'RE ONLY INTERESTED IN ROWS 3 TO N-4. HTML TABLE ROWS 1-2 CONTAIN
# MENU ITEMS AMD ROWS N-4 TO N CONTAIN TOTALS AND OTHER FORMATTING.
# ROW 3 IS HEADER ROW
print OUT "TEAM|" . join("|", @{$rows[3]}) . "\n";
```

```
# FOR REST OF ROWS, PIPE-DELIMIT DATA PLUS A LINEFEED
for $i (4 .. $N-4) {
    print OUT "$TeamID|";
    print OUT join("|", @{$rows[$i]});
    print OUT "\n";
}

# CLOSE OUTPUT FILE
close OUT;
```

The next script is an R program that will import the pipe-delimited text file
created using the Perl script, create a scatter plot of RBI versus HR, super-
impose the R^2 value, and save the file under the name **TeamID.png**. Type the
following listing into a file called *make_charts.r*:

```
# TELL R WHAT FOLDER AND FILE TO WORK WITH
setwd("C:/baseball_charts")
INFILE <- "data.txt"

# FETCH DATA DOWNLOADED FROM WEBPAGE
bbdata <- read.table(INFILE, header=TRUE, sep="|")
TeamID = as.character(bbdata$TEAM[1])

# TELL R TO OUTPUT THE PLOT TO FOLLOW A .PNG FILE
OUTFILE = paste(TeamID,".png", sep="")
png(filename=OUTFILE, bg="white")

# BG PROPERTY ABOVE DOESN'T WORK IN R 2.0.0 - BUG?
par(bg = "white")

# CREATE SCATTER PLOT
title = paste("TeamID =",TeamID)
plot(RBI~HR, data=bbdata, pch=19, cex=2, col="orange", main=title)

# APPEND LEAST SQUARES LINE
abline(lm(RBI~HR, data=bbdata))

# COMPUTE R^2 AND PLACE IT ONTO PLOT
r <- cor(cbind(bbdata$RBI, bbdata$HR))[2,1]
r2 <- formatC(r^2, format="f", digits=3)
mtext(paste("R^2 =",r2), line=-2, at=1, adj=0)

# CLOSE AND SAVE PNG FILE
dev.off( )
```

Running the Hack

To run this hack, you will need Perl and the `HTML::TableExtract` module.
For instructions on getting and installing Perl and Perl modules, see "Get
Perl" **[Hack #12]**. To download the batting statistics for the Detroit Tigers from

http://sports.espn.go.com/mlb/teams/batting?team=DET, parse the data, and create a delimited text file, you would call the Perl script as follows:

```
C:\baseball_charts>perl get_data.pl DET
```

This will produce a file called *data.txt*, as shown in Figure 4-19.

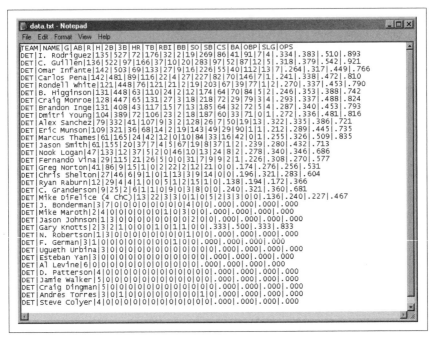

Figure 4-19. data.txt

Once you've got the data, it's easy to import this file into R and create a scatter plot that saves as a *.png* image file. Instead of typing the commands into R one by one (because we already have them saved in the *make_charts.r* file, right?), we'll just import the commands into R by using R's source() function. So in the R GUI, type the following (obviously, you'll need to update your path):

```
> source("C:/baseball_charts/make_charts.r")
```

If all went well, we should have *DET.png* sitting in the *C:\baseball_charts* folder. Simply use your favorite graphics editor or web browser to view it (see Figure 4-20).

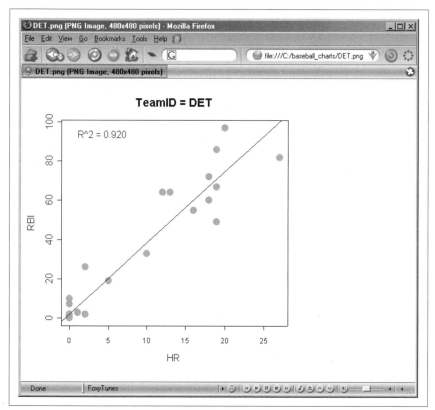

Figure 4-20. DET chart

Hacking the Hack

It's beyond the scope of this hack to explain how to set up a web server. But let's say you have access to a web server that supports Perl, or you have a web server installed on your local computer (such as IIS or the free Apache Web Server). You can skip creating a physical text file and just update the R script to import the data from the Perl script by supplying a URL rather than *data.txt*!

For example, let's say you rename *get_data.pl* to *get_data.cgi*, update it slightly to look like the following, and save it in a folder called *CGI-BIN* in your local web server:

```
#!/usr/bin/perl

# PERL LIBRARIES TO USE
use CGI;
use LWP::Simple;
use HTML::TableExtract;
```

```
# WHAT TEAM TO PULL?
$browser = new CGI;
$TeamID = $browser->param('team');

# TELL BROWSER TO EXPECT PLAIN TEXT
print "content-type: text/plain\n\n";

# GRAB HTML OF ESPN WEBPAGE FOR GIVEN TEAM
$URL  = "http://sports.espn.go.com/mlb/teams/batting?team=" . $TeamID;
$html = get($URL);

# PARSE HTML INTO NEW TABLEEXTRACT OBJECT
$te = new HTML::TableExtract( );
$te->parse($html);

# WE'RE INTERESTED IN THE 5TH HTML TABLE IN THE PAGE
$ts = $te->table_state(0,5);
@rows = $ts->rows;

# HOW MANY HTML TABLE ROWS?
$N = scalar(@rows);

# NOTE: WE'RE ONLY INTERESTED IN ROWS 3 TO N-4. HTML TABLE ROWS 1-2 CONTAIN
# MENU ITEMS AMD ROWS N-4 TO N CONTAIN TOTALS AND OTHER FORMATTING.
# ROW 3 IS HEADER ROW
print "TEAM|" . join("|", @{$rows[3]}) . "\n";

# FOR REST OF ROWS, PIPE-DELIMIT DATA PLUS A LINEFEED
for $i (4 .. $N-4) {
    print "$TeamID|";
    print join("|", @{$rows[$i]});
    print "\n";
}

# CLOSE OUTPUT FILE
close OUT;
```

Then you can call this script by pointing your browser to *http://localhost/
CGI-BIN/get_data.cgi?team=DET* to see the data dynamically fetched,
parsed, and delimited. Of course, you can supply a team= value if you want
(e.g., ATL, CIN, etc.).

Now, the really cool part is in the R script. Simply change the following:

```
INFILE <- "data.txt"
```

so that it reads:

```
INFILE <- "http://localhost/CGI-BIN/get_data.cgi?team=DET"
```

The scatter plot will be created for DET. Enter team=CIN, and a scatter plot
file will be created for CIN because R's read.table( ) function accepts not
only a filename but also any URL that will return a valid file that can be
read. Sweet!

Create a batch file to plow through several teams. You can actually run the R script in batch mode and not even have to open the R GUI at all. This allows you to create several plots en masse sequentially—say, for each team. On Windows, this is easy. Open Notepad, enter the following command, and save it as *make_charts.bat*:

```
"C:\Perl\bin\perl.exe" get_data.pl ATL
"C:\Program Files\R\rw2000\bin\RTerm.exe" --vanilla --quiet <make_charts.r

"C:\Perl\bin\perl.exe" get_data.pl BAL
"C:\Program Files\R\rw2000\bin\RTerm.exe" --vanilla --quiet <make_charts.r

"C:\Perl\bin\perl.exe" get_data.pl BOS
"C:\Program Files\R\rw2000\bin\RTerm.exe" --vanilla --quiet <make_charts.r

"C:\Perl\bin\perl.exe" get_data.pl CLE
"C:\Program Files\R\rw2000\bin\RTerm.exe" --vanilla --quiet <make_charts.r

"C:\Perl\bin\perl.exe" get_data.pl MIN
"C:\Program Files\R\rw2000\bin\RTerm.exe" --vanilla --quiet <make_charts.r

"C:\Perl\bin\perl.exe" get_data.pl TEX
"C:\Program Files\R\rw2000\bin\RTerm.exe" --vanilla --quiet <make_charts.r
```

Double-click the *make_charts.bat* file. When you're done, you should see six *.png* image files for the six teams mentioned in the code.

Still more automation. Those really ambitious among you will realize that you can automate this even more by doing one of the following:

- Update the Perl script to download separate text files for all teams, and then update the R script to search the folder containing the text files and loop through each found *.txt* file, importing each.

- Take the web-server approach and just update the R script to use the URL approach and loop through all teams you've defined in some sort of array.

Either approach requires that you turn the meat of the R script into a function so that it can be called easily and repeatedly.

Don't export individual PNG images. R can save plots in many formats. Instead of saving each plot as a separate image file, you can have R create a *.pdf* file and append one page per plot. Take a peek at the pdf( ) function in R. It can do amazing things!

—Tom Dierickx

Slice and Dice Teams with Cubes

HACK #39

Use Perl to create your very own local OLAP multidimensional cubes that you can explore using Microsoft's Office Web Components (OWC).

Many hacks in this book show you where to get data and how to store it in a database. Other hacks show you how to answer specific questions using this data. But what if you don't know exactly what question you want to ask? Oftentimes, so much data is available that you don't know where to start. Other times, you just want to kind of poke around and let one question lead you on a journey to five more, as if you were on some kind of data safari.

You can do this with a database, writing multiple SQL queries to fetch different subsets of data summarized in different ways. However, this quickly becomes tedious, especially if you ask the same types of questions repeatedly. A *data cube* is a popular tool for working with summarized, aggregated data that lets you easily slice and dice the data. Logically, these structures are called *cubes* because they're seen as 3D objects (or, more technically, as *n*D objects), where the qualitative things (such as teams, height, and season) that you typically like to group by are called *dimensions*, and the pre-aggregated data and any calculated expressions from them (such as hits and home runs), are seen as *measures*. This hack shows you how to use a cool tool from Microsoft to work with data cubes.

Well, let me back up. The Microsoft SQL Server product comes bundled with Microsoft SQL Server Analysis Services (it was called OLAP Services in earlier versions), which is devoted entirely to authoring, managing, and making "cube" data available online to connected network users. These network users can connect to this cube data using Microsoft Excel, as well as Microsoft OWC, which we shall see in a moment. This whole setup is, obviously, not within the price range of the casual home hobbyist, nor does it even make sense if money were no object because it's geared toward a larger enterprise environment. But here's the lesser-known fact: Microsoft made available a way that Excel (and other client products) can "cache" cube data offline. It created an MSOLAP data provider for its ActiveX Data Objects (ADO) library, which not only lets you connect to cube data on SQL Server through an ADO connection, but also allows you to create local cubes for offline use (via coding). The best part for us is that the originating data source does *not* need to be Microsoft SQL Server Analysis Services. You can use *any* ADO- *or* ODBC-compliant data source. So, we can use MySQL and connect through ODBC.

Once we create the cube, we will interact with it using Microsoft's OWC located on a local web page that we save with a special extension, *.hta*, to turn it into a lightweight application. When you've got the basic cube framework in place, you can use it to analyze anything you want. For example, you can load play-by-play data and answer some deep questions. How do teams bat by inning? How do teams compare on OBP by batting position? What team's 3-4-5 hitters are the most productive? Who had the most lead-off home runs? How many times did Frank Thomas fly out to left field versus right field? A cube provides a convenient interface for you to use.

Prerequisites

Microsoft's OWC consists of a few feature-rich, lightweight controls that provide enormous flexibility in enabling interactive content in web pages, and it is freely available to Microsoft Office users. In fact, if you have Microsoft Excel installed, you probably already have OWC installed. This hack assumes that you have Microsoft Office XP installed (if you have either an earlier or a later version installed, you might have to make a few tweaks to get this hack to work, which I'll explain later).

 If you don't have any version of Microsoft Office installed, this hack will not work for you. But there is some glimmer of hope. Take a look at the "Hacking the Hack" section of this hack. The freely available OpenOffice.org suite still promises to let you do some form of pivoting against MySQL, ODBC, and ADO data—just not local cubes—using the Calc program's DataPilot feature. It's just not as sophisticated or mature as Microsoft's pivot tables.

Now, back to the program. If you have Microsoft Office installed but you don't have (or you're not sure if you have) the OWC installed, you can either install them from your Microsoft Office install CD or download the most recent patches from Microsoft's web site, depending on which version you have:

Office 2000
    Look for *MSOWC.MSI* on your Microsoft Office CD.

Office XP
    Search Google for "OWC10.exe Web Components."

Office 2003
    Search Google for "OWC11.exe Web Components."

Finally, make sure you have an ODBC driver installed for MySQL [Hack #33].

The Code

Ah, finally! Now, for the good stuff. There are three steps to this hack: define the structure of our multidimensional cube, turn these blueprints into some physical cube file using Perl, and provide an interface.

Step 1: Define local cube contents. Sadly, there isn't a lot of good documentation out there (I managed to find one source: *http://www.localcubetask.com/createwithvb.htm*). So, hopefully, this will serve as some form of template for you. Tuck this pseudo-SQL-looking code into a text file; I named it *define_batting_cube.txt* and placed it in *C:\baseball_data directory*.

The key pieces of information are SOURCE_DSN=bbdatabank (which points to the ODBC DSN that we created earlier) and the DATA SOURCE = C:\baseball_data\batting.cub setting, which is completely counterintuitive because it doesn't refer to our "source" but, rather, to our "destination" file. Don't ask me!

```
PROVIDER=MSOLAP.2;
DATA SOURCE=C:\baseball_data\batting.cub;
SOURCE_DSN=bbdatabank;
CREATECUBE=CREATE CUBE [MyLocalCube] (

        DIMENSION [Seasons],
            LEVEL [All] TYPE ALL,
            LEVEL [Year],

        DIMENSION [Teams],
            LEVEL [All] TYPE ALL,
            LEVEL [League],
            LEVEL [Team],

        DIMENSION [Players],
            LEVEL [ALL] TYPE ALL,
            LEVEL [Player],
                PROPERTY [PlayerID] CAPTION [PlayerID],
                PROPERTY [HeightWeight] CAPTION [Height/Weight],

        MEASURE [G]   Function SUM,
        MEASURE [AB]  Function SUM,
        MEASURE [H]   Function SUM,
        MEASURE [HR]  Function SUM,
        MEASURE [RBI] Function SUM,

        COMMAND (
            CREATE MEMBER [MyLocalCube].[MEASURES].[AVG]
                AS 'IIF([MEASURES].[AB] > 0, [MEASURES].[H] / [MEASURES].[AB],
    NULL)',
                FORMAT_STRING = '0.000'
            )
);
```

```
INSERTINTO=INSERT INTO [MyLocalCube]
(
    [Seasons].[Year],
    [Teams].[League],
    [Teams].[Team],
    [Players].[Player].KEY,
    [Players].[Player].NAME,
    [Players].[Player].PlayerID,
    [Players].[Player].HeightWeight,
    [G],
    [AB],
    [H],
    [HR],
    [RBI]
)
SELECT
    B.YearID AS Year,
    B.lgID AS League,
    B.teamID AS Team,
    B.playerID AS Player_KEY,
    B.playerID AS PlayerID,
    CONCAT(M.nameLast,', ', M.nameFirst) AS Player_NAME,
    CONCAT(M.height, '"', ', ', M.weight, ' lbs') AS HeightWeight,
    B.G,
    B.AB,
    B.H,
    B.HR,
    B.RBI

FROM
    batting B, master M

WHERE
    B.playerID = M.playerID
```

Step 2: Create the local cube. Now that we have defined the code to create a local cube from our MySQL data, we'll use Perl to pass it into the Microsoft ADO object library, which will know what to do with it. I call this file *make_local_cube.pl*:

```perl
#!/usr/bin/perl

# WE WILL BE USING THE ADO OBJECT LIBRARY
use Win32::OLE;
use Win32::OLE::Const 'Microsoft ActiveX Data Objects';
Win32::OLE->Initialize(Win32::OLE::COINIT_OLEINITIALIZE);

# WHAT FILE HAS THE CREATE CUBE CODE?
$QueryFile = $ARGV[0];
```

```
# READ IN THE SYNTAX FROM THIS FILE
open INFILE, "$QueryFile" or die "can't open input file $QueryFile:$!\n";
$QueryText = '';
print "Reading contents of $QueryFile ...\n";
while (<INFILE>) {$QueryText = $QueryText . $_;}
close INFILE;

# INITIATE A NEW ADODB CONNECTION AND PASS IN THE CREATE CUBE CODE
print "Creating cube ...\n";
my $Conn = Win32::OLE->new('ADODB.Connection');
$Conn->Open($QueryText);

# IF THERE WAS AN ERROR, ALERT THE USER THAT IT FAILED
if (Win32::OLE->LastError) {die Win32::OLE->LastError( ), "\n";}

# CLOSE THE CONNECTION (IF EVEN STILL OPEN)
$Conn->Close;

# ELSE, PARSE OUT THE NAME OF THE CREATED .CUB FILE
$QueryText =~ /DATA SOURCE=(.*);/;
$CubeFile = $1;
print "$CubeFile created!\n";
```

Step 3: Create a local web application to interact with the cube. Last, but not least, we need some application to interact with the .*cub* file we created. A very lightweight local web application should work. Save the following code in a file called *cube_viewer.hta*:

```
<hta:application showintaskbar="YES" windowstate="MAXIMIZE"/>

<html>

<head>

<title>Interactive Cube Viewer</title>

<script language="VBScript">

Sub connectToCube(strFilename)

    'CONNECT TO THE DESIRED CUB FILE
    objPivot.ConnectionString = "provider=MSOLAP.2;Data Source=" &
strFilename
    objPivot.DataMember = "MyLocalCube"
    objPivot.ActiveView.TitleBar.Caption = strFilename

    'ONLY VISIBLE MEMBERS GO INTO TOTALS
    objPivot.ActiveView.TotalAllMembers = False
```

```
'SET DEFAULT PIVOT TABLE OPTIONS
objPivot.MaxWidth  = screen.availWidth - 50
objPivot.MaxHeight = screen.availHeight - 175
objPivot.AllowDetails = False
objPivot.DisplayFieldList = True
objPivot.DisplayToolbar  = True

'FORMAT PIVOT FIELDS
Set ptConstants = objPivot.Constants
for each fs in objPivot.ActiveView.FieldSets
    for each f in fs.fields

        'SET SUBTOTALS TO BOLD
        f.SubtotalLabelFont.bold = True
        f.SubtotalFont.bold = True

        'TURN MEMBER PROPERTIES INTO MOUSE-OVER SCREEN TIPS
        for each p in f.MemberProperties
            p.DisplayIn = ptConstants.plDisplayPropertyInScreenTip
        next

    next
Next

'HANDCUFF THE GRAPH TO THE PIVOT TABLE
objChart.DataSource = objPivot

'SET DEFAULT GRAPH OPTIONS
objChart.HasMultipleCharts = False
objChart.Width = screen.availWidth - 150
objChart.Height = screen.availHeight - 225
objChart.AllowPropertyToolbox = True
objChart.DisplayToolbar = True
objChart.DisplayFieldList = True
objChart.HasChartSpaceTitle = True
objChart.HasChartSpaceLegend = True
objChart.ChartSpaceTitle.Caption = strCubename
objChart.PlotAllAggregates = objChart.Constants.chPlotAggregatesSeries

'CHANGE THE VIEW BACK TO PIVOT TABLE VIEW
PickView (1)

End Sub

Sub PickView(opt)

    'HIDE/SHOW THE DESIRED OBJECT
    If (opt = 1) Then
        table_area.style.display = "block"
        chart_area.style.display = "none"
```

```
        Else
            table_area.style.display = "none"
            chart_area.style.display = "block"
        End If

    End Sub

</script>

</head>

<body bgcolor="rgb(240,240,240)" onload="connectToCube(cboCubeChooser.
value)">

<select id="cboCubeChooser" onchange="connectToCube(me.value)">
<option value="C:\baseball_data\batting.cub" SELECTED>Batting</option>
<option value="C:\baseball_data\pitching.cub">Pitching</option>
</select>

<a href="#" onclick="PickView(1)">View As Table</a> |
<a href="#" onclick="PickView(2)">View As Chart</a>
<hr>

<div id="table_area" style="display: block">
    <object id="objPivot"
        classid="clsid:0002E552-0000-0000-C000-000000000046">
    </object>
</div>

<div id="chart_area" style="display: none">
    <object id="objChart"
        classid="clsid:0002E556-0000-0000-C000-000000000046">
    </object>
</div>

</body>

</html>
```

Running the Hack

To run the hack, first you need to execute the Perl script to create the cube's data, and then open the cube viewer application. To perform the first step, call the *make_local_cube.pl* script and pass in the name of the file that has the CREATE CUBE syntax in it. Of course, nothing is stopping you from creating only this one. You can define many different cubes for different data sources and pass them into this reusable script (see Figures 4-21 and 4-22).

```
C:\baseball_data>perl make_local_cube.pl "define_batting_cube.txt"
Reading contents of define_batting_cube.txt ...
Creating cube ...
C:\baseball_data\batting.cub created!
```

Now for the fun part! To view the cube, open the *C:\baseball_data\cube_viewer.hta* application in Internet Explorer and, *voilà*, our data is alive! Just click and drag stuff around. You can also right-click on this and that to change fonts and number formats. Play around with it—you can't hurt anything. So now, let's see how easy it is to compare league batting averages between AL and NL.

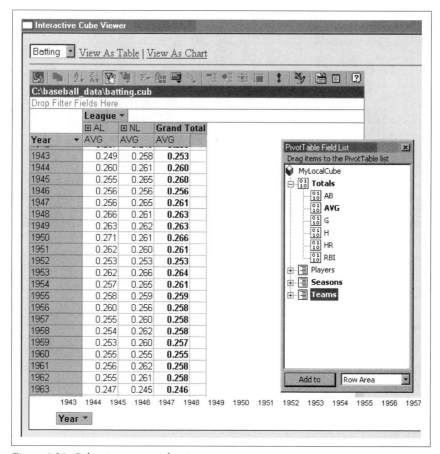

Figure 4-21. Cube viewer screenshot 1

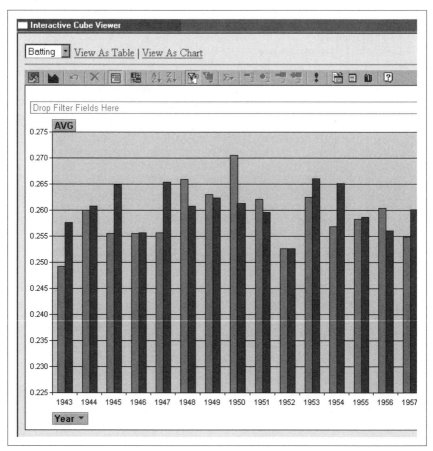

Figure 4-22. Cube viewer screenshot 2

Hacking the Hack

The OWC pivot table object is very flexible. You don't *have* to connect to a multidimensional cube (I simply prefer it because the pivot table object handles cube data a little better, and you can "pass in" extra information, such as rollover caption properties). But you certainly can connect to, for instance, the Baseball DataBank database stored in MySQL directly using ODBC. Simply replace the connection string information for *.cub* files:

```
objPivot.ConnectionString = "provider=MSOLAP.2;Data
Source=C:\baseball_data\batting.cub"

objPivot.DataMember = "MyLocalCube"
```

to the following:

```
objPivot.ConnectionString = "PROVIDER=MSDASQL.1;DRIVER={MySQL ODBC 3.
51 Driver};SERVER=localhost;DATABASE=bbdatabank;UID=username;PWD=password;"

objPivot.CommandText = "select * from batting;"
```

You also certainly can do your slicing and dicing from within Microsoft Excel (which I'm sure is what many people prefer to do). One advantage of doing that is you then have the full program at your disposal (if you're completely against Internet Explorer; also, you won't have to worry about any quirky OWC compatibility issues). And one really nice thing about Excel is that it's very easy to create a new pivot table and connect it to an external data source, be it live data via ODBC or a local *.cub* file you have stored. All you have to do is run the Pivot Table wizard in the Data menu and let it walk you through the process.

—*Tom Dierickx*

Formulas
Hacks 40–59

This chapter is a guide to some popular formulas for understanding baseball: common statistics that you remember from childhood and see displayed on the scoreboard during every game, more complicated statistics that illustrate the complexity of the game more clearly, and some advanced statistics developed by sabermetricians over the past 30 years.

The hacks in this chapter are a little different from the others in the book: each hack presents a single formula (or a set of formulas) as an equation (or a set of equations). I explain what each formula is designed to measure, and I present summary statistics for each formula that show the distribution of values by team and player over the past decade. I also give samples of a few exceptional seasons (by teams and/or players).

How I Chose the Formulas

I selected the hacks in this chapter by picking the simplest, cleverest, and most useful formulas I could find. A few of the best systems for evaluating players, such as Baseball Prospectus's PECOTA, Bill James's Win Shares, and TangoTiger's Base Runs, work well in practice but are too difficult to be called hacks. I was looking for simple, clever tricks that would be easy to understand.

Summary Statistics for the Formulas

In this chapter, each hack gives you summary statistics that provide you with some idea of what good, bad, and average values are for each statistic. This is a trick that I learned at work while analyzing data on network security, advertising effectiveness, and credit card fraud. When a statistician (or an econometrician) first gets a data set, he calculates the *summary statistics*.

These statistics are designed to give a feel for the data: what are the highest and lowest values, how are the values distributed, and which values are most common.

I didn't have a good feeling for what good or bad values meant for many different formulas, so I calculated summary statistics for each formula. Most readers probably know that a batting average of .300 is a good number, .260 is about average, and .200 is poor. But what is a good OPS, WHIP, or ISO?

I provide six distribution statistics for each formula:

Minimum
The smallest value seen.

25th percentile
The value at the 25th percentile (25% of values are smaller, 75% are larger).

Median
The value in the middle. Half of the values are smaller, half are larger.

Mean
The average value. This is not exactly the same as the median. You can tell something about the shape of the distribution by comparing the median and the mean.

75th percentile
The value at the 75th percentile (75% of values are smaller, 25% are larger).

Maximum
The highest value seen.

On the team level, I don't eliminate any players, regardless of their number of appearances. However, when analyzing single players, I often eliminate players who played in only a handful of games or had a handful of at bats. Many players play in only a few major league games (often during September, when the roster expands from 25 to 40 players). I exclude these players because including them would throw off the distribution of each measurement enormously and would not accurately reflect the level of talent in the game. Many measurements would have minima (and maybe even medians) at zero without this refinement. For more on how I thought about this problem, see "Significant Number of At Bats" [Hack #63].

Using Formulas for Fantasy Baseball

If you're an owner in a Rotisserie league, you'll probably read this chapter looking for ideas on how to outdraft and outmanage your opponents. Most of the formulas in this chapter try to do several things:

Properly value a player's total contribution
Some measures capture only one part of a player's contributions and ignore others. For example, batting average doesn't include walks. Some players, such as Garret Anderson, have high batting averages (a .298 career AVG) but never walk (a .327 career OBP), so they create a lot of outs.

Isolate a single player's contribution
Traditional measurements of performance often mix the contributions of several players. For example, runs batted in are as much a function of a player's hitting ability as is his place in the batting order.

Separate luck from skill
Some measures capture things that a player can't really control. For example, the winning pitcher in a game is (usually) the pitcher of record at the time his team takes the lead. Obviously, pitchers don't directly control how their team's batters fare against the opposing team's pitchers. A pitcher who gives up a lot of runs is not likely to win a lot of games, but a pitcher who gives up only a few runs can still lose a lot of games. (For example, during the 2005 season, Cleveland Indians starting pitcher Kevin Millwood won 9 games and lost 11 but had an incredible 2.86 ERA.)

Not all of these improvements will help fantasy owners. Let's start by considering whether it helps to measure a player's total contribution properly. Most fantasy leagues value players using simple measures such as batting average, home runs, runs batted in, earned run average, and strikeouts. So properly measuring a player's total contribution might not matter: if the league doesn't care about walks, it doesn't make sense to consider walks when choosing players.

Isolating a single player's contributions might be important if you know the players surrounding a player have changed. If you know a ground ball pitcher has moved to a team with a better defensive infield, you can use this information to better evaluate players.

Finally, let's consider measurements that separate luck and skill. These are very important for fantasy use because they help show undervalued and overvalued players. (In particular, look at some pitching statistics, such as DIPS and CERA.)

Who Came Up with These Things?

As much as I'd like to take credit for these formulas, most of them come from the hard work of other people. I just explain what each formula does, show you how to calculate it easily, and give some distribution statistics. I've tried to give proper credit to the inventor of each measurement.

HACK #40 Measure Batting with Batting Average

Use R to calculate the most familiar statistic in baseball: batting average.

Batting average (AVG) is, by far, the most popular baseball statistic. It's printed on baseball cards, flashed on scoreboards, and recounted by announcers during games. For more than 50 years, the best minds in baseball have talked about the problems with batting average, from Branch Rickey and Allan Roth's work with the Brooklyn Dodgers in the 1950s, through Bill James and Pete Palmer's work in the 1980s, to Michael Lewis's book, *Moneyball* (W. W. Norton & Company).

I agree that batting average isn't the best formula for measuring batting ability today, but I think it was once much more revealing. Batting average is one of the oldest statistics, dating back to the first time player statistics were published in the 19th century. In the early days of baseball, the pitcher's role was not the same as it is today. The pitcher wasn't supposed to trick batters with balls that looked like strikes, strikes that looked like balls, fastballs that flew past the batter, and changeups that slowly crossed the plate after the batter swung through the pitch. The early rules actually stated that a pitcher had to keep his arm stiff at the elbow and pitch underhand. The pitcher's role was to throw the ball over the plate, allowing the batter the chance to put the ball in play. So, naturally, batting average excludes walks and the number of times a player is hit by a pitch because these are the fault of a bad pitcher and have nothing to do with the skills of a good batter.

I'm including this hack for three reasons. First, this is the most familiar of all baseball formulas, and it's one of the simplest. I want to show you a few statistician tricks for quickly calculating, reading, and understanding numbers; with batting average, I know the formula itself won't confuse you. Second, batting average is one of the key statistics used to score teams in fantasy baseball. Regardless of whether batting average helps real teams win real games, it will help fantasy teams win fantasy leagues. Finally, we all grew up knowing batting averages, believing that .360 was MVP quality, .300 was a really good average, and .240 wasn't so hot. I know that batting average is a flawed statistic, but I have to admit that I still look at it.

Sample Code

Batting average formula. Batting average measures how often a player reaches base by his own efforts. It includes all balls in play (hits and outs) and all strikeouts. It excludes walks because no ball was put into play on a walk. It also excludes bases reached on error.

Each time a player safely reaches base by putting the ball in play, he is credited with a *hit*. (H is the abbreviation for the number of hits received.) Each time a player has an opportunity to reach base by putting the ball into play, and either reaches base or strikes out, he is credited with an *at bat*. (AB usually represents the number of at bats.) Batting average is the number of base hits divided by the total number of at bats. The formula is:

```
AVG = H / AB
```

There are a couple of special cases. If a batter is hit by a pitch, it doesn't count as an at bat. When a player makes an out on a fly ball to the outfield, but the runner on third base scores, this is a *sacrifice fly* (SF) and does not count as an at bat. When a player deliberately makes contact with the ball, advances the base runners, and is put out at first base, this is a *sacrifice hit* (SH) and does not count as an at bat either.

Running the Hack

Let's start simply, by just calculating AVG in R. As a starting point, let's load a database with data that you can get from several web sites, as explained in "Get Historical Play-by-Play Data" **[Hack #14]**. (If you don't want to install MySQL, you can load text files directly into R.)

To use any of the formulas in R, you will first have to load and attach this data set. If you have already loaded the data into R and saved it as an *.RData* file (as described in "Access Databases Directly from Excel or R" **[Hack #33]**), you should include an R statement like this to load and attach the file:

```
> load("bbdatabank.RData")
> attach(batting);
```

If you have MySQL installed and you have a copy of the Baseball DataBank database, you can access this in R through the following commands (as explained in "Access Databases Directly from Excel or R" **[Hack #33]**):

```
# this example uses RMySQL
library(RMySQL)
drv <- dbDriver("MySQL")
# change the username field as appropriate
bbdb.con <- dbConnect(drv, username="jadler",
    dbname="bbdatabank",host="localhost")
```

```
batting.query <- dbSendQuery(bbdb.con, "SELECT * FROM batting")
batting <- fetch(batting.query, n=-1)
```

In R, you can calculate batting average like this:

```
batting$AVG <- batting$H / batting$AB
```

I like to be able to refer to variables by their short names (like AVG) without specifying the data frame (in this case, batting), so I use the following command to attach the data frame:

```
attach(batting)
```

Summary statistics. The first thing that I like to do when trying to understand a formula is to calculate summary statistics in R. The idea is to calculate the mean and median values (so that you know where average players are), the maximum and minimum (so that you know where the worst and best players are), and the 25th and 75th percentiles. You calculate the values at the quartiles so that you can see where the middle is: half of all players are between the first and third quartiles.

Let's look at some summary statistics to understand how batting average has changed over time. Here are the summary statistics across the entire database (1871–2004):

```
> summary(AVG, digits=3)
    Min.  1st Qu.  Median    Mean  3rd Qu.     Max.       NA's
   0.000    0.151   0.232   0.211    0.275    1.000  10680.000
```

Notice the large number of NA values. Many players never had a single qualifying at bat. Also, the experience of many players in the major leagues was so short (or their number of at bats in a season was so small) that they never managed to get a hit, or never made an out.

To make this distribution more useful, let's cut this down to show only those players with a number of at bats that's large enough to qualify for a batting title. To qualify, a player needs an average of at least 3.1 plate appearances in every game played by his team. For a more detailed discussion of this rule, see "Significant Number of At Bats" [Hack #63].

Here's a straightforward way to do this in R alone:

```
> t <- subset(teams, select=c(teamID,yearID,G))
> names(t) <- c("teamID", "yearID", "teamG")
> b_and_t <- merge(batting, t, by=c("yearID", "teamID"))
> b_and_t$AVG <- b_and_t$H / b_and_t$AB
> b_and_t$qualify <- (b_and_t$AB + ifelse(is.na(b_and_t$BB),0, b_and_t$BB) +
+ ifelse(is.na(b_and_t$HBP),0,b_and_t$HBP) +
+ ifelse(is.na(b_and_t$SF),0,b_and_t$SF)) > 3.1 * b_and_t$teamG
> attach(b_and_t)
```

However, this code does not correctly deal with players who batted on more than one team in one year. You can use R to fix this problem (using the aggregate function), but the query takes a long time (more than 10 minutes) to run. I gave up on it and decided to get the data out of a MySQL database. This query takes less than 30 seconds:

```
> library(RMySQL)
> drv <-dbDriver("MySQL")
> con <- dbConnect(drv, username="jadler", dbname="bbdatabank",
host="localhost")
> bt.query <- dbSendQuery(con, statement = paste(
+    "select playerID, yearID, ",
+    "GROUP_CONCAT(teamID SEPARATOR ',') as teamIDs, ",
+    "sum(G / teamG) * sum(teamG) / count(teamID) as qualifyingG, ",
+    "sum(teamG) / count(teamID) as teamG, ",
+    "sum(G) as G, sum(AB) as AB, sum(R) as R, ",
+    "sum(H) as H, sum(2B) as X2B, sum(3B) as X3B, ",
+    "sum(HR) as HR, sum(RBI) as RBI, sum(SB) as SB, ",
+    "sum(CS) as CS, sum(BB) as BB, sum(SO) as SO, ",
+    "sum(IBB) as IBB, sum(HBP) as HBP, sum(SH) as SH, ",
+    "sum(SF) as SF, sum(GIDP) as GIDP ",
+    "from  (select b.*, t.G as teamG ",
+    "         from batting b inner join teams t ",
+    "         on b.teamID=t.teamID and b.yearID=t.yearID) i ",
+    "group by playerID, yearID"))> b_and_t <- fetch(bt.query, n=-1)
> b_and_t <- fetch(bt.query, n=-1)
> b_and_t$AVG <- b_and_t$H / b_and_t$AB
> b_and_t$qualify <- (b_and_t$AB + ifelse(is.na(b_and_t$BB),0, b_and_t$BB) +
+ ifelse(is.na(b_and_t$HBP),0,b_and_t$HBP) +
+ ifelse(is.na(b_and_t$SF),0,b_and_t$SF)) > 3.1 * b_and_t$teamG
> attach(b_and_t)
```

Here are the summary statistics across the entire database (1871–2004):

```
> summary(subset(AVG,qualify),digits=3)
    Min. 1st Qu.  Median    Mean 3rd Qu.    Max.
  0.0741  0.2580  0.2790  0.2800  0.3020  0.4920
```

Here are the summary statistics over the past decade (1995–2004):

```
> summary(subset(AVG,qualify & yearID > 1994),digits=3)
    Min. 1st Qu.  Median    Mean 3rd Qu.    Max.
   0.203   0.265   0.282   0.284   0.302   0.379
```

Top 10. To get an even better feel for the statistics, let's look at a few extreme values. Let's look at the top 10 batting averages of all time. Here is the SQL code that I used to calculate these results. I used the same MLB rule used to qualify for awards: an average of 3.1 plate appearances per game is required to qualify.

RMySQL and MySQL 5.0

I had some difficulty with RMySQL and MySQL 5.0. MySQL 5.0 includes slightly different information about column types than earlier versions of MySQL, confusing applications like R. In particular, I had problems with floating-point numbers. Here is a short example of the error message that I received:

```
There were 19 warnings (use warnings( ) to see them)
> warnings( )
Warning messages:
1: RS-DBI driver warning: (unrecognized MySQL field type 246 in column
3)
2: RS-DBI driver warning: (unrecognized MySQL field type 246 in column
4)
3: RS-DBI driver warning: (unrecognized MySQL field type 246 in column
5)
...
```

You need to fix the datatype of these fields in R (or else R considers them to be "character" types, and not numeric). To do this, I use the as.double and as.integer functions for decimal and integer values, respectively:

```
b_and_t$qualifyingG <- as.double(b_and_t$qualifyingG)
b_and_t$teamG <- as.integer(b_and_t$teamG)
b_and_t$G <- as.integer(b_and_t$G)
...
```

You can find the full version of the code I used at *http://www.oreilly.com/catalog/baseballhks*.

(If you want, you can skip the create index statements. A database index is an object that tells the database how to find values in a table quickly. It's a lot like an index in a book. Instead of flipping through a book to find *fielding runs*, you can just look up the page in an index. A database index works the same way. However, if you skip these statements, this query is likely to take substantially longer to run, maybe hours rather than seconds.)

```
create index batting_pidx on batting(idxLahman);
create index batting_tidx on batting(idxTeams);
create index master_pidx on master(idxLahman);
create index teams_idx on teams(idxTeams);
create index teams_fidx on teams(idxTeamsFranchises);
create index teamsFranchises_idx on teamsFranchises(idxTeamsFranchises);

create table b_and_t as
select idxLahman, yearID,
    GROUP_CONCAT(franchID SEPARATOR ",") as teamIDs,
```

```
       sum(G / teamG) * sum(teamG) / count(franchID) as qualifyingG,
       sum(teamG) / count(franchID) as teamG,
       sum(G) as G, sum(AB) as AB, sum(R) as R,
       sum(H) as H, sum(2B) as X2B, sum(3B) as X3B,
       sum(HR) as HR, sum(RBI) as RBI, sum(SB) as SB,
       sum(CS) as CS, sum(BB) as BB, sum(SO) as SO,
       sum(IBB) as IBB, sum(HBP) as HBP, sum(SH) as SH,
       sum(SF) as SF, sum(GIDP) as GIDP
from  (select b.*, t.yearID, t.G as teamG, f.franchID
       from batting b inner join teams t
       inner join TeamsFranchises f
       where b.idxTeams=t.idxTeams and
       t.idxTeamsFranchises=f.idxTeamsFranchises) i
group by idxLahman, yearID;

select f.franchName AS "First_Team",
    nameFirst, nameLast, b.yearID,
    b.AB, round(b.H/b.AB,3) as AVG
from b_and_t b inner join master m inner join teamsFranchises f
where b.idxLahman=m.idxLahman
    and substr(b.teamIDs,1,3)=f.franchID
    and b.AB + ifnull(b.BB, 0) + ifnull(b.HBP, 0) + ifnull(b.SF, 0)
    > 3.1 * b.teamG
    -- and b.yearID > 1994
order by AVG DESC limit 10;
```

Here are the top 10 batting averages of all time (note that the Athletics played only 28 games in 1871):

First_Team	nameFirst	nameLast	yearID	AB	AVG
Philadelphia Athletics	Levi	Meyerle	1871	130	0.492
Atlanta Braves	Hugh	Duffy	1894	539	0.440
St. Louis Cardinals	Tip	O'Neill	1887	517	0.435
Boston Red Stockings	Ross	Barnes	1872	229	0.432
Boston Red Stockings	Cal	McVey	1871	153	0.431
Chicago Cubs	Ross	Barnes	1876	322	0.429
Oakland Athletics	Nap	Lajoie	1901	544	0.426
Boston Red Stockings	Ross	Barnes	1873	322	0.425
St. Louis Cardinals	Rogers	Hornsby	1924	536	0.424
Baltimore Orioles	Willie	Keeler	1897	564	0.424

Here are the top 10 seasons over the past decade (1995–2004):

First_Team	nameFirst	nameLast	yearID	AB	AVG
Colorado Rockies	Larry	Walker	1999	438	0.379
Boston Red Sox	Nomar	Garciaparra	2000	529	0.372
San Diego Padres	Tony	Gwynn	1997	592	0.372
Colorado Rockies	Todd	Helton	2000	580	0.372
Seattle Mariners	Ichiro	Suzuki	2004	704	0.372

```
| San Francisco Giants | Barry   | Bonds   | 2002 | 403 | 0.370 |
| San Diego Padres     | Tony    | Gwynn   | 1995 | 535 | 0.368 |
| Colorado Rockies     | Larry   | Walker  | 1997 | 568 | 0.366 |
| Colorado Rockies     | Larry   | Walker  | 1998 | 454 | 0.363 |
| San Francisco Giants | Barry   | Bonds   | 2004 | 373 | 0.362 |
+----------------------+---------+---------+------+-----+-------+
```

Distribution. The third thing I like to do to understand a formula is plot a *histogram* of the distribution. The idea of a histogram is to create a set of evenly spaced bins across the range of values. Next, you count the number of items in each bin. (For batting average, the bins varied between about .20 and .40, and there were 40 bins of size .005. So, the first bin contained averages between .200 and .205, the second between .205 and .210, and so on.)

A simple command in R, called the hist( ) command, lets us plot this in one step:

```
> hist(subset(AVG,(qualify & yearID>1994)), breaks=40)
```

The left part of Figure 5-1 shows the plot that this statement generates. Here's one example of how to read this diagram. The little box whose left edge lines up with .25 contained players with batting averages of between .250 and .255, and it looks like there were about 75 players in that box.

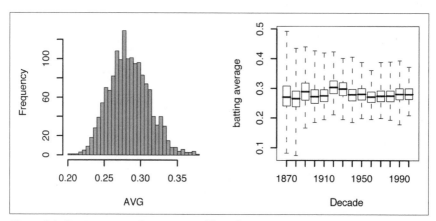

Figure 5-1. Batting average histogram and box plot

The thing to focus on here is that the general shape of the data resembles a bell curve. Notice also how common it is to be in the middle of the group, and how rare it is to be much better or much worse than average.

This isn't a perfect normal distribution; it's a little skewed toward low values. (Statistical terms like *skew* and *kurtosis* are used to explain how much a distribution deviates from a normal distribution.)

The Shape of the Distribution

Here's a little more to think about, if you're mathematically inclined. You might notice that the distribution resembles a bell curve and is called a Gaussian or normal distribution. Because of something called the Central Limit Theorem, bell curves occur naturally everywhere when plotting the distribution of sample means. A lot of baseball formulas are averages, so it is not surprising that their distributions look like bell curves. If you want to know more about how or why this occurs, check out a statistics book. I talk more about probability distributions and batting average in "Significant Number of At Bats" [Hack #63].

Box plot. As a final step, let's look at how batting averages have changed over time. I'll use a special type of plot to show not only how the median values have changed, but also how the middle quartile, maximum, and minimum values have changed. The plot is called a *box plot*, and you can see an example of it in Figure 5-1. These plots show five values for each decade. The lines at the top and bottom (the *whiskers*) represent the maximum and minimum values. The box in the middle of each plot shows the middle range of values. The bottom of the box represents the 25th percentile, the line in the middle represents the median, and the top of the box represents the 75th percentile.

I use a trick to group by decade. I divide the year by 10 (for example, changing 2004 to 200.4), then I use a floor function to truncate the decimal (turning 200.4 to 200), and then I multiply the result by 10 (turning 200 to 2,000). This is a quick way to group values together by decade. I then plot the results using the boxplot( ) command in R:

```
> b_and_t$decade <- as.factor(floor(b_and_t$yearID/10) * 10)
> boxplot(AVG~decade,data=b_and_t,subset=qualify,
+     pars=c(xlab="decade", ylab="batting average"),
+     range=0)
```

The right part of Figure 5-1 shows the box plot that this code generated. As you can see, the range of batting averages narrowed over the first 100 years but has been stable for the past couple of decades. A big reason for this has nothing to do with the players' skills: in the 1870s, teams played about 50 games a year; in the 1880s, most teams played only about 100 games; and by the 1890s, the average had increased to 140 games per year, which is close to today's 162.

Notice the tight range of values: most major league players have an average of between .260 and .300.

Measure Batting with On-Base Percentage

#41 Use on-base percentage as a simple measurement of a player's offensive contributions.

Batting average is easy to calculate, but its meaning is actually kind of complicated. It ignores important offensive contributions (walks) and it doesn't count sacrifices. Many baseball fans think that another statistic, on-base percentage (OBP), is a much better representation of hitting ability.

OBP is a measure of how many times a player makes it on base, whether he makes it on base through a hit (H), is awarded a walk (a base on balls, or BB), or is hit by a pitch (HBP). For batting average, we exclude walks, hits by pitches, and sacrifice flies (SF), but for OBP, we include all of these. The formula for OBP is a little more complicated than the formula for batting average:

```
OBP = (H + BB + HBP) / (AB + BB + HBP + SF)
```

However, I think its meaning is clearer. There are no caveats; it's just the percentage of time the player reaches base.

Sample Code

Here's the simple way to calculate OBP, if you have already loaded the Baseball Archive data into R:

```
attach(batting)
batting$OBP <- (H + BB + HBP) / (AB + BB + HBP + SF)
```

As I explain in "Measure Batting with Batting Average" **[Hack #40]**, I use a slightly more difficult method of calculation. Basically, I calculate the average number of games a player's teams played (when the player played on more than one team), and the total statistics for a player for a whole season. This lets me correctly calculate statistics for a player for the entire season and determine who qualified for batting awards.

```
attach(b_and_t)
b_and_t$OBP <- (H + BB + ifelse(is.na(HBP),0,HBP)) /
               (AB + BB + ifelse(is.na(HBP),0,HBP) + ifelse(is.na(SF),0,SF))
b_and_t$OBP <- (H + ifelse(is.na(BB),0,BB) + ifelse(is.na(HBP),0,HBP)) /
               (AB + ifelse(is.na(BB),0,BB) + ifelse(is.na(HBP),0,HBP) +
               ifelse(is.na(SF),0,SF))
```

Running the Hack

Summary statistics. Here are the summary statistics across the entire database (1871–2004):

```
> summary(subset(OBP, qualify), digits=3)
   Min. 1st Qu.  Median    Mean 3rd Qu.    Max.
 0.0968  0.3170  0.3450  0.3450  0.3730  0.6090
```

Here are the summary statistics over the past decade (1995–2004):

```
> summary(subset(OBP, qualify & yearID > 1994), digits=3)
   Min. 1st Qu.  Median    Mean 3rd Qu.    Max.
  0.259   0.331   0.354   0.357   0.381   0.609
```

Incidentally, when I first calculated these statistics, I was sure my calculations were wrong: how could anyone have an OBP as high as .609? It's a good idea to double-check your work if it looks wrong, so I took a closer look to figure out what was going on. The .609 OBP was from Barry Bonds's 2004 season. Here's how this worked: 373 at bats, 135 hits, 232 walks, 9 times hit by a pitch, and 3 sacrifice flies. By the way, he had 120 intentional walks.

Top 10. Let's look at the top 10 players of all time, ranked by OBP. Here is the SQL code that I used to calculate these results. (Notice the three indexes, which change the running time from hours to seconds.) I used the same MLB rule used to qualify for awards: an average of 3.1 plate appearances per game are required to qualify.

```
-- create b_and_t as shown in "Measure Batting with Batting Average" [Hack
#40]

select f.franchName AS "First_Team", b.yearID, nameFirst, nameLast,
    b.AB + ifnull(b.BB, 0) + ifnull(b.HBP, 0) + ifnull(b.SF, 0) as PA,
    round((b.H + ifnull(b.BB, 0) + ifnull(b.HBP, 0)) /
        (b.AB + ifnull(b.BB, 0) + ifnull(b.HBP, 0) + ifnull(b.SF, 0))
    ,3) as OBP
from b_and_t b inner join master m inner join teamsFranchises f
where b.idxLahman=m.idxLahman and
    substr(b.teamIDs,1,3)=f.franchID
    and b.AB + ifnull(b.BB, 0) + ifnull(b.HBP, 0) + ifnull(b.SF, 0)
    > 3.1 * b.teamG
order by OBP DESC limit 10;
```

Here are the top 10 on-base percentages of all time:

First_Team	yearID	nameFirst	nameLast	PA	OBP
San Francisco Giants	2004	Barry	Bonds	617	0.609
San Francisco Giants	2002	Barry	Bonds	612	0.582
Boston Red Sox	1941	Ted	Williams	606	0.553

```
| Baltimore Orioles      | 1899 | John    | McGraw    | 537 | 0.547 |
| New York Yankees       | 1923 | Babe    | Ruth      | 696 | 0.545 |
| New York Yankees       | 1920 | Babe    | Ruth      | 611 | 0.532 |
| San Francisco Giants   | 2003 | Barry   | Bonds     | 550 | 0.529 |
| Boston Red Sox         | 1957 | Ted     | Williams  | 546 | 0.526 |
| Philadelphia Phillies  | 1894 | Billy   | Hamilton  | 679 | 0.523 |
| New York Yankees       | 1926 | Babe    | Ruth      | 642 | 0.516 |
+-----------------------+--------+----------+----------+------+-------+
```

Here are the top 10 seasons over the past decade (1995–2004):

```
+-----------------------+--------+-----------+----------+------+-------+
| First_Team            | yearID | nameFirst | nameLast | PA   | OBP   |
+-----------------------+--------+-----------+----------+------+-------+
| San Francisco Giants  | 2004   | Barry     | Bonds    | 617  | 0.609 |
| San Francisco Giants  | 2002   | Barry     | Bonds    | 612  | 0.582 |
| San Francisco Giants  | 2003   | Barry     | Bonds    | 550  | 0.529 |
| San Francisco Giants  | 2001   | Barry     | Bonds    | 664  | 0.515 |
| Seattle Mariners      | 1995   | Edgar     | Martinez | 639  | 0.479 |
| Oakland Athletics     | 2001   | Jason     | Giambi   | 671  | 0.477 |
| Oakland Athletics     | 2000   | Jason     | Giambi   | 664  | 0.476 |
| Toronto Blue Jays     | 2000   | Carlos    | Delgado  | 711  | 0.470 |
| St. Louis Cardinals   | 1998   | Mark      | McGwire  | 681  | 0.470 |
| Colorado Rockies      | 2004   | Todd      | Helton   | 683  | 0.469 |
+-----------------------+--------+-----------+----------+------+-------+
```

Distribution and box plot. A third useful view of OBP is to look at a histogram of the distribution:

```
> hist(subset(OBP,(qualify & yearID>1994)), breaks=40)
```

See the left plot in Figure 5-2 for a histogram of OBP. Like AVG, the distribution of OBP appears to be normal (the famous bell curve shape). You'll notice a few outliers on the far right. A previous top 10 lists show you who the outliers were.

To help understand how batting averages have changed over time and what good and bad values for box plots are, let's use R to show box plots for batting average by decade:

```
> b_and_t$decade <- as.factor(floor(b_and_t$yearID/10) * 10)
> boxplot(OBP~decade,data=b_and_t,subset=qualify,
+     pars=c(xlab="decade", ylab="on base percentage"),
+     range=0)
```

Figure 5-2 shows the box plot this code generates.

As you can see, OBP rose during the first couple of decades of professional baseball and then was stable for decades. Only at the extremes was there much of a difference, with a noticeable decline in the 1960s and 1970s (as mound heights were increased to help pitchers) and a noticeable increase today (mostly due to Barry Bonds).

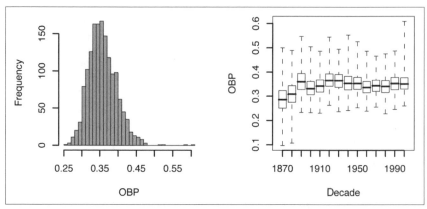

Figure 5-2. On-base percentage histogram and box plot

 Measure Batting with SLG

#42 Use slugging average to measure batting power.

Slugging average (SLG) is a kind of weighted batting average. In normal batting average, all hits count the same, but in SLG, doubles count twice, triples count three times, and home runs count four times. A high SLG means that a hitter hits the ball often and hits it hard. SLG is an old statistic, but writers such as Bill James have made it much more popular recently.

The Formula

For convenience, we'll use the expression *total bases* (TB) in this hack. Total bases is a weighted measurement of hits: singles count for 1, doubles count for 2, triples count for 3, and home runs count for 4. If you know how many hits (H), doubles (2B), triples (3B), and home runs (HR) a player hit, you can calculate TB:

```
TB = 1 * singles + 2 * doubles + 3 * triples + 4 * home runs
   = H + 2B + 2 * 3B + 3 * HR
```

Using TB, we can give a simple formula for SLG:

```
SLG = TB / AB
```

Sample Code

Here is some sample code for slugging average. To calculate SLG, we'll start by loading the Baseball Archive database. We'll then use the same technique we use in "Measure Batting with Batting Average" [Hack #40] to calculate SLG:

```
# assumes b_and_t data frame has been created
attach(b_and_t)
TB <- H + X2B + 2 * X3B + 3 * HR
b_and_t$TB <- TB
SLG <- TB / AB
b_and_t$SLG <- SLG
```

Running the Hack

Summary statistics. Let's look at some summary statistics to help understand how slugging average has changed over time. Here are the summary statistics across the entire database (1871–2004):

```
> summary(subset(SLG,qualify),digits=3)
   Min. 1st Qu. Median   Mean 3rd Qu.    Max.
 0.0741  0.3550 0.4070 0.4120  0.4620  0.8630
```

Here are the summary statistics over the past decade (1995–2004):

```
> summary(subset(SLG,qualify & yearID > 1994),digits=3)
  Min. 1st Qu. Median   Mean 3rd Qu.    Max.
 0.274   0.408  0.459  0.466   0.516   0.863
```

Top 10. Here's the SQL code that I used to fetch the top 10 players by slugging average:

```
-- create b_and_t as shown in "Measure Batting with Batting Average" [Hack
#40]

select f.franchName AS "First_Team", nameFirst, nameLast, b.yearID,
  b.AB + ifnull(b.BB, 0) + ifnull(b.HBP, 0) + ifnull(b.SF, 0) as PA,
  round((b.H + b.X2B + 2 * b.X3B + 3 * b.HR)/b.AB,3) as SLG
from b_and_t b inner join master m inner join teamsFranchises f
where b.idxLahman=m.idxLahman
    and substr(b.teamIDs,1,3)=f.franchID
    and b.AB + ifnull(b.BB, 0) + ifnull(b.HBP, 0) + ifnull(b.SF, 0)
    > 3.1 * b.teamG
order by SLG DESC limit 10;
```

There are a lot of great players and great teams on this list. The number three and number four hitters from "Murderer's Row," the lineup of the 1927 Yankees, are on this list, as are four of Barry Bonds's seasons.

```
+----------------------+-----------+----------+--------+------+-------+
| First_Team           | nameFirst | nameLast | yearID | PA   | SLG   |
+----------------------+-----------+----------+--------+------+-------+
| San Francisco Giants | Barry     | Bonds    | 2001   | 664  | 0.863 |
| New York Yankees     | Babe      | Ruth     | 1920   | 611  | 0.847 |
| New York Yankees     | Babe      | Ruth     | 1921   | 689  | 0.846 |
| San Francisco Giants | Barry     | Bonds    | 2004   | 617  | 0.812 |
| San Francisco Giants | Barry     | Bonds    | 2002   | 612  | 0.799 |
| New York Yankees     | Babe      | Ruth     | 1927   | 677  | 0.772 |
```

```
| New York Yankees    | Lou    | Gehrig   | 1927 | 696 | 0.765 |
| New York Yankees    | Babe   | Ruth     | 1923 | 696 | 0.764 |
| St. Louis Cardinals | Rogers | Hornsby  | 1925 | 589 | 0.756 |
| St. Louis Cardinals | Mark   | McGwire  | 1998 | 681 | 0.752 |
+---------------------+--------+----------+------+-----+-------+
```

Looking at the top 10 sluggers over the past decade, we see a lot of famous names. Barry Bonds made the list four times. Mark McGwire and Sammy Sosa (who both broke Roger Maris's home run record in 1998) are on the list. Rounding out the list are Larry Walker and Todd Helton, two very good hitters lucky enough to play in the thin air of Coors Field.

```
+---------------------+-----------+----------+--------+-----+-------+
| First_Team          | nameFirst | nameLast | yearID | PA  | SLG   |
+---------------------+-----------+----------+--------+-----+-------+
| San Francisco Giants | Barry    | Bonds    | 2001   | 664 | 0.863 |
| San Francisco Giants | Barry    | Bonds    | 2004   | 617 | 0.812 |
| San Francisco Giants | Barry    | Bonds    | 2002   | 612 | 0.799 |
| St. Louis Cardinals | Mark      | McGwire  | 1998   | 681 | 0.752 |
| San Francisco Giants | Barry    | Bonds    | 2003   | 550 | 0.749 |
| Chicago Cubs        | Sammy     | Sosa     | 2001   | 711 | 0.737 |
| Oakland Athletics   | Mark      | McGwire  | 1996   | 548 | 0.730 |
| Colorado Rockies    | Larry     | Walker   | 1997   | 664 | 0.720 |
| Colorado Rockies    | Larry     | Walker   | 1999   | 513 | 0.710 |
| Colorado Rockies    | Todd      | Helton   | 2000   | 697 | 0.698 |
+---------------------+-----------+----------+--------+-----+-------+
```

Distribution and box plot. Here is the code to create the histogram:

```
hist(subset(SLG,qualify & yearID>tenYearsAgo),breaks=Breaks,
     main="",xlab="SLG")
```

The histogram shown in the left half of Figure 5-3 is interesting. Notice that the distribution is a little lopsided; the bell curve looks as though it stretches a little to the right.

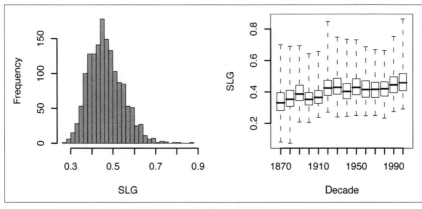

Figure 5-3. Slugging average histogram and box plot

```
b_and_t$decade <- as.factor(floor(b_and_t$yearID/10) * 10)
boxplot(SLG~decade,data=b_and_t,subset=qualify,
    pars=c(xlab="decade", ylab="slugging average"), range=0)
```

Looking at the box plot in the right half of Figure 5-3, we see that slugging averages have increased over time, dipping briefly in the 1960s and 1970s as the pitching mound height was increased.

Measure Batting with OPS

#43

Use OPS as a simple measurement of a player's offensive contributions.

The on-base percentage captures all of the times a play makes it on base, but it weighs them all the same. The slugging average weighs extra bases in rating hits, but it doesn't capture all of the times that players make it on base. So why not try adding the two together? That gives you on base plus slugging average, or OPS:

```
OPS = OBP + SLG
```

Pete Palmer came up with OPS in the 1970s. It's one of the best simple statistics for evaluating players. It captures the most important offensive attributes for a ballplayer: the ability to hit the ball hard, the ability to get on base, and the ability not to get out. It also correlates well with runs scored.

Running the Hack

Here's the simple way to calculate OPS, if you have already loaded the Baseball DataBank data into R:

```
attach(batting)
batting$OBP <- (H + BB + HBP) / (AB + BB + HBP + SF)
batting$TB <- (H + X2B + 2 * X3B + 3 * HR)
batting$SLG <- batting$TB / AB
batting$OPS <- batting$OBP + batting$SLG
```

As I explain in "Measure Batting with Batting Average" [Hack #40], I use a slightly more complicated method of calculation. Basically, I calculate the average number of games a player's teams played (when the player played on more than one team) and the total statistics for a player for a whole season. This lets me correctly calculate whole-season statistics for a player and determine who qualified for batting awards:

```
# assumes that b_and_t dataframe has been created as shown above
b_and_t$qualify <- (b_and_t$AB + ifelse(is.na(b_and_t$BB),0, b_and_t$BB) +
    ifelse(is.na(b_and_t$HBP),0,b_and_t$HBP) +
    ifelse(is.na(b_and_t$SF),0,b_and_t$SF)) > 3.1 * b_and_t$teamG
attach(b_and_t)
OBP <- (H + ifelse(is.na(BB),0,BB) + ifelse(is.na(HBP),0,HBP)) /
```

```
(AB + ifelse(is.na(BB),0,BB) + ifelse(is.na(HBP),0,HBP) +
ifelse(is.na(SF),0,SF))
TB <- H + X2B + 2 * X3B + 3 * HR
b_and_t$TB <- TB
SLG <- TB / AB
b_and_t$SLG <- SLG
OPS <- OBP + SLG
b_and_t$OPS <- OPS
```

Summary statistics. Here are the summary statistics across the entire database (1871–2004):

```
> summary(subset(OPS, qualify), digits=3)
   Min. 1st Qu.  Median    Mean 3rd Qu.    Max.
  0.179   0.680   0.754   0.757   0.829   1.420
```

Here are the summary statistics over the past decade (1995–2004):

```
> summary(subset(OPS, qualify & yearID > 1994), digits=3)
   Min. 1st Qu.  Median    Mean 3rd Qu.    Max.
  0.564   0.745   0.812   0.824   0.888   1.420
```

That crazy 1.420 OPS? Barry Bonds.

Top 10. Let's look at the top 10 players of all time, ranked by OPS. Here is the SQL code that I used to calculate these results. (Notice the three indexes, which change the running time from hours to seconds.) I used the same MLB rule used to qualify for awards: an average of 3.1 plate appearances per game.

```
select First_Team, concat(nameLast, ', ', nameFirst, ' (', yearID, ')')
       as name, SLG + OBP as OPS, SLG, OBP
FROM (
    select round((b.H + ifnull(b.BB, 0) + ifnull(b.HBP, 0)) /
       (b.AB + ifnull(b.BB, 0) + ifnull(b.HBP, 0) + ifnull(b.SF, 0))
       ,3) as OBP,
    round((b.H + b.X2B + 2 * b.X3B + 3 * b.HR)/b.AB,3) as SLG,
    b.AB + ifnull(b.BB, 0) + ifnull(b.HBP, 0) + ifnull(b.SF, 0) as PA,
    nameFirst, nameLast, b.yearID, f.franchName AS "First_Team"
    from b_and_t b inner join master m inner join teamsFranchises f
    where b.idxLahman=m.idxLahman and substr(b.teamIDs,1,3)=f.franchID
    and b.AB + ifnull(b.BB, 0) + ifnull(b.HBP, 0) + ifnull(b.SF, 0)
       > 3.1 * b.teamG) i
where yearID > 1994
order by OPS DESC limit 10;
```

Here are the top 10 players of all time, ranked by OPS:

```
+----------------------+----------------------+-------+-------+-------+
| First_Team           | name                 | OPS   | SLG   | OBP   |
+----------------------+----------------------+-------+-------+-------+
| San Francisco Giants | Bonds, Barry (2004)  | 1.421 | 0.812 | 0.609 |
| San Francisco Giants | Bonds, Barry (2002)  | 1.381 | 0.799 | 0.582 |
| New York Yankees     | Ruth, Babe (1920)    | 1.379 | 0.847 | 0.532 |
| San Francisco Giants | Bonds, Barry (2001)  | 1.378 | 0.863 | 0.515 |
| New York Yankees     | Ruth, Babe (1921)    | 1.358 | 0.846 | 0.512 |
| New York Yankees     | Ruth, Babe (1923)    | 1.309 | 0.764 | 0.545 |
| Boston Red Sox       | Williams, Ted (1941) | 1.288 | 0.735 | 0.553 |
| San Francisco Giants | Bonds, Barry (2003)  | 1.278 | 0.749 | 0.529 |
| New York Yankees     | Ruth, Babe (1927)    | 1.258 | 0.772 | 0.486 |
| Boston Red Sox       | Williams, Ted (1957) | 1.257 | 0.731 | 0.526 |
+----------------------+----------------------+-------+-------+-------+
10 rows in set (9.65 sec)
```

Here are the top 10 seasons over the past decade (1995–2004):

```
+----------------------+----------------------+-------+-------+-------+
| First_Team           | name                 | OPS   | SLG   | OBP   |
+----------------------+----------------------+-------+-------+-------+
| San Francisco Giants | Bonds, Barry (2004)  | 1.421 | 0.812 | 0.609 |
| San Francisco Giants | Bonds, Barry (2002)  | 1.381 | 0.799 | 0.582 |
| San Francisco Giants | Bonds, Barry (2001)  | 1.378 | 0.863 | 0.515 |
| San Francisco Giants | Bonds, Barry (2003)  | 1.278 | 0.749 | 0.529 |
| St. Louis Cardinals  | McGwire, Mark (1998) | 1.222 | 0.752 | 0.470 |
| Oakland Athletics    | McGwire, Mark (1996) | 1.197 | 0.730 | 0.467 |
| Chicago Cubs         | Sosa, Sammy (2001)   | 1.174 | 0.737 | 0.437 |
| Colorado Rockies     | Walker, Larry (1997) | 1.172 | 0.720 | 0.452 |
| Colorado Rockies     | Walker, Larry (1999) | 1.168 | 0.710 | 0.458 |
| Colorado Rockies     | Helton, Todd (2000)  | 1.161 | 0.698 | 0.463 |
+----------------------+----------------------+-------+-------+-------+
10 rows in set (3.25 sec)
```

Distribution and box plot. The left half of Figure 5-4 shows the distribution for OPS. Similar to many other batting statistics, OPS appears to be normally distributed, but it's very skewed toward low values. Of course, the outliers on the far right represent Barry Bonds's fabulous 2001–2004 seasons.

To help understand how OPS has changed over time and what good and bad values for box plots are, let's use R to show box plots for batting average by decade:

```
> b_and_t$decade <- as.factor(floor(b_and_t$yearID/10) * 10)
> boxplot(OPS~decade,data=b_and_t,subset=qualify,
+ pars=c(xlab="decade", ylab="OPS"), range=0)
```

The right half of Figure 5-4 shows the box plot for OPS, by decade.

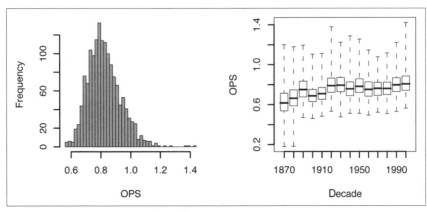

Figure 5-4. OPS histogram and box plot

As you can see, OPS rose during the first couple of decades of professional baseball and then was stable for decades. The low minima in the early years are interesting: a few players clearly had very low averages. Interestingly, the past decade most closely resembles the 1920s.

HACK Measure Power with ISO
#44 Use ISO to measure how well a player slugs the ball.

Isolated power (ISO) is a measurement of how well a player hits the ball, not just how often. A player wants to do several things during an at bat. First, he doesn't want to get out. Second, he wants to give base runners the opportunity to score. Third, he wants to put himself in a position to score on a future at bat, or better yet, to score on the current at bat.

Two popular statistics—AVG and OBP—measure how well a player gets on base without making an out. But they don't address how well a player helps base runners score, or how well he sets himself up to score a run from another player's hit. A batter can help other players score by hitting the ball harder, allowing him to advance to second, third, or home base on the play (clearing the bases). A batter makes it easier to score a run himself by advancing to second, third, or home base.

Any bases a player reaches beyond first base on a hit are *extra bases* (sometimes called XB). You can define XB as:

```
XB = TB - H
```

We want to measure how many extra bases a player gets: how many doubles, triples, and home runs. ISO is designed to measure the rate of extra bases hit by a batter.

Here is the formula for ISO:

```
ISO = XB / AB = (TB - H ) / AB = SLG - AVG
```

ISO is the part of slugging average that's independent of batting average. You can think of the relationship as:

```
SLG = AVG + ISO
```

For many players, ISO measures slugging ability better than slugging average. A player who hits a lot of singles will have a high SLG, even though he does not often hit the ball hard.

Branch Rickey and Allen Roth created isolated power while running the Dodgers in the 1950s. Incidentally, the folks at Baseball Prospectus prefer a slightly different formula. They believe that triples are really just doubles hit by fast runners (often in funky ballparks, or against teams with lousy fielders), so they count doubles and triples the same way in their ISO measurements.

Sample Code

To calculate ISO, we'll start off by loading the Baseball Archive database. We'll then use the same technique we use in "Measure Batting with Batting Average" [Hack #40] to calculate ISO:

```
# assumes that b_and_t data frame has been created
attach(b_and_t)
b_and_t$TB <- (H + X2B + 2 * X3B + 3 * HR)
b_and_t$qualify <- (b_and_t$AB + ifnull(b_and_t$BB,0) + ifnull(b_and_t$HBP,)
+ ifnull(b_and_t$SF,0)) > 3.1 * b_and_t$teamG
b_and_t$ISO <- (b_and_t$TB - H)/ AB
```

Summary statistics. Let's look at some summary statistics to help understand how isolated power has changed over time. Here are the summary statistics across the entire database (1871–2004):

```
> summary(subset(ISO,qualify),digits=3)
   Min. 1st Qu. Median   Mean 3rd Qu.   Max.
 0.0000  0.0836 0.1210 0.1320  0.1700 0.5360
```

Here are the summary statistics over the past decade (1995–2004):

```
> summary(subset(ISO,qualify & yearID > 1994),digits=3)
   Min. 1st Qu. Median   Mean 3rd Qu.   Max.
 0.0403  0.1330 0.1770 0.1820  0.2250 0.5360
```

Top 10. Let's look at the top 10 batting averages of all time. Here is the SQL code that I used to calculate these results. (Notice the three indexes that change the running time from hours to seconds.) I used the same MLB rule used to qualify for awards: an average of 3.1 at bats per game.

```
-- create b_and_t as shown in "Measure Batting with Batting Average" [Hack
#40]

select f.franchName AS "First_Team", nameFirst, nameLast, b.yearID,
    round((b.X2B + 2 * b.X3B + 3 * b.HR)/b.AB,3) as ISO, b.AB
from b_and_t b inner join master m inner join teamsFranchises f
where b.idxLahman=m.idxLahman
    and substr(b.teamIDs,1,3)=f.franchID
    and b.AB + ifnull(b.BB, 0) + ifnull(b.HBP, 0) + ifnull(b.SF, 0)
        > 3.1 * b.teamG
    -- and yearID > 1994
order by ISO DESC limit 10;
```

Here are the top 10 isolated power averages of all time:

First_Team	nameFirst	nameLast	yearID	ISO	AB
San Francisco Giants	Barry	Bonds	2001	0.536	476
New York Yankees	Babe	Ruth	1920	0.472	458
New York Yankees	Babe	Ruth	1921	0.469	540
St. Louis Cardinals	Mark	McGwire	1998	0.454	509
San Francisco Giants	Barry	Bonds	2004	0.450	373
San Francisco Giants	Barry	Bonds	2002	0.429	403
Oakland Athletics	Mark	McGwire	1996	0.418	423
St. Louis Cardinals	Mark	McGwire	1999	0.418	521
New York Yankees	Babe	Ruth	1927	0.417	540
Chicago Cubs	Sammy	Sosa	2001	0.409	577

Here are the top 10 seasons over the past decade (1995–2004):

First_Team	nameFirst	nameLast	yearID	ISO	AB
San Francisco Giants	Barry	Bonds	2001	0.536	476
St. Louis Cardinals	Mark	McGwire	1998	0.454	509
San Francisco Giants	Barry	Bonds	2004	0.450	373
San Francisco Giants	Barry	Bonds	2002	0.429	403
Oakland Athletics	Mark	McGwire	1996	0.418	423
St. Louis Cardinals	Mark	McGwire	1999	0.418	521
Chicago Cubs	Sammy	Sosa	2001	0.409	577
San Francisco Giants	Barry	Bonds	2003	0.408	390
San Francisco Giants	Barry	Bonds	2000	0.381	480
Cleveland Indians	Albert	Belle	1995	0.374	546

Distribution and box plot. We can show the distribution for ISO with the following R command:

```
> hist(subset(ISO,(qualify & yearID>1994)), breaks=40)
```

Looking only at isolated power (as shown in Figure 5-5) reveals an interesting pattern. It's basically a bell curve, but there is a long tail with a few exceptional players. Yes, the blip on the right is Barry Bonds.

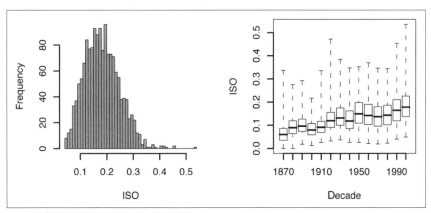

Figure 5-5. ISO histogram and box plot

To help understand how batting averages have changed over time and what good and bad values for box plots are, let's use R to show box plots for batting average by decade:

```
> b_and_t$decade <- as.factor(floor(b_and_t$yearID/10) * 10)
> boxplot(ISO~decade,data=b_and_t,subset=qualify,
+     pars=c(xlab="decade", ylab="isolated power"),
+     outline=FALSE)
```

ISO has not followed the same trend as batting average. On the contrary, it has increased over time (taking a breather in the 1960s and 1970s). ISO was very low in the 19th century, when baseballs were inelastic, bats were solid and heavy, and athletes played only part-time. In early baseball, a player would reach extra bases due to fielding errors, not hitting proficiency. In fact, players reached base often and advanced easily because baseball was played without gloves. At the turn of the 20th century, gloves were introduced, defensive ability increased, and ISO dropped slightly.

Then came Babe Ruth. Most players hit similarly to the past (see the box plot), but Babe Ruth and his imitators hit the ball hard, leading to a large increase in home runs. The war years led to a slight decline in the 1940s, followed by a steady increase in power over time. Isolated power is the essence of modern baseball.

While I was writing this book, the steroid scandal broke out. Several people asked me if I had anything to say about steroids. I wondered if I could say anything about modern baseball, steroids, and statistics. It seemed as though ISO was a good place to look for malfeasance. Sure enough, ISO has increased over the past few years.

However, it's not clear what steroid use does to batting statistics. There has been an increase in ISO over the past couple of decades, but it hasn't been dramatic. The opening of Coors Field in Denver, the decrease in the size of the strike zone (thanks to Questec), improvements in scouting and training techniques, and a change in the way the balls are made are some of the things that might have led to the increase we saw. It's clear that players are hitting the ball harder, but it's not clear that this is the result of steroid use.

If we ever get a definitive list of players who used steroids, which steroids they used, and during which period they were using steroids, we might be able to match this to performance data and look at the effects of steroid use. I doubt that will ever happen, and so I don't think we'll ever be able to say for sure how steroid use affects Major League Baseball players.

 ## HACK #45 Measure Batting with Runs Created

Measure how many runs a player would contribute to an average team with RC.

Runs created, or RC, is a measurement of the number of runs an offensive player contributed to a team during a season. Bill James developed this formula over time, publishing an initial version in his book *1979 Baseball Abstract*. (This book has been out of print for some time. See *http://baseballanalysts.com/archives/2004/07/abstracts_from_14.php* for a description of the contents.)

Run creation is a neat idea. Traditional statistics such as runs scored (R) and runs batted in (RBI) count the number of times a player did something. These are good measurements in one way because they measure what actually happened in a game. But they depend on context.

Suppose there is a league average player, whom we will call Joe Average. During one season, Joe is on a lousy team. When Joe hits the ball, players rarely are on base, so Joe gets few RBIs. After Joe reaches base, the other players rarely hit the ball, so Joe gets few runs.

Now suppose that in a different season, Joe is on a great team. When Joe hits the ball, players often are on base, so Joe gets many RBIs. After Joe reaches base, the other players often hit the ball, so Joe scores many runs.

Clearly, Joe's teammates help him out greatly. When his teammates hit better, Joe bats in more runs and scores more runs. We'd like to develop a statistic to measure how much Joe contributes to winning, independent of his teammates' performance. That's the idea of RC.

RC's appeal is its simplicity: the original formula is (H + BB) * (TB)/ (PA). We can use four easy measurements to calculate a player's total contribution. Other measurements are more accurate, but few are as easy.

Pete Palmer notes that he developed a closely related formula, called batter run average, during the 1970s, which was calculated as OBP * SLG. He refined this later to OPS because it was easier to calculate and better for measuring a player's contribution to a team. OBP * SLG works well for teams but not as well for individual players.

The Formula

We will look at a more complex version here that takes into account other ways of reaching base (being hit by a pitch or intentionally walked) or of getting out (grounding into double plays, failed steals, and sacrifices):

$$RC \equiv \frac{(H + BB + HBP - CS - GIDP) \cdot (TB + 0.26 \cdot (BB - IBB + HBP))}{AB + BB + HBP + SH + SF}$$

Bill James actually came up with 13 different versions of the RC formula for cases in which one of the components (SF, IBB, CS, etc.) was not available.

Sample Code

RC is easy to calculate, using only straightforward variables you can pull out of the Baseball DataBank data:

```
# assumes that batting table has been attached
attach(batting)
batting$TB <- H + X2B + 2 * X3B + 3 * HR
batting$RC <- (H + BB + HBP - CS - GIDP) *
    (batting$TB + .26 * (BB - IBB + HBP )) /
    (AB + BB + HBP + SH + SF)
```

One of the nice things about this formula is that it is not necessary to apply any qualifying rules to calculate it. Players with a small number of at bats have low RC scores.

Here is the SQL code that I used to calculate RC. For simplicity, I used a subquery. RC is calculated within the query, between the parentheses in the first from clause, and then this result is joined with the master table to get the players' names.

Note that you can't calculate these statistics with the Baseball Archive data before 1954.

Summary statistics. Here are the summary statistics over the past 50 years (1955–2004):

```
> summary(subset(batting$RC, batting$yearID > 1954))
    Min.   1st Qu.   Median     Mean   3rd Qu.     Max.      NA's
 -1.3330    0.5215   5.2940  21.2800   33.4000  226.5000 9333.0000
```

Here are the summary statistics over the past decade (1995–2004):

```
> summary(subset(batting$RC, batting$yearID > 1994))
    Min.   1st Qu.   Median     Mean   3rd Qu.     Max.      NA's
 -0.2500    0.3333   5.3260  23.1400   35.0600  226.5000 3099.0000
```

Top 10. Here is the code I used to calculate the top 10:

```
-- create b_and_t as shown in "Measure Batting with Batting Average" [Hack
#40]

select f.franchName AS first_team, m.nameFirst, m.nameLast,
    b.yearID, b.PA, round(b.RC, 1) as RC
FROM (select (H + BB + HBP - CS - GIDP) *
    (H + X2B + 2 * X3B + 3 * HR + .26 * (BB - IBB + HBP )) /
    (AB + BB + HBP + SH + SF) AS RC,
    (AB + BB + HBP + SH + SF) AS PA,
    yearID, teamIDs, idxLahman
    from b_and_t
    where yearID > 1953
) b inner join master m inner join teamsFranchises f
where m.idxLahman=b.idxLahman
    and substr(b.teamIDs,1,3)=f.franchID
    -- and yearID > 1994
order by RC DESC LIMIT 10;
```

Here are the top 10 players of all time, ranked by runs created:

```
+----------------------+-----------+----------+--------+------+-------+
| first_team           | nameFirst | nameLast | yearID | PA   | RC    |
+----------------------+-----------+----------+--------+------+-------+
| San Francisco Giants | Barry     | Bonds    | 2001   | 664  | 226.5 |
| San Francisco Giants | Barry     | Bonds    | 2002   | 612  | 204.8 |
| San Francisco Giants | Barry     | Bonds    | 2004   | 617  | 200.6 |
| St. Louis Cardinals  | Mark      | McGwire  | 1998   | 681  | 192.1 |
| Chicago Cubs         | Sammy     | Sosa     | 2001   | 711  | 190.5 |
| Colorado Rockies     | Todd      | Helton   | 2000   | 697  | 188.7 |
| Toronto Blue Jays    | Carlos    | Delgado  | 2000   | 711  | 184.7 |
| New York Yankees     | Mickey    | Mantle   | 1956   | 652  | 184.1 |
| Arizona Diamondbacks | Luis      | Gonzalez | 2001   | 728  | 180.5 |
| Colorado Rockies     | Larry     | Walker   | 1997   | 664  | 179.1 |
+----------------------+-----------+----------+--------+------+-------+
```

Here are the top 10 players over the past decade:

```
+----------------------+-----------+----------+--------+------+-------+
| first_team           | nameFirst | nameLast | yearID | PA   | RC    |
+----------------------+-----------+----------+--------+------+-------+
| San Francisco Giants | Barry     | Bonds    | 2001   | 664  | 226.5 |
| San Francisco Giants | Barry     | Bonds    | 2002   | 612  | 204.8 |
| San Francisco Giants | Barry     | Bonds    | 2004   | 617  | 200.6 |
| St. Louis Cardinals  | Mark      | McGwire  | 1998   | 681  | 192.1 |
| Chicago Cubs         | Sammy     | Sosa     | 2001   | 711  | 190.5 |
| Colorado Rockies     | Todd      | Helton   | 2000   | 697  | 188.7 |
| Toronto Blue Jays    | Carlos    | Delgado  | 2000   | 711  | 184.7 |
| Arizona Diamondbacks | Luis      | Gonzalez | 2001   | 728  | 180.5 |
| Colorado Rockies     | Larry     | Walker   | 1997   | 664  | 179.1 |
| St. Louis Cardinals  | Albert    | Pujols   | 2003   | 685  | 173.5 |
+----------------------+-----------+----------+--------+------+-------+
```

Looking at runs created over the past decade, we find that, like most offensive measurements, Barry Bonds tops the list with his 2001 and 2002 seasons.

You'll notice that these lists are loaded with modern sluggers: guys who hit lots of home runs and walk a lot. These kinds of players make a lot of money because they contribute a lot to their teams. In 2003, Albert Pujols and Todd Helton were good for an average of one run *per game*. In 2001, Barry Bonds generated almost one and a half runs in every game. When announcers talk about how he carries the Giants, they're not kidding.

Histogram and box plot. As shown in Figure 5-6, the majority of batters created a small number of runs. Only a few created a large number.

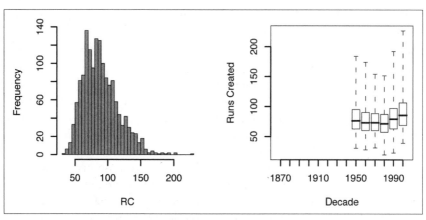

Figure 5-6. Runs created histogram and box plot

Here is some code to produce a box plot diagram of runs created over the past five decades:

```
> batting$decade <- as.factor(floor(batting$yearID/10) * 10)
> boxplot(RC~decade,data=batting,subset=(batting$yearID>1954),
+    pars=c(xlab="decade", ylab="runs created"),
+    outline=FALSE
```

As you can see, the average number of runs created has increased slightly over the past couple of decades. Additionally, a few great players have created a new maximum value.

HACK #46 Measure Batting with Linear Weights

Calculate one of the most accurate and intuitive measurements of offensive performance ever developed: linear weights.

The runs created formula in "Measure Batting with Runs Created" **[Hack #45]** measures the absolute performance of players. But what if we want to compare a player's contributions to an "average player?" The linear weights formula helps us do this.

The linear weights formula, also called batter runs (BR), is designed to reflect the offensive contributions of each batter accurately. The formula is weighted so that a league average player does not add or subtract value from his team; the BR for a league average player will be zero. The idea is to compare how much better or worse than average a player is.

The linear weights system assigns an average value to each baseball event. The BR formula sums the total value of a player's contributions, weighted by the value of each action. The idea is to measure the value of everything a batter does (hit a single, hit a home run, walk, steal a base, strike out, etc.), and rate hitters based on the number of times they performed each action.

Let's take a simple example. Suppose a batter is at the plate with no outs and no men on base. At this point, his team can expect to score .54 runs in that inning if an average player were batting (just take my word for it right now; I'll explain why later). Now, suppose this batter hits a home run. His team gains one run immediately and his team will be back where it started: another player will be at the plate, and his team could expect to score another .54 runs with an average player batting. Suppose instead that the player strikes out. Then, the bases will be empty with one out, and his team could expect to score .29 runs in the remainder of the inning, a difference of .54 − .29 = .25 runs. So the value of a strikeout in that situation is −.25 runs.

Pete Palmer and Jon Thorn developed the most famous version of these formulas and published it in their book, *The Hidden Game of Baseball* (Doubleday). Many people trace the idea to an article called "An Investigation of Strategies in Baseball," published in *Operations Research* magazine in 1963. But it turns out that this idea is much older than the article. Pete Palmer writes:

> Some years ago, Bob Kelterman sent me an article from a 1917 *Baseball* magazine by the legendary F.C. Lane, showing linear weights. He had the same problem that Lindsey had, namely no negative value for outs, but I think it was pretty remarkable. He compiled how many runs result from each event, and had pretty much the same values (of course) that came up later.

Over time, the weights for events have changed slightly, but they have remained remarkably consistent. We'll talk about that a little more, shortly.

Estimating the Weights from an Expected Runs Matrix

I'll show you how to calculate the average value of a home run, starting with an expected runs matrix. (If you want to know how to generate this matrix from play-by-play data, see "Calculate Expected Runs" **[Hack #60]**.) Table 5-1 shows the number of runs that can be expected in each situation and the number of times each situation occurs. Let's show how this works in the simplest case: home runs. First, we estimate the probability that the game is in a specific state (for example, no outs, no base runners or one out, runners on first and third). This appears in the Pr(state) column. Next, we estimate the number of runs that will be gained in the future. (For each number of outs, this is just the expected number of runs when the bases are empty with that number of outs: 0.54 for no outs, 0.29 for one out, 0.11 for two outs). Then, we calculate the total number of runs that will score (1 plus the number of base runners). I define the *baseline* number of runs as the expected number of runs that would score in that situation before the action. (So the Baseline column is the same as the ExpR column.) Then, I calculate the number of Net runs from the action as Future runs + Scoring runs – Baseline runs for each state. Finally, I multiply Net runs by the probability of being in that state. Table 5-1 shows my calculations from the 2004 season, showing the number of expected runs scored by each home run.

Table 5-1. Expected runs

Outs	1b	2b	3b	ExpR	N	Pr(state)	Future	Scoring	Baseline	Net runs	PR*NR
0	0	0	0	0.54	46180	0.2343	0.54	1	0.54	1	0.2343
1	0	0	0	0.29	32821	0.1665	0.29	1	0.29	1	0.1665
2	0	0	0	0.11	26009	0.1319	0.11	1	0.11	1	0.1319
0	0	0	1	1.46	512	0.0026	0.54	2	1.46	1.08	0.0028
1	0	0	1	0.98	2069	0.0105	0.29	2	0.98	1.31	0.0137
2	0	0	1	0.38	3129	0.0159	0.11	2	0.38	1.73	0.0275
0	0	1	0	1.17	3590	0.0182	0.54	2	1.17	1.37	0.0249
1	0	1	0	0.71	6168	0.0313	0.29	2	0.71	1.58	0.0494
2	0	1	0	0.34	7709	0.0391	0.11	2	0.34	1.77	0.0692
0	0	1	1	2.14	688	0.0035	0.54	3	2.14	1.4	0.0049
1	0	1	1	1.47	1770	0.0090	0.29	3	1.47	1.82	0.0163
2	0	1	1	0.63	1902	0.0096	0.11	3	0.63	2.48	0.0239
0	1	0	0	0.93	11644	0.0591	0.54	2	0.93	1.61	0.0951
1	1	0	0	0.55	13483	0.0684	0.29	2	0.55	1.74	0.1190
2	1	0	0	0.25	13588	0.0689	0.11	2	0.25	1.86	0.1282
0	1	0	1	1.86	1053	0.0053	0.54	3	1.86	1.68	0.0090
1	1	0	1	1.24	2283	0.0116	0.29	3	1.24	2.05	0.0237
2	1	0	1	0.54	3117	0.0158	0.11	3	0.54	2.57	0.0406
0	1	1	0	1.49	2786	0.0141	0.54	3	1.49	2.05	0.0290
1	1	1	0	0.97	4978	0.0253	0.29	3	0.97	2.32	0.0586
2	1	1	0	0.46	6545	0.0332	0.11	3	0.46	2.65	0.0880
0	1	1	1	2.27	805	0.0041	0.54	4	2.27	2.27	0.0093
1	1	1	1	1.6	1926	0.0098	0.29	4	1.6	2.69	0.0263
2	1	1	1	0.82	2380	0.0121	0.11	4	0.82	3.29	0.0397
										Total	1.4319

Notice that I got 1.43 runs. That's pretty similar to the 1.40 value that Palmer got in the early 1980s. You can continue this process yourself for all the other situations, but it gets a little complicated. (For example, sometimes the runner on second advanced to third on a single, sometimes the runner scored on a single, sometimes the runner was thrown out at home on a single, and sometimes the runner didn't even advance. You need to calculate the probability of each action to get the right answer.)

Palmer's Formula

Pete Palmer developed the weights in this formula. He analyzed play-by-play data from the World Series games between 1956 and 1960 using the method described earlier, and he calculated the estimated value of each action. (No large databases of play-by-play data were available at that time, so he used the only data he could get.) Since then, he has refined the formula slightly, and the version in this book reflects those refinements. Here is the linear weights formula:

$$BR \equiv \left(\begin{array}{l} 0.46 \cdot X1B + 0.85 \cdot X2B + 1.02 \cdot X3B + 1.40 \cdot HR + \\ 0.33 \cdot ((BB + HBP) + 0.22 - SB - 0.35 \cdot CS - 0.26 \cdot (AB - H)) \end{array}\right)$$

If you want a complete explanation of this formula and methodology, see Palmer and Thorn's *The Hidden Game of Baseball*, or *The 2006 ESPN Baseball Encyclopedia* (Sterling).

Sample Code

Let's start by just showing how to calculate BR in SQL:

```
-- create b_and_t as shown in "Measure Batting with Batting Average" [Hack
#40]

create table BRtbl AS
select f.franchName as Team_Name, m.nameLast, m.nameFirst, b.*,
    .46 * (b.H - b.X2B - b.X3B - b.HR) + .85 * b.X2B
    + 1.02 * b.X3B + 1.40 * b.HR
    + .33 * (b.BB + b.HBP) + .22 * b.SB
    - .35 * b.CS - .26 * (b.AB - b.H) as BR
from b_and_t b inner join master m inner join teamsFranchises f
where b.idxLahman=m.idxLahman
    and substring(b.teamIDs,1,3)=f.franchID;
```

In R, you can use this code:

```
attach(b_and_t)
b_and_t$X1B <- H - X2B - X3B - HR
attach(b_and_t)
b_and_t$BR <- 0.46 * X1B + 0.85 * X2B + 1.02 * X3B + 1.40 * HR +
              0.33 * (BB + HBP) + 0.22 * SB - 0.35 * CS - 0.26 * (AB - H)
```

Running the Hack

Summary statistics. Here are the summary statistics for all players across the entire database (1871–2004):

```
> summary(BR)
    Min.   1st Qu.   Median     Mean  3rd Qu.      Max.      NA's
 -47.010    -3.550   -0.320    1.073    0.460   136.400 22284.000
```

As expected, the median value is very close to zero. By design, an average player doesn't add or subtract much value from his team. Let's restrict the statistics to players with a qualifying number of plate appearances:

```
> summary(subset(BR, qualify))
    Min.   1st Qu.   Median     Mean  3rd Qu.      Max.      NA's
 -47.010     1.445   14.950   16.850   29.400   136.400  4885.000
```

As expected, good players get more playing time than mediocre players, so the median and mean values are higher among players who play often. Here are the summary statistics over the past decade (1995–2004):

```
> summary(subset(BR, qualify & yearID > 1994))
    Min.  1st Qu.  Median     Mean 3rd Qu.     Max.
 -31.650    9.682  22.610   25.730  38.960  135.200
```

Notice that the total over the past decade was slightly higher. The average player over the past five years scored a few more runs. (Pete Palmer notes that you can fix this problem by changing the weight for outs from −.26 to −.29.)

Top 10. Let's look at the top 10 players of all time, by BR. Here is the SQL code I used to calculate these results. (Notice that, unlike some other statistics, I don't use any qualification criteria. You can't get a high RC score unless you have a decent number of at bats, so these results are self-filtering.)

```
select concat(nameFirst, " ", nameLast) as Player, Team_Name, yearID, BR
from BRtbl
order by BR desc limit 10;
```

Here are the top 10 players of all time, by BR. Note the two representatives of "Murderer's Row" (also known as the greatest team of all time: the 1927 New York Yankees).

```
+---------------+-----------------------+--------+--------+
| Player        | Team_Name             | yearID | BR     |
+---------------+-----------------------+--------+--------+
| Babe Ruth     | New York Yankees      |   1921 | 136.42 |
| Barry Bonds   | San Francisco Giants  |   2004 | 135.23 |
| Barry Bonds   | San Francisco Giants  |   2001 | 133.97 |
| Babe Ruth     | New York Yankees      |   1923 | 129.06 |
| Barry Bonds   | San Francisco Giants  |   2002 | 128.54 |
| Babe Ruth     | New York Yankees      |   1920 | 123.27 |
| Lou Gehrig    | New York Yankees      |   1927 | 116.02 |
```

```
| Babe Ruth     | New York Yankees    |   1927 | 114.68 |
| Babe Ruth     | New York Yankees    |   1924 | 114.44 |
| Ted Williams  | Boston Red Sox      |   1941 | 112.51 |
+---------------+---------------------+--------+--------+
10 rows in set (1.37 sec)
```

Here are the top 10 seasons over the past decade (1995–2004):

```
+---------------+---------------------+--------+--------+
| Player        | Team_Name           | yearID | BR     |
+---------------+---------------------+--------+--------+
| Barry Bonds   | San Francisco Giants |  2004 | 135.23 |
| Barry Bonds   | San Francisco Giants |  2001 | 133.97 |
| Barry Bonds   | San Francisco Giants |  2002 | 128.54 |
| Mark McGwire  | St. Louis Cardinals |   1998 | 106.75 |
| Todd Helton   | Colorado Rockies    |   2000 | 103.69 |
| Larry Walker  | Colorado Rockies    |   1997 | 103.14 |
| Sammy Sosa    | Chicago Cubs        |   2001 | 101.84 |
| Carlos Delgado | Toronto Blue Jays  |   2000 |  99.70 |
| Barry Bonds   | San Francisco Giants |  2003 |  99.48 |
| Jason Giambi  | Oakland Athletics   |   2001 |  95.43 |
+---------------+---------------------+--------+--------+
10 rows in set (0.61 sec)
```

Barry Bonds, beyond any question, had remarkable seasons in 2001, 2002, 2003, and 2004. Regardless of whether you like him and whether you think he used illegal steroids, Barry Bonds's offensive numbers over the past few years show that he is a special player.

Amazingly, the five greatest seasons of the past 50 years occurred during the past 10 years. We don't see changes just at the extremes. The median number of runs per player has increased over time (compare the average of −.32 over the past 125 years to 14.95 over the past 10 years). It's not clear why this is happening. Are players hitting better? Are fewer players making it to the majors and then being sent back down to the minors, increasing the average? Are players stealing less often?

Histogram and box plot. A second useful view of batting average is to look at a histogram of the distribution:

```
> hist(subset(BR, qualify & yearID > 1994), breaks=40)
```

Looking only at batting runs for players qualifying for batting titles over the past decade, we see a picture similar to the one shown on the left side of Figure 5-7.

Like most metrics, this one gives us a funny-looking distribution. Almost all players have a BR of around zero. Some full-time players contribute less than zero. Players who really subtract value aren't allowed to play a lot, so the distribution is truncated at the low end. A few players performed incredibly well, leading to the long tail on the right.

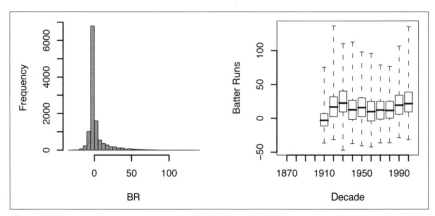

Figure 5-7. Batting runs histogram and box plot

That's because there are a lot of lousy offensive players with a small number of at bats. Many of these guys are pitchers, but a few of them are minor leaguers who are around for only a few games.

To help understand how batting averages have changed over time and what good and bad values for box plots are, let's use R to show box plots for batting average by decade. I have omitted results before 1900.

```
> b_and_t$decade <- as.factor(floor(b_and_t$yearID/10) * 10)
> boxplot(BR~decade,data=b_and_t,subset=qualify & yearID >= 1900,
+        pars=c(xlab="decade", ylab="Batting Runs"),
+        range=0)
```

Hacking the Hack

Estimate weights with linear regression. When Pete Palmer originally did this analysis, he came up with the coefficients through a lot of painstaking research and simulation. I'll show you how to come up with a formula in seven lines of R.

Here's the idea. The linear weights formula is essentially a linear model for runs: it predicts the runs scored by a team as a function of singles, doubles, triples, home runs, outs at the plate, walks, stolen bases, and times caught stealing. We can estimate the weights using an ordinary linear regression. I chose to estimate the coefficients based on MLB data between 1961 and 1977. You can choose any period you like.

There is one subtlety. Linear weights measures a player's offensive contribution to the contributions of an average player, not compared to no player. So, we need to fit a model that estimates the difference from the average number of runs, not the total number of runs.

```
 1  > # start by loading in the Baseball DataBank database
 2  > teams.query <- dbSendQuery(bbdb.con, "SELECT * from teams")
 3  > teams <- fetch(teams.query, n=-1)
 4  > teams$ERA <- as.double(teams$ERA)
 5  > teams$FP <- as.double(teams$FP)
 6  > teams.1961to1977 <- subset(teams, yearID > 1960 & yearID < 1978)
 7  > attach(teams.1961to1977)
 8  > X2B <- teams.1961to1977$"2B"
 9  > X3B <- teams.1961to1977$"3B"
10  > X1B <- H - X2B - X3B - HR
11  > Outs <- AB - H
12  > mean(R)
13  [1] 656.8963
14  > differenceFromMean <- R - 656.8963
15  > BR.lm <- lm(differenceFromMean~X1B+X2B+X3B+HR+BB+SB+CS+Outs+0)
16  > summary(BR.lm)
17
18  Call:
19  lm(formula = differenceFromMean ~ X1B + X2B + X3B + HR + BB +
20      SB + CS + Outs + 0)
21
22  Residuals:
23      Min       1Q   Median       3Q      Max
24  -68.7985 -15.5252  -0.8532  18.1816  65.5655
25
26  Coefficients:
27         Estimate Std. Error t value Pr(>|t|)
28  X1B    0.452681   0.019681  23.001  < 2e-16 ***
29  X2B    0.646003   0.058784  10.989  < 2e-16 ***
30  X3B    1.356543   0.137781   9.846  < 2e-16 ***
31  HR     1.473543   0.044423  33.171  < 2e-16 ***
32  BB     0.308156   0.019746  15.606  < 2e-16 ***
33  SB     0.243750   0.050715   4.806 2.24e-06 ***
34  CS    -0.377191   0.112970  -3.339 0.000927 ***
35  Outs  -0.241558   0.005043 -47.899  < 2e-16 ***
36  ---
37  Signif. codes:  0 '***' 0.001 '**' 0.01 '*' 0.05 '.' 0.1 ' ' 1
38
39  Residual standard error: 24.82 on 368 degrees of freedom
40  Multiple R-Squared: 0.9171,     Adjusted R-squared: 0.9153
41  F-statistic: 509.1 on 8 and 368 DF,  p-value: < 2.2e-16
```

Let me explain what's going on here. In line 15, I create a linear model for runs using R's lm( ) function. The argument to this function specifies the form of the equation: differenceFromMean~X1B+X2B+X3B+HR+BB+SB+CS+Outs+0, which means "create an equation for differenceFromMean in terms of singles, doubles, triples, home runs, walks, stolen bases, failed steal attempts, and outs." The coefficients in the equation appear in lines 26–35. This tells us that we estimate runs scored by a team using the following equation:

```
BR =
     X1B   *   0.452681  +
     X2B   *   0.646003  +
     X3B   *   1.356543  +
     HR    *   1.473543  +
     BB    *   0.308156  +
     SB    *   0.243750  +
     CS    *  -0.377191  +
     Outs  *  -0.241558
```

Neat, huh? (You don't really need all of those digits, and it might be better to round them off, but I wanted to show the default output from the lm( ) function and how it corresponds to a formula.) You can estimate a model for any period you like. You can also calculate different estimates for different leagues. (The designated hitter in the American League might have some interesting effects.) The estimates here aren't exactly the same as the original estimates, but they're very similar.

H A C K   Measure Pitching with ERA
#47   Calculate earned run average, the most popular statistic for comparing pitchers.

Earned run average (ERA) is a pitcher's counterpart to batting average. Like batting average, it's an old statistic (originating in the 19th century), it's familiar to most fans, and it has some serious faults.

Earned run average is the number of "earned runs" scored against a pitcher for every 27 outs pitched (there are 27 outs—3 outs per inning times 9 innings—in a game):

```
ERA = ER / IPOuts * 27
```

Earned runs are a funny concept, the counterpart to errors in batting and fielding. If a player makes it on base through a hit, walk, or fielder's choice and scores without any errors from the pitching team, that's considered an earned run. If the player reaches base on an error, or was not put out later because of an error, and later scores, that's considered an unearned run. Just like errors (in fact, because of errors), unearned runs are subjective.

There's another problem with earned run average: pitchers don't actually have much control over what happens once a ball is put in play. I explain more about this problem in "Measure Pitching with DIPS" [Hack #51].

The Code

Just like batters, pitchers can move between teams. This means we need to do some aggregation before looking at pitchers (we need to calculate full-season statistics for each pitcher). The following code does this. Besides this aggregation, ERA is simple.

```
-- assumes indexes from "Measure Batting with Batting Average" [Hack #40] are
there
create index pitching_idx on pitching(idxLahman);
create index pitching_tidx on pitching(idxTeams);
create table p_and_t as
select idxLahman, yearID,
    GROUP_CONCAT(franchID SEPARATOR ",") as teamIDs,
    sum(teamG) / count(franchID) as teamG,
    sum(W) as W, sum(L) as L, sum(G) as G, sum(GS) as GS,
    sum(CG) as CG, sum(SHO) as SHO, sum(SV) as SV,
    sum(IPouts) as IPouts, sum(H) as H, sum(ER) as ER,
    sum(HR) as HR, sum(BB) as BB, sum(SO) as SO,
    sum(BAOpp * BFP) / sum(BFP) as BAOpp,
    sum(ER) / sum(IPOuts) * 27 as ERA,
    sum(IBB) as IBB, sum(WP) as WP,
    sum(HBP) as HBP, sum(BK) as BK, sum(BFP) as BFP,
    sum(GF) as GF, sum(R) as R
from  (select p.*, t.G as teamG, t.yearID, f.franchID
        from pitching p inner join teams t
        inner join teamsFranchises f
        where p.idxTeams=t.idxTeams
        and t.idxTeamsFranchises=f.idxTeamsFranchises) i
group by idxLahman, yearID;

select f.franchName as Team,
    concat(m.nameFirst, " ", m.nameLast) as Player,
    p.yearID, p.ERA, p.ER, p.IPOuts, teamG
from p_and_t p inner join master m inner join teamsFranchises f
where substring(p.teamIDs,1,3)=f.franchID
    and p.idxLahman=m.idxLahman
    -- qualifying rule for ERA title:
    and p.IPOuts / 3 > teamG
order by ERA limit 10;
```

Running the Hack

Summary statistics. Let's start by calculating summary statistics for ERA. First, we'll suck the table defined earlier into R:

```
> drv <-dbDriver("MySQL")
> con <- dbConnect(drv, username="jadler", dbname="bbdatabank",
host="localhost")
> # assume that the table p_and_t has already been created in the db
> p_and_t.query <- dbSendQuery(con, statement = "select * from p_and_t")
> p_and_t <- fetch(p_and_t.query, n=-1)
```

Now, we'll define the requirements for qualifying for the ERA title:

```
> attach(p_and_t)
> p_and_t$qualify <- IPouts > 3 * teamG
```

Here are the summary statistics (among qualifying pitchers) in the whole
database (1871–2004):

```
> attach(p_and_t)
> summary(subset(ERA, qualify), digits=3)
   Min. 1st Qu. Median   Mean 3rd Qu.    Max.
   0.86    2.95   3.52   3.56    4.14   12.00
```

Here are the summary statistics for the past decade (1995–2004) only:

```
> summary(subset(ERA, qualify & yearID > 1994), digits=3)
   Min. 1st Qu. Median   Mean 3rd Qu.    Max.
   1.63    3.59   4.19   4.17    4.71    6.65
```

It's interesting that no pitcher pitched more than 162 innings and had an
ERA below 1.63 in the past decade, but it's even more interesting that this
did occur earlier than that. Note that a league average pitcher has an ERA of
about 4.2, and that half of all pitchers had an ERA of between 3.7 and 4.7.

Top 10. Here is the code for finding the top 10 players, by ERA:

```
select f.franchName as Team,
       concat(m.nameLast, ", ", m.nameFirst,
              " (", yearID, ")") as Player,
       round(p.ERA, 3) as ERA,
       concat(p.ER, "/", round(p.IPOuts/3,0)) as "ER/IP"
from p_and_t p inner join master m inner join teamsFranchises f
where substring(p.teamIDs,1,3)=f.franchID
      and p.idxLahman=m.idxLahman
      -- qualifying rule for ERA title:
      and p.IPOuts / 3 > teamG
order by ERA limit 10;
```

Now, let's look at the 10 best pitchers of all time, ranked by ERA:

```
+----------------------+--------------------------+-------+--------+
| Team                 | Player                   | ERA   | ER/IP  |
+----------------------+--------------------------+-------+--------+
| Troy Trojans         | Keefe, Tim (1880)        | 0.857 | 10/105 |
| Boston Red Sox       | Leonard, Dutch (1914)    | 0.961 | 24/225 |
| Milwaukee Brewers    | Cushman, Ed (1884)       | 1.000 | 4/36   |
| Chicago Cubs         | Brown, Mordecai (1906)   | 1.039 | 32/277 |
| St. Louis Cardinals  | Gibson, Bob (1968)       | 1.123 | 38/305 |
| San Francisco Giants | Mathewson, Christy (1909)| 1.144 | 35/275 |
| Minnesota Twins      | Johnson, Walter (1913)   | 1.145 | 44/346 |
| Chicago Cubs         | Pfiester, Jack (1907)    | 1.154 | 25/195 |
| Cleveland Indians    | Joss, Addie (1908)       | 1.163 | 42/325 |
| Chicago Cubs         | Lundgren, Carl (1907)    | 1.174 | 27/207 |
+----------------------+--------------------------+-------+--------+
10 rows in set (2.20 sec)
```

You'll notice that most of these seasons were quite a long time ago (other than Bob Gibson's remarkable performance in 1968). Over the past decade, these are the top pitchers:

```
+----------------------+--------------------------+-------+--------+
| Team                 | Player                   | ERA   | ER/IP  |
+----------------------+--------------------------+-------+--------+
| Atlanta Braves       | Maddux, Greg (1995)      | 1.631 | 38/210 |
| Boston Red Sox       | Martinez, Pedro (2000)   | 1.742 | 42/217 |
| Florida Marlins      | Brown, Kevin (1996)      | 1.893 | 49/233 |
| Washington Nationals | Martinez, Pedro (1997)   | 1.902 | 51/241 |
| Toronto Blue Jays    | Clemens, Roger (1997)    | 2.046 | 60/264 |
| Boston Red Sox       | Martinez, Pedro (1999)   | 2.067 | 49/213 |
| Atlanta Braves       | Maddux, Greg (1997)      | 2.205 | 57/233 |
| Boston Red Sox       | Martinez, Pedro (2003)   | 2.218 | 46/187 |
| Atlanta Braves       | Maddux, Greg (1998)      | 2.223 | 62/251 |
| Boston Red Sox       | Martinez, Pedro (2002)   | 2.258 | 50/199 |
+----------------------+--------------------------+-------+--------+
10 rows in set (0.82 sec)
```

You'll notice something funny about this list: where is Eric Gagne (the Cy Young Award winner in 2003 with a 1.2 ERA)? Where are all the other relievers? Well, a pitcher needs to pitch 162 innings to qualify for the ERA title, and few relievers get anywhere close. Reducing the qualifying threshold by two-thirds (more outs pitched than 162), we get the following list, dominated by elite closers:

```
+----------------------+-----------------------------+-------+-------+
| Team                 | Player                      | ERA   | ER/IP |
+----------------------+-----------------------------+-------+-------+
| Atlanta Braves       | Hammond, Chris (2002)       | 0.947 | 8/76  |
| Atlanta Braves       | Smoltz, John (2003)         | 1.119 | 8/64  |
| Cleveland Indians    | Mesa, Jose (1995)           | 1.125 | 8/64  |
| Los Angeles Dodgers  | Gagne, Eric (2003)          | 1.202 | 11/82 |
| Florida Marlins      | Benitez, Armando (2004)     | 1.292 | 10/70 |
| Washington Nationals | Urbina, Ugueth (1998)       | 1.298 | 10/69 |
| San Diego Padres     | Hoffman, Trevor (1998)      | 1.480 | 12/73 |
| Seattle Mariners     | Hasegawa, Shigetoshi (2003) | 1.480 | 12/73 |
| San Francisco Giants | Nen, Robb (2000)            | 1.500 | 11/66 |
| Baltimore Orioles    | Myers, Randy (1997)         | 1.508 | 10/60 |
+----------------------+-----------------------------+-------+-------+
10 rows in set (1.19 sec)
```

Distribution and box plot. To understand ERA better, let's look at how it has been distributed over the past decade:

```
hist(subset(ERA,yearID>1994 & qualify),breaks=40,
    main="", xlab="ERA")
```

Like many other statistics, ERA appears to be distributed normally (see Figure 5-8).

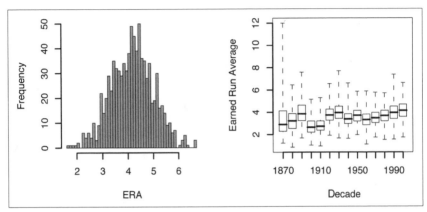

Figure 5-8. Earned run average distribution and box plot

To understand how ERA has changed over the history of baseball, let's use a box plot:

```
> p_and_t$decade <- as.factor(floor(p_and_t$yearID/10,0) * 10)
> boxplot(ERA~decade,data=p_and_t,subset=qualify,
+        pars=c(xlab="decade", ylab="Earned Run Average"),
+        range=0)
```

Earned run average seems to have bottomed out around the turn of the century, increasing sharply in the 1920s and not changing as much since then. A surge of great pitchers in the 1960s (and a change in mound height) led to a decline in ERA in the 1960s, but ERA has been increasing since then.

Since the 1970s, the average ERA has gone up for a number of reasons. The biggest reason is probably the explosion of new, smaller ballparks since the 1990s. Camden Yards in Baltimore kicked off the retro ballpark fad, and many cities (San Francisco, Philadelphia, Pittsburgh, Milwaukee, Cincinnati, and Houston) have followed suit. Unlike the dual-purpose ballparks of the 1970s (Veteran's Stadium in Philadelphia, Three Rivers Stadium in Pittsburgh, and the McAfee Coliseum in Oakland), with vast outfields and foul areas, these new ballparks are modeled after smaller, quirkier, more intimate ballparks. Many of these ballparks are designed for more home runs, which makes fans happier.

Another major cause is the addition of Coors Field, the ballpark in Denver. In the dry, thin air of Denver, balls travel much farther than they do at sea-level ballparks. Many more balls are hit out of the park, but many more balls land for hits in the vast outfield.

Even then, the differences are pretty small. Pitchers in the 1980s through the 2000s have been about the same, with maybe 5% to 10% higher ERAs.

HACK #48 Measure Pitching with WHIP

Measure how many base runners a pitcher allows by using WHIP.

Walks plus hits per inning pitched (WHIP) is a simple statistic for measuring pitcher effectiveness. In short, it measures the average number of base runners a pitcher allows per inning. WHIP is correlated with pitcher effectiveness, though its most important use is as a fantasy statistic (it's actually called *composite ratio* in the book *Rotisserie League Baseball* [Bantam Books]). Here is the formula for WHIP:

```
WHIP = (BB + H) / (IPOuts / 3)
```

Running the Hack

Summary statistics. We'll start with the p_and_t table from "Measure Pitching with ERA" [Hack #47], and we'll use this code to load the table into R (using Open Database Connectivity, or ODBC, this time):

```
attach(p_and_t)
WHIP <- (BB + H) / IPouts * 3
p_and_t$WHIP <- WHIP
```

Now, let's calculate summary statistics for consistency:

```
> qualify <- IPouts > 3 * teamG
> p_and_t$qualify <- qualify
> summary(subset(WHIP, yearID > 1910 & qualify))
   Min. 1st Qu. Median    Mean 3rd Qu.    Max.
 0.7373  1.2110 1.3090  1.3150  1.4150  1.9820
```

Top 10. We'll start with the p_and_t table from "Measure Pitching with ERA" [Hack #47], and we'll use this SQL code to calculate the top 10 players of all time, by WHIP:

```
select f.franchName as Team,
    concat(m.nameLast, ", ", m.nameFirst, " (", p.yearID, ")") as Player,
    round((p.H + p.BB)/p.IPOuts * 3,3) as WHIP,
    p.IPOuts
from p_and_t p inner join master m inner join teamsFranchises f
where substring(p.teamIDs,1,3)=f.franchID
    and p.idxLahman=m.idxLahman
    -- qualifying rule for ERA title:
    and p.IPOuts / 3 > teamG and p.yearID > 1900
order by WHIP limit 10;
```

Here is the list of the top 10 pitchers of all time, by WHIP:

```
+-----------------------+-------------------------+-------+--------+
| Team                  | Player                  | WHIP  | IPOuts |
+-----------------------+-------------------------+-------+--------+
| Boston Red Sox        | Martinez, Pedro (2000)  | 0.737 |    651 |
| Minnesota Twins       | Johnson, Walter (1913)  | 0.780 |   1038 |
| Cleveland Indians     | Joss, Addie (1908)      | 0.806 |    975 |
| Atlanta Braves        | Maddux, Greg (1995)     | 0.811 |    629 |
| Chicago White Sox     | Walsh, Ed (1910)        | 0.820 |   1109 |
| San Francisco Giants  | Mathewson, Christy (1909) | 0.828 |  826 |
| San Francisco Giants  | Mathewson, Christy (1908) | 0.837 | 1172 |
| Chicago Cubs          | Brown, Mordecai (1908)  | 0.842 |    937 |
| Baltimore Orioles     | McNally, Dave (1968)    | 0.842 |    819 |
| Philadelphia Phillies | Alexander, Pete (1915)  | 0.842 |   1129 |
+-----------------------+-------------------------+-------+--------+
10 rows in set (2.03 sec)
```

Here is a list of the top pitchers over the past decade, by WHIP:

```
+-----------------------+-------------------------+-------+--------+
| Team                  | Player                  | WHIP  | IPOuts |
+-----------------------+-------------------------+-------+--------+
| Boston Red Sox        | Martinez, Pedro (2000)  | 0.737 |    651 |
| Atlanta Braves        | Maddux, Greg (1995)     | 0.811 |    629 |
| Arizona Diamondbacks  | Johnson, Randy (2004)   | 0.900 |    737 |
| Minnesota Twins       | Santana, Johan (2004)   | 0.921 |    684 |
| Boston Red Sox        | Martinez, Pedro (1999)  | 0.923 |    640 |
| Boston Red Sox        | Martinez, Pedro (2002)  | 0.923 |    598 |
| Washington Nationals  | Martinez, Pedro (1997)  | 0.932 |    724 |
| Florida Marlins       | Brown, Kevin (1996)     | 0.944 |    699 |
| Atlanta Braves        | Maddux, Greg (1997)     | 0.946 |    698 |
| San Francisco Giants  | Schmidt, Jason (2003)   | 0.953 |    623 |
+-----------------------+-------------------------+-------+--------+
10 rows in set (0.80 sec)
```

Distribution and box plot. Now, let's take a look at the distribution of WHIP:

```
> hist(subset(WHIP, yearID > 1994 & qualify), breaks=40)
```

As shown in the left plot in Figure 5-9, WHIP appears to be normally distributed.

Here's the code to generate the box plot:

```
> boxplot(WHIP~decade,data=p_and_t,subset=qualify,
+         pars=c(xlab="decade", ylab="WHIP"),
+         range=0)
```

As you can see from the right plot in Figure 5-9, WHIP has fluctuated over time, increasing through the 1920s and 1930s, dropping in the 1950s and 1960s, and steadily increasing since then. A big reason why the range of WHIP was so much wider in the 1870s and 1880s is simply the number of games. Teams played far fewer games at that time than modern teams play, increasing the range of many statistics (including WHIP). Interestingly, the range has also been increasing recently, with the best and worst pitchers moving farther apart.

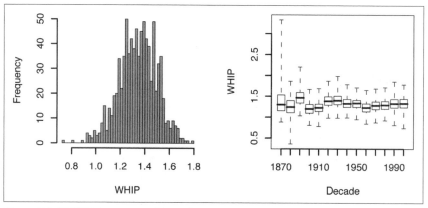

Figure 5-9. WHIP histogram and box plot

HACK #49 Measure Pitching with Linear Weights

Estimate the number of runs prevented by pitchers, compared to a league average player.

Pitching runs is a formula for measuring a pitcher's contribution compared to an average pitcher. It's another formula from Pete Palmer. It measures the number of runs that the pitcher prevented from scoring compared to the league average.

This formula is based on another popular formula: earned run average (ERA). This formula compares a player's ERA to the league average ERA, yielding the difference in earned runs per nine innings pitched. This figure is then multiplied by innings pitched to yield a player's contribution over a season. Finally, this total is adjusted to account for the number of runs, beyond average, credited to the defense.

(Incidentally, the original version of this formula measured only the difference between a player's ERA and the league average ERA. But Pete Palmer later revised the formula to take into account the number of outs due to the defense. I like the improved formula much better, and I show how to compute only this version in this book.)

This statistic separates the pitcher's performance from the defensive performance. To adjust a pitcher's performance to his team's defensive performance, the formula relies on the fielding runs formula (see "Measure

Fielding with Linear Weights" [Hack #55]). Here's the formula for pitching runs:

```
PR = IPOuts / 27 * (lgERA - ERA) - (IPOuts / tmIPOuts) * tmFR
```

In this equation, lgERA represents the league average ERA, tmIPOuts represents the total defensive outs played by the teams, and tmFR represents the total fielding runs for the teams' defenders.

Sample Code

To calculate pitching runs, start by calculating fielding runs using the code for fielding runs from "Measure Fielding with Linear Weights" [Hack #55]. Then run the following SQL code:

```
-- let's start by figuring out earned runs for the league by year
create temporary table pitching_lgER_totals AS
select sum(p.ER) as lgER, sum(p.IPOuts) as lgIPOuts, t.yearID, t.lgID
from pitching p inner join teams t
on p.idxTeams=t.idxTeams
group by yearID, lgID;

-- now, let's merge player stats with league totals
create index pitching_idx on pitching(idxPitching);
create index pitching_tmidx on pitching(idxTeams);

create temporary table pitching_w_lg_totals as
select p.*, t.lgER, t.lgIPOuts
from pitching p inner join pitching_lgER_totals t inner join teams t2
where t.yearID=t2.yearID and t.lgID=t2.lgID and p.idxTeams=t2.idxTeams;

-- now, count outs pitched by team
create temporary table tm_IPOuts  as
select idxTeams, sum(IPOuts) tmIPOuts
from pitching
group by idxTeams;

-- now, let's merge fielding runs with these team stats
create index fielding_w_fr_ytidx on fielding_w_fr(idxTeams);

create temporary table tmFR_t  as
select f.idxTeams, sum(FR) as tmFR, tmIPOuts
from fielding_w_fr f inner join tm_IPOuts p
ON f.idxTeams=p.idxTeams
group by idxTeams;

-- finally, let's calculate pitching runs
create index pitching_w_lg_totals_idx on pitching_w_lg_totals(idxTeams);
create index tmFR_t_idx on tmFR_t(idxTeams);
create table pitching_w_PR AS
```

```
select  (IPOuts / 27 * ((lgER / lgIPOuts * 27) - (ER / IPOuts * 27)) -
              tmFR * IPOuts/tmIPOuts) AS PR,
         tmIPOuts, p.*
from pitching_w_lg_totals p inner join tmFR_t t
on p.idxTeams=t.idxTeams
where IPOuts > 0
order by PR;
```

Here's the code I used to load this into R. I needed to change the default number of fetched records to get the whole table out of MySQL.

```
> library(RMySQL)
Loading required package: DBI
> drv <- dbDriver("MySQL", fetch.default.rec=1000000)
> con <- dbConnect(drv, username="jadler", dbname="bbdatabank",
host="localhost")
> pitching_w_pr.query <- dbSendQuery(con, statement="select * from pitching_
w_pr")
> pitching_w_pr <- fetch(pitching_w_pr.query, n=-1)
> attach(PRtbl)
```

Running the Hack

Summary statistics. To calculate these statistics, I started by creating the pitcher runs table in MySQL, and then I imported the results into R:

```
> summary(PR, yearID>1910)
     Min.     1st Qu.    Median      Mean    3rd Qu.       Max.      NA's
-223.90000   -5.90000  -1.01400   0.02412   4.33200  214.60000  227.00000
```

Top 10. Here's the code for showing the top 10 pitcher seasons, by pitching runs:

```
select concat(m.nameFirst, " ", m.nameLast) as Player,
       t.name, t.yearID as year,
       round(p.PR, 3) as PR, round(p.ERA, 3) as ERA, p.IPOuts as outs
from pitching_w_PR p inner join master m inner join teams t
where p.idxLahman=m.idxLahman and p.idxTeams=t.idxTeams
    and yearID>1910
order by PR DESC limit 10;
```

Here are the top 10 pitcher seasons between 1910 and 2004, ranked by pitching runs:

Player	name	year	PR	ERA	outs
Walter Johnson	Washington Senators	1912	80.196	1.390	1107
Pedro Martinez	Boston Red Sox	2000	77.576	1.740	651
Whit Wyatt	Brooklyn Dodgers	1943	77.121	2.490	542
Lefty Grove	Philadelphia Athletics	1931	75.302	2.060	866
Roger Clemens	Toronto Blue Jays	1997	74.894	2.050	792

```
| Dolf Luque      | Cincinnati Reds       | 1923 | 72.721 | 1.930 |  966 |
| Lefty Gomez     | New York Yankees      | 1937 | 71.367 | 2.330 |  835 |
| Lefty Gomez     | New York Yankees      | 1934 | 68.855 | 2.330 |  845 |
| Lefty Grove     | Philadelphia Athletics| 1930 | 68.142 | 2.540 |  873 |
| Dazzy Vance     | Brooklyn Robins       | 1930 | 67.640 | 2.610 |  776 |
+-----------------+-----------------------+------+--------+-------+------+
```

One of the greatest things about this statistic is that it works so far back in time, showing great performances from the turn of the century and great performances by modern pitchers.

Distribution and box plot. Here's the code to generate the histogram:

```
> hist(subset(PR, yearID>1910), breaks=50, xlab="PR")
```

Here is the code to generate the box plot:

```
> pitching_w_pr$decade <- as.factor(floor(yearID/10) * 10)
> boxplot(PR~decade, data=pitching_w_pr, subset=(yearID>1910),
+         pars=c(xlab="decade", ylab="Pitching Runs"), range=0)
```

Figure 5-10 shows the distribution of pitching runs.

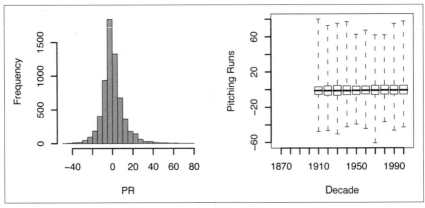

Figure 5-10. Pitching runs histogram and box plot

Not surprisingly, this statistic is centered at around zero (it measures how much better or worse than average a player performed). Additionally, almost all players performed very similarly, making a difference of only ± 5 runs over the course of a season. Extreme performances haven't changed much either. (In case you were wondering why Ron Guidry and Sandy Koufax didn't crack the top 10 list, take a look at the extreme values in the 1960s and 1970s. These guys were great pitchers, but the range was much narrower than other periods. For example, Pedro Martinez was much, much better than the average pitcher in 2000.)

Measure Defense with Defensive Efficiency
A quick-and-dirty way to measure a team's defensive skills.

Defensive efficiency (DER) is a very simple statistic for measuring how well a team's defense performs. It is simply the percentage of balls put in play that are turned into outs. Bill James developed this statistic in one of his abstracts during the 1980s. This statistic applies only to whole teams.

This formula might look a little out of place here; I describe most fielding statistics later in the chapter. However, DER is strongly related to the defense independent pitching statistics (DIPS) formula (see "Measure Pitching with DIPS" [Hack #51] for more information). This formula is essentially the same as batting average on balls in play (with a couple of subtle differences). Before we start talking about DIPS, we need to talk (just a little bit) about defense.

The Formula

Standard statistics don't tell us much about how a team performed defensively. We're stuck with only a few coarse measurements:

HA
  Hits allowed

SOA
  Strikeouts of opponents

HRA
  Home runs allowed

E
  Errors

IPouts
  Outs pitched

We want to show how well a team created outs from balls put in play. Unfortunately, errors create some problems for us. First, the difference between a hit and an error can be subjective. Additionally, errors can occur at times other than when balls are put in play (for example, passed balls by the catcher, missed fouls, or bad throws on putouts). So, the formula here is just an approximation if we use team statistics:

```
DER = (IPOuts - HRA - SOA) / (HA + E + I1POuts - HRA - SOA)
```

For some improvements on this formula, see "Calculate Fan Save Value" [Hack #57].

Sample Code

Here's some sample R code for this operation:

```
> # start by loading the Baseball Archive data
> load("lahman51-csv.RData")
> attach(teams)
> DER <- (IPOuts - HRA - SOA) / (HA + E + IPOuts - HRA - SOA)
> summary(subset(DE, yearID == 2003))
```

Here's some sample SQL code:

```
create temporary table teams_de as
select *,
    (IPOuts - HRA - SOA) /(HA + E + IPOuts - HRA - SOA) as DER
from teams;

select name, yearID, DER
from teams_de
where yearID>1994
order by DER limit 5;
```

Summary Statistics

The distribution for DER remains relatively constant over time (though a few notable teams did exceptionally well or poorly).

Distribution in last 10 years (1994–2003). Over the past 10 years, defensive efficiency also did not vary greatly. Half of all teams had a DER between .6527 and .6696.

```
> summary(subset(DER, yearID > 1994)
Min. 1st Qu.  Median    Mean 3rd Qu.    Max.
 0.6239  0.6527  0.6609  0.6609  0.6696  0.6982
```

Here are the summary statistics for the top five teams in the last decade:

```
+---------------------+--------+--------+
| name                | yearID | DER    |
+---------------------+--------+--------+
| Seattle Mariners    |  2001  | 0.6982 |
| Atlanta Braves      |  2002  | 0.6946 |
| Seattle Mariners    |  2003  | 0.6915 |
| San Francisco Giants|  2002  | 0.6901 |
| Anaheim Angels      |  2002  | 0.6901 |
+---------------------+--------+--------+
```

Here are the summary statistics for the bottom five teams:

```
+-------------------+--------+--------+
| name              | yearID | DER    |
+-------------------+--------+--------+
| Colorado Rockies  |  1999  | 0.6239 |
| Detroit Tigers    |  1996  | 0.6281 |
```

```
| Oakland Athletics |  1997 | 0.6319 |
| Boston Red Sox    |  1996 | 0.6346 |
| Texas Rangers     |  2000 | 0.6353 |
+-------------------+-------+--------+
```

Distribution and box plot. DER does not vary greatly between teams at any time, though it has varied across decades. Here is the R code that I used to create these plots:

```
teams.query <- dbSendQuery(bbdb.con, "SELECT * FROM teams")
teams <- fetch(teams.query, n=-1)
teams$ERA <- as.double(teams$ERA)
teams$FP <- as.double(teams$FP)
attach(teams)
DER <- (IPouts - HRA - SOA) / (HA + E + IPouts - HRA - SOA)
teams$DER <- DER

pdf("der.pdf", height=Height, width=Width,
    paper="special", horizontal=FALSE, onefile=FALSE,
    pointsize=Pointsize.Def)
par(mfrow=c(1,2), lwd=1, mar=c(5.1,4.1,2.1,2.1))
hist(subset(DER, yearID>1994), main="", xlab="DER", breaks=20)
teams$decade <- as.factor(floor(teams$yearID/10) * 10)
boxplot(DE~decade,data=teams,
        pars=c(xlab="decade", ylab="Defensive Efficiency"),
        range=0)
dev.off()
```

As you can see from the diagram in Figure 5-11, defensive efficiency for most teams varied within a very narrow range over the past decade. Most teams managed to put out approximately 66% of balls in play. It was very uncommon for a team to do 2% to 3% better or worse than average.

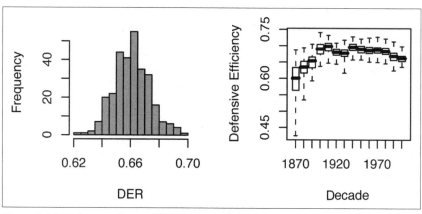

Figure 5-11. Defensive efficiency histogram and box plot

Over time, we observe a couple of interesting trends. First, defensive play improved a lot in the first few decades of professional ball, with defensive efficiency rising from about .6 to about .7. But after this point, defensive efficiency began a long decline, leaving us where we are today, with efficiency of about .66. What's going on here?

Modern baseball has more strikeouts and more home runs. This has decreased the importance of defensive play; teams put far more value in pitchers who can strike out batters or batters who can hit the ball out of the park than they do in players with sound defensive skills.

Measure Pitching with DIPS

Measure a pitcher's performance independent of the fielders' performance using DIPS.

In December 1999, baseball fan Voros McCracken came up with a new method of measuring pitching. McCracken started to wonder whether a pitcher could really do anything about balls in play; were outs from balls in play a function of a pitcher's skill, the defense's skill, or dumb luck? He set out to test this hypothesis and discovered (much to his surprise) that it wasn't pitcher skill. He concluded that what happens after a ball is put in play depends on the defense. Only on walks, strikeouts, and home runs is the defense not involved.

To help measure a pitcher's performance independent of the fielders' performance, McCracken came up with a system he called defensive independent pitching stats (DIPS). If you want to know more about the story behind this formula, Michael Lewis's book *Moneyball* has a nice write-up on Voros McCracken. If you want to learn how the formula works, read on.

The Formula

The formula for DIPS is, unfortunately, a little complicated. See the sample code that follows for an explanation of DIPS calculations. I'll just launch into the code to explain how to calculate this measurement. (I used Voros McCracken's own explanation for DIPS 2.0 numbers to make the following calculations.)

The process proceeds in two phases. First, a set of defense-independent measurements are calculated: DIPS intentional walks allowed (dIBB), DIPS hit batsmen (dHP), DIPS total walks (dBB), DIPS home runs (dHR), DIPS hits (dH), and DIPS innings pitched (dIP). A couple of other numbers are calculated that are used in later calculations. A few more variables are calculated based on a mix of actual values and DIPS values: strikeouts per ball in play (sSO), home runs per ball in play (sHR), and hits per ball in play (sH). These also are used in some later calculations. Finally, DIPS earned runs (dER) and DIPS ERA (dERA) are calculated.

 The normal abbreviation for defensive efficiency is DER. Don't confuse that with DIPS earned runs, which is abbreviated here as dER.

Sample Code

Here is some sample code for calculating DIPS in R:

```
# 4
dIBB <- BFP * .0074
# 5
sHP <- HBP / (BFP - IBB)
dHP <- sHP * (BFP - dIBB)
# 6
sBB <- (BB - IBB) / (BFP - IBB - HBP)
dBB <- sBB * (BFP - dIBB - dHP) + dIBB
# 7
sSO <- SO / (BFP - HBP - BB)
dSO <- sSO * (BFP - dBB - dHP)
# 8
sHR <- HR / (BFP - HBP - BB - SO)
dHR <- sHR * (BFP - dBB - dHP - dSO)
# 9
sH <- .304396 + .002321 * (throws == "L") - .04782 * sSO - .08095 * sHR
# 10
dH <- sH * (BFP - dHR - dBB - dSO - dHP) + dHR
# 11
dIP <- (1.048 * (BFP - dBB - dHP - dSO - dH) + dSO) / 3
# 12
dER <- (dH-dHR)*.49674 + dHR*1.294375 + (dBB-dIBB)*.3325 + dIBB*.0864336 +
dSO*(-.084691) + dHP*.3077 + (BFP-dHP-dBB-dSO-dH)*(-.082927)
# 13
dERA <- dER * 9  / dIP Summary Statistics
# calculate summary stats for 2003
> summary(subset(dERA, yearID == 2003 & BFP > 249))
```

To compute this in SQL, you can use the following code. This code creates a temporary table called dipsERAs from which you can query DIPS ERA results. Notice the nine subqueries in this statement; I calculated each formula in sequence, just as I did in the R code.

```
CREATE TEMPORARY TABLE dipsERAs AS
SELECT nameFirst, nameLast, idxTeams,
       lgID, ERA, dERA, IPOuts
  FROM ( -- p_w_d
   SELECT *, dER * 9  / dIP AS dERA
   FROM ( -- p9
```

```
SELECT *,
    (dH-dHR)*.49674 + dHR*1.294375
    + (dBB-dIBB)*.3325 + dIBB*.0864336
    + dSO*(-.084691) + dHP*.3077
    + (BFP-dHP-dBB-dSO-dH)*(-.082927) AS dER
FROM ( -- p8
  SELECT *,
        (1.048 * (BFP - dBB - dHP - dSO - dH)
        + dSO) / 3 AS dIP
    FROM ( -- p7
    SELECT *,
        sH * (BFP - dHR - dBB - dSO - dHP)
        + dHR AS dH
      FROM ( -- p6
      SELECT *,
        .304396
        + .002321 * (CASE WHEN throws='L' THEN 1 ELSE 0 END)
        - .04782 * sSO - .08095 * sHR AS sH
      FROM ( -- p5
      SELECT *,
            sHR * (BFP - dBB - dHP - dSO) AS dHR
        FROM ( -- p4
        SELECT *,
            sSO * (BFP - dBB - dHP) AS dSO,
          HR / (BFP - HBP - BB - SO) AS sHR
          FROM ( -- p3
          SELECT *,
          sBB * (BFP - dIBB - dHP)
          + dIBB AS dBB,
          SO / (BFP - HBP - BB) AS sSO
          FROM ( -- p2
          SELECT *,
          sHP * (BFP - dIBB) AS dHP,
          (BB - IBB) / (BFP - IBB - HBP) as sBB
          FROM ( -- p1
          SELECT p.*, m.nameFirst, m.nameLast, m.throws,
            BFP * .0074 AS diBB,
            HBP / (BFP - IBB) AS sHP
          FROM pitching p inner join master m
          ON p.idxLahman=m.idxLahman
                ) p1
                ) p2
                ) p3
                ) p4
              ) p5
              ) p6
            ) p7
          ) p8
        ) p9
        ) p_w_d
  ;
```

To better understand DIPS ERA, let's look at the distribution of DIPS ERA, as shown in Figure 5-12. Notice that the range and shape of the distribution is similar to ERA.

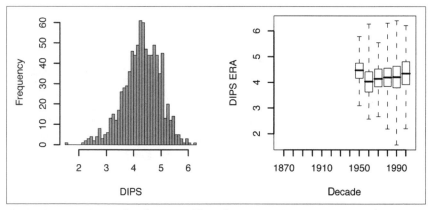

Figure 5-12. DIPS ERA distribution and box plot

Last year (2003). What can we learn from looking at DIPS numbers? Well, the top pitchers by ERA come out as the top pitchers by dERA. However, a closer look reveals that a couple of pitchers (LaTroy Hawkins and Guillermo Mota) might have been overperformers. In 2004, this proved to be true. Mota's ERA went up to 2.14 in the beginning of 2004, when he played with the Dodgers, and then climbed up to 4.81 when he was traded to the Marlins, leaving the Dodgers' super defense.

In 2004, LaTroy Hawkins played for the Cubs (as their closer), ending the year with a 2.63 ERA. This was higher than his 1.86 ERA with the Twins, probably because of the step down in defensive ability.

```
Min. 1st Qu. Median   Mean 3rd Qu.   Max.
1.048   3.821  4.339  4.360  4.946  6.652
```

Table 5-2 shows the players with the lowest DIPS ERAs in 2003.

Table 5-2. Five lowest DIPS ERAs in 2003

First name	Last name	Year	Team	League	ERA	DIPS ERA	Outs pitched
Eric	Gagne	2003	LAN	NL	1.202	1.006	247
John	Smoltz	2003	ATL	NL	1.119	1.691	193
Pedro	Martinez	2003	BOS	AL	2.218	2.236	560
LaTroy	Hawkins	2003	MIN	AL	1.862	2.609	232
Guillermo	Mota	2003	LAN	NL	1.971	2.609	315

Last 10 years (1994–2003).

```
Min.  1st Qu. Median  Mean  3rd Qu.  Max.
1.048  3.895  4.419  4.409  4.943  7.676
```

Table 5-3 shows the five best pitcher seasons (ranked by DIPS ERA) between 1994 and 2003.

Table 5-3. Five best DIPS ERAs, 1994–2003

First name	Last name	Year	Team	League	ERA	DIPS ERA	Outs pitched
Eric	Gagne	2003	LAN	NL	1.202	1.006	247
Pedro	Martinez	1999	BOS	AL	2.067	1.519	640
John	Smoltz	2003	ATL	NL	1.119	1.691	193
Mariano	Rivera	1996	NYA	AL	2.09	1.768	323
Eric	Gagne	2002	LAN	NL	1.968	1.829	247

Last 50 years (1955–2003). DIPS ERA gives us some interesting insight into Dennis Eckersley's 1990 season. Eckersley always ranks at the top of pitching lists for this performance, a 0.61 ERA for the season. DIPS tells us something interesting: Eckersley got very lucky. He still had a super season, but an expected ERA of 1.68 based on his strikeouts, home runs, and walks is much less remarkable.

```
Min.  1st Qu. Median  Mean  3rd Qu.   Max.     NA's
1.048  3.816  4.276  4.291  4.747   7.676  141.000
```

Table 5-4 shows the five best pitcher seasons over the past 50 years, by DIPS ERA.

Table 5-4. Five best DIPS ERAs, 1954–2003

First name	Last name	Year	Team	League	ERA	DIPS ERA	Outs pitched
Eric	Gagne	2003	LAN	NL	1.202	1.006	247
Pedro	Martinez	1999	BOS	AL	2.067	1.519	640
Dave	Smith	1987	HOU	NL	1.65	1.643	180
Dennis	Eckersley	1990	OAK	AL	0.614	1.68	220
John	Smoltz	2003	ATL	NL	1.119	1.691	193

Lucky and Unlucky Players

As I noted earlier, when a ball is put into play, it's the defense's responsibility to convert it into an out. If a pitcher is lucky, the defense will convert a lot of balls in play into outs, and a pitcher will have very few earned runs. If a pitcher is unlucky, the defense will miss a lot of balls, and a pitcher will have many earned runs. DIPS is designed to estimate a pitcher's ERA independent of defense. So, we can use DIPS to determine which pitchers were lucky and which were unlucky.

We'll just calculate the difference between actual ERA and dERA to measure how lucky or unlucky each pitcher has been. Interestingly, the five luckiest and five unluckiest players had similar DIPS ERAs. The lucky players had great ERAs (all under 3) and the unlucky players had poor ERAs (all over 7).

Here's the SQL code I used. It's almost identical to the earlier code, except I added a luck variable to measure the difference between DIPS ERA and ERA.

```
select nameFirst, nameLast, yearID, teamID, lgID, round(ER / IPOuts * 27,3)
ERA, dERA,
       round(dERA - ERA, 3) AS luck, IPOuts
FROM (select *, round(dER * 9  / dIP, 3) AS dERA
FROM (select *,
(dH-dHR)*.49674 + dHR*1.294375 + (dBB-dIBB)*.3325 + dIBB*.0864336 +
dSO*(-.084691) + dHP*.3077 + (BFP-dHP-dBB-dSO-dH)*(-.082927) AS dER
FROM (select *,
(1.048 * (BFP - dBB - dHP - dSO - dH) + dSO) / 3 AS dIP
FROM (select *,
sH * (BFP - dHR - dBB - dSO - dHP) + dHR AS dH
FROM (SELECT *,
.304396 + .002321 * (CASE WHEN throws='L' THEN 1 ELSE 0 END) - .04782 * sSO
- .08095 * sHR AS sH
FROM (SELECT *,
sHR * (BFP - dBB - dHP - dSO) AS dHR
FROM (SELECT *,
sSO * (BFP - dBB - dHP) AS dSO,
HR / (BFP - HBP - BB - SO) AS sHR
FROM (select *,
sBB * (BFP - dIBB - dHP) + dIBB AS dBB,
SO / (BFP - HBP - BB) AS sSO
FROM (select *,
sHP * (BFP - dIBB) AS dHP,
(BB - IBB) / (BFP - IBB - HBP) as sBB
FROM (select p.*, m.nameFirst, m.nameLast, m.throws,
BFP * .0074 AS dIBB,
HBP / (BFP - IBB) AS sHP
FROM pitching p inner join master m
ON p.playerID=m.playerID
where yearID>1954 AND IPOuts > 161
) p1) p2) p3) p4) p5) p6) p7) p8) p9) p_w_d
ORDER BY luck DESC
LIMIT 5
;
```

Table 5-5 shows the luckiest pitcher seasons; Table 5-6 shows the unluckiest pitcher seasons. Interestingly, Roy Halladay made the list in 2000. He's now Toronto's ace pitcher, and he won the Cy Young Award in 2003.

Table 5-5. Lucky pitchers

First name	Last name	Year	Team	League	ERA	DIPS ERA	Diff	Outs pitched
Terry	Fox	1961	DET	AL	1.413	4.334	2.924	172
Darold	Knowles	1972	OAK	AL	1.371	4.227	2.857	197
Dave	Tobik	1981	DET	AL	2.685	5.44	2.75	181
Jerry	Bell	1972	ML4	AL	1.656	4.386	2.726	212
Terry	Forster	1985	ATL	NL	2.275	4.971	2.691	178

Table 5-6. Unlucky pitchers

First name	Last name	Year	Team	League	ERA	DIPS ERA	Diff	Outs pitched
Roy	Halladay	2000	TOR	AL	10.64	5.972	-4.66	203
Andy	Ashby	1993	COL	NL	8.5	4.476	-4.02	162
Andy	Larkin	1998	FLO	NL	9.643	5.887	-3.75	224
Jesse	Jefferson	1976	CHA	AL	8.519	4.987	-3.53	187
Bobby	Ayala	1998	SEA	AL	7.288	3.844	-3.44	226

Measure Base Running Through EqBR

HACK #52 Measure base running proficiency through equivalent batter runs or extra base running percentage (XBRpct).

Twenty years ago, Bill James devised a set of formulas for measuring batting speed using readily available statistics. If you're curious, here are the formulas:

SpS1: speed score based on SB percentage
SpS1 = ((SB + 3) / (SB + CS + 7) - 0.4) * 20

SpS2: speed score based on SB attempts
SpS2 = SQRT ((SB + CS) / ((H - 2B - 3B - HR) + BB + HP)) / 0.07

SpS3: speed score based on triples
SpS3 = 3B / (AB - HR - K) / 0.02 * 10

SpS4: speed score based on runs per time on base
SpS4 = ((R- HR) / (H + BB - HR - HP) - 0.1) / 0.04

SpS5: speed score based on GDPs
SpS5 = (0.055 - GDP / (AB - HR - K)) / 0.005

Net speed score
Average of top four speed scores in the list

These measurements are useful, but they don't take individual situations into account. For example, let's consider SpS5. On average, a slow runner who follows a batter with a high on-base percentage will hit into fewer double plays than a similar runner who follows a batter with a high on-base percentage.

The *Baseball America 2005 Prospect Handbook* (Baseball America) has a great essay by James Click on a method for measuring base running. Aside from steals (successful and failed), good statistics aren't available for measuring how well players run around the bases. In this hack, I explain quickly how to measure this statistic from the play-by-play data.

Equivalent Batter Runs

Click's measurements are nice because they do a better job of separating a runner's performance from the batters preceding and following him. Click described three different situations where a good base runner can get an extra base:

A single is hit with a base runner on first and no runners on second or third
An average runner will reach second base, and a good base runner will reach third or home.

A double is hit with a base runner on first and no runners on second or third
An average base runner will reach third base, and a good base runner will score.

A single is hit with a base runner on second and no runner on third
An average base runner will reach third base, and a good base runner will score.

We can search for these situations in the play-by-play data and count the number of times each player reached the expected base and the extra base. The next step is to compare each player's total to the league average.

The Code

First, we will use play-by-play data, as described in "Load Baseball Data into MySQL" [Hack #20]. Now, we want to calculate each base runner's statistics in each situation. I'll use a SQL trick to calculate these in one type of statement: a CASE statement. The idea is to perform a logical test on each line— for example, to check whether the play was a single with one runner on second. Then we set a column to 1 or 0, depending on whether the player reached the expected base or extra bases, and sum the totals by player.

Here's the code I used to count these situations, and to count the number of times each player got the expected number of bases and extra bases:

```
create table pbp.baserunning2k as
select year,
   if(case1 OR case2, first_runner, second_runner) as pid,
   sum(case1) as case1,
   sum(if(runner_on_1st_dest>2 AND case1,1,0)) as case1_extra,
   sum(case2) as case2,
   sum(if(runner_on_1st_dest>3 AND case2,1,0)) as case2_extra,
   sum(case3) as case3,
   sum(if(runner_on_2nd_dest>3 AND case3,1,0)) as case3_extra,
   group_concat(distinct teamID separator ',') as teamIDs
from (select first_runner, second_runner, runner_on_1st_dest, runner_on_2nd_
dest,
   if(hit_value=1 AND first_runner != "" AND second_runner = "" AND third_
runner = "",1,0) CASE1,
   if(hit_value=2 AND first_runner != "" AND second_runner = "" AND third_
runner = "",1,0) CASE2,
   if(hit_value=2 AND second_runner != "" AND third_runner = "",1,0) CASE3,
   if(batting_team=1, substr(game_id,1,3), visiting_team) teamID,
   substr(game_id,4,4) as year
   from  pbp2k) p
where case1=1 or case2=1 or case3=1
group by if(case1 OR case2, first_runner, second_runner), year;
create index baserunning2k_idx on baserunning2k(year, pid);
create index rosters_idx on rosters(year, retroID);
```

I wanted a percentage measurement, and not just an absolute number of extra runs, for each base runner. So I devised a measurement called extra base running percent (XBRpct) that measured the percentage of equivalent batter runs scored out of all opportunities. Here is the R code that I used to calculate XBRpct. (You'll have to load the RODBC library and configure an ODBC connection called pbp to use this code.)

```
# modify dbname, username, and password fields to match your database
pbp.com <- dbConnect(drv, username="jadler",
    dbname="retrosheet",host="localhost",
    password="p@ssw0rd")
baserunning.query <- dbSendQuery(pbp.con, statement = paste (
    "SELECT l.*, r.lastName, r.firstName, r.team ",
    "from pbp.baserunning2k l inner join pbp.rosters r ",
    "on l.year=r.year and l.pid=r.retroID"
    )
)
baserunning <- fetch(baserunning.query, n=-1)

# corrections, if using MySQL 5.0
baserunning$year <- as.integer(baserunning$year)
baserunning$case1 <- as.integer(baserunning$case1)
```

```
baserunning$case2 <- as.integer(baserunning$case2)
baserunning$case3 <- as.integer(baserunning$case3)
baserunning$case1_extra <- as.integer(baserunning$case1_extra)
baserunning$case2_extra <- as.integer(baserunning$case2_extra)
baserunning$case3_extra <- as.integer(baserunning$case3_extra)

# the calculations (finally)
attach(baserunning)
EBR <- case1+case2+case3
XBR <- case1_extra+case2_extra+case3_extra
XBRpct <- XBR / EBR
baserunning$EBR <- EBR
baserunning$XBR <- XBR
baserunning$XBRpct <- XBRpct
```

Summary statistics. Now, let's take a look at summary statistics for XBRpct. Here is the distribution for all base runner seasons between 2000 and 2004:

```
> summary(XBRpct)
   Min. 1st Qu. Median    Mean 3rd Qu.    Max.
 0.0000  0.1818 0.4091  0.4050  0.5385  1.0000
```

Let's take a quick look at EBR (the number of opportunities for each player in each season):

```
> summary(EBR)
   Min. 1st Qu. Median    Mean 3rd Qu.    Max.
   1.00    2.00   5.00   10.06   17.00   50.00
```

As you can see, most base runners were rarely in these situations. To get some amount of statistical significance, let's limit ourselves to base runners with at least 20 opportunities:

```
> summary(subset(XBRpct, EBR > 19))
   Min. 1st Qu. Median    Mean 3rd Qu.    Max.
 0.1000  0.3333 0.4286  0.4240  0.5000  0.8077
```

Top 10. Here's the SQL code that I used to find the top 10 base runner seasons:

```
SELECT lastName, firstName, team, year,
       XBR/EBR as XBRpct
FROM
(SELECT l.year, r.lastName, r.firstName, r.team,
       case1+case2+case3 AS EBR,
       case1_extra+case2_extra+case3_extra as XBR
 FROM pbp.baserunning2k l inner join pbp.rosters r
 ON l.year=r.year and l.pid=r.retroID) i
 -- only include seasons with at least 20 chances
 WHERE EBR > 19
 ORDER BY XBRPct DESC LIMIT 10;
```

Here are the top 10 base running seasons (2000–2004):

```
+----------+-----------+------+------+--------+
| lastName | firstName | team | year | XBRpct |
+----------+-----------+------+------+--------+
| Soriano  | Alfonso   | NYA  | 2002 | 0.8065 |
| Guzman   | Cristian  | MIN  | 2001 | 0.8000 |
| Wilson   | Jack      | PIT  | 2004 | 0.7931 |
| Erstad   | Darin     | ANA  | 2000 | 0.7778 |
| Tejada   | Miguel    | OAK  | 2003 | 0.7778 |
| Wells    | Vernon    | TOR  | 2004 | 0.7500 |
| Walker   | Larry     | COL  | 2003 | 0.7391 |
| Goodwin  | Tom       | COL  | 2000 | 0.7308 |
| Goodwin  | Tom       | LAN  | 2000 | 0.7308 |
| Holliday | Matt      | COL  | 2004 | 0.7308 |
+----------+-----------+------+------+--------+
```

Histogram. Here is the code for calculating the distribution of base running ratings in 2004. Figure 5-13 shows the histogram. Note that the distribution is roughly normal, with the average rating near 43%.

```
hist(subset(XBRpct, EBR>19), main="", xlab="XBRpct", breaks=20)
```

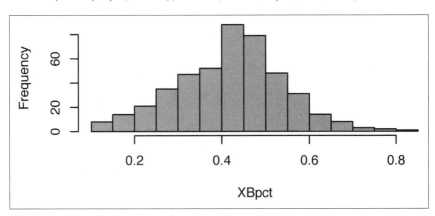

Figure 5-13. Distribution of extra base running percentage

Hacking the Hack

It would be great to fit these measurements into the linear weights system, and doing so is straightforward. From the expected runs matrix, we know how many runs are expected with runners on first and third (instead of first and second) after a single, to score from first after a double (as opposed to leaving a runner on third), and to score from second on a single (instead of holding at third). We can easily extrapolate the value of these moves in terms of runs.

Additionally, you can adjust these figures to account for differences between ballparks. I skipped this step to keep this hack simple. For information on calculating ballpark effects, see "Measure Park Effects" [Hack #56].

Measure Fielding with Fielding Percentage
#53
Measure how well a defensive player performed with fielding percentage.

Fielding percentage is a very simple measurement. It measures the number of successfully fielded balls (putouts and assists) divided by the number of opportunities (putouts, assists, and errors).

Sabermetric types don't like this measurement, for several reasons. First, it is somewhat subjective. Fielding percentage only counts errors as missed opportunities, and the official scorer decides errors. Second, errors are rare compared to putouts and assists. Fielding percentages are very high for most major league players, more than 98% on average. Third, fielding percentage misses a lot of subtlety. It doesn't include badly fielded plays such as ground balls missed by infielders, and great plays such as fly balls caught just over the fence to prevent home runs.

Finally, fielding percentage penalizes players who try to make good plays and fail. If a player can't even make it to a ball, he can't get an error. This is important: slow infielders or outfielders might end up nowhere near the ball, so they don't mess up fielding the ball or catching it as often as do players with better range. (Hence the reason for this statistic: *range* factor.) This is the principal objection to Derek Jeter as a fielder: just because he doesn't get a lot of errors doesn't mean he's a good shortstop. He has poor range.

Fielding percentage has one thing going for it: it's easy to calculate. Let's look at fielding percentage, the simplest defensive statistic.

The Formula
Fielding percentage is just the percentage of successfully fielded balls divided by the number of fielding opportunities:

```
FCPT = (PO + A) / (PO + A + E)
```

Sample Code
Here is some simple code for calculating fielding percentage:

```
attach(fielding_w_fr)
fpct <- (PO + A) / (PO + A + E)
fops <- PO + A + E
fielding_w_fr$fpct <- fpct
fielding_w_fr$fops <- fops
```

Ranking at the top for fielding percentage means not making any errors. Fielding percentage reminds me of the current Scholastic Aptitude Test (SAT) scoring scheme. The SAT scoring changed in the last 10 years so that more students would receive perfect scores. This makes a lot of pretty bright high school students feel good about themselves, but it doesn't do very much to distinguish between performances at the top.

Is that a bad thing? Well, a single error in 500 opportunities is a great performance. It's probably just as easy for a baseball player to miss a ball once as it is for a high school student to miss one question in an analogy. These sorts of mistakes are just noise; the measurement isn't sensitive enough to distinguish properly between different ability levels.

Fielding percentage reminds me of the SAT in another way, as well. At top schools, the scores aren't precise enough to measure great performances. For example, about 8% of MIT students score perfectly on the SAT.* Similarly, almost all Major League Baseball players have fielding percentages that are nearly perfect.

In most of this book, I've tried to keep my opinion of "classic" baseball statistics quiet, but I can't resist taking a swipe at fielding percentage. Here are the summary statistics for fielding percentage for the past decade (1995–2004):

```
> summary(subset(fpct,fops>99 & yearID>1994))
  Min. 1st Qu. Median  Mean 3rd Qu.   Max.
 0.873   0.974  0.985 0.981   0.992  1.000
```

Here are the summary statistics for fielding percentage for the whole database (1874–2003):

```
> summary(subset(fpct,fops>99))
  Min. 1st Qu. Median  Mean 3rd Qu.   Max.
 0.646   0.953  0.974 0.963   0.987  1.000
```

Do you notice anything funny about these statistics? Well, almost every single player who plays regularly fields almost every ball perfectly. Over the past decade, the median was .985, meaning that half of all players made less than one error in 67 opportunities. I'm skipping the box plot and histogram for this formula because they just don't tell us very much. Fielding percentage might be more valuable when looking at minor league (or little league) players, but at the major league level, it just doesn't tell us anything.

---

* *http://admissions.mit.edu/AdmissionsWeb/appmanager/AdmissionsWeb/Main?_nfpb=true&_pageLabel=pageMITToday.*

Measure Fielding with Range Factor

#54 Use range factor to measure how much a defensive player works.

Range factor (RF) represents the number of balls fielded by a player per inning. It's a pretty simple metric that you can calculate from readily available statistics (putouts, assists, and innings), and it does a pretty good job of ranking players by defensive ability. Bill James created the statistic and included it in his book *1977 Baseball Abstract*.

As described in the previous hack, FP does a poor job of differentiating between players. RF is a much better statistic. RF simply measures the average number of putouts plus assists (successful defensive players) per inning. The idea is that all players will have about the same number of fielding opportunities, so we should measure players by the number of successfully fielded balls. It excludes errors because they just don't tell you very much. Here's the formula:

```
RF = (PO + A) / (InnOuts / 3)
```

Sample Code

Let's calculate range factor in SQL first. We'll start by building a table with a summary of fielding statistics by player (in all positions played by that player):

```
-- assumes indexes from "Measure Batting with Batting Average" [Hack #40] are
there
create index fielding_idx on fielding(idxLahman);
create index fielding_tids on fielding(idxTeams);
create table f_and_t as
select idxLahman, GROUP_CONCAT(franchID SEPARATOR ",") as teamIDs,
    pos, sum(i.G) as G, sum(i.GS) as GS, sum(i.InnOuts) as InnOuts,
    sum(i.PO) as PO, sum(i.A) as A, sum(i.E) as E,
    sum(i.DP) as DP, sum(i.PB) as PB, teamG, yearID
from (select f.*, t.G as teamG, tf.franchID, t.yearID
        from fielding f inner join teams t inner join teamsFranchises tf
        where f.idxTeams=t.idxTeams
        and t.idxTeamsFranchises=tf.idxTeamsFranchises) i
group by idxLahman, yearID, pos;
```

We want to use the number of outs played to calculate range factor, but this information is not available for all players during all seasons. When this is not available, we'll approximate range factor by using the number of games played:

```
create table rf_t as
select *, (PO + A) / (InnOuts / 27) as exactRF,
    (PO + A) / G as approxRF,
    (PO + A) /
```

```
                (CASE WHEN InnOuts is not null
                    THEN InnOuts / 27
                    ELSE G END) as RF
        from f_and_t;
```

As a standard for range factor, we'll consider only players who played in at least seven innings for every game played by their team in a year.

Summary statistics. Here is the code for calculating summary statistics in R. Range factor depends greatly on position, so we'll calculate it separately for each position in our database:

```
f_and_t.query <- dbSendQuery(bbdb.con, "SELECT * FROM f_and_t")
f_and_t <- fetch(f_and_t.query, n=-1)
f_and_t$G <- as.integer(f_and_t$G)
f_and_t$GS <- as.integer(f_and_t$GS)
f_and_t$InnOuts <- as.integer(f_and_t$InnOuts)
f_and_t$PO <- as.integer(f_and_t$PO)
f_and_t$A <- as.integer(f_and_t$A)
f_and_t$E <- as.integer(f_and_t$E)
f_and_t$DP <- as.integer(f_and_t$DP)
f_and_t$PB <- as.integer(f_and_t$PB)
f_and_t$yearID <- as.integer(f_and_t$yearID)
f_and_t$qualify <- f_and_t$InnOuts > 6 * f_and_t$teamG
attach(f_and_t)
RF <- (PO + A) / ifelse(is.na(InnOuts), G, InnOuts / 27)
f_and_t$RF <- RF
```

To show a summary of range factor by position, we can use R's tapply( ) function. This function lets us calculate summary statistics separately for each fielding position. (See the R help files for more information.)

```
> tapply(RF,INDEX=pos,FUN=summary)
$"1B"
   Min. 1st Qu.  Median    Mean 3rd Qu.    Max.    NA's
  0.000   5.667   8.333   7.482   9.727  27.000   3.000

$"2B"
   Min. 1st Qu.  Median    Mean 3rd Qu.    Max.    NA's
  0.000   3.000   4.385   3.971   5.196  18.000   1.000

$"3B"
   Min. 1st Qu.  Median    Mean 3rd Qu.    Max.    NA's
  0.000   1.500   2.403   2.231   3.000   9.000   2.000

$C
   Min. 1st Qu.  Median    Mean 3rd Qu.    Max.
  0.000   3.732   4.867   4.727   5.909  27.000

$CF
   Min. 1st Qu.  Median    Mean 3rd Qu.    Max.
  0.000   1.667   2.308   2.281   2.750  18.000
```

```
$DH
    Min. 1st Qu.  Median    Mean 3rd Qu.    Max.    NA's
                                                    6154

$LF
    Min. 1st Qu.  Median    Mean 3rd Qu.    Max.    NA's
   0.000   1.000   1.684   1.651   2.114  18.000   1.000

$OF
    Min. 1st Qu.  Median    Mean 3rd Qu.    Max.
   0.000   1.209   1.762   1.657   2.150   8.000

$P
    Min. 1st Qu.  Median    Mean 3rd Qu.    Max.    NA's
   0.000   1.432   1.990   2.108   2.613  54.000  76.000

$RF
    Min. 1st Qu.  Median    Mean 3rd Qu.    Max.    NA's
   0.000   1.031   1.791   1.729   2.213  18.000   1.000

$SS
    Min. 1st Qu.  Median    Mean 3rd Qu.    Max.
   0.000   2.500   4.000   3.623   4.833  18.000
```

Let's look at the values taken by range factor. The players who rank at the top in terms of range factor are not the best fielders in baseball. Infielders get more fielding opportunities than outfielders do. First basemen (especially) get a lot of fielding opportunities. These guys get credit for a lot of putouts, which probably means that the other infielders are doing a great job throwing them the ball.

Also, notice the high putout rates for catchers. One reason for this is that catchers are credited with putouts on strikeouts. This isn't to demean catching; catching is a very tough position, probably the hardest defensive position in baseball. But you can't compare RF for catchers to RF for outfielders.

Clearly, the only way you can meaningfully compare players with range factor is on a position-by-position basis. Even then, you need to be careful. This statistic can be interesting and informative, but it's not just a competency measurement.

Top 10. Here are the top 10 players by range factor for shortstop, third base, second base, and outfield positions. I chose to include only players who played in more than half of their team's games. (This isn't a perfect restriction. I'd rather include only players who played in at least half of the innings played, or in more than half of the opponents' plate appearances. But we don't have the information to do that.) I also include only players during the past 50 years.

```
mysql> -- top ten shortstops by range factor
mysql> select substr(teamIDs,1,3) as teamID, pos,
    -> m.nameLast, m.nameFirst, f.yearID, f.RF, f.G
    -> from rf_t f inner join master m
    -> on f.idxLahman = m.idxLahman
    -> where pos="SS" and yearID > 1954
    -> and G * 2 > teamG
    -> order by RF DESC LIMIT 10;
```

teamID	pos	nameLast	nameFirst	yearID	RF	G
STL	SS	Templeton	Garry	1980	5.8609	115
STL	SS	Smith	Ozzie	1982	5.8561	139
SDP	SS	Smith	Ozzie	1981	5.8364	110
SDP	SS	Smith	Ozzie	1980	5.7532	158
MIL	SS	Yount	Robin	1981	5.7097	93
STL	SS	Templeton	Garry	1981	5.6842	76
TBD	SS	Martinez	Felix	2000	5.6778	106
CHW	SS	Aparicio	Luis	1960	5.5948	153
MIL	SS	Yount	Robin	1978	5.5920	125
LAD	SS	Zimmer	Don	1958	5.5877	114

```
10 rows in set (0.40 sec)

mysql> -- top ten second basemen by range factor
mysql> select substr(teamIDs,1,3) as teamID, pos,
    -> m.nameLast, m.nameFirst, f.yearID, f.RF, f.G
    -> from rf_t f inner join master m
    -> on f.idxLahman = m.idxLahman
    -> where pos="2B" and yearID > 1954
    -> and G * 2 > teamG
    -> order by RF DESC LIMIT 10;
```

teamID	pos	nameLast	nameFirst	yearID	RF	G
ATL	2B	Hubbard	Glenn	1985	6.2714	140
PIT	2B	Cash	Dave	1972	6.2062	97
PIT	2B	Mazeroski	Bill	1963	6.1304	138
BAL	2B	Grich	Bobby	1975	6.0467	150
PIT	2B	Mazeroski	Bill	1961	6.0197	152
STL	2B	Blasingame	Don	1956	5.9490	98
PIT	2B	Stennett	Rennie	1974	5.9481	154
PIT	2B	Stennett	Rennie	1976	5.9363	157
PHI	2B	Trillo	Manny	1980	5.9071	140
SDP	2B	Fuentes	Tito	1975	5.8944	142

```
10 rows in set (0.44 sec)

mysql> -- top ten third basemen by range factor
mysql> select substr(teamIDs,1,3) as teamID, pos,
    -> m.nameLast, m.nameFirst, f.yearID, f.RF, f.G
    -> from rf_t f inner join master m
```

```
    -> on f.idxLahman = m.idxLahman
    -> where pos="3B" and yearID > 1954
    -> and G * 2 > teamG
    -> order by RF DESC LIMIT 10;
+----------+-----+----------+-----------+--------+--------+------+
| teamID   | pos | nameLast | nameFirst | yearID | RF     | G    |
+----------+-----+----------+-----------+--------+--------+------+
| NYY      | 3B  | Boyer    | Clete     | 1962   | 3.7134 | 157  |
| NYY      | 3B  | Boyer    | Clete     | 1966   | 3.6824 | 85   |
| TEX      | 3B  | Bell     | Buddy     | 1982   | 3.6345 | 145  |
| OAK      | 3B  | Lopez    | Hector    | 1955   | 3.6237 | 93   |
| TEX      | 3B  | Bell     | Buddy     | 1981   | 3.6146 | 96   |
| CLE      | 3B  | Nettles  | Graig     | 1971   | 3.6139 | 158  |
| CHC      | 3B  | Santo    | Ron       | 1967   | 3.6025 | 161  |
| NYY      | 3B  | Boyer    | Clete     | 1961   | 3.5745 | 141  |
| CHC      | 3B  | Santo    | Ron       | 1966   | 3.5592 | 152  |
| STL      | 3B  | Boyer    | Ken       | 1958   | 3.5139 | 144  |
+----------+-----+----------+-----------+--------+--------+------+
10 rows in set (0.41 sec)

mysql> -- top ten outfielders by range factor
mysql> select substr(teamIDs,1,3) as teamID, pos,
    -> m.nameLast, m.nameFirst, f.yearID, f.RF, f.G
    -> from rf_t f inner join master m
    -> on f.idxLahman = m.idxLahman
    -> where pos IN ("LF", "CF", "RF", "OF") and yearID > 1954
    -> and G * 2 > teamG
    -> order by RF DESC LIMIT 10;
+----------+-----+----------+-----------+--------+--------+------+
| teamID   | pos | nameLast | nameFirst | yearID | RF     | G    |
+----------+-----+----------+-----------+--------+--------+------+
| MIN      | OF  | Puckett  | Kirby     | 1984   | 3.5469 | 128  |
| CHW      | OF  | Lemon    | Chet      | 1977   | 3.5168 | 149  |
| SEA      | CF  | Cameron  | Mike      | 2003   | 3.4206 | 147  |
| ANA      | CF  | Erstad   | Darin     | 2002   | 3.3942 | 143  |
| PHI      | OF  | Ashburn  | Richie    | 1956   | 3.3377 | 154  |
| PHI      | OF  | Ashburn  | Richie    | 1957   | 3.3333 | 156  |
| PHI      | OF  | Ashburn  | Richie    | 1958   | 3.3092 | 152  |
| MIN      | CF  | Hunter   | Torii     | 2001   | 3.2934 | 147  |
| OAK      | OF  | Murphy   | Dwayne    | 1980   | 3.2911 | 158  |
| WSN      | OF  | Dawson   | Andre     | 1981   | 3.2718 | 103  |
+----------+-----+----------+-----------+--------+--------+------+
10 rows in set (0.44 sec)
```

Histogram. There's a twist on the way I'm presenting statistics in this section. In most sections, I've shown just one histogram for the past 10 years. However, range factors vary greatly by position. So, instead, I'm showing histograms of range factors for all positions, using lattice charts as a trick. For more on using these plots, see "Compare Teams and Players with Lattices" [Hack #35].

Using the same qualifying rule (an average of six innings per game), plus including range factors for players over the last 25 years, let's plot the distribution of range factor by defensive position:

```
> library(lattice)
> trellis.device(color=FALSE)
> histogram(~RF|pos,xlab="Range Factor", data=subset(f_and_t,
    f_and_t$yearID > 1980),nint=30)
```

In Figure 5-14, notice the much greater range factors for infielders than for outfielders.

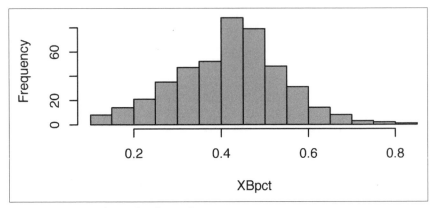

Figure 5-14. Range factor distribution by position

Also notice that first basemen and catchers tend to have a wider distribution of range factors.

Box plot. For lack of space, I'm omitting box plots (I'd want to show them separately for all positions). See "Measure Fielding with Linear Weights" **[Hack #55]** for a discussion of how fielding has changed over time.

Hacking the Hack

STATS, Inc. publishes a statistic called zone rating (ZR) that is related to RF. STATS divides the playing field into a set of "zones," each of which is the primary responsibility of a defensive player. STATS scorekeepers carefully record where each ball lands and use this information to measure the quality of defensive players.

Zone rating is defined as:

$$ZR = \frac{\text{Number of balls in outs} + \text{Balls turned into double plays}}{\text{Balls in zone} + \text{Balls outside zone that were turned into outs}}$$

ZR seems as though it should be a better measurement than RF. RF doesn't take into account how many balls are hit near a fielder. Many things distort RF, including ballpark shapes (for example, the Green Monster in left field at Fenway Park), pitcher types (for example, sinkerball pitchers who get mostly ground ball outs), and luck. ZR counts actual fielding opportunities, so it should be more accurate.

Unfortunately, the Baseball Archive and Baseball DataBank databases don't include the raw data to calculate ZR. (They do include ZR from some recent years.) You can calculate an approximate zone rating, maybe a ZRjr, from the Retrosheet event files.

I decided to try to calculate a quick-and-dirty version of ZR, which I'm calling Zone Rating Jr. (ZRjr), from Retrosheet event files. I started with the database described in "Make a Historical Play-by-Play Database" [Hack #22]. First, I decided to determine roughly where each ball landed and track whether the ball was turned into an out. The event files sometimes include extra information on where balls were hit. The BEVENT program will write this information to the hit_location field. (You can find a chart to interpret the hit_location field at *http://www.retrosheet.org/location.htm.*) In cases where the hit_location field was not blank and a ball did not go between two defensive players or go out of the park, I assigned responsibility to the player whose position matched the location. In cases where the hit_location field was blank, I assigned responsibility to the player who fielded the ball.

I created a temporary table with this information and called it zrjr_inner:

```
create table zrjr_inner
as select outs_on_play,
    if (mid(hit_location,2,1) IN (1,2,3,4,5,6,7,8,9), 0, 1)
        as opportunities,
    hit_location,  event_text, fielded_by,
    mid(game_id,4,4) as yearID,
    if(length(hit_location) > 0 and mid(hit_location,2,1)
        NOT IN (1,2,3,4,5,6,7,8,9),
        left(hit_location,1), fielded_by) as pos,
    case when batting_team=0
        then left(game_id,3)
        else visiting_team end as teamID,
    case
        if(outs_on_play=0 and batted_ball_type='G'
            and fielded_by IN (7, 8, 9) and sf_flag='F'
            and length(hit_location) > 0,
        left(hit_location,1), fielded_by)
        when '1' then pitcher
        when '2' then catcher
        when '3' then first_base
        when '4' then second_base
        when '5' then third_base
```

```
      when '6' then shortstop
      when '7' then left_field
      when '8' then center_field
      when '9' then right_field
    end as player
 from pbp.pbp2k
 where fielded_by > 0 -- fielded_by=0 for HR, SO
 ;
```

Next, I created an index on this table for fast summaries, and then I calculated ZRjr values for each player during each season. I decided to use the following formula:

```
ZRjr = Outs made on plays fielded by fielder / Balls fielded by
fielder
```

Here is the code that I used to calculate these values:

```
create index zrjr_inner_idx on zrjr_inner(yearID,teamID,player);

create table zrjr as
select yearID, teamID, player, pos,
       sum(outs_on_play) as outs,
       sum(opportunities) as opportunities,
       if(sum(opportunities) > 0,
         sum(outs_on_play) / sum(opportunities),
         null) as ZRjr
from zrjr_inner
where player is not null
group by yearID, teamID, player, pos
;
```

To show the top fielders with this ranking (for example, the top shortstops), you can use a query like this:

```
mysql> select r.lastName, r.firstName, yearID, teamID, ZRjr
    -> FROM ZRJR l inner join rosters r
    -> on l.player=r.retroID and l.teamID=r.team and l.yearID=r.year
    -> where opportunities > 100 AND pos=6
    -> ORDER BY zrjr desc limit 10;
+-----------+-----------+--------+--------+--------+
| lastName  | firstName | yearID | teamID | ZRjr   |
+-----------+-----------+--------+--------+--------+
| Sanchez   | Rey       | 2001   | KCA    | 1.1150 |
| Bordick   | Mike      | 2002   | BAL    | 1.1008 |
| Rodriguez | Alex      | 2000   | SEA    | 1.0985 |
| Tejada    | Miguel    | 2000   | OAK    | 1.0981 |
| Vizquel   | Omar      | 2000   | CLE    | 1.0948 |
| Clayton   | Royce     | 2002   | CHA    | 1.0935 |
| Lopez     | Felipe    | 2002   | TOR    | 1.0917 |
| Cruz      | Deivi     | 2000   | DET    | 1.0911 |
| Valentin  | Jose      | 2002   | CHA    | 1.0909 |
| Sanchez   | Rey       | 2000   | KCA    | 1.0907 |
+-----------+-----------+--------+--------+--------+
10 rows in set (0.03 sec)
```

This is a very coarse calculation, but it might be a little better than range factor is in some cases.

 Measure Fielding with Linear Weights
#55 Use fielding runs to measure a player's defensive performance with the linear weights system.

Fielding runs (FR) is a formula for measuring a defense's contribution compared to an average defense. FR is the fielding part of the linear weights system for measuring player contributions. It measures the number of runs that a defense prevented from scoring compared to the league average fielder.

The Formula

Computing FR is a little bit more complicated than computing some other formulas in this chapter. First, I will explain how the system works. Then, I'll explain how to compute fielding runs in four steps.

Comparisons to league average for position
For each measurement (A, PO, DP, E, PB), we compare the total fielded by each player to the league average. We call the league averages the *expected numbers.*

Adjustment for time played
We adjust the expected amounts by the time each player fielded each position. Ideally, we would use the number of batters or balls in play. But we don't know this information. We do know innings played in each position, so we will use that measurement instead.

Weight by impact and position
We weight the impact of each defensive statistic differently. Assists count more than putouts, double plays, and errors (assists count twice as much for infielders) because they are harder. All of those count more than passed balls (a catcher-only statistic that's half the pitcher's fault). Outfield assists count twice as much as infield assists (because they are harder). Finally, double plays and putouts for first basemen don't count (because they're so easy).

Adjustments for strikeouts
We adjust the catcher numbers to take away strikeouts (for which catchers receive credit).

That's the idea behind fielder runs: it makes all of these adjustments to give a fair measurement of the runs saved by each player.

To see how this works, let's look at the formula for different players:

Shortstop, second baseman, and third baseman
The basic form of the linear weights formula compares a player's assists, putouts, double plays, and errors to league averages:

```
FR = .2 * (2 (A - expA) + (PO - expPO) + (DP - expDP) - (E - expE))
```

Catcher
The formula for catchers is similar. However, there is a correction to the number of putouts: catchers are credited with a putout for every strikeout, which is really due to the pitcher.

```
FR = .2 * (2 (A - expA) + ((PO - SO) - (expPO - expSO)) + (DP - expDP) -
.5 * (PB - expPB) - (E - expE))
```

First baseman
First base is considered such an easy position that first basemen don't get credit for putouts.

```
FR = .2 * (2 (A - expA) - (E - expE))
```

Outfielders
Assists are harder for outfielders than for infielders. Otherwise, this formula is similar.

```
FR = .2 * (4 (A - expA) + (PO - expPO) + (DP - expDP) - (E - expE))
```

Pitcher
Pitchers don't make as many defensive plays as infielders, so the weight is different.

```
FR = .1 * (2 (A - expA) + (PO - expPO) + (DP - expDP) - (E - expE))
```

Designated hitter
Designated hitters don't contribute anything to fielding.

```
FR = 0
```

Calculating Fielding Runs

Now, let's look at the procedure to calculate FR.

Step 1: Calculate league totals. The first step in calculating FR is to calculate the total number of assists (A), putouts (PO), double plays (DP), errors (E), passed balls (PB), strikeouts (SO), and balls in play (BIP). Later, we will use these numbers to estimate the league average at each position.

Step 2: Calculate team totals. We need to split up fielding plays between different players on teams, according to the time that each player played each position, so we will use outs played. We also need the number of strikeouts per team (to adjust catcher numbers), so we will total outs played (InnOuts) and strikeouts (SO) for each team.

Step 3: Calculate expected values for each player. We calculate the expected number of assists, putouts, double plays, passed balls, strikeouts, and errors that we expect each player to make (or see). To do this, we first calculate the number seen by the average player in each league (in each year). We then adjust this number by the number of innings played by each player (in each year).

Step 4: Calculate fielding runs for each player. Finally, we calculate FR using the preceding formulas.

Sample Code

This formula is a little trickier than pitching runs and batting runs because the fielding runs formula varies slightly by position. To calculate the statistics shown here with MySQL, I used the following code. Incidentally, I initially tried doing all the joins in one statement, but the code ran too slowly, so I split it into smaller statements.

```
-- calculate league totals for pitching
create temporary table pitching_lg_totals as
select sum(p.BFP - p.BB - p.SO - p.HR - p.HBP) as lgBIP,
    sum(p.SO) as lgSO, t.yearID, t.lgID
from pitching p inner join teams t
on p.idxTeams=t.idxTeams
group by yearID, lgID;

-- calculate team totals for pitching
create temporary table pitching_tm_totals
as select sum(p.BFP - p.BB - p.SO - p.HR - p.HBP) as tmBIP,
    sum(p.SO) as tmSO, t.yearID, t.idxTeamsFranchises,
    t.idxTeams, t.lgID
from pitching p inner join teams t
on p.idxTeams=t.idxTeams
group by yearID, idxTeamsFranchises, idxTeams;

create index plt_idx on pitching_lg_totals(yearID);
create index ptt_idx on pitching_tm_totals(yearID);

-- join the pitching totals together
create temporary table pitching_totals
as select plt.*, ptt.tmBIP, ptt.tmSO, ptt.idxTeams
from pitching_lg_totals plt inner join pitching_tm_totals ptt
where plt.yearID=ptt.yearID and plt.lgID=ptt.lgID;

-- calculate league totals for fielding
create temporary table fielding_lg_totals as
select sum(f.A) as lgA, sum(f.PO) as lgPO, sum(f.DP) as lgDP,
    sum(f.E) as lgE, sum(f.PB) as lgPB,
    t.yearID, Pos, t.lgID
```

```
from fielding f inner join teams t
on f.idxTeams=t.idxTeams
group by yearID, pos, lgID;

-- calculate team totals for fielding
create temporary table fielding_tm_totals as
select sum(f.InnOuts) tmInnOuts, t.yearID, f.idxTeams, f.pos, t.lgID
from fielding f inner join teams t
on f.idxTeams=t.idxTeams
group by yearID, idxTeams, pos;

create index ftt_idx on fielding_lg_totals(yearID,pos);
create index flt_idx on fielding_tm_totals(yearID,pos);

-- join the fielding totals together
create temporary table fielding_totals as
select flt.*, ftt.tmInnOuts, ftt.idxTeams
from fielding_tm_totals ftt inner join fielding_lg_totals flt
ON flt.yearID=ftt.yearID AND flt.pos=ftt.pos AND flt.lgID=ftt.lgID;

create index ft_idx on fielding_totals(idxTeams);
create index pt_idx on pitching_totals(idxTeams);

-- put together the fielding and pitching totals
create temporary table fielding_aggregates AS
select f.idxTeams, f.yearID, f.Pos,
       p.lgBIP, p.lgSO, p.tmBIP, p.tmSO,
       f.lgA, f.lgPO, f.lgDP, f.lgE, f.lgPB,
       f.tmInnOuts
from fielding_totals f inner join pitching_totals p
on f.idxTeams=p.idxTeams;

create index fa_idx on fielding_aggregates(idxTeams, pos);
-- calculate expected fielding totals
create temporary table fielding_w_expected AS
select f.*,
    a.lgBIP, a.lgSO, a.tmBIP, a.tmSO,
    a.lgA, a.lgPO, a.lgDP, a.lgE, a.lgPB,
    a.tmInnOuts,
    lgA * tmBIP / lgBIP * InnOuts / tmInnOuts as expA,
    lgE * tmBIP / lgBIP * InnOuts / tmInnOuts as expE,
    (lgPO - if(f.pos='C',1,0) * lgSO) *
        tmBIP / lgBIP * InnOuts / tmInnOuts as expPO,
    lgPB * tmBIP / lgBIP * InnOuts / tmInnOuts as expPB,
    lgDP * tmBIP / lgBIP * InnOuts / tmInnOuts as expDP
from fielding f inner join fielding_aggregates a
    inner join teams t
where f.idxTeams=a.idxTeams
  AND f.idxTeams=t.idxTeams AND f.pos=a.pos;

-- finally, calculate fielding runs for each player
create table fielding_w_fr AS
select f.*,
```

```
((0.2 - 0.1 * if(Pos="P",1,0)) *
 ((2 + 2 * if(Pos IN ("CF","LF","RF"),1,0)) *
 (A - expA) +
 ((PO - if(Pos="C",1,0) * tmSO *
   (InnOuts / tmInnOuts)) - expPO) *
 if(Pos="1B",0,1) +
 (1 + if(Pos IN ("CF","LF","RF"),1,0)) *
 (DP - expDP) * if(Pos="1B",0,1) - (E - expE) -
 0.5 * ifnull(PB,0) - ifnull(expPB,0))) as FR
FROM fielding_w_expected f;
```

Here's the code to load this into R:

```
> library(RMySQL)
Loading required package: DBI
> drv <-dbDriver("MySQL")
> con <- dbConnect(drv, username="jadler", dbname="bbdatabank",
host="localhost")
> fr.query <- dbSendQuery(con, statement="select * from fielding_w_fr")
> fielding_w_fr <- fetch(fr.query, n=-1)
```

Before about 1910, the figures for batters faced by pitcher (BFP) were not accurately reported in the Baseball Archive data, so these formulas don't work quite right.

Summary Statistics

Descriptive statistics. Let's take a quick look at the distribution of values for FR:

```
> attach(fielding_w_fr)
> summary(subset(FR,yearID > 1910))
     Min.    1st Qu.     Median      Mean    3rd Qu.      Max.
NA's
 -58.06000   -0.55580   -0.05835   -0.01287   0.44710   38.26000
63855.00000
```

Most players are clustered around zero FR (meaning they performed at about the average level for a major league player).

Top 10. Here is the SQL statement I used to select the 10 best fielding seasons by FR:

```
select t.name,
    concat(m.nameFirst, ' ', m.nameLast, ' (',t.yearID, ')') as name,
    f.pos, f.FR
from fielding_w_fr f inner join master m inner join teams t
where f.idxLahman=m.idxLahman and f.idxTeams=t.idxTeams
and yearID>1910
order by FR DESC
limit 10;
```

Here's the top 10 list:

```
+---------------------+-----------------------+-----+--------------+
| name                | name                  | pos | FR           |
+---------------------+-----------------------+-----+--------------+
| Toronto Blue Jays   | Orlando Hudson (2003) | 2B  | 41.328716186 |
| Toronto Blue Jays   | Orlando Hudson (2004) | 2B  | 35.293815642 |
| Toronto Blue Jays   | Alex Gonzalez (2001)  | SS  | 34.661324816 |
| Colorado Rockies    | Neifi Perez (2000)    | SS  | 34.480802536 |
| Los Angeles Dodgers | Alex Cora (2003)      | 2B  | 33.682829918 |
| Oakland Athletics   | Eric Chavez (2003)    | 3B  | 33.399151186 |
| Tampa Bay Devil Rays| Felix Martinez (2000) | SS  | 32.511943136 |
| Kansas City Royals  | Rey Sanchez (2001)    | SS  | 31.642047458 |
| Baltimore Orioles   | Miguel Tejada (2004)  | SS  | 30.849571158 |
| Oakland Athletics   | Bobby Crosby (2004)   | SS  | 28.824352106 |
+---------------------+-----------------------+-----+--------------+
```

There are a couple of interesting things to notice. First, the highest-impact players were shortstops and second basemen. Second, it seems as though the best defensive seasons occurred very recently (over the past few years). Well, it turns out that we can see why this happened if we also look at the 10 worst seasons of all time:

```
select t.name,
       concat(m.nameFirst, ' ', m.nameLast, ' (',t.yearID, ')') as name,
       f.pos, f.FR
from fielding_w_fr f inner join master m inner join teams t
where f.idxLahman=m.idxLahman and f.idxTeams=t.idxTeams
and yearID>1910 and FR is not null and pos IN ('SS', '2B')
order by FR
limit 10;
```

As you might notice, I am only including shortstops and second basemen.

```
+-----------------+-----------------------+-----+---------------+
| name            | name                  | pos | FR            |
+-----------------+-----------------------+-----+---------------+
| Minnesota Twins | Luis Rivas (2001)     | 2B  | -56.353273254 |
| New York Yankees| Derek Jeter (2002)    | SS  | -41.432782878 |
| New York Yankees| Derek Jeter (2000)    | SS  | -37.447310276 |
| Minnesota Twins | Luis Rivas (2003)     | 2B  | -33.715415308 |
| Seattle Mariners| Bret Boone (2004)     | 2B  | -33.558463106 |
| New York Yankees| Derek Jeter (2003)    | SS  | -33.157131056 |
| Minnesota Twins | Jay Canizaro (2000)   | 2B  | -31.705916250 |
| Anaheim Angels  | David Eckstein (2004) | SS  | -29.177353744 |
| Minnesota Twins | Cristian Guzman (2003)| SS  | -29.033513958 |
| Minnesota Twins | Luis Rivas (2002)     | 2B  | -29.029130766 |
+-----------------+-----------------------+-----+---------------+
```

Yup, that's right: the worst seasons also occurred within the past few years. Right now, we're seeing the largest range of fielding ability. Because fielding runs compared players to league average, players are getting much higher and lower scores than usual. (I took a quick look at assists, putouts, errors, and double plays to see whether there was anything funny about the past few years. It turns out that there wasn't. The figures were completely consistent with the past.)

As a Yankees fan (hey, I grew up in Northern Jersey, got a problem with that?), it saddens me a little bit to see Jeter rank as one of the worst defensive shortstops ever. In case you're wondering, Derek Jeter had another below-average season in 2004. But, thanks to A-Rod's presence at third base, his fielding runs total was −13.4097. I guess you could consider his Golden Glove Award in 2004 to be fair if it were awarded for the biggest improvement.

Distribution and box plot. The vast majority of player seasons are clustered around zero, so we plot the distribution with a little more resolution than usual:

```
> hist(subset(FR,yearID>1994), breaks=100)
```

As you can see in Figure 5-15, this is a very tightly clustered distribution, with almost all fielders breaking even and only a few giving away or taking more than a couple of runs through their fielding ability. This is not surprising; the statistic is designed to have an average of zero, and part-time players can't do much better or worse than zero.

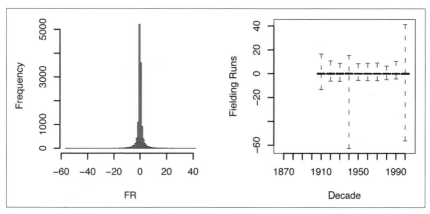

Figure 5-15. Fielding runs distribution and box plot

Finally, let's look at how fielding runs have changed over time:

```
> fielding_w_fr$decade <- as.factor(floor(fielding_w_fr$yearID/10)*10)
> boxplot(FR~decade,data=fielding_w_fr,subset=yearID>1910,
+         pars=c(xlab="decade", ylab="Fielding Runs"),
+         range=0)
```

As this plot shows, there is a huge difference in fielding runs between the best and worst players over the past decade.

See Also

To calculate pitching runs, you need to know fielding runs; see "Measure Pitching with Linear Weights" [Hack #49] for another way to use this.

Measure Park Effects

H A C K
#56 Measure the impact on pitchers and hitters from each major league park.

Unlike other sports, baseball is not played on identically sized fields. Some parks are built at different elevations (most notably Coors Field in Colorado), some have large amounts of foul territory (such as McAfee Coliseum in Oakland), and some have odd-shaped outfields (such as Wrigley Field in Chicago). Most fans notice the short right-field porch at Yankee Stadium or the huge green wall in left field at Fenway Park. Many web sites adjust statistics to compensate for park effects. But how do you measure these?

Approaches

We want to come up with a "fudge factor" that tells us how well a batter or a pitcher is expected to perform in a particular park. If a player's home park is a hitter's park (a park where more runs are scored than normal), we might want to discount his stats appropriately. Similarly, if a batter plays in a pitcher's park (where fewer runs than average are scored), we might want to boost his stats. We're looking for a simple number that we can multiply by a batter's AVG, a pitcher's ERA, or other ballpark-dependent statistics to compare players' performances fairly.

Requirements for a good park factor. We're looking for a few characteristics in an ideal park factor:

Stability
   If the park doesn't change, the park effect shouldn't change. This means park effects should be the same from year to year.

Player independent
   A park factor should measure the park's effect on an average hitter; it should not just measure how a team performs at home versus away.

Symmetry
   Park effects should help predict both offensive (hitting) performance and defensive (pitching) performance. If a park factor predicts that 10% more runs will be scored by a team's batters, it should predict that 10% fewer runs should be allowed by the pitching staff.

Predictive

Park effects need to be predictive: we should be able to tell how a team (or a batter) will perform in a park based upon the park effect.

In reality, parks do change from year to year—weather changes from year to year, teams move ads around, ground crews change the field, etc.—so it's hard to get stable rankings. Also, teams select players based on their individual parks, most significantly by acquiring left- or righthanded pitchers or hitters. Subtler effects are possible, too: Minnesota, Toronto, and Tampa Bay need quality infielders who are effective on their stadiums' artificial surfaces; New York (American League) needs lefty pitchers to deal with the short right-side outfield line; etc. So, it's hard to make a player-independent measurement, or a measurement that works the same way for batters and pitchers.

There are many different types of park factors: park factors for batters, park factors for pitchers, park factors for lefties, park factors for home runs…you get the idea. If you can measure something, you can compare it among ballparks.

In this book, we'll focus on a run-based park factor. You can use this factor directly in comparing players by run-based statistics, such as the linear weights statistics (batter runs, pitcher runs, fielder runs) and ERA-like statistics. You can use it indirectly in comparing figures, including batting average, OBP, and slugging average. I explain how to do this next.

Methodology

In this book, I will use a simple park factor measurement. This is the approach used on many web sites, including ESPN.com. Here is a simple formula for comparing the runs scored and allowed at home to the runs scored and allowed away:

$$simplePF = \frac{(HomeRS + HomeRA)/(HomeG)}{(RoadRS + RoadRA)/(Roadg)}$$

This is a good start to a park factor because it factors in both hitting and pitching, and it adjusts for the number of games played. However, we can make several adjustments to yield a better park factor.

First, remember that if the home team is leading in the middle of the ninth, the game ends and the home team bats for only eight innings (not nine). This means that a team will actually bat slightly more on the road than at home and will pitch slightly more at home than on the road. So, we need to adjust the number in the formula to account for the number of innings pitched and batted at home and away.

Here's a formula that makes this adjustment, using innings in place of games and weighing runs scored and allowed by innings batted and pitched, respectively:

$$PF = \frac{\dfrac{HomeRS \cdot HomeIB + HomeRA \cdot HomeIP}{HomeIB + HomeIP}}{\dfrac{AwayRS \cdot AwayIB + AwayRA \cdot AwayIP}{AwayIB + AwayIP}}$$

We need data on individual games to calculate park effects. We can do this from play-by-play files, but it's easier to start with game logs. (See "Make Box Scores or Database Tables from Play-by-Play Data with Retrosheet Tools" [Hack #15].) Game logs give us lots of data for both the home team and the visiting team, such as runs scored, hits, doubles, home runs, and several other stats.

Let's start by loading the game log files into a database using the procedure in "Load Retrosheet Game Logs" [Hack #21], and using SQL queries. (By the way, game logs are different from event files. They don't have play-by-play information, but they do tell you how many runs were scored in each game, so they're ideal for this exercise.)

Sample Code

Here is some example SQL code for estimating park effects. I used only the 2003 data, for simplicity. If you have data over a longer period, it's better to use several years of data and average it together (this decreases the variance from year to year).

```
-- collect opponents, scores, and innings from each game
create temporary table scores as
select length(VisitorLineScore) as VisitorInnings,
    -- no explicit inning count, so we'll use
    -- line scores (runs per inning) to
    -- determine the number of innings
    if(locate('x',HomeLineScore)>0,
        length(HomeLineScore) - 1,
        length(HomeLineScore)) as HomeInnings,
    HomeRunsScore, VisitorRunsScored,
    HomeTeam, VisitingTeam as AwayTeam
from ALLGL
where floor(Date/10000) = 2003;

-- calculate a table of the home figures
create temporary table home_sums as
select HomeTeam,
    sum(HomeRunsScore) as HomeRS, sum(VisitorRunsScored) as HomeRA,
    sum(VisitorInnings) as HomeIP, sum(HomeInnings) HomeIB
```

```
from scores
group by HomeTeam;

-- calculate a table of the away figures
create temporary table away_sums as
select AwayTeam,
    sum(VisitorInnings) as AwayIB, sum(HomeInnings) AwayIP,
    sum(HomeRunsScore) as AwayRA, sum(VisitorRunsScored) as AwayRS
from scores
group by AwayTeam;

-- estimate park factor
create table pf as
select
    (((HomeRS * HomeIB) + (HomeRA * HomeIP)) / (HomeIB + HomeIP)) /
    (((AwayRS * AwayIB) + (AwayRA * AwayIP)) / (AwayIB + AwayIP))
    as PF,
    HomeTeam
from home_sums h inner join away_sums a
on h.hometeam=a.awayteam;
```

Here are the estimated park factors in 2003:

```
mysql> select t.teamID as ID, t.park, p.pf
    -> from pf p inner join bbdatabank.teams t
    -> on p.HomeTeam=t.teamID
    -> where t.yearID=2003;


ID    park                                       round(PF,3)
-----  ------------------------------------       -------------
ANA   Edison International Field                  0.877
ARI   Bank One Ballpark                          1.214
ATL   Turner Field                               0.929
BAL   Oriole Park at Camden Yards                0.890
BOS   Fenway Park II                             1.095
CHA   U.S. Cellular Field                        0.968
CHN   Wrigley Field                              0.969
CIN   Great American Ball Park                   0.998
CLE   Jacobs Field                               0.856
COL   Coors Field                                1.246
DET   Comerica Park                              0.902
FLO   Pro Player Stadium                         0.869
HOU   Minute Maid Park                           1.070
KCA   Royals Stadium                             1.247
LAN   Dodger Stadium                             0.867
MIL   Miller Park                                1.052
MIN   Hubert H Humphrey Metrodome                1.034
MON   Stade Olympique,Hiram Bithorn Stadium      1.383
NYA   Yankee Stadium II                          0.930
NYN   Shea Stadium                               0.967
OAK   Oakland Coliseum                           0.866
PHI   Veterans Stadium                           0.897
PIT   PNC Park                                   0.981
```

```
SDN    Qualcomm Stadium                  0.829
SEA    Safeco Field                      0.940
SFN    PacBell Park                      0.996
SLN    Busch Stadium II                  0.922
TBA    Tropicana Field                   1.000
TEX    The Ballpark at Arlington         1.223
TOR    Skydome                           1.103
```

Using Park Factors

Park factors for run-based measurements. You measure park factors in terms of their effect on runs scored in a stadium (compared to runs scored elsewhere). This means you can use park factors to adjust any statistic denominated in terms of runs.

Additionally, teams play half their games at home and half their games away from home, so you can't use park factors directly. Instead, you use the average of a team's park factor and the park factor for the league average park (which should be 1). For example, to adjust Toronto hitters, you would use a factor of (1.103 + 1) / 2 = 1.0525.

The adjustments are easiest for normalized measurements, such as those in terms of runs per at bat, runs per inning, or runs per game. For example, let's use the 2003 park factors to adjust ERAs for pitchers in 2003 and select the top 10 pitchers. We join the pitching statistics from 2003 with the park factors table and divide each player's ERA by their park factor (to remove the park effects):

```
select round(p.ER / p.IPOuts * 27, 3) as ERA,
    round(p.ER / p.IPOuts * 27 / ((pf + 1)/2),3) as adjERA,
    p.teamID, m.nameLast, m.nameFirst
from bbdatabank.pitching p inner join bbdatabank.master m
    inner join pf pf
on p.playerID=m.playerID AND pf.Hometeam=p.teamID
where p.IPOuts > 162 * 3 and p.yearID=2003
order by adjERA LIMIT 10;
```

ERA	adjERA	teamID	nameLast	nameFirst
2.218	2.118	BOS	Martinez	Pedro
2.340	2.344	SFN	Schmidt	Jason
2.427	2.465	CHN	Prior	Mark
2.389	2.559	LAN	Brown	Kevin
2.839	2.566	ARI	Webb	Brandon
2.946	2.662	ARI	Schilling	Curt
3.201	2.687	MON	Hernandez	Livan
3.238	2.718	MON	Vazquez	Javier
2.700	2.893	OAK	Hudson	Tim
2.903	2.950	CHA	Loaiza	Esteban

You'll notice that most of these effects are pretty subtle because most parks are close to neutral, but a few pitchers were helped by pitching in pitchers' parks (e.g., Tim Hudson) or were hurt by pitching in batters' parks (e.g., Javier Vazquez).

If you're using a statistic denominated in terms of runs per season, you can't use a park adjustment directly. First, normalize the measurement to calculate runs per game, inning, or at bat (for the specific player or team). Next, apply the park factor to the normalized measurement. Then, change the measurement back to runs per season.

Park factors for other statistics. You can also use park factors to adjust other statistics that are not directly denominated in runs, using one of Pete Palmer's tricks. He observed that OBP * SLG is an even better predictor of runs scored than OBP + SLG. (This formula actually relates closely to runs created; see "Measure Batting with Runs Created" **[Hack #45].**) So, he suggested using the square root of park factor to adjust OBP and SLG because of this relationship:

$$\frac{OBP}{\sqrt{PF}} \cdot \frac{SLG}{\sqrt{PF}} = \frac{OBP \cdot SLG}{PF}$$

(Intuitively, this makes sense, but it's just an approximation not a rigorous mathematical truth.) So, let's apply this relationship to rank the top batters by OBP in 2003:

```
select round((b.BB + b.HBP + b.H) /
       (b.AB + b.BB + b.SF + b.HBP), 3)  as OBP,
   round((b.BB + b.HBP + b.H) / (b.AB + b.BB + b.SF + b.HBP)
       / sqrt((pf + 1)/2),3) as adjOBP,
   b.teamID, m.nameLast, m.nameFirst
from bbdatabank.batting b inner join bbdatabank.master m
   inner join pf pf
on b.playerID=m.playerID AND pf.Hometeam=b.teamID
where (b.AB + b.HBP + b.SF + b.BB) > 162 * 3.1 and b.yearID=2003
order by adjOBP DESC LIMIT 10;
```

OBP	adjOBP	teamID	nameLast	nameFirst
0.529	0.53	SFN	Bonds	Barry
0.439	0.448	SLN	Pujols	Albert
0.458	0.432	COL	Helton	Todd
0.419	0.427	ATL	Sheffield	Gary
0.409	0.42	PHI	Abreu	Bobby
0.412	0.419	NYA	Giambi	Jason
0.427	0.417	BOS	Ramirez	Manny
0.426	0.415	TOR	Delgado	Carlos
0.406	0.413	SEA	Martinez	Edgar
0.405	0.412	NYA	Posada	Jorge

Again, you'll see that this is a subtle effect for most players (most ballparks are close to neutral).

Hacking the Hack

I'm sure readers have a lot of ideas about where to go next. Here are just a few ideas for refining these measurements.

Enhancements. Not every team plays against every other team an equal number of times. Teams play other teams within their own divisions far more often than they play teams from other divisions. So, it would be helpful to equally weight games at all stadiums. You can weight the runs in each stadium evenly by dividing the number of runs scored and allowed by the away team in each stadium by the number of innings batted or pitched by that team in each stadium.

Additionally, no team's batters faced their own team's pitchers, nor did any team's pitchers face their own team's batters. It would be helpful to compensate for this. Other park factor calculations (such as Palmer's calculation in *Total Baseball* [Total Sports]) account for these factors; read Palmer's book if you want to learn more.

Compare individual offensive stats (singles, doubles, triples, home runs, etc.). I used a simple, run-based park factor as an example, but you can calculate park factors on any part of the offense or defense. Park effects are due to different surfaces (grass versus turf) and shapes, so they should have a different impact on different statistics. For example, a large foul territory means more fly outs in foul territory. A large foul territory might slightly reduce the number of home runs (a home run hitter might be more likely to foul out before hitting home runs), but the primary effect is on foul outs. You can even look at strikeout rates per park. (Shea Stadium, home of the New York Mets, is infamous for its poor visibility. Presumably, batters have a tough time picking out the ball from the sun, the outfield scoreboards, and planes flying in and out of JFK International Airport.)

Fancy statistical approaches. I'm not crazy about the classical park factors because they're so closely tied to the home teams' performances. I think it would be worthwhile to examine park factors as one factor that affects performance, along with pitcher/batter matchups, weather, defensive ability, and other things. Here are a couple of approaches that I'd like to investigate:

Build a regression model for run rate with the park as a categorical factor
    This approach is a bit more complicated, but it will help isolate some of the different effects that determine run rate.

Use Bayesian methods to estimate the probability of each event for every combination of batter, pitcher, and park

This is an even better approach, kind of a grand, unified theory of baseball statistics. See "Fitting Game Scores to a Strength Model" [Hack #71] for a more sophisticated approach to park factors.

See Also

Visit *http://www.ballparksofbaseball.com* to see pictures of current and past ballparks.

In "Use Microsoft Excel Web Queries to Get Stats" [Hack #24], I show how to create a spreadsheet for calculating park factors that is automatically refreshed throughout the baseball season.

HACK #57 Calculate Fan Save Value

Calculate a more accurate assessment of the save statistic based on the lead and the number of outs to pitch when the relief pitcher enters the game.

I (Ari Kaplan, the author of this hack) came up with the save value when I was with the Baltimore Orioles in 1990. Teams were bringing in relief pitchers with two outs in the ninth, with a two-run lead to get the save. The pitchers being pulled were usually doing just fine. The pitcher pulled most often was a middle reliever named Curt Schilling. My analysis revealed that he was a much better pitcher than his "standard" pitching statistics, such as win/loss, save, and ERA—it all depended on how he was being used by the team.

Relievers were, and still are, brought in, despite the risk that the new pitcher will have an off night. This was nothing more than padding standard statistics to look good to fans. It is illogical and sometimes counterproductive for winning games.

Saves

According to Section 10.20 of the official rules of Major League Baseball:

SAVES FOR RELIEF PITCHERS

Credit a pitcher with a save when he meets all three of the following conditions: (1) He is the finishing pitcher in a game won by his club; and (2) He is not the winning pitcher; and (3) He qualifies under one of the following conditions: (a) He enters the game with a lead of no more than three runs and pitches for at least one inning; or (b) He enters the game, regardless of the count, with the potential tying run either on base, or at bat, or on deck (that is, the potential tying run is either already on base or is one of the first two batsmen he faces); or (c) He pitches effectively for at least three innings. No more than one save may be credited in each game.

Why was the save statistic created? Jerome Holtzman (the first official Major League Baseball historian) wanted to credit relief pitchers for performing well. Today, the save statistic is one of the primary tools to analyze relief performance and to determine, for example, the Rolaids Relief Pitcher of the Year Award. For salary determination, trade factor, and day-to-day pitcher usage, teams inaccurately use the save statistic.

Saves are subjective. In Major League Baseball, there are only a few *subjective statistics*—that is, statistics that are ruled not by the umpires but by an official scorer. Balls and strikes, safe at the plate, failing to tag up, fair, and foul are all subjective, but the umpire makes the official ruling on the field. Only with errors and the save value can an off-the-field official record the statistic. With an error, the official scorer determines whether a play is a hit or an error. With a save, in addition to some actual rules, the official scorer can judge, regardless of the lead or number of innings pitched, that a relief pitcher who finishes a game (and pitches at least three innings and doesn't get the win) deserves a save. A pitcher might have a seven-run lead, a pitcher might pitch six innings—there is no rule, no guideline, and no standard.

Why is the save statistic flawed? Here are seven big problems with the save statistic:

- It has a subjective component in the ruling. There is no standard definition of "pitches effectively for at least three innings."
- The number of runs a team is in the lead does not count. One save with a one-run lead counts the same as one save with a three-run lead, although it is many times more difficult.
- The number of outs needed to pitch does not count. One save with nine outs remaining in the game counts the same as one save with one out remaining, although it is nine times more difficult.
- Whether there are base runners, and which bases they are on, do not count. One save with two outs and bases loaded is counted the same as one save with two outs and bases empty.
- The pitcher gets more saves with better team run support during the innings pitched.
- The pitcher is at the mercy of the manager to be placed into a save opportunity. Some pitchers are used when teams are losing or are tied. Some pitchers pitch for teams with fewer save opportunities.

  For example, in 2004, the Cardinals had 86 games with save opportunities, well over 50% more than the Royals and the White Sox, who had only 51 games with save opportunities. When looking at overall save opportunities (with the possible multiple opportunities in one game, such as three pitchers getting a "hold" and the fourth pitcher getting a save), in 2004, the Cardinals had 185 overall save opportunities, 85% more than the Royals, who had 100.

- The pitcher must complete the game, but he is at the mercy of the manager to finish. If the manager brings in another pitcher, the first pitcher loses the save opportunity.

Fan Save Value

I came up with this formula to measure save value:

FSV = [X/Y] / 2

Here's what the formula means:

- X = outs left in the game (X = 5 for the eighth inning, one out; X = 1 for the 15th inning, two outs).
- Y = number of run lead (1, 2, 3, 4, 5). Note that there is never a no-run lead for a save opportunity. Otherwise, if Y = 0, the formula is a "divide by zero" undefined. Also, there is never more than a five-run lead in a save opportunity, even with bases loaded.

The fan save value is an easy-to-compute statistic for the fans. It is simply the number of outs needed to pitch to end the game, divided by the number of runs in the lead, and then divided in half. The more outs needed to pitch, the more valuable the performance, and the greater the team's lead, the less valuable the performance.

Fans can calculate this value using simple math, which is why it is called the fan save value, but this value is less accurate than the more complex save value (described in "Calculate Save Value" [Hack #58]). We divide by 2 to get this value so that the average fan save value is close to 1, making it easy to compare against the standard save value. For all 2004 games, there is only a 5% difference between the total number of fan save values and the total number of actual save values. This is remarkably close, considering the simplicity of the formula.

The fan save value does not take into account runners on base, which is a major factor in the difficulty of a pitcher converting a save opportunity into a save. But the standard save value doesn't factor it in either. Nor does the standard save give credit for the number of innings left to pitch, nor for the size of the lead a team has at the start of the save opportunity.

How does a fan save value compare to the standard save value? One example in which a fan save value compares to the standard save value is a save opportunity of entering the ninth inning with one out and a one-run lead, which is exactly one fan save value ([2 outs to pitch / 1-run lead] / 2). Another is entering the eighth inning with a three-run lead ([6 outs to pitch / 3-run lead] / 2). On the tough end, entering the seventh inning with a one-run lead is worth a 4.5 fan save value. On the easy end, entering a game in the ninth inning with two outs and a two-run lead is worth a 0.25 fan save value.

Sample Code

First, let's build a table of saving pitchers. We can do this by using game logs, as described in "Load Retrosheet Game Logs" **[Hack #21]**. (I started with a massive table, called ALLGL, containing game logs from all games between 1871 and 2004.)

```
CREATE TABLE SAVES2K AS
SELECT HomeTeam, VisitingTeam, concat(HomeTeam,Date, DoubleHeader)as GameID,
SavingPitcherID
FROM gamelogs.ALLGL A
WHERE DATE > 20000000;
```

Second, we can join this table with the play-by-play data to determine the value of each save. We don't need to know everything about the game. We just need to know the difference between the two teams' scores, the inning, and the number of outs when the relief pitcher entered the game. So, when we merge the save and play-by-play tables, we will keep only a couple of values: the minimum scores and the minimum number of outs pitched.

```
-- create indexes for fast joining
CREATE INDEX SAVES2K_IDX ON SAVES2K(GameID, SavingPitcherID);
CREATE INDEX pbp2K_SIDX ON pbp2k(game_id, res_pitcher);

CREATE TABLE FSVs AS
select i.game_id, i.res_pitcher,
  if(inning > 9,
      27 - outs_pitched_on_entrance,
      inning * 3 - outs_pitched_on_entrance)
  / if(batting_team=0,
      home_score - vis_score,
      vis_score - home_score)
  / 2 as FSV
from (select r.game_id, r.res_pitcher,
      min((inning - 1) * 3 + outs) as outs_pitched_on_entrance,
      min(home_score) as home_score,
      min(vis_score) as vis_score,
      min(inning) as inning,
      batting_team
```

```
from saves2k l inner join pbp2k r
on l.GameID=r.game_id and l.SavingPitcherID=r.res_pitcher
group by r.game_id, r.res_pitcher) i;
```

Using the Fan Save Value Formula

Example 1: How did the 2004 AL and NL save leaders fare?
Mariano Rivera of the Yankees led the AL with 53 saves (in 74 appearances). His fan save value was 49.55, down 6.5% from his 2003 value, showing that he had slightly easier opportunities than the average.

Armando Benitez of the Marlins and Jason Isringhausen of the Cardinals led the NL with 47 saves each (in 64 and 74 games, respectively). Benitez's fan save value was 42.1, down 10.5% from the previous year, showing that he had easier opportunities than the average. Isringhausen's fan save value was 40.5, down 13.9% from the previous year, showing that he had much easier opportunities than the average, and that he received more credit than he should have.

Example 2: What was the biggest difference between saves and fan save value to make the pitcher seem better?
Technically, Aaron Fultz of Minnesota's fan save value of 0.125 was eight times easier than his actual save, but that is with a sample space of 1. And LaTroy Hawkins of the Cubs had 25 saves with an 18.4 save value (27% easier than it appeared).

Example 3: What was the biggest difference between saves and fan save value to make the pitcher seem worse?
Technically, Jorge Sosa of Tampa Bay had a 300% difference (one save with a save value of 4), but that is with a sample space of 1. For a significant number of saves, Brad Lidge of the Houston Astros had 32 saves with a 41.875 save value (31% harder than it appeared).

Example 4: What was the biggest team difference between saves and fan save value to make the team seem better?
The 2004 Colorado Rockies had 36 total saves (added up for all of their pitchers) but only a 27.35 total fan save value, a difference of 24%. In other words, the 36 saves the Rockies achieved should have been worth only 27.35 saves, due to each of their save opportunity situations. The next-closest team was the 2004 Toronto Blue Jays, with 36 total saves but a 29.3 total fan save value, a difference of 18.7%.

Example 5: What was the biggest team difference between saves and fan save value to make the team appear worse?
The 2004 Tampa Bay Devil Rays had only 36 total saves but a 43.5 total fan save value, a difference of 20.7%. In other words, the 36 saves the Devil Rays achieved should have been worth 43.5 saves, due to each of

their save opportunity situations. The next-closest team was the 2004 Houston Astros, with 50 total saves but a 59.5 total fan save value, a difference of 19.1%.

—Ari Kaplan

HACK #58   Calculate Save Value

Calculate a more accurate assessment of the save statistic based on the lead, the number of outs to pitch, the outs in the inning, and the location of base runners when the relief pitcher enters the game.

For background information on the save statistic, its limitations, and the fan save value, see "Calculate Fan Save Value" [Hack #57], where we examine why the save statistic is flawed. The fan save value is limited because it does not take into account whether there are base runners or which bases they are on when the pitcher enters the game. One fan save value with a pitcher entering the ninth with a two-run lead and the bases empty is counted the same as one fan save value with a pitcher entering the ninth with a two-run lead and the bases loaded. And the latter is a much more difficult situation (2.27 runs are expected to score with the bases loaded and no outs).

The Formula

The save value is the most accurate statistic for determining the value of the save relative to the effort needed to convert the particular situation into a save. This is straightforward to calculate, but it requires knowledge of the expected run matrix. Fans do not easily memorize the matrix, which is why I came up with the simpler fan save value:

```
Save Value= 1.12 * X / ( L + Y - E )
```

Here's how to read the equation:

- X = outs left in the game (X = 5 for the eighth inning, 1 out; X = 1 for the 15th inning, two outs).
- Y = number of run lead (1, 2, 3, 4, 5).
- L = expected runs with no outs and bases loaded = 2.27.
- E = expected runs to score based on number of outs and base runners. See "Calculate Expected Runs" [Hack #60] for additional information on calculating the expected run matrix.

The save value is more complicated to calculate than the fan save value, which was a statistic for fans reading from a newspaper or box score. The save value is the number of outs divided by (1) the sum of the number of expected runs to score with the bases loaded and no outs, plus (2) the lead, minus (3) the expected number of runs to score, given the situation. Then multiply this result by 1.12. The more outs needed to pitch, the more valuable the performance. The greater the team's lead, the less valuable the performance. The more runs expected to score in the inning, the more valuable the performance.

Using the Save Value

We multiply by 1.12 so that the median save value is close to 1, making it easy to compare against the standard save.

Example 1: How does the save value compare to the fan save value?
Because the fan save value does not take into account base runners when the relief pitcher appears, let's look at three examples:

Example A
> Ninth inning, no outs, three-run lead, bases loaded: save value is 1.12; fan save value is 0.5.

Example B
> Eighth inning, two outs, two-run lead, bases loaded: save value is 1.30; fan save value is 1.

Example C
> Seventh inning, two outs, two-run lead, runners on first and second: save value is 2.06; fan save value is 1.75.

The fan save value is simplistic in the approach of leads, so even with the bases empty, a one-run lead will have slightly more weight (about 18% more) in terms of fan save value than save value. This is somewhat skewed, but keep in mind that the fan save value is a statistic for the fans; it's still much better than the standard save.

Example 2: How does the save value compare to the standard save?
One example is a save opportunity of entering the ninth inning with no outs, a two-run lead, and a runner on first, which is exactly one save value: 1.12 * ([3 outs to pitch] / (2.27 + [2 run lead] − 0.93 runs expected to score). Another example is entering the eighth inning with two outs, a three-run lead, and bases loaded. On the tough end, entering the seventh inning with a one-run lead and bases loaded is worth a 10.1 save value. On the easy end, entering a game in the ninth inning, with two outs and a runner on first and a three-run lead, is worth a 0.22 save value.

Sample Code

Here is some SQL code to create a table of save values from the play-by-play data. This code assumes that you have created a table of saves, as shown in "Calculate Fan Save Value" [Hack #57], and that you have a database of play-by-play data similar to the one created in "Make a Historical Play-by-Play Database" [Hack #22].

This code works a little differently from the code shown in "Calculate Fan Save Value" [Hack #57], to demonstrate a second way to find the play when a relief pitcher entered the game. The innermost query identifies all plays where the saving pitcher is pitching, and it finds the lowest event_num for each of those games. The next query merges this map to the play-by-play table using the event_num and game_id fields. This gives only the first play of each game when the saving pitcher was pitching.

The long case statements use the information from "Calculate Expected Runs" [Hack #60] to calculate the expected number of runs that the opponent will score in the current inning, given the set of base runners and number of outs. Finally, the outermost function computes save value, as described previously.

```
CREATE TABLE pbp.SVs AS
select d.game_id, d.res_pitcher,
  1.12 * if(inning > 9, 3 - outs, 30 - (3 * inning + outs)) /
  (2.27 +
   if(batting_team=0,home_score-vis_score,vis_score-home_score) -
   CASE outs
     WHEN 0 THEN CASE
       WHEN first_runner is not null and second_runner is not null
         and third_runner is not null THEN 2.27
       WHEN first_runner is not null and second_runner is not null
         and third_runner is null THEN 1.49
       WHEN first_runner is not null and second_runner is null
         and third_runner is not null THEN 1.86
       WHEN first_runner is null and second_runner is not null
         and third_runner is not null THEN 2.14
       WHEN first_runner is not null and second_runner is null
         and third_runner is null THEN .93
       WHEN first_runner is null and second_runner is not null
         and third_runner is null THEN 1.17
       WHEN first_runner is null and second_runner is null
         and third_runner is not null THEN 1.46
       WHEN first_runner is null and second_runner is null
         and third_runner is null THEN 0.54
       END
     WHEN 1 THEN CASE
       WHEN first_runner is not null and second_runner is not null
         and third_runner is not null THEN 1.6
```

```
      WHEN first_runner is not null and second_runner is not null
        and third_runner is null THEN  .97
      WHEN first_runner is not null and second_runner is null
        and third_runner is not null THEN 1.24
      WHEN first_runner is null and second_runner is not null
        and third_runner is not null THEN  1.47
      WHEN first_runner is not null and second_runner is null
        and third_runner is null THEN .93
      WHEN first_runner is null and second_runner is not null
        and third_runner is null THEN .71
      WHEN first_runner is null and second_runner is null
        and third_runner is not null THEN .98
      WHEN first_runner is null and second_runner is null
        and third_runner is null THEN .29
      END
    WHEN 2 THEN CASE
      WHEN first_runner is not null and second_runner is not null
        and third_runner is not null THEN .82
      WHEN first_runner is not null and second_runner is not null
        and third_runner is null THEN .46
      WHEN first_runner is not null and second_runner is null
        and third_runner is not null THEN .54
      WHEN first_runner is null and second_runner is not null
        and third_runner is not null THEN .63
      WHEN first_runner is not null and second_runner is null
        and third_runner is null THEN  .55
      WHEN first_runner is null and second_runner is not null
        and third_runner is null THEN .34
      WHEN first_runner is null and second_runner is null
        and third_runner is not null THEN .38
      WHEN first_runner is null and second_runner is null
        and third_runner is null THEN .11
      END
    END
  )
  AS SV
from (
  select c.game_id, c.batting_team, c.inning, c.outs,
  c.first_runner, c.second_runner, c.third_runner,
  c.vis_score, c.home_score, c.res_pitcher
  from (
    select game_id, min(event_num) as event_num
    from pbp.saves2k l inner join pbp.pbp2k r
    on l.GameID=r.game_id and l.SavingPitcherID=r.res_pitcher
    group by r.game_id, r.res_pitcher
  ) b inner join pbp.pbp2k c
  on b.game_id=c.game_id and b.event_num=c.event_num
) d;
```

Using the Save Value Formula

Example 1: How did the 2004 AL and NL save leaders fare?

Mariano Rivera of the Yankees led the AL with 53 saves (in 74 appearances). His save value was 51.1, down 3.6% from the previous year, showing that he had slightly easier opportunities than the average.

Armando Benitez (Marlins) and Jason Isringhausen (Cardinals) led the NL with 47 saves each (in 64 and 74 games, respectively). Benitez's save value was 45.7, down 2.8%, showing that he also had slightly easier opportunities than the average. Isringhausen's save value was 43.38, down 7.7%, showing about the same difficulty as the average.

Example 2: What was the biggest difference between saves and save value to make the pitcher seem better?

Technically, Aaron Fultz of Minnesota's save value of 0.19 was five times easier than his actual one save, but that is with a sample space of 1. And LaTroy Hawkins of the Cubs had 25 saves with a 21 save value (16.1% easier than it appeared).

Example 3: What was the biggest difference between saves and save value to make the pitcher seem worse?

Technically, Rob Bell of Tampa Bay had a 522% difference (one save with a 6.2 save value), but that is with a sample space of 1. For a significant number of saves, Brad Lidge of Houston had 32 saves with a 40.6 save value (26.9% harder than it appeared).

Example 4: What was the biggest team difference between saves and save value to make the team seem better?

The 2004 Colorado Rockies had 36 total saves (added up for all of their pitchers) but only a 31.1 total save value, a difference of 13.6%. In other words, the 36 saves the Rockies achieved should have been worth only 31.1 saves, due to each of their save opportunity situations. The next-closest team was the Cincinnati Reds, with 47 total saves but a save value of 42.5, a 9.6% difference.

Example 5: What was the biggest team difference between saves and save value to make the team appear worse?

The 2004 Tampa Bay Devil Rays had only 36 total saves but a 47.8 total save value, a difference of 32.9%. In other words, the 36 saves the Devil Rays achieved should have been worth 47.8 saves, due to each of their save opportunity situations. The next-closest team was the 2004 Detroit Tigers, with 34 total saves but a 42.4 total save value, a difference of 24.8%.

—Ari Kaplan

HACK #59

Calculate Holds and Decent Holds for Relief Pitchers

Calculate the hold statistic for evaluating middle relief pitcher performance, and the decent hold for a more insightful analysis.

The mainstream statistics for evaluating relief pitchers are ERA, win–loss, and save. For a middle relief pitcher, there is little chance to get wins, losses, and saves—while the ERA can be misleading for describing pitcher performance. The hold statistic gives some insight into how a middle relief pitcher performs in holding the lead during a game. This hack will discuss why a hold is helpful and how it can be misleading.

What Is a Hold?

The hold is not an official Major League Baseball statistic. Despite this, many media outlets, including the Associated Press (AP) and MLB organizations, use the hold to better evaluate talent. According to the Major League Baseball's web site definition:

> The hold is not an official statistic, but it was created as a way to credit middle relief pitchers for a job well done. Starting pitchers get wins, and closers—the relief pitchers who come in at the end of the game—get saves, but the guys who pitch in between the two rarely get either statistic. So what's the most important thing one of these middle relievers can do? "Hold" a lead. If a reliever comes into a game to protect a lead, gets at least one out and leaves without giving up that lead, he gets a hold. But you can't get a save and a hold at the same time.

John Dewan and Mike O'Donnell, the creators of the hold, define it as:

> HOLD FOR RELIEF PITCHERS: Credit a pitcher with a Hold when he enters a game in a Save situation, preserves the lead, and does not finish the game.

Currently, there are two definitions: the traditional version of the hold, for which no outs need to be recorded, and the MLB unofficial definition that requires at least one out. Fewer than 6% of the situations in 2004 (121 of 2,114) occurred in which no outs were recorded. To be sure, this hack will show results for both definitions, as well as describe the decent hold—a statistic I created for more meaningful pitching performances. Why was the hold statistic created? It was because of the flaws of using traditional pitching statistics for middle relief pitchers.

Analysis of reliever statistics. Why are relief pitcher statistics flawed? Here are several big problems:

ERA can be misleading
> If the middle relief pitcher pitches only a few innings for the season, there is not a statistically significant threshold for meaningful information. Also, if the relief pitcher strands many runners before the end of the inning, the subsequent pitchers greatly affect the previous pitchers' ERA by allowing the runs to score (or not).

Saves can be misleading
> Saves are elusive, especially for middle relievers, because the pitcher is at the mercy of the manager to finish the game to get a save. See "Calculate Save Value" [Hack #58] for additional reasons why the save statistic can be misleading.

Wins can be misleading
> A middle relief pitcher must have the go-ahead run score during his pitching performance to get a win. This is out of the pitcher's hands and is pure luck. Once in that situation, the pitcher must still hold the lead for the win, so some degree of skill is needed, but still.... Also, no weights are assigned to wins and losses. A relief pitcher can pitch eight innings with a one-run lead to get a win, or pitch one inning with a 10-run lead to get a win, all depending on when the single go-ahead run scored.
>
> For example, a middle relief pitcher enters and allows no runs to score in four innings. When the closer comes in, the team has a five-run lead in the ninth inning. The closer then allows five runs to score, but the team rallies to win in the bottom of the ninth. Regardless, the win is not granted to the middle reliever because the closer blew the opportunity.

Losses can be misleading
> Although a pitcher is usually to blame for blowing a lead (which can result in a loss), it is largely out of the pitcher's hands (or completely out of his hands, if there is a designated hitter) if the team can go ahead and score to avoid a loss.
>
> For example, a middle relief pitcher comes into the game at the start of the sixth inning with a tied game. He allows five runs in the inning, and his team scores six at the bottom of the inning. The relief pitcher is replaced in the top of the seventh, but he still gets the win, all while allowing five runs to score in a single inning!

Analysis of the hold statistic. All of the following can make the hold statistic misleading or flawed:

- The hold statistic does not take into account runners on base, which is a major factor in the difficulty of a pitcher converting a hold opportunity into a hold.

- The hold statistic does not give credit proportionate to the number of innings pitched. A hold for pitching five innings is credited the same as a hold for pitching one inning, although it is five times as difficult. In the traditional definition of a hold, a pitcher can technically walk a runner and be relieved, yet still get a hold. This happened 121 times in the 2004 season. This understandably upsets many analysts, so some further define a hold so that the pitcher must get at least one out.

- The hold statistic does not give credit proportionate to the size of the lead a team has at the start of the hold opportunity. Getting a hold with a five-run lead is much easier than getting a hold with a one-run lead.

- The pitcher can pitch effectively, but the team is tied or behind in the score, so he does not get a hold. The pitcher must be put into a game in which his team is winning, which is at the mercy of the manager and how good the pitcher's team is.

The Code

To calculate the number of holds (according to the original creators' definition of not needing to record an out) for a pitcher, issue this SQL:

```
SELECT count(*), pitcher
FROM fullpbp2004
ON [save opp]="T" AND last_pitcher_flag="F" AND
    (if (batting_team=0,
        end_home_score - end_vis_score,
        end_vis_score - end_home_score) > 0
GROUP BY pitcher
ORDER BY pitcher
```

The code returns the number of holds each pitcher received for the season. For a pitcher to get a hold, he must enter with a save opportunity ([save opp] = "T"). He must not finish the game ("last_pitcher_flag="F"). And he must preserve the lead: if batting_team=0, this is end_home_score minus end_vis_score; otherwise, it is end_vis_score minus end_home_score. This difference must be greater than 0. 0 means that the pitcher allowed the tying run to score, and a negative number indicates the pitcher blew the lead and the team is now behind in runs.

Decent Hold

A more effective way to define a hold is to require that the relief pitcher record at least three outs, which I devised as a decent hold.

Here is some pseudocode to calculate decent holds. (This code won't work exactly as written; it requires a "save opportunity" flag to be derived.)

```
SELECT count(*), pitcher
FROM pbp2k
ON [save opp]="T" AND last_pitcher_flag="F" AND
    (if (batting_team=0,
            end_home_score - end_vis_score,
            end_vis_score - end_home_score) > 0 AND
        outs_pitched > 2
GROUP BY pitcher
ORDER BY pitcher
```

Of the 2,114 holds in 2004, 928 (44% of them) occurred with the relief pitcher getting zero, 1, or 2 outs; 121 holds were granted when the pitcher got no outs; 445 with just one out recorded; and 362 with two outs recorded. Thirteen outs recorded is the longest for any hold (Sun-Woo Kim of the Expos pitched the third out in the seventh inning against the Royals with a 2–0 lead—a very decent hold indeed).

Example 1: Which 2004 teams had the most holds?
For the definition of not needing to record an out, there were 2,114 holds for all pitchers in 2004. The San Francisco Giants led with 106 holds, and the St. Louis Cardinals were a close second with 105. The next team (New York Yankees) drops off at 89 holds.

For the definition of needing to record at least one out, there were 1,993 holds for all pitchers in 2004. The St. Louis Cardinals led with 100 holds, the San Francisco Giants had 90, and the Philadelphia Phillies had 84.

Example 2: Which 2004 teams had the most decent holds?
There were 1,186 decent holds for all pitchers in 2004. The San Diego Padres led with 59 decent holds, and the Philadelphia Phillies and Houston Astros were a close second with 57. The next team (New York Yankees) drops off at 53 decent holds.

Example 3: Which 2004 teams had the fewest holds?
For the definition of not needing to record an out, the average team had 70 holds. The Seattle Mariners had just 48 holds, with the Minnesota Twins and Tampa Bay Devil Rays having 50 holds each.

For the definition of needing to record at least one out, the average team had 66.5 holds. The Seattle Mariners had just 42 holds, with the Minnesota Twins, Kansas City Royals, and Tampa Bay Devil Rays having 49 holds each.

Example 4: Which 2004 teams had the fewest decent holds?
The average team had 39.5 decent holds. The Seattle Mariners had just 18 decent holds, with the Kansas City Royals having 23 decent holds and the Oakland Athletics having 28 decent holds.

Example 5: Which 2004 pitchers had the largest discrepancy, depending on which definition of holds was used?
Seventy-one pitchers would receive a hold based on the definition stating that they do not need to record an out, but these pitchers would not have received credit for a hold from the MLB definition. Jason Christiansen had seven holds without recording an out, Felix Heredia had five, and four tied with four holds each.

Example 6: Which 2004 pitchers had the most holds?
For the definition of not needing to record an out, 272 pitchers had at least one hold (47 had exactly one hold and 39 had exactly two holds). Tom Gordon of the New York Yankees led the Majors with 40 holds. Considering that he had only four saves (and six blown saves), you can see how the hold adds to the analysis of middle relievers. Ray King of the St. Louis Cardinals had 35 holds (and no saves and one blown save). Akinori Otsuka of the San Diego Padres had 34 holds (and two saves and five blown saves).

For the definition that requires at least one out, 268 pitchers had at least one hold (47 had exactly one hold and 38 had exactly two holds). Tom Gordon led with 40 holds (same as with the other hold definition). Akinori Otsuka had 34, as did Ray King. Ray King dropped one hold because he did not get an out during one of his appearances.

Example 7: Which 2004 pitchers had the most decent holds?
Two hundred forty-one pitchers had at least one decent hold (69 had exactly one decent hold and 44 had exactly two decent holds). Akinori Otsuka led with 32 decent holds, Tom Gordon with 28, Francisco Rodriguez of the Anaheim Angels had 27, Guillermo Mota with 23, and Salomon Torres and Chris Reitsma with 21.

—*Ari Kaplan*

CHAPTER SIX

Sabermetric Thinking
Hacks 60–71

I think that this chapter contains the most fun set of hacks in the book. I like scoring games, searching for data, and compiling databases. But the reason for doing all of these things is to learn more about baseball, which is what this chapter is all about.

The term *sabermetrics* comes from SABR, the Society for American Baseball Research (see *http://www.sabr.org* for more information). In 1974, Bill James, Pete Palmer, and Dick Cramer started a statistics committee to encourage the exchange of ideas on baseball. These three pioneers, and many other committee members, popularized thinking about baseball statistics and strategy. As described in Chapter 5, they developed some of the most famous formulas in baseball. Over time, this type of numbers-based thinking has come to be known as sabermetrics.

In this chapter, I examine some classic questions about baseball and some questions of my own. Some fellow baseball fans have contributed to this chapter, and I hope you enjoy reading their hacks as much as I did. These hacks aren't designed just to answer questions about baseball, but to teach you how to answer questions about baseball.

Thinking About Baseball

Although it's hard to see it at first, all of the hacks in this chapter follow a similar pattern. Each hack begins with a problem or question about baseball—for example, is bunting a good strategy?

Next, we formulate a hypothesis that we can test. In this example, we might hypothesize that bunting reduces the expected number of runs scored.

Then we ask what data is needed to solve the problem. To answer whether sacrifice bunts are a good strategy, we need to determine the number of runs we expect to score in different situations. To calculate the expected number of runs in different situations, we need data on a lot of baseball plays. (See "Calculate Expected Runs" [Hack #60] for a more thorough explanation.)

Finally, we use the data to test the hypothesis. In the case of sacrifice bunts, we find that they do make sense in some situations.

Some of these hacks make these steps explicit. Some of them skip a step or two. But all of them fit into this model. If you choose to explore the baseball data and you try to learn more about the game, I encourage you to think about the game in this way.

Calculate Expected Runs

Calculate the expected number of runs, given the number of outs and the number of players on base.

One of the most frequent decisions a manager makes during a game is to tell the batter what to do. Should the batter have discretion to do what he thinks is best? Should the batter be told not to swing, hoping for a ball outside the strike zone? Should the batter bunt? This hack shows you how to figure out what is most likely to happen in different situations, helping you to judge a manager's decisions.

The Code

To understand managers' decisions better, we're going to answer a simple question: if your team has a certain number of outs and a certain number of men on base, how many runs can you expect your team to score in that inning?

To answer this question, we need to use detailed, play-by-play data. (To learn where to get this data, see "Get Recent Play-by-Play Data" [Hack #28]. To learn how to turn this data into a database table, see "Make Box Scores or Database Tables from Play-by-Play Data with Retrosheet Tools" [Hack #15] and "Make a Historical Play-by-Play Database" [Hack #22]. Or, you can download preprocessed files from this book's web site: *http://www.oreilly.com/catalog/baseballhks*.)

Here is a simple strategy for calculating how many runs you expect a team to score in an inning. For each play, we can figure out the state of the game: the score before the play, the number of outs before the play, and the set of men on base. We can also determine the score at the end of every half-inning in every game. So, if we create a table telling us the score at the end of every half-inning of every game, we can merge this with the detailed play-by-play information and figure out the number of runs scored in the remainder of every inning.

Let's do this analysis using a database. First, let's create a table showing the number of runs at the end of every inning. We'll add the score at the beginning of the inning (the minimum score in any of the records) to the number of runs scored. This will give us the total number of runs scored.

```
create table runs_by_inning2004 AS
    select game_id, inning, batting_team,
           if (batting_team=0,
               min(vis_score) +
                   sum(if(runner_on_1st_dest>3,1,0)) +
                   sum(if(runner_on_2nd_dest>3,1,0)) +
                   sum(if(runner_on_3rd_dest>3,1,0)) +
                   sum(if(batter_dest>3,1,0)),
               min(vis_score)) AS vis_score_end_of_inning,
           min(vis_score) AS vis_score_beginning_of_inning,
           if (batting_team=1,
               min(home_score) +
                   sum(if(runner_on_1st_dest>3,1,0)) +
                   sum(if(runner_on_2nd_dest>3,1,0)) +
                   sum(if(runner_on_3rd_dest>3,1,0)) +
                   sum(if(batter_dest>3,1,0)),
               min(home_score)) AS home_score_end_of_inning,
           min(home_score) AS home_score_beginning_of_inning
    from pbp.pbp2k
    where substring(game_id,4,4)="2004"
    group by game_id, inning, batting_team;
```

We're going to merge this table with the play-by-play data. To ensure that this query finishes quickly (in minutes rather than hours), let's create an index on this table. For more information on indexes, see the section titled "7.4.5 How MySQL Uses Indexes" in the *MySQL Reference Manual*.

```
create index runs_by_inning2004_idx
ON runs_by_inning2004(game_id, inning, batting_team);
```

Next, we will merge this new table with the play-by-play data. We will create indicators to show if there is a runner on each base.

```
select p.outs,
       if (p.first_runner  != "", 1, 0) AS runner_on_1st,
       if (p.second_runner != "", 1, 0) AS runner_on_2nd,
       if (p.third_runner  != "", 1, 0) AS runner_on_3rd,
       sum(if (p.batting_team=0,
               r.vis_score_end_of_inning - p.vis_score,
               r.home_score_end_of_inning - p.home_score)
          ) / count(*)
       AS expected_runs,
       count(*) AS N
from fullpbp2004 p inner join runs_by_inning2004 r
on p.game_id=r.game_id AND p.inning=r.inning
    AND p.batting_team=r.batting_team
group by runner_on_1st, runner_on_2nd, runner_on_3rd, outs;
```

That's it! You'll get a table of the number of runs scored in each situation.

Running the Hack

Running this code produces the results shown in Table 6-1.

Table 6-1. Expected runs table

Outs	Runner on first	Runner on second	Runner on third	Expected runs	N
0	0	0	0	0.54	46180
1	0	0	0	0.29	32821
2	0	0	0	0.11	26009
0	0	0	1	1.46	512
1	0	0	1	0.98	2069
2	0	0	1	0.38	3129
0	0	1	0	1.17	3590
1	0	1	0	0.71	6168
2	0	1	0	0.34	7709
0	0	1	1	2.14	688
1	0	1	1	1.47	1770
2	0	1	1	0.63	1902
0	1	0	0	0.93	11644
1	1	0	0	0.55	13483
2	1	0	0	0.25	13588
0	1	0	1	1.86	1053
1	1	0	1	1.24	2283
2	1	0	1	0.54	3117
0	1	1	0	1.49	2786
1	1	1	0	0.97	4978
2	1	1	0	0.46	6545
0	1	1	1	2.27	805
1	1	1	1	1.6	1926
2	1	1	1	0.82	2380

I find the data a little hard to read in this format, so I imported it into Microsoft Excel and used pivot tables to rearrange it. Here is how to do this:

Run the query in Aqua Data Studio

Aqua Data Studio (or other GUI tools) makes it much easier to write and execute database queries than the MySQL terminal program. After you run the query, select Save Results from the File menu. Select Grid

Results as the Results type, Comma Delimited as the Data Format, and Include Column Headers as an option, and save the results to a file with the *.csv* extension.

Import the data into Excel

You can now double-click the file and it should open in Excel. If it does not, open Excel, select Open... from the File menu, and select the file you saved. It should open into a new workbook window, like the one shown in Figure 6-1.

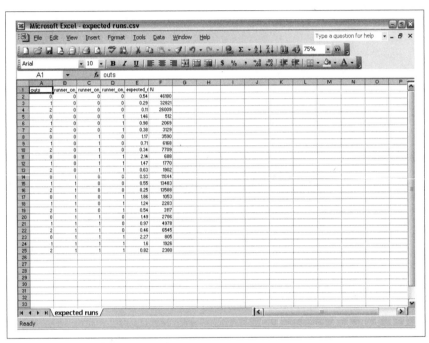

Figure 6-1. Expected runs in Excel

Create a pivot table

Select the data in the spreadsheet, and then select Pivot Table Report from the Data menu. This will open the PivotTable wizard. The first screen asks, "Where is the data that you want to analyze?" Select "Microsoft Excel list or database" and then click the Next button. The second screen asks, "Where is the data that you want to use?" The Range should say $A$1:$F$25; if it doesn't, select the data in the workbook and click the Next button. Finally, the wizard asks, "Where do you want to put the PivotTable?" Select "New worksheet" and click Finish. You will see a new worksheet with a blank pivot table and a palette.

Place the fields into the pivot table

Now, you can drag-and-drop each field into the pivot table. Drag "expected runs" into the Data area. Drag "outs" onto the Columns area (this will now say Total; just drop the field on top of cell B3). Drag the "runner_on_1st," "runner_on_2nd," and "runner_on_3rd" fields into the "rows" area (drag the first one onto the word *Total* in cell A5, drag the second onto the words "runner_on_1st" in cell A4, and then drag-and-drop the third onto the words "runner_on_2nd."

Clean up the pivot table

The pivot table now contains some Total columns that make it hard to read. From the PivotTable palette, click on the PivotTable menu and select the Table Options... menu item. (Alternately, right-click anywhere in the pivot table and select the same item.) In the dialog box, deselect "Grand totals for columns" and "Grand totals for rows." Click the OK button. Now, double-click on the "runner_on_1st" label in cell A4 to open the PivotTable Field Options dialog box. Under Subtotals, select the None radio button and click OK. Finally, double-click on the "runner_on_2nd" label in cell B4 to open the PivotTable Field Options dialog box. Under Subtotals, select the None radio button and click OK.

The data is now in a pivot table in Excel. You should see a table in your workbook that looks like the pivot table shown in Figure 6-2.

Pivot tables make it much easier to manipulate and change data. For example, suppose that you also want to show the total number of plays that fit each situation. Drag-and-drop the N field from the palette onto the data area of the table. The pivot table will now show you both figures at once!

Many adherents of statistical baseball (like the Oakland Athletics, as managed by Billy Beane) are opposed to sacrifice bunts. Their claim is that a sacrifice bunt is a bad strategic move because a team is less likely to score a run after a sacrifice bunt than it was before the bunt. This pivot table helps illustrate their logic. Look at the expected number of runs with a man on first (runner_on_1st=1), no men on second or third (runner_on_2nd=0, runner_on_3rd=0), and no outs (outs=0). In the pivot table in Figure 6-2, this is cell D9. As you can see, this analysis implies that a team can expect to score 0.93 runs in this inning.

After a successful sacrifice bunt, a team will have a man on second (runner_on_2nd=1), no men on first or third (runner_on_1st=0, runner_on_3rd=0), and one out (outs=1). In the pivot table in Figure 6-2, this is cell E7. This analysis implies that a team can expect to score only 0.71 runs in this inning.

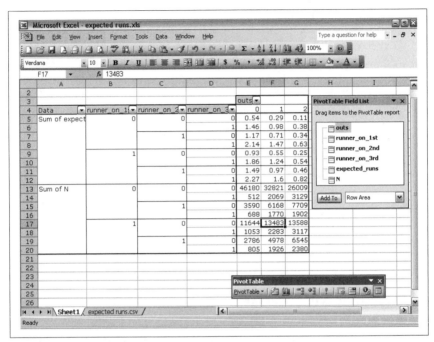

Figure 6-2. Expected runs pivot table

Clearly, a team can expect to score more runs in the first situation than in the second. This is the standard argument against sacrifice bunts.

Hacking the Hack

Our play-by-play database has very rich information about every play. A flag (called bunt_flag) tells us if the play actually was a bunt. A field tells us who was batting. Another field tells us who the player was on first base. This lets us easily explore situational strategies in much more detail.

What actually happened when teams bunted? Let's start with the bunt flag. We can easily modify this SQL code, to group by not just the number of outs and the men on base, but also by the bunt indicator:

```
select p.outs,
        if (p.first_runner  != "", 1, 0) AS runner_on_1st,
        if (p.second_runner != "", 1, 0) AS runner_on_2nd,
        if (p.third_runner  != "", 1, 0) AS runner_on_3rd,
        bunt_flag,
        sum(if (p.batting_team=0,
                r.vis_score_end_of_inning - p.vis_score,
                r.home_score_end_of_inning - p.home_score)
        ) / count(*)
```

```
        AS expected_runs,
        count(*) AS N
from (select * from pbp.pbp2k where substring(game_id,4,4)="2004") p
    inner join runs_by_inning2004 r
on p.game_id=r.game_id AND p.inning=r.inning
    AND p.batting_team=r.batting_team
group by runner_on_1st, runner_on_2nd, runner_on_3rd,
        outs, bunt_flag;
```

In situations where players did bunt, the expected number of runs in the inning was actually 0.83. This is lower than the number of runs expected when a bunt wasn't attempted (0.94), but it's higher than the overall number of runs expected when there was one runner on second and one out (0.71). What is going on here?

Could it be that the batter is often not put out on a bunt, leaving men on first and second with no outs? (That's a good situation to be in; a team can expect to score 1.49 runs in this situation.) Of course, sometimes a bunt goes badly, and the runner on first is put out (or the batter fouls out on the bunt, striking out). Let's add another cut to our data, this time looking at the number of situations in which the bunt resulted in the batter and/or runner being put out. Let's modify our SQL code to include splits for everywhere that the runners ended up:

```
select p.outs,
        if (p.first_runner  != "", 1, 0) AS runner_on_1st,
        if (p.second_runner != "", 1, 0) AS runner_on_2nd,
        if (p.third_runner  != "", 1, 0) AS runner_on_3rd,
        bunt_flag,
        runner_on_1st_dest, runner_on_2nd_dest,
        runner_on_3rd_dest, batter_dest,
        sum(if (p.batting_team=0,
                r.vis_score_end_of_inning - p.vis_score,
                r.home_score_end_of_inning - p.home_score)
            ) / count(*)
        AS expected_runs,
        count(*) AS N
from (select * from pbp.pbp2k where substring(game_id,4,4)="2004") p
    inner join runs_by_inning2004 r
on p.game_id=r.game_id AND p.inning=r.inning
    AND p.batting_team=r.batting_team
group by runner_on_1st, runner_on_2nd, runner_on_3rd,
        outs, bunt_flag,
        runner_on_1st_dest, runner_on_2nd_dest,
        runner_on_3rd_dest, batter_dest;
```

I exported the results into Excel (see "Move Data from a Database to Excel" [Hack #19] for instructions on how to do this) and used a pivot table to look at how often each situation occurred. I set up this pivot table slightly differently, placing the outs, runner, and bunt indicators into the "page" section and then making a table of batter_dest and runner_on_1st_dest fields. The results are shown in Figure 6-3.

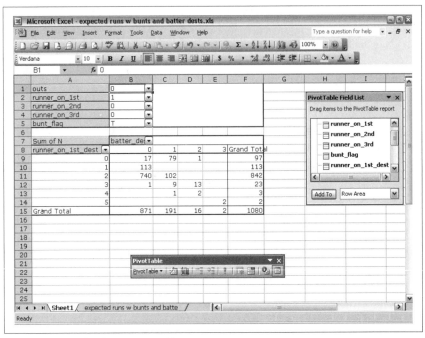

Figure 6-3. Sacrifice bunts pivot table

As you can see, there were 1,080 attempted bunts with a runner on first and no outs in 2004. The batter was put out 81% of the time, but he made it on base 19% of the time. The runner on first was put out almost 9% of the time. Double plays were rare, occurring only 17 times during the season (about 1.6% of the time). Both players made it on base almost 12% of the time.

By looking at what happens after a bunt and combining this with the initial expected runs matrix, we can calculate the expected number of runs from a bunt as a weighted average. (I did this by converting the data in Figure 6-3 into percentages and multiplying the expected number of runs by the percentage of the time that each event occurred.) Using this method, the estimated number of runs scored from bunting is .77. This is higher than the total would have been if bunting always resulted in a runner on second, no runner on first or third, and one out (.71), but it's lower than the actual number in 2004 (.83). What is going on here?

Bunting teams might have had good base runners who were more likely than average runners to score. Or they might have chosen to bunt when above-average hitters were following the bunter; these hitters might have been much more likely to get extra base hits. Interested readers can try looking at the data to see if this was true. Whatever the answer, this analysis still makes bunting look like a losing strategy.

Is bunting ever a good strategy? Clearly, bunting is not a very good choice when an average hitter is facing an average pitcher during an arbitrary inning. But what if the hitter is way below average? What if the hitter rarely gets extra base hits, has a low average, strikes out often, and hits into double plays? (In the National League, these rotten hitters are called pitchers.)

From this table, we can see what a bad at bat can do. A strikeout reduces the expected number of runs from .93 to .55. A double play reduces the expected number of runs from .93 to .29. Clearly, if these things are likely to happen, it's better to have a man on second base and one out (and it's better to expect to score .71 runs).

To answer this question, I tried another twist on the same query. First, I created a table with the on-base percentage (and some other information) for each batter in 2004, and then I created an index on this table for fast merging:

```
create table obps_2004 AS
select playerID,
    INSERT(playerID, LENGTH(playerID) - 1, 1, "") AS pbpID,
    sum(H + BB + HBP) / sum(AB + BB + HBP +SF) AS OBP,
    sum(H + BB + HBP) as OB, sum(AB + BB + HBP +SF) as PA,
    sum(H) as H, sum(BB) as BB, sum(HBP) as HBP,
    sum(AB) as AB, sum(SF) as SF
from Batting
where yearID=2004
group by pbpID
order by OBP;
alter table obps_2004 add id
    INT UNSIGNED NOT NULL AUTO_INCREMENT PRIMARY KEY;
create index obps_2004_idx ON obps_2004(pbpID);
```

Next, I merged this table into the results of this query to classify at bats based on how good the batter was. I classified the batter as "bad" if the player was in the bottom 50th percentile of all batters ranked by on-base percentage. (The number of at bats from bad batters is still very small, only 3.6% of all batters in this situation. This is because many players had a very low number of at bats.)

```
select p.outs,
       if (p.first_runner  != "", 1, 0) AS runner_on_1st,
       if (p.second_runner != "", 1, 0) AS runner_on_2nd,
       if (p.third_runner  != "", 1, 0) AS runner_on_3rd,
       bunt_flag,
       if (o.id > 0.5 * (select count(*) from obps_2004),
           1, 0) as good_batter,
       sum(if (p.batting_team=0,
               r.vis_score_end_of_inning - p.vis_score,
               r.home_score_end_of_inning - p.home_score)
          ) / count(*)
       AS expected_runs,
       count(*) AS N
from (select * from pbp.pbp2k where substring(game_id,4,4)="2004") p
     inner join runs_by_inning2004 r
     inner join obps_2004 o
on p.game_id=r.game_id
   AND p.inning=r.inning
   AND p.batting_team=r.batting_team
   AND p.res_batter=o.pbpID
group by runner_on_1st, runner_on_2nd, runner_on_3rd,
         outs, bunt_flag, good_batter;
```

Here is what we find when there is a runner on first, there are no other base runners, and there are no outs:

	No bunt	Bunt
Bad batter	0.63	0.80
Good batter	0.95	0.84

Incidentally, most bunts in this situation occurred when there was a below-average base runner. When a bad batter came to the plate, the manager usually had him bunt.

	No bunt	Bunt
Bad batter	184	236
Good batter	10380	844

Bunting with good batters does not appear to have been a good strategic move. But bunting with the poorest batters improved the average number of runs scored from .63 to .80.

What about the pitcher? And the runners? What if there are two runners on base? What happened in other years? What about lefties versus righties? What about the postseason? What about late innings? At this point, you probably have many more questions about bunting and expected runs. I recommend that you use the same strategy to answer these questions that I used earlier. The key idea behind this hack is to use indicator variables to group plays into different buckets (e.g., bunts and other plays) and then look at the number of runs generated within each group.

(One interesting idea in particular is the use of sacrifices in late innings. Although a sacrifice can reduce the total number of runs expected in a game, a sacrifice can also increase the probability of scoring at least one run. In a close game—a tie game or a game in which a team is leading or trailing by one run—it might be more important to score at least one run than it is to maximize the expected number of runs scored.)

See Also

Expected runs matrices were published for the first time in a paper called "Statistical Data Useful for the Operation of a Baseball Team," written by George Lindsey and appearing in the March/April 1959 issue of the journal *Operations Research*. If you'd like to know more about this story, see the book *The Numbers Game: Baseball's Lifelong Fascination with Statistics* (St. Martin's Griffin).

HACK #61 Calculate an Expected Hits Matrix

Calculate the probability of a hit, walk, or out based on the ball–strike count.

The ball–strike count is one of the most important ways pitchers and hitters determine their strategy. Most batters will be ready to swing on an 0,2 (no balls, two strikes) count, but many batters won't swing on a 3,0 count (three balls, no strikes). Of course, if the pitcher has generally good control, he might be able to throw the ball into the strike zone at this point, so it might be a good idea for the batter to swing. But then again, if the batter is planning to swing and the pitcher knows the batter is expecting a ball in the strike zone, the pitcher might decide to throw something unhittable and outside the strike zone...you get the idea. The count is at the core of baseball strategy. It drives the mental battle between the hitter and the pitcher.

This hack examines what is likely to happen on different counts. Clearly, a walk is more likely if the pitcher has thrown more balls, and a strikeout is more likely if the pitcher has thrown more strikes. But are extra base hits more likely in some situations? This hack shows you how to count the number of situations in which each of these things happened.

The Code

The key to understanding this code is to understand the possible set of counts and how a batter can move between them. Figure 6-4 illustrates how this works (the first number is the number of balls and the second is the number of strikes).

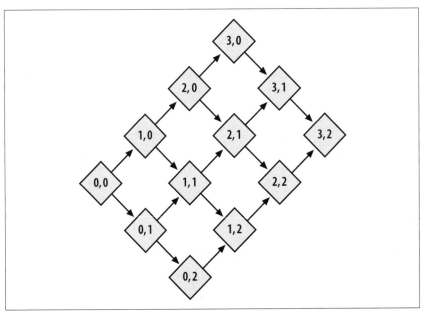

Figure 6-4. How the count progresses in a plate appearance

A batter can put a ball into play at any time. That means that from an 0,0 count, a batter can go to a 1,0 count or an 0,1 count, can stay in the same place (if there is a balk, a pitcher throws to first base, a base is stolen, or something else), can get a hit, can get on base on an error, can get on base on a fielder's choice, or can be put out.

As you can tell, there is more than one path to certain states. As a simple example, consider a 1,1 count. A batter can get there in two ways: 0,0 to 1,0 to 1,1, or 0,0 to 0,1 to 1,1. But notice something else: many destinations cross through the same intermediate states. Batters with 3,1 counts and 2,2 counts once had 2,1 counts.

When we count the number of plays in which a batter had a certain count, we have to count all previous counts. For example, if a pitch sequence was "ball, ball, called strike, ball, swinging strike, and ball put in play as a single," that means the counts would have been 0,0, 1,0, 2,0, 2,1, 3,1, and 3,2.

So, here is how we will count the number of situations that a batter was in each count. We'll use a play-by-play database in MySQL, and we'll use the REGEXP operator to help us search for pitch strings that start off with each pattern we want. We'll code a flag for each situation.

To make the results a little easier to read, I summed the indicators (yielding a count of the number of times batters were in each situation). Here is the code:

```
select sum(CNT_10) AS c10, sum(CNT_20) AS c20, sum(CNT_30) AS c30,
       sum(CNT_11) AS c11, sum(CNT_12) AS c12, sum(CNT_21) AS c21,
       sum(CNT_31) AS c31, sum(CNT_22) AS c22, sum(CNT_32) AS c32,
       sum(CNT_01) AS c01, sum(CNT_02) AS c02, count(*) AS c00, event_type
FROM (select
  IF(pitch_sequence REGEXP
    '^[.>123N]*[BIPV]',1,0) AS CNT_10,
  IF(pitch_sequence REGEXP
    '^[.>123N]*[BIPV][.>123N]*[BIPV]',1,0) AS CNT_20,
  IF(pitch_sequence REGEXP
    '^[.>123N]*[BIPV][.>123N]*[BIPV][.>123N]*[BIPV]',1,0) AS CNT_30,
  IF(pitch_sequence REGEXP
    '^[.>123N]*[CFKLMOQRST]',1,0) AS CNT_01,
  IF(pitch_sequence REGEXP
    '^[.>123N]*[CFKLMOQRST][.>123N]*[CFKLMOQRST]',1,0) AS CNT_02,
  IF(pitch_sequence REGEXP
    '^[.>123N]*[CFKLMOQRST][.>123N]*[BIPV]'
      or pitch_sequence REGEXP
      '^[.>123N]*[BIPV][.>123N]*[CFKLMOQRST]',1,0) AS CNT_11,
  IF(   pitch_sequence REGEXP
      '^[.>123N]*[CFKLMOQRST][.>123N]*[BIPV][.>123N]*[BIPV]'
      or pitch_sequence REGEXP
      '^[.>123N]*[BIPV][.>123N]*[CFKLMOQRST][.>123N]*[BIPV]'
      or pitch_sequence REGEXP
      '^[.>123N]*[BIPV][.>123N]*[BIPV][.>123N]*[CFKLMOQRST]',1,0) AS CNT_
21,
  IF(   pitch_sequence REGEXP  -- SBBB
      '^[.>123N]*[CFKLMOQRST][.>123N]*[BIPV][.>123N]*[BIPV][.>
123N]*[BIPV]'
      or pitch_sequence REGEXP  -- BSBB
      '^[.>123N]*[BIPV][.>123N]*[CFKLMOQRST][.>123N]*[BIPV][.>
123N]*[BIPV]'
      or pitch_sequence REGEXP  -- BBSB
```

```
                    '^[.>123N]*[BIPV][.>123N]*[BIPV][.>123N]*[CFKLMOQRST][.>
        123N]*[BIPV]'
            or pitch_sequence REGEXP  -- BBBS
                    '^[.>123N]*[BIPV][.>123N]*[BIPV][.>123N]*[BIPV][.>
        123N]*[CFKLMOQRST]'
            ,1,0) AS CNT_31,
          IF(    pitch_sequence REGEXP -- SSB
                    '^[.>123N]*[CFKLMOQRST][.>123N]*[CFKLMOQRST][.>123NF]*[BIPV]'
            or pitch_sequence REGEXP -- BSS
                    '^[.>123N]*[BIPV][.>123N]*[CFKLMOQRST][.>123N]*[CFKLMOQRST]'
            or pitch_sequence REGEXP -- SBS
                    '^[.>123N]*[CFKLMOQRST][.>123N]*[BIPV][.>123N]*[CFKLMOQRST]',1,0) AS
        CNT_12,
          IF(    pitch_sequence REGEXP -- SSBB
                    '^[.>123N]*[CFKLMOQRST][.>123N]*[CFKLMOQRST][.>123NF]*[BIPV][.>
        123NF]*[BIPV]'
            or pitch_sequence REGEXP -- BBSS
                    '^[.>123N]*[BIPV][.>123N]*[BIPV][.>123N]*[CFKLMOQRST][.>
        123N]*[CFKLMOQRST]'
            or pitch_sequence REGEXP -- BSBS
                    '^[.>123N]*[BIPV][.>123N]*[CFKLMOQRST][.>123N]*[BIPV][.>
        123N]*[CFKLMOQRST]'
            or pitch_sequence REGEXP -- BSSB
                    '^[.>123N]*[BIPV][.>123N]*[CFKLMOQRST][.>123N]*[CFKLMOQRST][.>
        123NF]*[BIPV]'
            or pitch_sequence REGEXP -- SBSB
                    '^[.>123N]*[CFKLMOQRST][.>123N]*[BIPV][.>123N]*[CFKLMOQRST][.>
        123NF]*[BIPV]'
            or pitch_sequence REGEXP -- SBBS
                    '^[.>123N]*[CFKLMOQRST][.>123N]*[BIPV][.>123N]*[BIPV][.>
        123N]*[CFKLMOQRST]'
            ,1,0) AS CNT_22,
          IF(    pitch_sequence REGEXP
                    '^[.123NCFKLMOQRST]*[BIPV][.123NCFKLMOQRST]*[BIPV][.
        123NCFKLMOQRST]*[BIPV]'
            and pitch_sequence REGEXP
                    '^[.123BIPV]*[CFKLMOQRST][.123BIPV]*[CFKLMOQRST]',1,0) AS CNT_32,
            event_type
            FROM pbp.pbp2k where substring(game_id,4,4)="2004") pc
        group by event_type;
```

Running the Hack

Running this code produces the results shown in Table 6-2.

Table 6-2. Calculating an expected hits matrix

c10	c20	c30	c11	c12	c21	c31	c22	c32	c01	c02	c00	Event type
36761	10803	1864	33638	18549	16602	5116	14844	6811	41081	12465	93196	2
10639	2710	477	15956	18432	6704	1607	13034	5030	21664	13559	32326	3
1263	384	75	943	483	475	150	414	3	1016	301	2297	4
128	30	2	64	29	25	7	14	0	123	30	253	5
374	118	19	354	136	174	65	107	2	352	80	731	6
195	60	10	156	76	80	21	53	20	196	54	500	8
745	201	36	535	427	232	47	321	119	612	262	1361	9
193	59	13	128	61	65	20	54	21	130	42	323	10
51	11	2	40	23	14	3	16	7	62	20	159	11
31	11	0	19	19	11	2	15	6	26	13	59	12
27	10	2	30	15	17	3	16	9	38	9	66	13
10987	7674	5247	6457	2627	7158	7155	4846	6796	4094	934	15084	14
1361	1324	1317	76	4	79	79	4	2	42	2	1403	15
562	134	16	613	412	225	44	237	71	939	319	1886	16
5	1	0	7	9	2	1	7	4	15	7	20	17
712	202	45	667	385	308	102	295	133	781	249	1811	18
202	66	12	159	99	84	35	84	39	196	65	477	19
11566	3398	583	10894	5992	5381	1660	4779	2183	13195	3931	29674	20
3763	1178	195	3207	1648	1733	578	1430	731	3801	1137	9046	21
403	131	19	306	176	183	61	155	76	359	124	909	22
2475	840	182	2006	965	1165	436	916	505	2094	564	5554	23

It's a little hard to understand the data when it's presented in this way, so I imported the data into Excel so that I could easily reformat it. The event_ code field is generated by the Retrosheet BEVENT program, or by Chadwick. This is what these values mean:

Code	Meaning	Classification
0	Unknown event	Other
1	No event	Other
2	Generic out	Out
3	Strikeout	Out
4	Stolen base	Other
5	Defensive indifference	Other
6	Caught stealing	Other
7	Pickoff error	Other
8	Pickoff	Other
9	Wild pitch	Other
10	Passed ball	Other
11	Balk	Other
12	Other advance	Other
13	Foul error	Other
14	Walk	Walk
15	Intentional walk	Walk
16	Hit by pitch	Walk
17	Interference	Other
18	Error	Other
19	Fielder's choice	Out
20	Single	Hit
21	Double	Hit
22	Triple	Hit
23	Home run	Hit

In Excel, I assigned one of the classification values in the preceding table to each event type and used a pivot table to summarize the results. As you can see, I skipped interference calls and errors. Errors are subjective, but they are often caused by someone other than the pitcher or batter, so I think it's best to ignore them. Here is what I found about getting on base, based on the 2004 data:

On base	No strikes	One strike	Two strikes
No balls	33.5%	28.0%	21.2%
One ball	39.5%	32.1%	24.2%
Two balls	51.9%	40.5%	30.7%
Three balls	76.3%	59.7%	46.6%

And here is what I found about getting a hit:

Hits	No strikes	One strike	Two strikes
No balls	23.8%	22.2%	17.4%
One ball	23.1%	22.4%	18.0%
Two balls	19.6%	21.5%	18.1%
Three balls	9.9%	16.3%	15.7%

In general, as the number of strikes increases, the odds of getting on base decrease, except if there are three balls. (In particular, look at what happens on 3,0 counts—the odds of getting on base are enormous (76.3%), but nearly always from walking (only 9.9% hits). Additionally, as the number of balls increases, the chances of getting on base increase, but the chances of getting a hit decrease. This is pretty intuitive: if a pitcher is having trouble throwing strikes, he's likely to walk batters. Additionally, if the pitcher is throwing balls, he's likely to be unhittable.

Hacking the Hack

Without even running another query, we can use this data to answer a hand-ful of other questions about what happens on different pitch counts.

Strikeouts and the count. Let's start with a simple question: what is the per-centage of at bats ending in a strikeout? We can calculate this by dividing the number of strikeouts by the total number of hits, walks, and outs:

Strikeouts	No strikes	One strike	Two strikes
No balls	17.1%	24.8%	41.0%
One ball	13.5%	21.8%	37.7%
Two balls	9.6%	17.1%	32.3%
Three balls	4.8%	9.6%	22.6%

Not surprisingly, a pitcher is most likely to get a strikeout on an 0,2 count and is least likely on a 3,0 count. The odds of a strikeout go way up with each strike, no matter what.

Extra base hits and the count. Announcers often say things during games such as "It's a 3,0 count, the batter knows a fastball is coming, he's going to hit this ball hard!" If pitchers were more likely to throw hittable balls on certain counts, and batters could control where the ball went, we should be able to see it in the data. In particular, we should see a different percentage of extra base hits on different counts. Using exactly the same data as before, let's look at what actually happened in 2004. Here are the extra base hits:

Extra base hits	No strikes	One strike	Two strikes
No balls	34.3%	32.2%	31.7%
One ball	36.5%	33.6%	31.8%
Two balls	38.7%	36.4%	34.4%
Three balls	40.4%	39.3%	37.5%

And here is the number of home runs:

Home runs	No strikes	One strike	Two strikes
No balls	12.3%	10.8%	9.8%
One ball	13.6%	12.2%	11.0%
Two balls	15.1%	13.8%	12.6%
Three balls	18.6%	15.9%	14.4%

There appears to be a subtle effect here. As the number of balls increases, it's slightly more likely that a player is going to be able to hit the ball hard. Additionally, a player seems slightly more likely to hit the ball hard on no strikes than on one or two strikes. This probably means that pitchers are more likely to throw fastballs than off-speed pitches.

Balls in play and the count. Another interesting question: what happens on balls in play, based on the count? Is a ball in play less likely to end up in an out on certain counts? I looked at the number of hits on balls in play (which were defined as generic outs, fielder's choices, singles, doubles, triples, and home runs). Here's what I found:

Hits/balls in play	No strikes	One strike	Two strikes
No balls	32.5%	32.0%	31.5%
One ball	33.0%	32.7%	32.0%
Two balls	33.8%	33.6%	32.8%
Three balls	34.3%	34.7%	33.8%

It looks as though there is a slight increase in the number of hits when there are more balls. On zero, one, or two balls, it appears that the play is more likely to result in a hit on fewer strikes (but not on three balls). Either way, this is a very subtle effect.

HACK #62 Look for Evidence of Platoon Effects
Do lefties hit better against righties (and vice versa)?

In the 1950s, Branch Rickey's Dodgers pioneered a lot of baseball thinking, including "platoon effects." Based on observations that lefthanded batters fared better (on average) when facing righties than lefties, the Dodgers began to change pitchers and batters to better fit their opponents.

This hack looks at this classic sabermetric effect, showing you how to measure the effect of handedness.

Average Platoon Effects

Let's start by looking at how lefty and righty hitters fared, on average, against lefty and righty pitchers over the past year.

To run these queries, you'll need a play-by-play database such as the one I created in "Make a Historical Play-by-Play Database" **[Hack #22]**. You'll also find it helpful to index the play-by-play tables by hand so that the queries run quickly. You can do this by executing the following SQL commands through your SQL client:

```
-- create an index to expedite processing
create index pbp2k_hands_idx on pbp.pbp2k
    (res_batter_hand, res_pitcher_hand, res_batter, res_pitcher);
```

Now, let's look at how players do by hand. Here is a query that calculates league batting averages and league average on-base percentage for each combination of batter and pitcher hand. I used a subquery to make this easy to read. The subquery calculates H, AB, BB, HBP, SF, and SH for each play. The main query calculates the league averages of these amounts.

```
select res_batter_hand, res_pitcher_hand, count(*) as N,
    sum(H) / sum(AB) as AVG,
    SUM(H + BB + HBP) / SUM(AB + BB + HBP + SF) as OBP
from (select res_batter_hand, res_pitcher_hand,
 CASE WHEN hit_value > 0 THEN 1 ELSE 0 END AS H,
 CASE WHEN EVENT_TYPE IN (14, 15) THEN 1 ELSE 0 END AS BB,
 CASE WHEN EVENT_TYPE=16 THEN 1 ELSE 0 END AS HBP,
 CASE WHEN SF_FLAG="T" THEN 1 ELSE 0 END AS SF,
 CASE WHEN SH_FLAG="T" THEN 1 ELSE 0 END AS SH,
 CASE WHEN AB_FLAG="T" THEN 1 ELSE 0 END AS AB
 FROM pbp.pbp2k) inner_query
group by res_batter_hand, res_pitcher_hand;
```

This query produces the following results on the 2000–2004 data:

```
+-----------------+------------------+--------+--------+--------+
| res_batter_hand | res_pitcher_hand | N      | AVG    | OBP    |
+-----------------+------------------+--------+--------+--------+
| L               | L                |  35258 | 0.2573 | 0.3273 |
| L               | R                | 169180 | 0.2742 | 0.3494 |
| R               | L                |  86645 | 0.2727 | 0.3392 |
| R               | R                | 163214 | 0.2646 | 0.3257 |
+-----------------+------------------+--------+--------+--------+
```

As you can see, lefty batters hit better against righty pitchers (.274 AVG and .345 OBP) than against lefty pitchers (.257 AVG and .327 OBP). Likewise, righty batters hit better against lefty pitchers (.273 AVG and .340 OBP) than against righty pitchers (.265 AVG and .326 OBP). That's about a 5% to 6% higher average in each case. With a sample size this large, this is clearly a statistically significant effect. I think that this observation is applied more than any other statistical observation in baseball.

Switch Hitters

I got curious about switch-hitters while reading Bill Ferber's *The Book on the Book* (St. Martin's Press), a recent book on baseball strategy with a chapter titled "The Vogue Era of Bad Switch-Hitters." The title says it all; Ferber thinks a lot of switch-hitters bat much better from one side than the other.

Most switch-hitters face lefties from the right side and righties from the left side. Is there a difference in the platoon effect if we take out switch-hitters? Do switch-hitters bat equally well from both sides?

To examine switch-hitters, I modified this query slightly. I joined the information from the pbp table with the rosters table to find batting hands. To keep the query from taking a week to run, I used temporary tables and indexes:

```
create temporary table temp_pbp as
    select res_batter, res_batter_hand, res_pitcher_hand,
    substr(game_id,4,4) as year,
    CASE WHEN hit_value > 0 THEN 1 ELSE 0 END AS H,
    CASE WHEN EVENT_TYPE IN (14, 15) THEN 1 ELSE 0 END AS BB,
    CASE WHEN EVENT_TYPE=16 THEN 1 ELSE 0 END AS HBP,
    CASE WHEN SF_FLAG="T" THEN 1 ELSE 0 END AS SF,
    CASE WHEN SH_FLAG="T" THEN 1 ELSE 0 END AS SH,
    CASE WHEN AB_FLAG="T" THEN 1 ELSE 0 END AS AB
    FROM pbp.pbp2k;

create temporary table temp_rosters as
    select year, retroid, bats from pbp.rosters
    group by year, retroid, bats;
```

```
create index rosters_idx on temp_rosters(year, retroid);
create index pbp_idx on temp_pbp(year, res_batter);

select res_pitcher_hand, res_batter_hand,  bats, count(*) as N,
    sum(H) / sum(AB) as AVG,
    SUM(H + BB + HBP) / SUM(AB + BB + HBP + SF) as OBP
from temp_pbp l inner join temp_rosters r
    on l.res_batter=r.retroid and l.year=r.year
group by res_batter_hand, res_pitcher_hand, bats;
```

The preceding code returns the following output:

```
+-----------------+-----------------+------+--------+--------+--------+
| res_pitcher_hand | res_batter_hand | bats | N      | AVG    | OBP    |
+-----------------+-----------------+------+--------+--------+--------+
| L               | L               | B    |     37 | 0.2667 | 0.3889 |
| L               | L               | L    |  34565 | 0.2579 | 0.3280 |
| R               | L               | B    |  57901 | 0.2671 | 0.3406 |
| R               | L               | L    | 109149 | 0.2780 | 0.3540 |
| L               | R               | B    |  21178 | 0.2667 | 0.3321 |
| L               | R               | R    |  63413 | 0.2746 | 0.3414 |
| R               | R               | B    |    136 | 0.2411 | 0.3411 |
| R               | R               | R    | 157637 | 0.2643 | 0.3254 |
+-----------------+-----------------+------+--------+--------+--------+
```

Notice how uncommon it is for switch-hitters to bat with the same hand as the pitcher; this happened much less than 1% of the time. We'll ignore these cases; they occur so rarely that the numbers aren't statistically significant.

Let's start by scrambling these results a little bit, to make it easier to compare how batters do against pitchers, based on hand. (I made these changes by hand.) First, let's focus on the statistics for switch-hitters. On average, switch-hitters bat almost identically against lefties and righties:

```
+-----------------+-----------------+------+--------+--------+--------+
| res_pitcher_hand | res_batter_hand | bats | N      | AVG    | OBP    |
+-----------------+-----------------+------+--------+--------+--------+
| L               | R               | B    |  21178 | 0.2667 | 0.3321 |
| R               | L               | B    |  57901 | 0.2671 | 0.3406 |
+-----------------+-----------------+------+--------+--------+--------+
```

Now, let's examine how switch-hitters fare compared to lefties and righties when facing lefthanded and righthanded pitchers:

```
+-----------------+-----------------+------+--------+--------+--------+
| res_pitcher_hand | res_batter_hand | bats | N      | AVG    | OBP    |
+-----------------+-----------------+------+--------+--------+--------+
| L               | L               | L    |  34565 | 0.2579 | 0.3280 |
| L               | R               | B    |  21178 | 0.2667 | 0.3321 |
| L               | R               | R    |  63413 | 0.2746 | 0.3414 |
| R               | L               | L    | 109149 | 0.2780 | 0.3540 |
| R               | L               | B    |  57901 | 0.2671 | 0.3406 |
| R               | R               | R    | 157637 | 0.2643 | 0.3254 |
+-----------------+-----------------+------+--------+--------+--------+
```

Against lefthanded pitchers, switch-hitters bat worse than righties but better than lefties. Against righthanded pitchers, switch-hitters bat better than lefties but worse than righties.

Hacking the Hack

More than anything else, I'm amazed by the symmetry of these statistics. If you'd like to take this analysis further, here are a few ideas:

Ballpark effects
> Baseball parks are often asymmetrical: Fenway Park has the Green Monster in left field, Yankee Stadium has the short right field porch, and Wrigley Field has those crooked corners. Some players hit better to one particular side of the field, so it might be interesting to see how platoon effects vary between ballparks.

Power differences
> Do switch-hitters often have more power from one side or the other?

Primary hand versus secondary hand for switch-hitters
> We know the throwing hand for each switch-hitter, which we can guess is the player's preferred hand. Do switch-hitters fare differently depending on their throwing hands?

Fielding and handedness
> Second basemen, third basemen, and shortstops are almost always righthanded. Lefties are stuck in the outfield or at first base because they are more likely to be lefty throwers. Lefties typically earn playing time by batting really well because defense isn't as valuable in these positions. (There is a greater difference in ability between, say, shortstops than first basemen. A manager will rarely pick a lousy defensive shortstop for his batting ability but will often pick a lousy defensive first baseman for his batting ability.) This means that major league lefties are, on average, better batters.

Opposing pitcher frequency
> Righthanded pitchers are much more common than lefthanded pitchers. So, lefties typically have more experience with righthanded pitchers than righties have with lefthanded pitchers.

H A C K

#63

Significant Number of At Bats

How to choose a threshold for a statistically significant number of at bats.

Here's a good trivia question for you: of all players who have played more than 15 seasons, who had the highest batting average? The answer is Michael Stanton. Yup, that's correct: lefthanded pitcher Mike Stanton (relief pitcher for the Braves, Mets, and Yankees between 1989 and 2005) had a career batting average of .421, making him the greatest batter of all time, better than Ted Williams, Babe Ruth, and Barry Bonds.

Obviously, I'm kidding; Stanton was not the greatest batter of all time. He got 8 hits in 19 at bats over a 16-year career, making him lucky. This is a problem with a lot of baseball statistics: how can you tell if they're significant? This hack explains how to think about this problem, and it shows a few things about baseball statistics that I think are remarkable.

Major League Baseball uses two thresholds to decide which players qualify for titles such as Highest Batting Average. (In case you're wondering, these are actually part of the Official Rules; see rule 10.23, if you're curious.) For batters, they require that a batter had an average of 3.1 at bats in every game of the season (that's about 502.2 at bats). For pitchers, they require that the pitcher pitched an average of one inning in each game played over the course of the season (that's 162 innings). Are these reasonable assumptions?

But often, baseball teams and announcers use less-stringent criteria when presenting data. At the beginning of the season, teams show batting averages based on very small numbers of at bats. In the middle of the season, announcers say things such as "He's been hitting .500 in his last 20 at bats." Are these numbers at all meaningful?

This hack shows you how to determine how precise these averages are, based on the number of at bats.

Find the Distribution of At Bats

As a first step, let's see how many at bats most players actually have in one year. (We don't want to set our standard too high or we could exclude some, or all, players!)

As an example, let's pick one season and look at the number of at bats for each player. You can do this analysis in Excel if you want (it's one row of numbers, and there are only about 1,000 of them), but this example uses R.

Let's start by loading the batting data into R using the procedure in "Load Text Files into R" [Hack #34]. Let's subset the at bat data for 2003 and attach the data frame for easy reference:

```
> batting2003 <- subset(batting, batting$yearID == 2003)
> attach(batting2003)
```

Next, let's look at the number of players in this data set, and the distribution of at bats:

```
> length(AB)
[1] 1347
```

```
> summary(AB)
   Min. 1st Qu.  Median    Mean 3rd Qu.    Max.
    0.0     1.0    18.0   123.8   189.0   682.0
```

So, 1,347 players were listed as batters in 2003. It looks as though a very large number of players had a very low number of at bats (we know that 25% of players had, at most, one!). Let's check the number of players with zero or one at bat:

```
> length(subset(AB, AB == 0))
[1] 327
> length(subset(AB, AB == 1))
[1] 82
```

Almost 25% of players in our table had zero or one at bats. You might wonder what's going on. Why does this "batting table" contain all of these players who have never batted? Who are these guys? To look at them, I selected them as a subset and used the edit( ) function in R to display the values. (Notice the R trick: I assigned the results to a variable called trash; otherwise, the edit( ) procedure would print the contents of the data frame to the console.)

```
trash <- edit(subset(batting2003, AB < 2))
```

Did these guys all have just walks? Were they only pinch runners? A quick look at the data shows an occasional 1 in the BB column (so a few did walk once) and a handful of stolen bases (SB) or failed attempts (CS), but that doesn't explain what these guys are doing here. Maybe all of these guys are pitchers. Let's check by calling out all the players with zero at bats, merging this table with the fielding table, and looking at the distribution of the position (Pos) variable:

```
> batting2003.0AB <- subset(batting2003, batting2003$AB == 0)
> batting2003.0AB.POS <- merge(batting2003.0AB, fielding, by="playerID")
> summary(batting2003.0AB.POS$Pos)
  1B   2B   3B    C   CF   DH   LF   OF    P   RF   SS
   0    0    0    0    0    3    0    6 1967    1    0
```

Yes, almost all of them are pitchers (with a handful of pinch runners and guys who walked once). Now, let's eliminate batters who were seen zero or one time and look at the remaining distribution:

```
> batting2003.ABgt1 <- subset(batting2003, batting2003$AB > 1)
> length(batting2003.ABgt1$playerID)
[1] 938
> attach(batting2003.ABgt1)
> summary(AB)
   Min. 1st Qu.  Median    Mean 3rd Qu.    Max.
    2.0    13.0    83.5   177.7   312.5   682.0
```

Hmmm, there are still a lot of players with very few at bats. Let's draw a couple of graphs to understand this better:

```
> # plot a histogram with bins of 20 AB and range of 0 to 700
> hist(AB, seq(0, 700, 20), prob=TRUE)
> # let's add a line showing the approximate density
> lines(density(AB, bw=10))
```

This shows a plot like the one in Figure 6-5. It looks as though there are still many, many players with fewer than 20 at bats.

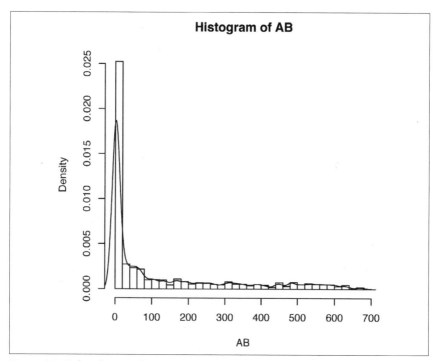

Figure 6-5. At bats bar graph

Statistical Significance

We still haven't gotten to the point of this hack yet, which is to ask, "How many at bats do we need to judge a batter accurately?" We want to estimate how many at bats are required to get a statistically significant sample. Here are the assumptions I am going to use:

Batting is a stochastic (nondeterministic, probabilistic) process
   This is a key assumption. We assume that every time a batter comes to the plate to bat, the results are somewhat random; they're not fated ahead of time. This is a subtle philosophical point. Each at bat is kind of like rolling dice, spinning a roulette wheel, or flipping a coin.

At bats are independent events
Any time a batter is given a chance to hit the ball, this event is not correlated with anything that has happened before. (In practice, this might not be a valid assumption: batters get to know pitchers over the course of a game or a season, and pitchers tire out over the course of a game. On the other hand, major league pitchers adjust their pitching during a game to counteract this effect.) In probability lingo, these are called *Bernoulli trials*.

The mean batting average in MLB is .260
From observed values, the mean batting average is about .260, meaning that the probability that a batter gets a hit in any at bat is p = .26.

Batting average is a good way to measure statistical significance of playing time
To help you understand why I am stating this assumption, I'll first explain why it's not a good assumption and then I'll explain why it makes things easier. In practice, really good batters don't always either put the ball in play or make an out. They walk. Really good players walk a lot; some players (like Jason Giambi) walk almost 15% of the time they bat. Walks aren't counted in at bats.

So, let's consider two players: Felix Freeswinger and Dirk Discipline. Felix never walks and has about a .300 batting average and a .300 OBP. Dirk walks all the time and has a .270 batting average but a .400 OBP. Suppose both of these guys come to the plate 720 times during a season. Felix Freeswinger will be credited with 720 at bats. Now let's consider Dirk Discipline. Dirk makes an out 60% of the time. That implies 432 outs this season. His batting average is .270, meaning that his rate of outs per at bat is .770. We can solve for his at bats by setting .770 * AB = 432, so Dirk would be credited with approximately 592 at bats per year.

As you can see, there is something a little fishy about this batting average thing and this "at bat" thing. It kind of seems as though comparing Felix and Dirk is like comparing apples and oranges. Dirk would need to come to the plate 840 times during the year if he was to have the same number of at bats as Felix.

Batting average is definitely not the best measurement, but it's intuitive and everyone knows it. If this bothers you, try to repeat this analysis with OBP.

Now, let's ask a simple question. Suppose the probability that a specific batter (let's call him Bert Batter) gets a hit during an at bat is .260. Clearly, he isn't always going to hit exactly the same number (batting is a probabilistic process, by assumption). It's very likely that he'll hit within a certain range.

We want to find the range for the number of hits we expect from Bert, given a certain number of at bats. We'd like to set bounds so that the probability that he hits outside the range is only 10% (5% of the time he hits more than the maximum number in the range, and 5% of the time he hits fewer than the minimum number in the range). These bounds are called *confidence intervals*.

The number of hits Bert will get in a season is determined by the binomial distribution. Let's use R to calculate a few confidence intervals for Bert's hits for a few different numbers of at bats. We'll pick 25, 50, 100, 200, 400, and 682 at bats for our calculations. (All of these are plausible numbers; 682 is the maximum anyone had in 2003.) We could work backward and determine the exact number of at bats required to estimate batting average with a specified accuracy (say, ±.05 with 90% confidence), but let's take a different approach. It's easy to calculate the values at the high and low ends of the range for a given sample size and probability, so that's what I'd like to try here.

We will use the R function qbinom(*p*, *size*, *prob*). This function returns the values at different quantiles (*p*) for a binomial distribution with a given number of observations (*size*) and a given probability (*prob*). The quantiles are specified in an array.

```
> qbinom(c(0.95, 0.05), 25, 0.260)
[1] 10  3
> qbinom(c(0.95, 0.05), 50, 0.260)
[1] 18  8
> qbinom(c(0.95, 0.05), 100, 0.260)
[1] 33 19
> qbinom(c(0.95, 0.05), 200, 0.260)
[1] 62 42
> qbinom(c(0.95, 0.05), 400, 0.260)
[1] 119  90
> qbinom(c(0.95, 0.05), 682, 0.260)
[1] 196 159
```

That looks like quite a range. Remember how R lets you divide a column by a single value? We'll divide each confidence interval (for a number of hits) by the number of at bats to give ranges for batting average:

```
> qbinom(c(0.95, 0.05), 25, 0.260) / 25
[1] 0.40 0.12
> qbinom(c(0.95, 0.05), 50, 0.260) / 50
[1] 0.36 0.16
> qbinom(c(0.95, 0.05), 100, 0.260) / 100
[1] 0.33 0.19
> qbinom(c(0.95, 0.05), 200, 0.260) / 200
[1] 0.31 0.21
```

```
> qbinom(c(0.95, 0.05), 400, 0.260) / 400
[1] 0.2975 0.2250
> qbinom(c(0.95, 0.05), 680, 0.260) / 680
[1] 0.2882353 0.2323529
>
```

The result is kind of shocking. Obviously, 25 at bats is a small number, but look at 200. An average batter can appear to be a terrible batter (.210 average) or a great batter (.310 average), just by chance. (In fact, 5% of average batters will hit above .310, and 5% will hit below .210, according to this model!)

Let's take another look at this problem. Suppose Bert has 200 at bats and gets fewer than 40 hits. What is the probability that this happens and that he is a .300 hitter, a .250 hitter, or a .200 hitter?

To answer this question, we will use the pbinom( ) function in R. This formula gives the distribution function. In this example, this corresponds to the probability that Bert got only 40 hits in 200 at bats, given that his "true" batting average was really .300, .250, or .200.

```
> pbinom(c(40), 200, 0.30)
[1] 0.0009283146
> pbinom(c(40), 200, 0.25)
[1] 0.05784983
> pbinom(c(40), 200, 0.20)
[1] 0.5421796
# Does that number seem a little odd to you? Did
# you expect the value to be about 50%? This is just
# a rounding problem; take a look at nearby values:
> pbinom(c(41), 200, 0.20)
[1] 0.6108329
> pbinom(c(39), 200, 0.20)
[1] 0.47181
```

Well, that's sort of comforting. A "true" .300 hitter (a guy who has a probability of getting a hit of .3) will hit less than .200 in 200 at bats with a probability of less than 0.1%. A true .250 hitter will hit .200 with a probability of about 6%. And a true .200 hitter will hit less than .200 about half of the time.

But that gets us back to our original question. How many at bats do we need to be comfortable? Suppose we want an answer that's correct within ±5% of the true value, with confidence intervals of 5% to 95%. For a batting average of .260, that means our estimate would need to be correct within a range of ±.013, or a range of .247 to .273. Here is the number I got after a little trial and error:

```
> qbinom(c(0.95, 0.05), 3000, 0.260) / 3000
[1] 0.2733333 0.2470000
```

Yes, that's right: 3,000 at bats. We're shooting too high; no player has more than 682 at bats! Let's shoot for a value that's correct to within ±10% of the true value, with confidence intervals of 10% to 90%. That's a range of .234 to .286.

```
> qbinom(c(0.9, 0.1), 500, 0.260) / 500
[1] 0.286 0.234
```

That's right: 500 at bats. (Notice that this answer is very close to the MLB standard of 3.1 at bats per game.) How many players had that many at bats?

```
> length(subset(batting2003.ABgt1$AB,batting2003.ABgt1$AB > 499))
[1] 103
> length(subset(batting2003.ABgt1$AB,batting2003.ABgt1$AB > 249))
[1] 286
> length(subset(batting2003.ABgt1$AB,batting2003.ABgt1$AB > 99))
[1] 446
```

Let's back into this the other way and ask what the confidence intervals would be with 100 at bats:

```
> qbinom(c(0.9, 0.1), 100, 0.260) / 100
[1] 0.32 0.20
> qbinom(c(0.8, 0.2), 100, 0.260) / 100
[1] 0.30 0.22
> qbinom(c(0.75, 0.25), 100, 0.260) / 100
[1] 0.29 0.23
```

Gosh, 50% of the time, Bert's average will be between .230 and .290, and 50% of the time it will be higher or lower. That's not very accurate. For 250 at bats, here is what we get:

```
> qbinom(c(0.90, 0.10), 250, 0.260) / 250
[1] 0.296 0.224
> qbinom(c(0.80, 0.20), 250, 0.260) / 250
[1] 0.284 0.236
> qbinom(c(0.75, 0.25), 250, 0.260) / 250
[1] 0.28 0.24
```

If I were short on data, I would be comfortable with a threshold of 250 at bats; that gives us an answer that is ±10% of the correct answer 80% of the time.

OBP, AVG, and accuracy. By the way, let's go back to Dirk Discipline and Felix Freeswinger for a minute. Clearly, Dirk is a greater asset to his team than Felix is, as Dirk makes an out far less frequently (432 outs for Dirk versus 504 for Felix). But another strange effect is at work here. Dirk is credited with only 592 at bats, compared to Felix's 720. This has some interesting implications for the expected range of their batting averages.

There is more variance with a smaller sample size. Because Dirk bats less frequently, we would expect his average to span over a wider range for the same confidence interval:

```
> qbinom(c(0.10, 0.90), 720, 0.300) / 720
[1] 0.2777778 0.3222222
> qbinom(c(0.10, 0.90), 592, 0.270) / 592
[1] 0.2466216 0.2939189
> .32222222 - .27777777
[1] 0.04444445
> .2939189 - .2466216
[1] 0.0472973
```

This is not a large difference, in practice. I doubt many batters are underappreciated because they walk a lot and get unlucky. But it's another reason not to like batting average.

Testing the hypothesis. Now that I've argued for a few pages about why we need a lot of at bats, it's time to answer the question about whether this actually makes any sense. The methodology we used here is a good way to test the hypothesis that independent at bats are independent events. In short, we would expect that batting averages for players are stable from year to year, but within a very wide range.

Let's consider only batters with more than 250 at bats. Let's pick data from three consecutive years—1999, 2000, and 2001—to use as an estimator of a hitter's "true" hitting probability. Then we'll look at each hitter's 2002 performance and check whether it is within the expected range.

To do this, we'll subset the variables we need from these four years and then merge them. Next, we'll use the qbinom( ) function in R to estimate the values at the 10th and 90th percentiles in the binomial distribution, using the players' average from 1999 to 2001 as an estimate of their "true" batting average. Then, we'll check each player's 2002 performance to see whether it is inside or outside the confidence interval. We would expect that 80% of players should perform within this interval. Finally, we will count the number of players whose average falls inside and outside the interval and check if *that* number falls within the expected interval for another binomial distribution (this one with 140 observations and p = 0.8).

```
> batting1999 <- subset(batting, batting$yearID == 1999 & batting$AB > 249,
    select=c("H", "AB","playerID"))
> batting2000 <- subset(batting, batting$yearID == 2000 & batting$AB > 249,
    select=c("H", "AB","playerID"))
> batting2001 <- subset(batting, batting$yearID == 2001 & batting$AB > 249,
    select=c("H", "AB","playerID"))
> batting2002 <- subset(batting, batting$yearID == 2002 & batting$AB > 249,
    select=c("H", "AB","playerID"))
```

```
> names(batting1999) <- c("H99", "AB99", "playerID")
> names(batting2000) <- c("H00", "AB00", "playerID")
> names(batting2001) <- c("H01", "AB01", "playerID")
> names(batting2002) <- c("H02", "AB02", "playerID")
> batting.test <- merge(merge(merge(batting1999, batting2000,
by="playerID"),
  batting2001, by="playerID"), batting2002, by="playerID")
> batting.test$sample.AVG <- (H99 + H00 + H01) / (AB99 + AB00 + AB01)
> batting.test$ci.p10 <- qbinom(c(0.1), batting.test$AB02, batting.
test$sample.AVG)
> batting.test$ci.p90 <- qbinom(c(0.9), batting.test$AB02, batting.
test$sample.AVG)
> batting.test$ci.low <- batting.test$H02 < batting.test$ci.p10
> batting.test$ci.high <- batting.test$H02 > batting.test$ci.p90
> # see what the expected range of confidence interval is
> qbinom(c(0.1, 0.9), 140, .8)
[1] 106 118
> summary(batting.test$ci.high | batting.test$ci.low)
   Mode   FALSE    TRUE   .
logical     106      34
# looks like it's within range, but barely
# check for symmetry
> summary(batting.test$ci.low)
   Mode   FALSE    TRUE
logical     111      29
> summary(batting.test$ci.high)
   Mode   FALSE    TRUE
logical     135       5
```

It appears that the overall test passed: the number of players whose expected 2002 AVG was within the expected confidence range was 75.7%, a little short of the expected 80% but within the 10% to 90% confidence interval that we're using today. The only problem is that the final distribution is a little asymmetrical: 29 players fell below the expected value and 5 were above. We can probably use some sort of time series analysis to refine the methodology here, but I'll leave that to advanced readers.

So, what was the point of all this? Well, first you should note that batting averages are very imprecise. You can't meaningfully quantify a player's total batting average at the end of a season to any better than ±10% with any degree of confidence.

This should also tell you something else about batting averages at the beginning of the season: they are totally insignificant. Next year, when you read about all the "breakthrough" players who have .400 averages in April, just ignore it. Here's a simple calculation:

```
> qbinom(c(0.95), 50, .30) / 50
[1] 0.4
```

meaning that, on average, 5% of players whose true hitting ability is a .300 average will hit .400 over the course of 50 at bats. Here's another quick calculation:

```
> qbinom(c(0.98), 50, .26) / 50
[1] 0.4
```

So, 2% of players (that's 1 in 50!) with average hitting ability will hit .400 over the course of 50 at bats.

HACK **#64** Find "Clutch" Players

Help find "clutch" players, if they really exist.

Perhaps no subject in baseball is more hotly contested than the concept of clutch players. If you want to start a fight with a member of the SABR statistics committee, insist that clutch players exist. Tell him they absolutely exist, beyond any doubt. Tell him Alex Rodriguez is obviously not a clutch player, and David Ortiz is a clutch player. If you want to start a fight with a traditional baseball fan, tell him there is no such thing as a clutch player. Tell him there is absolutely no statistical evidence that any player has ever performed better in "clutch" situations.

Making the debate even more contentious, Bill James recently switched sides. He used to be a clutch atheist ("there are no clutch players"), but recently he became a clutch agnostic ("we can't measure whether there are any clutch players"). (If you want to read the article, see *http://www.sabr.org/ cmsfiles/underestimating.pdf*.)

In this hack, I'll show you some quick ways to answer this question yourself using play-by-play data. Let's break down this problem into four parts: defining what makes a player a clutch player, measuring player performance in clutch situations, comparing player performance in clutch situations, and understanding the results.

Identify Clutch Players

The dictionary definition of *clutch* is "tending to be successful in tense or critical situations" (well, the relevant meaning). Here are a few examples of clutch situations:

Last batter in a game, with his team down by one point
    Suppose a team is down by one point, and a batter comes to the plate with two outs in the bottom of the ninth inning. If the player doesn't get a hit, the game will end.

Last game of the season for a pennant contender
Suppose a team is tied for first place in its division and it's the last game of the season. If the starting pitcher for that team performs badly, the team is less likely to make it to the playoffs.

A closing pitcher in a save situation
A closing pitcher always performs in save situations; if he fails to hold the lead, his team risks losing the game.

Late inning pressure situations
One standard way to quantify clutch situations is *late inning pressure* (LIP) situations. (The Elias Sports Bureau invented this term and publishes statistics for batters hitting in these situations.) A batter is hitting in an LIP situation if the game is tied, or if his team is trailing by one, two, or three runs, in the seventh inning or later.

Let's focus on clutch situations by batters and leave aside clutch performances by pitchers or teams. We want to pick a definition of clutch situations that is broad enough to provide a reasonable sample size for measuring player ability, but is narrow enough so that players' performances can really be considered clutch. For example, if a team is losing by 10 runs in the bottom of the ninth inning, a bad performance by a batter doesn't really matter. A batter shouldn't feel too much pressure in that situation because his team is likely to lose anyway. A definition that includes this situation would be too broad. On the other hand, if we include only those situations in which a team is losing by one point in the bottom of the ninth inning with two outs, the definition would be way too narrow.

A convenient way to define clutch situations might be to just say that a batter is hitting in a clutch situation if the pitcher is pitching in a save situation. A relief pitcher is in a save situation if he has the opportunity to be the finishing pitcher and one of the following occurs:

- He enters the game with a lead of three or fewer runs and has the opportunity to pitch for one full inning.
- He enters the game with the potential tying run on base, at bat, or on deck.
- He pitches three or more innings, regardless of the score, and the official scorer credits him with a save.

In this book, let's keep it simple and say that a batter is batting in a clutch situation if it's at least the ninth inning and his team trails by one, two, or three runs.

Measure Player Performance in Clutch Situations

The second step in measuring clutch performances is to find all situations in which a player is batting in a clutch situation and measure the player's performance in those situations. You could measure all types of different statistics in these situations: batting average, slugging average, isolated power, batting runs, etc. In this book, we'll just focus on OBP: the number of times a player makes it on base in these situations. I'll call this stat cOBP (clutch OBP).

Compare Players

There's one last question to answer here: what's considered a good performance in these clutch situations? Does a player have to perform better in clutch situations than in average situations to be considered a clutch player? Does he have to perform better than his peers do? Does he just have to perform no worse in these situations?

I think the best approach is to measure the ratio of a player's OBP in clutch situations to all situations (cOBP / OBP) and compare a player's ratio to other ratios in the league.

Understanding the Results

We're not done yet. Suppose one player with a .350 OBP overall had 10 plate appearances in clutch situations and got on base 5 times. This implies a cOBP of .500. Clearly, this player did pretty well in clutch situations. But is this meaningful? Could this player actually not be a clutch player? If we put him in 1,000 clutch situations, is it possible that his cOBP would be only .100?

The Code

Let's start out by using SQL to identify all of the clutch situations in the 2004 play-by-play data. We'll use the event_type_code field to calculate OBP directly for each player. I use a few SQL tricks here to make this statement short. I use an IN statement to check event_type against a list of ways to get on base and ways to end a plate appearance, I use an if( ) statement that returns 1 or 0, and I use a SUM statement to sum the results. This is a quick way to count the number of plays matching each case.

Here's a quick way to count the OBP in all clutch (and non-clutch) situations during 2004. Enter the following code into a SQL client:

```
select count(*) as N, count(distinct res_batter) as N_batters,
    -- Event type codes:
```

```
--   0  =>  Unknown event, 1 =>  No event, 2  =>  Generic out
--   3  =>  Strikeout, 4  =>  Stolen base, 5  =>  Defensive indifference
--   6  =>  Caught stealing, 7  =>  Pickoff error, 8  =>  Pickoff
--   9  =>  Wild pitch, 10 =>  Passed ball, 11 =>  Balk
--   12 =>  Other advance, 13 =>  Foul error, 14 =>  Walk
--   15 =>  Intentional walk, 16 =>  Hit by pitch, 17 =>  Interference
--   18 =>  Error, 19 =>  Fielder's choice, 20 =>  Single
--   21 =>  Double, 22 => Triple, 23 => Home run, 24 => Missing play
  sum(if(event_type IN (14,15,16,20,21,22,23),1,0)) /
  sum(if(event_type IN (2,3,5,14,15,16,17,18,19,20,21,22,23),1,0)) as OBP,
  if(batting_team=1,
      vis_score - home_score IN (1, 2, 3),
      vis_score - home_score IN (1, 2, 3)) AND
  inning >= 9 as clutch_situation
from pbp.pbp2k where substring(game_id,4,4)="2004") and visiting_team != ''
group by clutch_situation
;
```

The preceding code returns the following results:

```
N         N_batters    OBP       clutch_situation
------    -----------  -------   -------------------
191157    960          0.33214   0
5897      573          0.31547   1
```

Notice something worrying: the average number of plate appearances for a batter in non-clutch situations was 191,157 / 960 ≈ 200, and the average number of plate appearances in clutch situations was 5,897 / 573 ≈ 10.

Also, notice that the mean OBP is very similar in both situations but is slightly lower in clutch situations. This is probably an artifact of the way that I defined clutch situations as the counterpart to save situations. Most teams ask their closer to pitch in save situations. Most teams select their best relief pitcher to be their closer, so it's not surprising that batters have a hard time reaching base in these situations.

Next, let's calculate statistics for each player. Let's start by creating indexes on the play-by-play and master tables so that we can quickly match name information to players:

```
create index fullpbp2004_btridx on fullpbp2004(res_batter);
create temporary table master_w_pbpid_tmp as select * from master_w_pbpid;
create index master_w_pbpid_tmp_idx on master_w_pbpid_tmp(pbpID);
```

Now, let's calculate a table of statistics for each batter:

```
create table pbp.clutch_obps as
select
  sum(if(p.clutch_situation=1, OBP, 0)) as clutchOBP,
  sum(if(p.clutch_situation=0, OBP, 0)) as otherOBP,
  sum(if(p.clutch_situation=1, N, 0)) as clutchN,
  sum(if(p.clutch_situation=0, N, 0)) as otherN,
  p.res_batter, r.lastName, r.firstName
```

```
from (select count(*) as N,
        sum(if(event_type IN (14,15,16,20,21,22,23),1,0)) /
        sum(if(event_type IN (2,3,5,14,15,16,17,18,19,20,21,22,23),1,0)) as OBP,
        if(batting_team=1,
            vis_score - home_score IN (1, 2, 3),
            home_score - vis_score IN (1, 2, 3)) AND
        inning >= 9 as clutch_situation, res_batter
        from pbp.pbp2k
        where substring(game_id,4,4)="2004"
            and res_batter != '' and visiting_team != ''
        group by res_batter, clutch_situation
    ) p inner join pbp.rosters r
        on p.res_batter=r.retroID
    group by p.res_batter, r.lastName, r.firstName;
```

Top players in clutch situations. You can show which players performed best in clutch situations by querying this table. But first let's try to come up with a fair number of clutch at bats to make the list. Let's examine this table from R. Type this code into R to load the RODBC library and fetch this table:

```
> library(RODBC)
> channel <- odbcConnect("pbp")
> clutch.obps <- sqlFetch(channel, "clutch_obps")
> attach(clutch.obps)
```

First, look at the number of times each player bats in clutch situations:

```
> summary(clutchN)
   Min. 1st Qu. Median   Mean 3rd Qu.   Max.
  0.000   0.000  2.000  5.826 11.000  31.000
```

This is very low, compared to the number of at bats in non-clutch situations:

```
> summary(otherN)
   Min. 1st Qu. Median   Mean 3rd Qu.   Max.
    1.0    8.0   76.0  198.6  359.3  796.0
```

Let's pick a threshold of 11 at bats (yielding 25% of players) to make our list of the top clutch performers. Type the following SQL code into your database client to give the top 10 clutch performers in 2004:

```
mysql> select nameFirst, nameLast, clutchOBP, clutchN, otherOBP, otherN
    -> from pbp.clutch_obps
    -> where clutchN > 10
    -> order by clutchOBP DESC LIMIT 10;
```

nameFirst	nameLast	clutchOBP	clutchN	otherOBP	otherN
Hee Seop	Choi	0.61538	13	0.35891	409
Mark	Loretta	0.58824	18	0.38406	716
Mike	Cuddyer	0.58333	12	0.33420	396
Aubrey	Huff	0.57143	22	0.34969	684
Jim	Thome	0.57143	14	0.39238	635
Mark	Bellhorn	0.57143	16	0.36921	695
Juan	Rivera	0.56250	16	0.35610	421

```
| Corey    | Patterson | 0.52941 | 17 | 0.31343 | 681 |
| Michael  | Tucker    | 0.52632 | 19 | 0.34280 | 542 |
| Ryan     | Klesko    | 0.52632 | 19 | 0.39009 | 474 |
+----------+-----------+---------+---------+---------+--------+
10 rows in set (0.01 sec)
```

Significant clutch performances. As you can see, each of them performed better in clutch situations than they did normally, so these guys deserve some credit.

But why did they perform well in these situations? Were they really "clutch" players, who could pull something extra out of themselves when the game was on the line? Were they players who didn't try as hard as they could in ordinary, "non-clutch" situations? Or did they get really lucky and just get on base a lot when their teams needed them?

One way to look at this question is to ask if this is a statistically significant difference. Let's use a simple test to find out. Suppose a player performs the same in clutch situations as he does in other situations. (This is called the *null hypothesis* in statistics lingo.) Based on the player's OBP in non-clutch situations and the number of at bats in clutch situations, a player would be expected to have an OBP within a narrow range.

As an example, consider Jim Thome's performance in clutch situations. We'd expect him to reach base with a probability of .392 in non-clutch situations. What are the 90% confidence intervals for Jim Thome, given his 14 at bats in clutch situations? Let's use the qbinom( ) function in R to calculate this value:

```
> qbinom(c(0.05, 0.95), 14, .392) / 14
[1] 0.2142857 0.6428571
```

Here's how to understand what this means. Suppose we could place Jim Thome in a clutch situation anytime we wanted to see how he batted. Now, suppose we play the following game. First, we place Jim Thome in a clutch situation 14 times, then we calculate his OBP. If we played this game over and over again, over time we would have a set of different OBPs. This equation means that 90% of the time, Jim Thome's OBP will be between .214 and .643 in these games.

So, what does this mean to us? Suppose we want to be 90% sure that Jim Thome batted exceptionally well in clutch situations. Then, he'd need an OBP of more than .643. In actuality, he batted only .571. That doesn't mean he wasn't a clutch player, it just means that we can't be sure with that degree of confidence. If we lower our standards a little bit (to be only 80% sure), here are the bounds we get:

```
> qbinom(c(0.1, 0.9), 14, .392) / 14
[1] 0.2142857 0.5714286
```

By these standards, Jim Thome had an exceptional performance.

If you want to find all players with exceptional clutch performances, you can do this in R. Simply calculate a threshold for an exceptional performance from the binomial distribution and then select only those players whose performance exceeded the threshold. Here is the R code to show these players:

```
> clutch.obps$threshold <- qbinom(c(.95), clutchN, otherOBP) / clutchN
> attach(clutch.obps)
> subset(clutch.obps, clutchOBP > threshold & clutchN > 10)
    clutchOBP otherOBP clutchN otherN res_batter nameLast nameFirst
51    0.57143  0.36921      16    695   bellhma1  Bellhorn      Mark
435   0.57143  0.34969      22    684   huffau1       Huff    Aubrey
541   0.58824  0.38406      18    716   loretma1   Loretta      Mark
874   0.52632  0.34280      19    542   tuckemi1    Tucker   Michael

     threshold
51   0.5625000
435  0.5000000
541  0.5555556
874  0.5263158
```

By the way, only about 100 players had 11 or more plate appearances in these situations. That means about 5% of players performed outside the 90% confidence range. This, by the way, is completely consistent with what we would expect if these performances were random.

 # Calculate Expected Number of Wins
HACK #65
Use Pythagorean Wins formulas to estimate the expected number of wins for a team, given their other statistics.

Ultimately, baseball comes down to wins. Winning is what the game is all about, and the only reason to measure anything else (batting, pitching, or fielding) is to measure its effect on wins.

Win estimates can be useful for measuring how lucky or unlucky a team was. (A lucky team will exceed its expected number of wins, and an unlucky team will have fewer wins.)

Many fans have developed different formulas for estimating the expected number of wins based on different statistics. In this hack, I'll show a couple of the most popular formulas for estimating the number of wins and losses.

The Pythagorean Wins Formula

Bill James invented a formula for expected wins that has been nicknamed Pythagorean Wins (because of its resemblance to the Pythagorean theorem). The idea of this formula is that the expected win/loss ratio for a team is proportional to the square of runs scored to runs allowed:

$$E\left(\frac{W}{L}\right) = \left(\frac{R}{RA}\right)^2$$

How well does this equation do in practice? First, let's solve for the expected number of wins using this formula:

$$E\left(\frac{W}{L}\right) = \frac{E(W)}{E(L)} = \frac{E(W)}{G - E(W)}$$

$$\frac{E(W)}{G - E(W)} = \left(\frac{R}{RA}\right)^2$$

$$E(W) = (G - E(W)) \cdot \left(\frac{R}{RA}\right)^2$$

$$E(W) \cdot \left(1 + \left(\frac{R}{RA}\right)^2\right) = G \cdot \left(\frac{R}{RA}\right)^2$$

$$E(W) = G \cdot \frac{\left(\frac{R}{RA}\right)^2}{1 + \left(\frac{R}{RA}\right)^2}$$

The code. Let's measure the effectiveness of this formula using R. First, let's load the team data and create a subset of the 2004 data:

```
> library(RODBC)
> channel <- odbcConnect('bballdata')
> teams <- sqlFetch(channel,'teams')
> teams2004 <- subset(teams, yearID==2004)
> attach(teams2004)
```

Now, let's calculate the expected wins for each team in 2004 based on runs scored and allowed, using these formulas:

```
> teams2004$expWLratio <- (R / RA) ^ 2
> teams2004$expW <- G * (teams2004$expWLratio / (1 + teams2004$expWLratio))
> teams2004$difference <- W - teams2004$expW
```

Here are the results:

```
> subset(teams2004, select=c("teamID", "W", "expW", "difference"))
       teamID  W      expW  difference
2446     ANA  92  91.48060  0.51939641
2447     ARI  51  51.64456 -0.64456106
2448     ATL  96  95.74326  0.25673834
2449     BAL  78  82.16262 -4.16261954
2450     BOS  98  97.88977  0.11022896
```

```
2451   CHA  83   84.24634  -1.24633684
2452   CHN  89   94.71592  -5.71592474
2453   CIN  76   65.78715  10.21285364
2454   CLE  80   81.09446  -1.09446061
2455   COL  68   72.71879  -4.71879225
2456   DET  72   79.35206  -7.35205566
2457   FLO  83   83.05609  -0.05608618
2458   HOU  92   92.27726  -0.27726007
2459   KCA  58   62.79290  -4.79290428
2460   LAN  93   89.60808   3.39191692
2461   MIL  67   66.37393   0.62606756
2462   MIN  92   88.03019   3.96981132
2463   MON  67   65.67803   1.32196914
2464   NYA 101   89.43333  11.56667396
2465   NYN  71   75.62501  -4.62501135
2466   OAK  91   86.37648   4.62352458
2467   PHI  86   86.88856  -0.88855933
2468   PIT  72   73.27863  -1.27863172
2469   SDN  87   87.91607  -0.91606562
2470   SEA  63   67.77571  -4.77570752
2471   SFN  91   88.98054   2.01946176
2472   SLN 105  101.62657   3.37343153
2473   TBA  70   67.34481   2.65519380
2474   TEX  89   87.45405   1.54594770
2475   TOR  67   69.69055  -2.69054501
```

As you can see, this formula does a pretty good job of predicting wins. The mean values for wins and expected wins are almost the same:

```
> mean(W)
[1] 80.93333
> mean(expW)
[1] 80.90141
```

The differences from the expected totals are mostly just a few games apart:

```
> summary(difference)
    Min.   1st Qu.   Median     Mean   3rd Qu.     Max.
-7.35200  -2.33800  -0.16670  0.03192  1.90100  11.5700
```

The Pythagenport Formula

The Pythagorean Wins formula works pretty well, but Clay Davenport of Baseball Prospectus developed an improved version of this formula, nicknamed the Pythagenport formula:

$$E\left(\frac{W}{G}\right) = \frac{R^p}{R^p + RA^p}$$

$$p \equiv 1.5 \cdot \log_{10}\left(\frac{R + RA}{G}\right) + 0.45$$

(Notice that this formula gives the expected winning percentage, not the expected ratio of wins.) Let's see how this formula compares to Pythagorean Wins:

```
> p <- 1.5 * log10((R + RA) / G) + 0.45
> expWPctpthgnprt <- R ^ p / (R ^ p + RA ^ p)
> teams2004$expWpthgnprt <- expWPctpthgnprt * G
> teams2004$pthgnprtErr <- W – teams2004$expWpthgnprt
> teams2004$pthgrnErr <- W - expW
> subset(teams2004, select=c("teamID", "W", "expW", "pthgrnErr",
"expWpthgnprt", "pthgnprtErr"))
```

	teamID	W	expW	pthgrnErr	expWpthgnprt	pthgnprtErr
2446	ANA	92	91.48060	0.51939641	91.11548	0.88451550
2447	ARI	51	51.64456	-0.64456106	52.90926	-1.90926007
2448	ATL	96	95.74326	0.25673834	94.92833	1.07166652
2449	BAL	78	82.16262	-4.16261954	82.14552	-4.14552080
2450	BOS	98	97.88977	0.11022896	97.79041	0.20959048
2451	CHA	83	84.24634	-1.24633684	84.21369	-1.21369086
2452	CHN	89	94.71592	-5.71592474	93.90454	-4.90454136
2453	CIN	76	65.78715	10.21285364	66.04937	9.95062545
2454	CLE	80	81.09446	-1.09446061	81.09385	-1.09385246
2455	COL	68	72.71879	-4.71879225	72.70845	-4.70845459
2456	DET	72	79.35206	-7.35205566	79.37661	-7.37660987
2457	FLO	83	83.05609	-0.05608618	82.91555	0.08445277
2458	HOU	92	92.27726	-0.27726007	91.72184	0.27815772
2459	KCA	58	62.79290	-4.79290428	63.21545	-5.21545452
2460	LAN	93	89.60808	3.39191692	89.07603	3.92396899
2461	MIL	67	66.37393	0.62606756	67.38085	-0.38085290
2462	MIN	92	88.03019	3.96981132	87.67223	4.32777034
2463	MON	67	65.67803	1.32196914	66.75160	0.24839528
2464	NYA	101	89.43333	11.56667396	89.36347	11.63652973
2465	NYN	71	75.62501	-4.62501135	75.99528	-4.99527547
2466	OAK	91	86.37648	4.62352458	86.14831	4.85168999
2467	PHI	86	86.88856	-0.88855933	86.74303	-0.74302506
2468	PIT	72	73.27863	-1.27863172	73.74564	-1.74564399
2469	SDN	87	87.91607	-0.91606562	87.53061	-0.53060504
2470	SEA	63	67.77571	-4.77570752	68.36789	-5.36788823
2471	SFN	91	88.98054	2.01946176	88.78227	2.21772942
2472	SLN	105	101.62657	3.37343153	100.69501	4.30409284
2473	TBA	70	67.34481	2.65519380	67.81181	2.18818532
2474	TEX	89	87.45405	1.54594770	87.33685	1.66314973
2475	TOR	67	69.69055	-2.69054501	70.10792	-3.10791906

Let's compare the average errors for each formula:

```
> summary(teams2004$pthgrnErr)
    Min.  1st Qu.   Median     Mean  3rd Qu.      Max.
-7.35200 -2.33800 -0.16670  0.03192  1.90100  11.57000
> summary(teams2004$pthgnprtErr)
   Min. 1st Qu.  Median    Mean 3rd Qu.     Max.
-7.3770 -2.8080 -0.1482  0.0134  2.0570  11.6400
```

Looking at the residual values, we see that both formulas are very slightly biased (overestimating the number of wins), that the range of residuals from both formulas is very similar, and that the Pythagenport formula is a little bit better.

The Back-of-the-Envelope Method

Pete Palmer points out a simple formula for estimating the number of expected wins for a team:

$$E(W) \approx \frac{R - RA}{10} + 81$$

The nice thing about this formula is that you can estimate wins without using a calculator. Amazingly, this method is almost as accurate as the Pythagorean Wins method:

```
> boeW <- (R - RA) / 10 + 81
> teams2004$boeW <- boeW
> teams2004$boeDiff <- W - boeW
> teams2004$pythDiff <- W - teams2004$expW
> summary(teams2004$boeDiff)
    Min. 1st Qu.  Median    Mean 3rd Qu.    Max.
-7.30000 -3.35000 -0.75000 -0.06667 1.72500 11.10000
> summary(teams2004$pythDiff)
    Min. 1st Qu.  Median    Mean 3rd Qu.    Max.
-7.35200 -2.33800 -0.16670  0.03192 1.90100 11.57000
```

Measure Hits by Pitch Count
HACK #66   Determine whether pitchers are more effective earlier in games than they are later.

In Game 7 of the 2003 American League Championship Series, Pedro Martinez was dominant. In the first seven innings of the game, Pedro allowed the Yankees to score only two runs. The Red Sox were leading the game, 5 to 2. Pedro got the first batter (Nick Johnson) to pop out to short, but then he allowed Derek Jeter to hit a one-out double. Red Sox fans knew that Pedro became less effective after pitching his first 80 pitches, and, at this point in the game, he was well over that mark. Red Sox manager Grady Little decided to stick with his ace. Bernie Williams hit a single to center, scoring Jeter. Matsui then hit a double, followed by a double from Posada to tie the game.

The rest is history. The game went into extra innings and ended with a walk-off home run by Aaron Boone; the Yankees went on to lose the World Series, and Grady Little lost his job.

Part of the "conventional wisdom" of baseball is that pitchers become less effective as the game progresses. This is partly because pitchers tire out and can't throw the ball as hard (or can't follow through as well on their pitches), and partly because batters learn to recognize what the pitcher is throwing. But is this true?

This hack shows you how to use play-by-play data to examine what happens to starting pitchers as a game progresses.

The Code

To show how a pitcher performs as a game progresses, you need to calculate a cumulative pitch count. The first step in calculating a pitch count is to filter the pitch sequence strings, to remove pickoff throws, stolen bases, and other things that aren't really pitches. You can do this in SQL using a procedure like this:

```
create view fullpbp2003_w_npitches as
select game_id, res_pitcher, batting_team, event_type, outs,
  event_num, event_text, pitch_sequence,
  length(
    replace(
      replace(
        replace(
          replace(
            replace(
              replace(
                replace(pitch_sequence,
                        '>',''), -- runner going on pitch
                  '.',''), -- play not involving the batter
                '1',''), -- throw to first
              '2',''), -- throw to second
            '3',''), -- throw to third
          'N',''), -- no pitch (on balks and interference calls)
        'V','') -- called ball because pitcher went to mouth
    ) as npitches
from pbp.pbp2k
where substring(game_id,4,4)="2003");
```

The second step is to calculate the cumulative pitch count. We need to make sure not to calculate duplicate pitches, so we include only records that either end the inning or end a plate appearance. There is a trick for doing this in SQL: a self-join. You join a table with itself and add a where clause to restrict the set of records with which you join any given record. Here's an example of how to do this:

```
create index fullpbp2003_idx on fullpbp2003(game_id, batting_team,
  event_num, res_pitcher);
select l.game_id, l.res_pitcher, l.batting_team,
  sum(r.npitches) as cum_pitches
```

```
from fullpbp2003_w_npitches l inner join fullpbp2003_w_npitches r
on l.game_id=r.game_id and l.res_pitcher=r.res_pitcher and l.batting_team=r.
batting_team
where r.event_num <= l.event_num and
    (-- caught stealing or pickoff with two outs
    (r.event_type IN (6, 8) and r.outs=2) or
    -- ball in play
    r.event_type IN (2,3,14,15,17,18,19,20,21,22,23))
group by l.game_id, l.res_pitcher, l.batting_team;
```

Unfortunately, this method takes a very, very long time to run. (I stopped this query after it ran for 10 minutes.) All of that self-joining takes time, and MySQL isn't very smart about using indexes to optimize operations like this. A faster way to calculate cumulative pitch counts is to use a procedural language. We know that the play-by-play tables are sorted by event number, so we can count just the number of pitches as we read through the table.

To solve this problem, let's use a Perl script. This script reads all of the plays in 2003, determines the starting pitchers, and saves the results in hashes by game and event number. It then calculates the cumulative pitch counts while writing the output results to standard output.

```
use DBI;
use DBD::mysql;

my $dsn = "DBI:mysql:host=localhost;database=pbp";
my $dbh = DBI->connect($dsn, "jadler", "", {PrintError => 0, RaiseError =>
1});

my $query = "SELECT * FROM fullpbp2003_w_npitches";

my $sth = $dbh->prepare($query);
$sth->execute( );
while (my $ref = $sth->fetchrow_hashref ( )) {
    $game_id = $ref->{game_id};
    $batting_team = $ref->{batting_team};
    $event_num = $ref->{event_num};
    if (!defined($starting_pitchers{$game_id}[$batting_team])) {
    $starting_pitchers{$game_id}[$batting_team] = $ref->{res_pitcher};
    }
    if ($ref->{res_pitcher} eq $starting_pitchers{$game_id}[$batting_team])
{
    $pitch_counts{$game_id}{$event_num} = $ref->{npitches};
    $outcomes{$game_id}{$event_num} = $ref->{event_type};
    $batting_teams{$game_id}{$event_num} = $ref->{batting_team};
    $events{$game_id}{$event_num} = $ref->{event_text};
    }
}
```

```
print "gameid,starter,pitch_count,event_type,pitches,event_text\n";
foreach $game_id (keys %pitch_counts) {
    $cumulative_pitch_count[0] = 0;
    $cumulative_pitch_count[1] = 0;
    $start[0] = $starting_pitchers{$game_id}[0];
    $start[1] = $starting_pitchers{$game_id}[1];
    foreach $event_num (sort keys %{$pitch_counts{$game_id}}) {
        $batting_team = $batting_teams{$game_id}{$event_num};
        $cumulative_pitch_count[$batting_team]
            = $cumulative_pitch_count[$batting_team] +
            $pitch_counts{$game_id}{$event_num};
        print "$game_id,"
            , $start[$batting_team], ","
            , $cumulative_pitch_count[$batting_team], ","
            , $outcomes{$game_id}{$event_num}, ","
            , $pitch_counts{$game_id}{$event_num}, ","
            , $events{$game_id}{$event_num}, "\n";
    }
}
```

This script outputs a file with a game ID, a player ID, a pitch count at the start of the at bat, the number of pitches during the at bat, an event type, and a description of the event.

Running the Hack

Save this script in a file called *hits_by_pitchcount_2003.pl* and run it with the following command:

```
% perl hits_by_pitchcount_2003.pl > pitchcounts2003.csv
```

(Incidentally, this script took 12 seconds to run on my iMac G5.) This script output 127,204 lines, which is unfortunate because it means this file is too big to analyze in Excel. To deal with this data, we'll need to use another tool to work with it. Well, at least, we'll need to use a tool to do a little preprocessing so that we can use Excel later because it's going to be easiest to work with the results if we can get them into a pivot table.

Let's start by pulling this data back into MySQL. The easiest way to do this is to use the script from "Load Baseball Data into MySQL" [Hack #20] to generate the import code. You can generate the import code and load the file with the following commands:

```
% perl check_field_sizes.pl -h -s "," -i pitchcounts2003.csv >
pitchcounts2003.sql
% mysql pbp < pitchcounts2003.sql
```

Let's shrink this table by summarizing how each pitcher performed, depending on the pitch count at the start of the at bat. We'll break these pitch counts into bands of 10 (0–9, 10–19, 20–29, etc.) using the floor function, and then we'll count the number of hits, walks, and plate appearances.

```
create index pitchcounts2003_idx on pitchcounts2003(starter);

create temporary table names
as select nameLast, nameFirst, pbpID
from master_w_pbpid;
create index names_idx on names(pbpID);

select nameFirst, nameLast,
    floor(pitch_count / 10) * 10 as pitch_count_band,
    count(*) as opportunities,
    sum(if(event_type IN (20,21,22,23), 1, 0)) as hits,
    sum(if(event_type IN (14,15,16), 1, 0)) as walks
from pitchcounts2003 l inner join master_w_pbpid r
on l.starter=r.pbpID
group by nameFirst, nameLast, floor(pitch_count / 10) * 10
;
```

This new table has 3,538 rows of cuts, perfect for pivot tables in Excel. You can run the query in your database query tool (such as your MySQL Query tool), copy the results of the query, and paste them into Excel. To make the analysis easy, select the whole table in Excel and then select PivotTable Report... from the Data menu. Click Finish to end the wizard (just accept the default values). Next, drag pitch_count_band to the "drag rows here" section of the pivot table, and drag opportunities onto the "drag data fields here" section of the pivot table.

To make this easier to read, let's add a couple of calculated fields to this pivot table. Calculated fields are a great feature because they allow you to calculate values, such as averages, dynamically, based upon the counts in the table. (You don't get the right result if you just calculate averages in MySQL. Using calculated fields gives you the properly weighted answer.)

To add calculated fields, select Calculated Field... from the Formulas submenu of the PivotTable menu on the Pivot Table palette. An illustration of this dialog box is shown in Figure 6-6. (Alternately, you can right-click on the pivot table to reach this dialog box.) Enter an expression on the Formula line and a name for the field in the Name box, and click the Insert Field button to add the field. Click OK when finished.

Let's create two fields: an approximate batting average (hits divided by opportunities minus walks) and OBP (hits plus walks divided by opportunities). If you like, you can change the number format of these fields through the Field Settings menu option in the PivotTable menu, and change the number format.

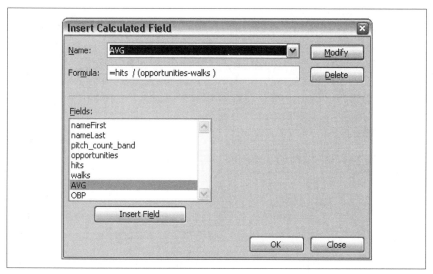

Figure 6-6. Insert Calculated Field dialog box

Now that we have the data in a pivot table, let's calculate a few neat things. First, let's break this down by pitcher. Drag the nameLast and nameFirst fields onto the "drag page fields here" section of the pivot table. You can now select results for specific pitchers through these menus. Let's pick Pedro Martinez, to see how his performance changes by pitch count. Figure 6-7 shows Pedro's performance by pitch count.

As you can see, his performance early in the game was phenomenal: opponents averaged less than .200 against him when his pitch count was less than 60 (pitch_count_bands of 0 through 50), but he began to slip as his pitch count increased. There are a couple of exceptions: pitches 90–99 and 120–129. We can explain these partly through statistical significance and partly by noting that Pedro was allowed to pitch deep into games only if he was pitching phenomenally well.

Let's add a chart to make this table easier to read. First, open the Pivot Table Options dialog box (either by right-clicking on the table or from the Pivot-Table menu) and remove the Grand Total fields (they clutter the charts). Next, select the whole table and click the Chart button to open the Chart wizard. (To select the whole table, try clicking cell A4.) Select a line chart and click Finish to close the wizard and view the chart.

You'll notice a problem with the chart: you can't read the averages (which go up to only .50) and the opportunities (which go up to 82) on the same chart. To fix this problem, we'll move the opportunities to a second axis.

	Microsoft Excel - pitch counts pivot charts.xls					

File Edit View Insert Format Tools Data Window Help   Type a question for help

Verdana   10   B I U

B6   fx 60

	A	B	C	D	E	F
1	nameLast	Martinez				
2	nameFirst	Pedro				
3						
4		Data				
5	pitch_count_band	Sum of opportunities	Sum of AVG	Sum of OBP		
6	0	60	0.133	0.133		
7	10	75	0.186	0.240		
8	20	70	0.188	0.257		
9	30	69	0.197	0.290		
10	40	80	0.187	0.238		
11	50	67	0.188	0.224		
12	60	79	0.253	0.291		
13	70	65	0.237	0.308		
14	80	82	0.264	0.354		
15	90	51	0.143	0.176		
16	100	35	0.303	0.343		
17	110	19	0.353	0.421		
18	120	10	0.000	0.300		
19	130	2	0.500	0.500		
20						
21						

Sheet4 / Sheet1 / Sheet2 / Sheet3 /

Ready   SCRL

Figure 6-7. Pivot table of Pedro's performance

Select the opportunities line by clicking on it, and select "format data series" by right clicking on the line. Go to the Axis pan and select Secondary Axis. This will make the graph readable. See Figure 6-8 for an example chart (I changed the formatting so that it would look OK in print). As you can see, opponents did have an easier time hitting off Pedro in later innings.

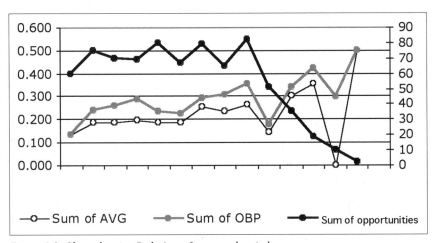

Figure 6-8. Chart showing Pedro's performance by pitch

Hacking the Hack

Is Pedro's performance typical? To find out, let's show the same chart for all pitchers. You can just deselect the nameFirst and nameLast values, and the chart will change to reflect this. You should see a chart such as the one shown in Figure 6-9. Somewhat surprisingly, pitcher performance seems flat; opponent averages stay the same (or even decrease) as the number of innings pitched increases. Is this effect real, or did we do something wrong?

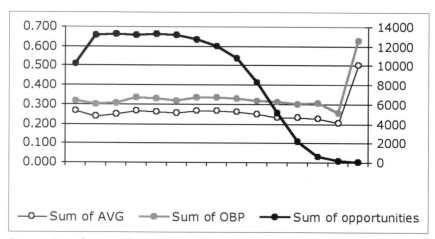

Figure 6-9. Performance by pitch for all pitchers

One possibility is that these results are being distorted because pitchers are pulled from games as they begin to give up hits, so our figures primarily show pitchers who are performing well. A way to test this hypothesis is to group performances by the maximum number of pitches thrown, not by name.

To figure this out, let's start by creating a temporary table containing the total number of pitches thrown by each starter in each game:

```
create temporary table total_pitches as
select gameid, starter, max(pitch_count + pitches) as totalpitches
from pitchcounts2003 group by gameid, starter;
```

Then, we'll create two indexes to make the merge fast:

```
create index total_pitches_idx on total_pitches(gameid, starter);
create index pitchcounts2003_gmidx on pitchcounts2003(gameid, starter);
```

Finally, we'll break down performance by pitch count at each point in the game and by total number of pitches thrown:

```
select
    floor(pitch_count / 10) * 10 as pitch_count_band,
    floor(totalpitches / 20) * 20 as total_pitches_band,
```

```
        count(*) as opportunities,
        sum(if(event_type IN (20,21,22,23), 1, 0)) as hits,
        sum(if(event_type IN (14,15,16), 1, 0)) as walks
    from pitchcounts2003 l inner join total_pitches r
    on l.starter=r.starter and l.gameid=r.gameid
    group by floor(pitch_count / 10) * 10, floor(totalpitches / 20) * 20
    ;
```

Run this code in your SQL Query client and then copy the results and paste them into Excel. Select the data and create a pivot table, then create a new calculated field for OBP. Drag pitch_count_band to the "drop columns here" part of the pivot table, and total_pitches_band to the "drop rows here" part of the pivot table. You should have a table of approximately 15×15 rows, where the lower-left corner is filled with #DIV/0! values. Very few pitchers got beyond 140 pitches in a game, and they'll make the resulting chart unreadable, so you might want to change the field settings for total_pitches_band to hide any games with fewer than 20 or more than 140 pitches thrown. Plot this chart as explained earlier. You should see a chart similar to the one shown in Figure 6-10.

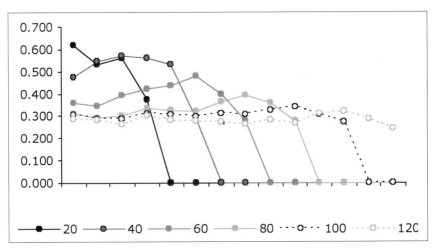

Figure 6-10. Batting average by endurance

Not surprisingly, pitchers who exit games very early have higher on-base percentages. (They are probably taken out of games early because of their ineffectiveness.) But surprisingly, pitchers don't actually seem to perform much worse as their pitch counts increase. Some pitchers get a little less effective (take a look at the 60–79 pitch band) as the game progresses, but it's not a dramatic difference, and it does not appear to be typical.

OBP, SLG, and Scoring Runs

#67 Calculate the relative strengths of how you can use OBP and SLG to estimate runs.

In his 2003 best-selling book, *Moneyball* (W. W. Norton & Company), Michael Lewis communicated that in the evaluation of players, the Oakland Athletics organization placed a weight on on-base percentage that was worth roughly three times the weight of slugging percentage:

> ...OPS was the simple addition of on-base and slugging percentages. Crude as it was, it was a much better indicator than any other offensive statistic of the number of runs a team would score. Simply adding the two statistics together, however, implied that they were of equal importance. If the goal was to raise a team's OPS, an extra percentage point of on-base was as good as an extra percentage point of slugging.

> Before his thought experiment Paul [DePodesta] had felt uneasy with this crude assumption; now he saw that the assumption was absurd. An extra point of on-base percentage was clearly more valuable than an extra point of slugging percentage—but by how much? ... In his model an extra point of on-base percentage was worth three times an extra point of slugging percentage.

In this hack, we'll show how to calculate how much more important OBP is than SLG, using a simple linear regression analysis. And we'll demonstrate that this number is closer to two than it is to three.

The Data and the Code

In this hack, we take a very simple approach to calculating the relative values of OBP and SLG, as they pertain to scoring runs. With the help of the Baseball Archive database (as described in "Get a MySQL Database of Player and Team Statistics" **[Hack #10]**), we will look at actual team outcomes over a time period to determine the best linear fit.

For each team and each season, we will consider the three values of OBP, SLG, and RS. For example, from the 2004 season, the two World Series teams would give us the following (OBP, SLG, RS) data:

```
STL    .344    .460    855
BOS    .360    .472    949
```

We can express the problem we are trying to solve as follows: *which values of A, B, and C will provide the best fit between actual team data and the following linear model?*

```
A * OBP + B * SLG + C = RS
```

The ratio | "= A / B will give us the importance of OBP, relative to SLG, as it pertains to scoring runs. We will use the statistical analysis tool R and this simple linear model to calculate the best fit, but first we need to get our hands on the relevant data. We will use team totals for all 30 major league teams over the past five seasons (2000–2004) as the starting point of our investigation.

See "Learn Perl" [Hack #13] to see how you can obtain the data from the Baseball Archive database. For the time being, we will assume you have downloaded the data and that it resides on your local hard drive, in your current folder. Using the read.csv( ) function in R, we can read the data directly from a CSV file and load it into a data frame that we will call Teams:

```
Teams <- read.csv("Teams.csv", header=TRUE)
```

Since the Baseball Archive database does not contain the explicit values for OBP and SLG, we will calculate these values and store them in columns within the data frame. We will also explicitly calculate and store singles and total bases along the way for simplicity.

First, we will calculate the number of singles per team by adding another column that we will call X1B (R doesn't let column names start with a digit):

```
Teams <- cbind(Teams, X1B = (Teams$H - (Teams$X2B + Teams$X3B + Teams$HR)))
```

Next, we will calculate the total bases values:

```
Teams <- cbind(Teams, TB = (Teams$X1B + 2 * Teams$X2B + 3* Teams$X3B +
4*Teams$HR))
```

We will calculate and store the slugging percentages with the following:

```
Teams <- cbind(Teams, SLG = (Teams$TB / Teams$AB))
```

Finally, we will calculate the OBP by including walks but ignoring HBP. We exclude HBP because the data is not always available; also, the exclusion of HBP is a minor one that will not affect the results tremendously.

```
Teams <- cbind(Teams, OBP = ((Teams$H + Teams$BB) / (Teams$AB + Teams$BB)))
```

From this full collection of data, we will extract only those years and teams of interest by using the subset( ) function as follows:

```
RecentTeams <- subset(Teams, yearID>=2000)
```

Now, because we have set up this data frame nicely, we can take advantage of R's linear fit tool to fit runs to a linear combination of SLG and OBP by issuing the following R command:

```
fm <- lm(R ~ OBP + SLG, RecentTeams)
```

The Results

We can get a quick summary of the results by just typing the name of the result object as follows:

```
fm

Call:
lm(formula = R ~ OBP + SLG, data = RecentTeams)

Coefficients:
(Intercept)          OBP          SLG
   -928.3        2863.7       1783.9
```

The simple way to interpret this output is that R is telling us that the best linear fit between runs, OBP, and slugging comes in the form of the following linear equation:

```
Runs = 2863.7 * OBP + 1783.9 * SLG - 928.3
```

Because our original question was concerned with the relative importance of OBP and SLG in determining runs, we can divide the coefficients to find the following:

$$\rho = 2863.7 / 1783.9 = 1.61$$

In other words, the best (linear) explanation of how much more significant OBP was to SLG during the years 2000–2004 is that OBP was about 1.61 times more "important."

But just how well did the data fit the model? We can obtain more detailed output of the results by looking at the result object's summary:

```
summary(fm)

Call:
lm(formula = R ~ SLG + OBP, data = RecentTeams)

Residuals:
    Min     1Q  Median     3Q    Max
-75.207 -14.753 -1.445 14.676 57.881

Coefficients:
            Estimate Std. Error t value Pr(>|t|)
(Intercept)  -933.07      48.46  -19.26   <2e-16 ***
SLG          1779.89     131.56   13.53   <2e-16 ***
OBP          2882.99     239.44   12.04   <2e-16 ***
---
Signif. codes:  0 '***' 0.001 '**' 0.01 '*' 0.05 '.' 0.1 ' ' 1

Residual standard error: 24.9 on 147 degrees of freedom
Multiple R-Squared: 0.9164,    Adjusted R-squared: 0.9153
F-statistic: 805.6 on 2 and 147 DF,  p-value: < 2.2e-16
```

Most importantly, we see that the R^2 value is roughly 0.92, which is a good indication that the quantities correlate well. For the purposes of this hack, we aren't going to dwell on how well the data fits the model, but instead we will choose to investigate different year ranges to see if we can gain any insight into how this quantity changes from one year to the next.

To make it easy to calculate the coefficient for many different groups of seasons, we next create a function called rho that takes the start year and end year of a range of seasons for which we want to calculate the ratio of the OBP coefficient to the SLG coefficient:

```
> rho <- function (year1, year2)
  TheTeams <- subset(Teams, yearID >= year1 & yearID <= year2)
  fm1 <- lm(R ~ OBP + SLG, TheTeams)
  (fm1$coef)[2] / (fm1$coef)[3]
  }
```

We can use this function to recalculate the previous quantity by simply typing the following:

```
> rho(2000,2004)
     OBP
1.605250
```

With this function, one can easily generate the following matrix by entering the year in the lefthand column as the start year, with the year in the top row as the end year:

Start /End	1995	1996	1997	1998	1999	2000	2001	2002	2003	2004
1995	2.2	1.0	1.4	1.5	1.6	1.7	1.7	1.6	1.5	1.4
1996		1.0	1.7	2.2	2.0	2.2	2.3	2.1	1.9	1.9
1997			2.6	2.8	2.3	2.5	2.4	2.1	2.0	1.9
1998				3.3	2.2	2.5	2.5	2.1	1.9	1.8
1999					1.7	2.2	2.2	1.9	1.7	1.6
2000						3.9	3.0	2.0	1.7	1.6
2001							3.2	1.5	1.4	1.3
2002								0.8	0.9	1.0
2003									1.1	1.2
2004										1.2

You can make several very interesting observations from this matrix alone:

- This number is not particularly stable from one year to the next. It certainly could be the case in which an outlier or two from that season dramatically altered the best fit. Excluding such outliers could lead to more-consistent ratios from year to year.

- If you did this exercise for a year or two and ended in 2001, the resulting ratio would have appeared to be around 3.0, more or less.

- However, looking at more-recent years, especially with more and more history, the results tend to be closer to 2.0.

What does all of this tell us? The most important result, in our opinion, is that the inconsistency from one season to the next could indicate that the relationship between OBP, SLG, and RS might in fact not be linear. This shouldn't be taken as news, in our opinion, because OBP and SLG do, in fact, double-count certain statistics, so you should instead appeal to a more sensible metric such as linear weights to gain a much better understanding of the correlation between baseball's discrete events and the outcomes of those events.

—*Mark E. Johnson and Matthew S. Johnson*

Measure Skill Versus Luck
#68   How many wins can you attribute to skill, and how many to luck, in the course of a baseball season?

Baseball is a game of luck and skill, and, fortunately, we can measure both quite accurately. The amount of luck involved is probably higher than most people think, and it's higher than the Lords of Baseball would like to admit.

First, let's look at team performance over a season. Take 16 evenly balanced teams that have an equal likelihood of winning or losing any game. The actual results should show a normal distribution with a mean of .500, with some variation. A common measure of variation is the standard deviation, called *sigma*, which you can calculate by simply taking the sum of the squares of the difference between the team's actual wins and the expected value, which would be 81 wins in a 162-game season. For a simple example, take four teams with wins of 89, 84, 77, and 73. The mean is 81 and the sum of the squares is 64 + 16 + 16 + 64, or 160. Divide 160 by the number of teams (4) and take the square root, and you get ≈6.

Calculating the expected sigma for team wins involves a formula derived for a binomial distribution. The formula is the square root of $p \times q \times n$, where p is the probability of success (.5), q is the probability of failure (also .5), and n is the number of samples (162). This gives a value of the square root of .25 $\times$ 162 (40.5), or 6.36.

Another characteristic of sigma in a normal distribution is that approximately two-thirds of the values differ from the mean by an amount less than or equal to it, and about 5% will be off by more than double. Only about 1 in 400 will stray more than 3 sigma from the mean, indicating that over the course of a season, 1 team in 20 might be expected to have a win total of either less than 69 or greater than 93.

Now, we can measure exactly the actual standard deviation of team wins for any season or seasons, and we know exactly what the expected variation due to chance or luck should be. Because there is no reason to suspect that the two are correlated, we can say with confidence that the variation due to skill is equal to the square root of the total variation squared, minus the variation due to luck squared.

Let's look at some numbers. Here is the standard deviation in wins per season for various periods:

period	total	luck	skill
1901-1920	15.0	6.1	13.8
1921-1940	14.3	6.2	12.8
1941-1960	13.6	6.2	12.0
1961-1980	12.0	6.4	10.0
1981-1997	9.8	6.3	7.5
1998-2004	12.7	6.4	10.9

For 1998–2004, $6.4^2 + 10.9^2 = 12.7^2$. As you can see, the difference in team skill was reduced almost equal to that of luck for an entire season in the 1980s, but recently it has gone back to historical levels. Of the top 13 variations by league since 1981, 10 have occurred in the 14 league seasons from 1998 to 2004, and only 3 in the 34 league seasons from 1981 to 1997. This variation might be due to a higher spread in team salaries. Subtracting expansion, when variation understandably shoots up, it is still 8 to 2 in favor of the current period.

An interesting question concerns the probability of the best team coming in first over the course of a season. Unfortunately, that question cannot be answered exactly, except for a specific definition of preseason win probabilities for all teams. You can calculate exactly the chances of one team beating another if you know the win probabilities of each team, but if they are the top two teams, the chances of another team beating them both is a function of the league as a whole. Using the normal distribution, here are the values for one team beating another. Because two teams are involved, the standard deviation on the expected difference in wins between the two teams is the square root of 2 times the one-team deviation, which is 9.

difference in expected wins between team a and team b	probability team a will finish ahead of team b
0	50%
1	54%
2	59%
4	67%

6	75%
8	81%
10	86%
15	95%
21	99%

The best way to determine the probability of the best team coming in first in a season is to set the preseason win probabilities and run a simulation. To do this, you need to know the probability of any one team beating any other team.

Because team win percentages are almost always between .400 and .600, a reasonable rule of thumb is that the probability of Team A beating Team B in a given game is win percent (a) minus win percent (b) plus .500. If you want to add in a home team advantage, a typical value is to add .040 for the home team, based on actual home winning percentage data for 1961 through today.

However, if you use the actual winning percentage for each team for the season being studied, you will get a variation that is too high in wins in the simulation because the actual winning percentages already include a luck factor that tends to spread the team further from the mean. For example, in 1939 the Yankees set an all-time record for runs scored minus runs allowed (even without Lou Gehrig) and coasted to their fourth pennant in a row. Using actual team winning percentages gives a sigma of about 24 wins for the distribution of all team wins in the simulation of 1,000 seasons, where the actual number was only 19. To get a sigma of 19 in the simulation, you have to use only 80% of the team difference in percentage from .500. So, a .600 team would be simulated at .580, and a .400 team would be simulated at .420. In general, the fraction of actual winning percentage used is sigma skill over sigma total from the first table. This is usually around 80%, except for 1981–1997, when it was closer to 70%.

This raises an important point. Because a good amount of luck is involved, even over the course of a full season, and teams will tend to win 5 or 10 games more or less than what they would win if they achieved their exact expected number of wins based on true talent, teams with high win totals will tend to have more good luck and teams with low win totals will tend to have more bad luck. One way of looking at this is that a .600 team could be a .550 team with good luck or a .650 team with bad luck. However, because there are many more .550 teams, the odds are that it is the former.

You can show this even more dramatically when you look at team winning percentages from one season to the next. Here, the effect is intensified because the factors that brought a team to a successful season can deteriorate, and the expected change due to luck would tend to be neutral. Here are the results of season winning percentage based solely on the previous season:

1981-2004					1902-2004			
n	prev	curr	pct		n	prev	curr	pct
					5	.248	.374	50
					9	.277	.384	52
1	.265	.444	24		13	.301	.358	72
3	.332	.473	16		36	.326	.402	56
11	.347	.407	61		71	.349	.399	67
17	.375	.459	33		74	.375	.419	64
40	.399	.461	39		123	.400	.439	61
52	.423	.462	48		144	.424	.445	73
70	.449	.482	36		188	.449	.483	34
102	.473	.483	64		228	.474	.486	54
84	.501	.499	-		225	.501	.505	-
85	.527	.517	65		231	.526	.511	42
77	.552	.524	46		212	.550	.534	67
52	.576	.534	44		165	.574	.535	48
38	.599	.535	35		152	.600	.566	66
20	.626	.567	53		94	.625	.580	64
6	.645	.574	51		36	.649	.591	61
1	.667	.568	41		22	.674	.613	65
2	.699	.610	55		10	.697	.621	61
1	.716	.574	34		4	.719	.599	45
					2	.752	.677	70

The pct column shows the amount of retained winning percentage from .500 from the previous season. For example, in the 1981–2004 period, teams from .545 to .555 averaged .552 the first year and .524 the second, and .024 divided by .052 is 46%. This shows that teams tend to fall back to .500 in the following season. If you have only the previous year's percentage to go on, your best estimate for the current season is about halfway between .500 and the previous year. The effect in recent years has been a bit more drastic in a smaller sample. In statistical terms, this is called *regression to the mean*.

Of course, we do have more information. We have the performance over past years. However, this does not change things very much. Multivariate linear regression is a tool that gives you an exact answer for the weights of each variable, to give a minimum prediction error for a given sample. The formula is current year = m1 × year1 + m2 × year2, etc., plus a constant, called the *intercept*. Here are the values for one-, two-, and three-year tests when tested on the years 1981–2004:

	m1	m2	m3	intercept	correlation	sigma
1 year	.437			.282	44%	.0624
2 year	.369	.147		.243	46%	.0618
3 year	.367	.142	.012	.240	46%	.0619

This shows that using the past two years results in a slight improvement over just one year, and that three years makes no difference. If you want to predict a team's winning percentage for next year, take .369 times this year, plus .147 times last year, plus .243.

The 66 teams that played .550 or better for two years between 1981 and 2004 fared no better. Their average percentages for the three years were .598, .602, and .558, where the general formula would predict .147 × .598 + .369 × .602 + .242, or .552, less than one game different from the actual and well within expected differences (1 sigma for a sample of 66 teams would be .061 over the square root of 66, or .008).

Some people say that runs scored and runs allowed is a better predictor of future team performance than wins and losses, which seems logical. However, at least for the years 1981–2004, the difference is negligible. Here we used runs less opponent runs per game for past performance, instead of team winning percentage:

```
           m1      m2      m3      intercept   correlation   sigma
1 year   .0512                       .500         47%        .0615
2 year   .0447   .0126                .501         48%        .0611
3 year   .0447   .0124   .0006        .500         48%        .0612
```

Because it takes about 10 runs to produce one win, the multipliers are about one-tenth of the values in the wins calculation. So, if a team outscored its opponent by 50, 100, and then 150 runs, that would be .309, .617, and .926 delta runs per game. The predicted winning percentage using the three-year model would be .549. However, the correlation increases from 46% to only 48%, and the standard deviation between predicted and actual percentage is reduced from .0619 to .0612, less than one percentage point, or about a one-eighth win. Again, only two years of data are needed—even one year works pretty well. The one-year model would predict .547 (calculated as .0517 × .926 + .500).

The actual sigma between wins compared to the previous year (normalized to the 162-game schedule to account for strikes) was 11.7 for the years 1981–2004, where the difference due to chance was 9 (the square root of 2 times 6.36). Thus, the true difference between teams from year to year is the square root of $11.7^2 - 9^2$, or 7.5. This says that the wins difference from year to year is actually more from luck than from skill.

In the years 1981–2004, 2.5% of the 632 teams, or 16 teams, would expect to lose 18 or more games than they did in the previous year by chance. Thirty-five teams actually did that, meaning that if a team increases its loss total by 18 or more games over two seasons, there is a 50–50 chance it is just bad luck. Only 11 of the managers involved did not start the following year, indicating reasonably that they are usually given another chance. However, in 2004, three of the four managers had already been fired, so maybe patience is wearing thin these days.

A good second-half performance is supposed to bode well for the following season. In reality, second-half performance does correlate slightly better with the following year than with the first half, but overall performance was still better, mainly because it is a larger sample:

	m1	m2	intercept	correlation	sigma
1st half	.303		.348	34%	.0661
2nd half	.366		.317	43%	.0633
each half	.144	.283	.284	45%	.0622
full season	.437		.282	44%	.0624

Counting both halves separately gave an insignificant improvement over the season as a whole.

How close should an expert be able to predict future performance? We know it should be better than 11.7 wins, which you can get by picking each team to win the same number of games as it did in the previous year. The simple two-season formula using wins or runs gets you down to 10.0 (.0618 ×162). Looking at Las Vegas over and under wins for the season from 1996 to 2004, we get an error of 9.4. This prediction includes trades, free agent gains or losses, potential rookies, players who retired or might be coming back from injury, or aging of current players—all of which is quite a bit more information than just the team record for the past two years. Because overall predictability in that period has been slightly better than average, only 11.5 wins from the previous year instead of 11.7, the actual number for the 23-year period is probably a bit higher. Anyway, a prediction off by 11 wins is pretty bad, 10 is fair, and anything close to 9 is super.

The Code

I write my programs in BASIC and I use my own datafiles, which I have accumulated over the years from official sources. I originally made my team file on punch cards, so my datafiles are text-file card images. I used these to create *Total Baseball* editions 1 through 7 (Total Sports); a newly created database from the same sources was used for *The 2005 ESPN Baseball Encyclopedia* by Pete Palmer and Gary Gillette (Sterling). (You can use the team statistics from the Baseball DataBank or Baseball Archive databases described in "Get a MySQL Database of Player and Team Statistics" [Hack #10].)

For each year, set SSQ and N to zero, then read in each team's wins and losses, setting SSQ = SSQ + ((W - L) / 2) ** 2 and N = N + 1. If a team wins 91 games and loses 71, W - L is 20, but this is 10 games above the average of 81.

Then I found the total standard deviation for the year by taking SQRT (SSQ/ N). Say SSQ equals 2,016 and N equals 14, for example. Then the total sigma is SQRT (2,016/14), or 12. The standard deviation expected by chance from the binomial distribution is SQRT (P×Q×N), where P is the probability of success (set to .5), Q is the probability of failure (set to 1 − P, or also .5), and N is the number of games (usually 162). So, this would be SQRT (40.5), or 6.36. The standard deviation due to skill would be SQRT (sigma (total) ** 2 − sigma (chance) ** 2) or SQRT (144 − 40.5), or 10.2.

I have a FORTRAN multivariate linear regression program I copied out of an old IBM manual in the 1970s. It works fine, but it is pretty complicated and runs about 300 lines, including a frontend that allows using variable-size arrays. Many sites on the Web have statistical utility programs that you can use.

I will list my program for reference:

```
      PROGRAM PALMR
C     CHANGED TO READ IN DATA DIRECTLY WITHOUT MANIPULATION
      DIMENSION RX1(2500),R(2500),RX(2500)
      CHARACTER*3 LN(50)
      CHARACTER*12 OFILE
      INTEGER*2 Y [HUGE] (1500,50)
      REAL*4 X [HUGE] ( 75000)
      DATA Y / 75000*0/
      OPEN(UNIT=5,FILE='REGRESS.III',STATUS='OLD')
C     READ IN OUTPUT FILE
      READ(5,102) OFILE
102   FORMAT(A12)
      OPEN(UNIT=6,FILE=OFILE)
      WRITE(6,*) OFILE
C     READ IN NUMBER OF SAMPLES, NO OF VARIABLES
      READ(5,104) N,M
104   FORMAT(50I5)
C     READ IN VARIABLES NAMES
      READ(5,105) (LN(I),I=1,M)
105   FORMAT(20(2X,A3))
C     READ IN DATA (1500 SAMPLES MAX)
      DO 2000 N=1,1500
      READ(5,104,END=3000) (Y(N,K),K=1,M)
2000  CONTINUE
3000  CONTINUE
      N=N-1
      WRITE(0,104) M,N
      DO 9500 K=1,M
      DO 9500 J=1,N
      X(J+N*(K-1))=Y(J,K)
9500  CONTINUE
      WRITE(0,104) 99,99
      CALL PALM1(M,N,X,RX1,R,RX,LN)
```

```
          CLOSE(UNIT=5)
          CLOSE(UNIT=6,STATUS='KEEP')
          STOP
          END

          SUBROUTINE PALM1(M,N,X[HUGE],RX1,R,RX,LN)
          DIMENSION XBAR(50),STD(50),D(50),B(50),T(50),ISAVE(50),
      X     RY(50),L(50),MM(50),SB(50),ANS(10),
         *RX1(1),R(1),RX(1),X(1)
          CHARACTER*3 LN(1)
          CHARACTER*12 ANN(10)
          DATA ANN /
         X12HINTERCEPT    ,
         X12HCORRELATION ,
         X12H            ,
         X12H            ,
         X12HDEP VAR      ,
         X12H            ,
         X12H            ,
         X12HDEG/FREEDOM ,
         X12H            ,
         X12H            /
          IO=1
          CALL CORRE(N,M,IO,X,XBAR,STD,RX1,R,D,B,T)
          NDEP=M
          K=M-1
          DO 130 I=1,K
130       ISAVE(I)=I
          CALL ORDER(M,R,NDEP,K,ISAVE,RX,RY)
          WRITE(6,*) 'CROSS CORRELATION'
          WRITE(6,12) (LN(I),I=1,M-1)
12        FORMAT(1H ,10(5X,A3))
          I1=1
          DO 132 I=1,K
          I2=I*K
          WRITE(6,15) (RX(J),J=I1,I2)
          I1=I2+1
132       CONTINUE
          WRITE(6,13) ' CORRELATION WITH ',LN(M)
13        FORMAT(A18,A3)
          WRITE(6,12) (LN(I),I=1,M-1)
          WRITE(6,15) (RY(I),I=1,K)
15        FORMAT(1H ,10F8.5)
          CALL MINV(RX,K,DD,L,MM)
          IF(DD)140,135,140
135       WRITE(6,20)
20        FORMAT(1H ,3HD=0)
          RETURN
140       CALL MULTR(N,K,XBAR,STD,D,RX,RY,ISAVE,B,SB,T,ANS)
          WRITE(6,*) ' N     ITEM       M      SIGMA          T'
          WRITE(6,30)(I,LN(I),B(I),SB(I),T(I),I=1,K)
```

```
30    FORMAT(1H ,I3,3X,A5,F10.5,F10.5,F10.5)
      WRITE(6,*) '  N     ITEM                MEAN                SIGMA'
      WRITE(6,31)(I,LN(I),XBAR(I),STD(I),I=1,M)
31    FORMAT(1H ,I3,3X,A5,F20.5,F20.5)
      WRITE(6,32)(ANN(K),ANS(K),K=1,10)
32    FORMAT(1H ,A12,F20.10)
      RETURN
      END

      SUBROUTINE CORRE(N,M,IO,X[HUGE],XBAR,STD,RX,R,B,D,T)
      DIMENSION X(1),XBAR(1),STD(1),RX(1),R(1),B(1),D(1),T(1)
      DO 100 J=1,M
      B(J)=0.0
100   T(J)=0.0
      K=(M*M+M)/2
      DO 102 I=1,K
102   R(I)=0.0
      FN=N
      L=0
      IF(IO)105,127,105
105   DO 108 J=1,M
      DO 107 I=1,N
      L=L+1
107   T(J)=T(J)+X(L)
      XBAR(J)=T(J)
108   T(J)=T(J)/FN
      DO 115 I=1,N
      JK=0
      L=I-N
      DO 110 J=1,M
      L=L+N
      D(J)=X(L)-T(J)
110   B(J)=B(J)+D(J)
      DO 115  J=1,M
      DO 115  K=1,J
      JK=JK+1
115   R(JK)=R(JK)+D(J)*D(K)
      GO TO 205
127   GO TO 205
205   JK=0
      DO 210 J=1,M
      XBAR(J)=XBAR(J)/FN
      DO 210 K=1,J
      JK=JK+1
210   R(JK)=R(JK)-B(J)*B(K)/FN
      JK=0
      DO 220 J=1,M
      JK=JK+J
220   STD(J)=SQRT(ABS(R(JK)))
      DO 230 J=1,M
      DO 230 K=J,M
      JK=J+(K*K-K)/2
      L=M*(J-1)+K
```

```
      RX(L)=R(JK)
      L=M*(K-1)+J
      RX(L)=R(JK)
      IF(STD(J)*STD(K))225,222,225
222   R(JK)=0.0
      GO TO 230
225   R(JK)=R(JK)/(STD(J)*STD(K))
230   CONTINUE
      FN=SQRT(FN-1.0)
      DO 240 J=1,M
240   STD(J)=STD(J)/FN
      L=-M
      DO 250 I=1,M
      L=L+M+1
250   B(I)=RX(L)
      RETURN
      END

      SUBROUTINE ORDER (M,R,NDEP,K,ISAVE,RX,RY)
      DIMENSION R(1),ISAVE(1),RX(1),RY(1)
      MM=0
      DO 130 J=1,K
      L2=ISAVE(J)
      IF(NDEP-L2)122,123,123
122   L=NDEP+(L2*L2-L2)/2
      GO TO 125
123   L=L2+(NDEP*NDEP-NDEP)/2
125   RY(J)=R(L)
      DO 130 I=1,K
      L1=ISAVE(I)
      IF(L1-L2)127,128,128
127   L=L1+(L2*L2-L2)/2
      GO TO 129
128   L=L2+(L1*L1-L1)/2
129   MM=MM+1
130   RX(MM)=R(L)
      ISAVE(K+1)=NDEP
      RETURN
      END

      SUBROUTINE MINV(A,N,D,L,M)
      DIMENSION A(1),L(1),M(1)
      D=1.0
      NK=-N
      DO 80 K=1,N
      NK=NK+N
      L(K)=K
      M(K)=K
      KK=NK+K
      BIGA=A(KK)
      DO 20 J=K,N
      IZ=N*(J-1)
      DO 20 I=K,N
```

```
        IJ=IZ+I
        IF(ABS(BIGA)-ABS(A(IJ)))15,20,20
15      BIGA=A(IJ)
        L(K)=I
        M(K)=J
20      CONTINUE
        J=L(K)
        IF(J-K)35,35,25
25      KI=K-N
        DO 30 I=1,N
        KI=KI+N
        HOLD=-A(KI)
        JI=KI-K+J
        A(KI)=A(JI)
30      A(JI)=HOLD
35      I=M(K)
        IF(I-K)45,45,38
38      JP=N*(I-1)
        DO 40 J=1,N
        JK=NK+J
        JI=JP+J
        HOLD=-A(JK)
        A(JK)=A(JI)
40      A(JI)=HOLD
45      IF(BIGA)48,46,48
46      D=0.0
        RETURN
48      DO 55 I=1,N
        IF(I-K)50,55,50
50      IK=NK+I
        A(IK)=A(IK)/(-BIGA)
55      CONTINUE
        DO 65 I=1,N
        IK=NK+I
        HOLD=A(IK)
        IJ=I-N
        DO 65 J=1,N
        IJ=IJ+N
        IF(I-K)60,65,60
60      IF(J-K)62,65,62
62      KJ=IJ-I+K
        A(IJ)=HOLD*A(KJ)+A(IJ)
65      CONTINUE
        KJ=K-N
        DO 75 J=1,N
        KJ=KJ+N
        IF(J-K)70,75,70
70      A(KJ)=A(KJ)/BIGA
75      CONTINUE
        D=D*BIGA
        A(KK)=1.0/BIGA
80      CONTINUE
        K=N
```

```
100    K=(K-1)
       IF(K)150,150,105
105    I=L(K)
       IF(I-K)120,120,108
108    JQ=N*(K-1)
       JR=N*(I-1)
       DO 110 J=1,N
       JK=JQ+J
       HOLD=A(JK)
       JI=JR+J
       A(JK)=-A(JI)
110    A(JI)=HOLD
120    J=M(K)
       IF(J-K)100,100,125
125    KI=K-N
       DO 130 I=1,N
       KI=KI+N
       HOLD=A(KI)
       JI=KI-K+J
       A(KI)=-A(JI)
130    A(JI)=HOLD
       GO TO 100
150    RETURN
       END

       SUBROUTINE MULTR(N,K,XBAR,STD,D,RX,RY,ISAVE,B,SB,T,ANS)
       DIMENSION XBAR(1),STD(1),D(1),RX(1),RY(1),ISAVE(1),
      *B(1),SB(1),T(1),ANS(1)
       MM=K+1
       DO 100 J=1,K
100    B(J)=0.0
       DO 110 J=1,K
       L1=K*(J-1)
       DO 110 I=1,K
       L=L1+I
110    B(J)=B(J)+RY(I)*RX(L)
       RM=0.0
       BO=0.0
       L1=ISAVE(MM)
       DO 120 I=1,K
       RM=RM+B(I)*RY(I)
       L=ISAVE(I)
       B(I)=B(I)*(STD(L1)/STD(L))
120    BO=BO+B(I)*XBAR(L)
       BO=XBAR(L1)-BO
       SSAR=RM*D(L1)
       RM=SQRT(ABS(RM))
       SSDR=D(L1)-SSAR
       FN=N-K-1
       SY=SSDR/FN
       DO 130 J=1,K
```

```
        L1=K*(J-1)+J
        L=ISAVE(J)
        SB(J)=SQRT(ABS((RX(L1)/D(L))*SY))
130     T(J)=B(J)/SB(J)
        SY=SQRT(ABS(SY))
        FK=K
        SSARM=SSAR/FK
        SSDRM=SSDR/FN
        F=SSARM/SSDRM
        ANS(1)=B0
        ANS(2)=RM
        ANS(3)=SY
        ANS(4)=SSAR
        ANS(5)=FK
        ANS(6)=SSARM
        ANS(7)=SSDR
        ANS(8)=FN
        ANS(9)=SSDRM
        ANS(10)=F
        RETURN
        END
```

—Pete Palmer

Odds of the Best Team Winning the World Series
#69
What are the odds of the best team winning the World Series or any seven-game series?

Let's look at the probability of the best team winning the World Series. Obviously, this was much more likely before division play in 1969. The best team has a much better chance of getting to the Series based on a full season than on a playoff series. We can't figure out exactly what the odds are of the best team winning. But if we take a sample for the years 1961–1968, using our simulation and assuming that the true winning percentage of each team was downgraded 20% toward the mean and that the best team was the team with the highest percentage, we get these results (where the probability of winning is based on 1,000 simulated seasons):

year	AL winner	wins	prob of winning	NL winner	wins	prob of winning
1961	NY	109	.730	CIN	93	.497
1962	NY	96	.551	SF	103	.373
1963	NY	104	.766	LA	99	.565
1964	NY	99	.385	STL	93	.254
1965	MIN	102	.616	LA	97	.414
1966	BAL	97	.644	LA	95	.382
1967	BOS	92	.306	STL	101	.709
1968	DET	103	.781	STL	97	.649

This says that, on average, the best team in the league wins the pennant a little more than half the time, which seems reasonable. The best team over-all increases that probability to around 60%.

We already stated that the probability of winning a given game is equal to .500, plus the difference in winning percentages of the two teams. Extending the series to three, five, seven, or nine games increases the odds of the best team winning:

1-game	probability of winning a series			
pct.	3 games	5 games	7 games	9 games
.510	.515	.519	.522	.529
.520	.530	.537	.544	.549
.530	.545	.556	.565	.573
.540	.560	.575	.587	.598
.550	.575	.593	.608	.621
.560	.590	.611	.629	.645
.580	.619	.647	.671	.690
.600	.648	.683	.710	.733
.700	.784	.837	.874	.901

For example, take a five-game series, where p is the probability of winning one game and q is the probability of losing. The probability of winning the series is $p^3 + 3 \times p^3 \times q + 6 \times p^3 \times q^2$. There is only one way to win 3 straight, but there are three ways to win 3 to 1 (lwww, wlww, wwlw) and six ways to win 3 to 2.

Next, let's look at the difference in team season winning percentage and the results in the postseason to see if the actual results track the expected. Unfortunately, even 100 years of postseason play do not provide enough data to show a very good relationship. In the following table, p is the expected winning percentage for one game for the favored team based on the season record, which is .500 plus pct-favorite minus pct-underdog. This assumes that leagues and schedules are equal, although we know they are not. Sigma is the expected standard deviation in winning percentage based on the square root of pqn, and z is the difference in actual and expected winning percentage divided by sigma. Typically, as stated before, about two-thirds of the samples would be expected to be under 1 sigma and 5% over 2 sigma. In the data shown next, 11 of 15 are under 1 sigma and one is over 2 sigma, so the results are reasonably close to expected, but not compelling.

		-- series --			------- games -----------			
p	w	l	pct	w	l	pct	sigma	z
.501	4	2	0.667	19	12	0.613	.087	1.279
.509	16	19	0.457	89	94	0.486	.037	-0.617
.520	16	17	0.485	90	86	0.511	.038	-0.224
.528	11	15	0.423	73	75	0.493	.041	-0.848
.538	14	16	0.467	76	74	0.507	.041	-0.777
.549	10	8	0.556	51	42	0.548	.052	-0.005

.559	7	10	0.412	48	48	0.500	.051	-1.154
.571	13	5	0.722	55	38	0.591	.051	0.400
.579	5	2	0.714	22	17	0.564	.079	-0.189
.591	5	1	0.833	18	6	0.750	.088	1.801
.601	9	1	0.900	32	6	0.842	.059	4.078
.611	1	0	1.000	4	0	1.000	.000	0.000
.623	1	1	0.500	4	4	0.500	.177	-0.693
.650	2	1	0.667	9	8	0.529	.121	-0.996
.658	2	0	1.000	7	2	0.778	.139	0.864

So, if we assume that the odds of winning a playoff series agree with theory, we can continue to examine the probability of the best team making it to, and winning, the World Series.

The average advantage in season winning percentage in the playoffs is about 43 points (45 in the Divisional Series, 43 in the Championship Series, and 42 in the World Series). This translates to about a 60% chance of winning any series. Thus, in the current two-preliminary-round setup, the probability of the best playoff team getting into the Series is about 36%, and the odds of that team winning the Series is about 22%. If all teams were even, these numbers would be 25% and 12%, respectively.

However, the chances of the best team making the playoffs have increased because now eight teams qualify instead of two. Again, this is difficult to measure, but by simulating seasons, we can give it a try. You can calculate the probability of making the playoffs by playing out 1,000 seasons under the assumption that the team with the best record in the real season was the best team. Here are the results for the two-division play, adding the League Championship series:

year	AL winner	wins	prob of making playoffs	NL winner	wins	prob of making playoffs
1969	BAL	109	.947	NY	100	.671
1970	BAL	108	.906	CIN	102	.873
1971	BAL	101	.843	PIT	97	.705
	OAK	101	.929			
1972	OAK	93	.657	PIT	96	.814
1973	BAL	97	.672	CIN	99	.563
1974	BAL	91	.430	LA	102	.627
1975	OAK	98	.756	CIN	108	.964
1976	NY	97	.805	CIN	102	.805
1977	KC	102	.671	PHI	101	.689
1978	NY	100	.421	LA	95	.480
1979	BAL	102	.692	PIT	98	.558
1980	NY	103	.616	HOU	93	.369
1981	OAK	64	.643	CIN	66	.619
1982	MIL	95	.440	STL	92	.451
1983	CHI	99	.944	LA	91	.451
1984	DET	104	.847	CHI	96	.665
1985	TOR	99	.498	STL	101	.626

1986	BOS	95	.532	NY	108	.970
1987	DET	98	.467	STL	95	.505
1988	OAK	104	.901	NY	100	.892
1989	OAK	99	.601	CHI	93	.587
1990	OAK	103	.750	PIT	95	.567
1991	MIN	95	.548	PIT	98	.868
1992	OAK	96	.604	ATL	98	.739
	TOR	96	.518			
1993	TOR	95	.526	ATL	104	.592

Allowing two teams from each league to play in the playoffs increased the probability of the best team in the league playing in the postseason from around 50% to 67%, and the best team overall from 60% to 75%.

Adding a division and a wildcard team in 1994 again increased the probability of the best team making the playoffs, but the extra round of games again decreased its chances of winning the World Series. Although there were no playoffs that year because of the strike, we can still calculate the odds. The best team in the league had about an 87% chance of making the playoffs, and the best team overall made it 91% of the time.

year	AL winner	wins	prob of making playoffs	NL winner	wins	prob of making playoffs
1994	NY	70	.873	MON	74	.966
1995	CLE	100	1.000	ATL	90	.982
1996	CLE	99	.926	ATL	96	.870
1997	BAL	98	.917	ATL	101	.918
1998	NY	114	.998	ATL	106	.923
1999	NY	98	.850	ATL	103	.669
2000	CHI	95	.828	ATL	95	.453
				STL	95	.970
2001	SEA	116	.975	STL	93	.745
				HOU	93	.711
2002	NY	103	.959	ATL	101	.886
	OAK	103	.758			
2003	NY	101	.894	ATL	101	.675
2004	NY	101	.933	STL	105	.985

At any rate, the probability of the best team winning the World Series has been reduced from 36% under the one-division plan (60% to make the Series and 60% of winning) to 27% under the two-division plan (75% playoffs and 60% times 60% overall) and to around 20% under the three-division and a wildcard plan (90% to make the postseason and 60% times 60% times 60% to win out). However, baseball is a business, and the objective is not to maximize the probability of the best team winning the World Series, but to maximize revenues, and they have done a pretty good job of that.

To calculate the probability of making the playoffs, I read in the won–lost records of all teams for a given year and then played 1,000 seasons to see how often each team made the playoffs. This was simple in the pre-1969 period, during which only the pennant winner in each league made the playoffs. After that, there was an East/West playoff through 1993. After the 1994 strike, the wildcard team was added, which made things more complicated.

In the BASIC program, first I read in P (T%), which is the adjusted winning percentage of team T% (TC% teams total). Remember, we are reducing the percentage toward the mean by a factor of sigma(skill) over sigma(total), usually around 80%. When Team A plays Team B, the expected winning percentage for Team A is P(A) minus P(B) plus .500. I used a random number to determine the winner. Wins and losses were kept in W%(T%) and L%(T%). I kept losses just to make sure the number of games for each team came out OK. The division, used to calculate the number of games between the two teams, is set in array DIV%(T%+TD%), where TD% is 0 for the NL and 16 for the AL. I made an approximation of the number of games between teams, which usually came out to 160, so I arbitrarily added one win and one loss to each team to get to 162.

In practice, the number of games between teams varies a bit to get to 162. The leading team in each division is in TMAX%(DIVT%), and the number of wins is in WMAX%(DIVT%). Ties were a problem, so I set a flip-flop flag (TF%), and, in case of a tie, I would take either the current team or the new team, depending on the flag value. This spread the ties out among the teams and resulted in a reasonable answer without too much figuring. After each season is played, the three division champs and the nonwinner with the most wins have the playoff appearances incremented (F%(T%)) and after 1,000 seasons, the data is stored. In addition, the distribution of wins for each team is kept (WD%(T%,W%)) and stored. TWL%(1,T%) is the original team wins for the season from the team file. SSQ is the sum of squares of the difference from average in team wins, used to calculate the standard deviation for the 1,000-season simulation; VAT, VAC, and VAS are the standard deviations for total, chance, and skill, based on the team data. VAT should be about equal to the 1,000-season standard deviation if the simulation worked correctly. The FA array is used to show how often a team with a given expected win difference from another team actually finished ahead of that team in the simulation.

```
200 'SIMULATE 1000 SEASONS
210 TF%=0   :FOR T%=1 TO 16   :F%(T%)=0   :FOR W%=0 TO 100   :WD%(T%,W%)=0
215 NEXT W%   :NEXT T%

220 SSQ=0   :N=0   :FOR S%=1 TO 1000   :WMAX%(1)=0   :WMAX%(2)=0   :WMAX%(3)=0
```

```
225 FOR T%=1 TO 16   :W%(T%)=1   :L%(T%)=1   'SCHEDULE COMES OUT TO 160 OR 161
232 NEXT T%

235 FOR T%=1 TO TC%   :DIVT%=DIV%(T%+TD%)   :GT%=0
238 RANDOMIZE TIMER
240 FOR U%=T%+1 TO TC%   :DIVU%=DIV%(U%+TD%)   'OPPONENT
241 IF L%=1 AND Y%>1997 GOTO 250   '16-TEAM NL
242 G2%=20   :IF DIVT%=DIVU% GOTO 260   'SAME DIVISION
244 G2%=8   'DIFFERENT DIVISION (20 X 4 + 8 X 5 + 10 X 4 = 160)
245 IF DIVT%=3 OR DIVU%=3 THEN G2%=10   'WEST DIVISION HAS 4 IN, 10 OUT
246 'THIS MAKES 20 X 3 + 10 X 10 = 160)
248 GOTO 260
250 G2%=22   :IF DIVT%=2 THEN G2%=20   '20 VS DIV, UNLESS NL CENTRAL
252 IF DIVT%=DIVU% GOTO 260
254 G2%=7   :IF DIVT%=2 OR DIVU%=2 THEN G2%=6
255 '6-TEAM CENTRAL 20 X 5 + 6 X 10 = 160
258 '5-TEAM EAST/WEST 22 X 4 + 6 X 6 + 7 X 5 = 159
260 FOR G%=1 TO G2%   :GT%=GT%+1
265 X=RND(X)   :PWT=.500+P(T%)-P(U%)
270 IF X<PWT THEN W%(T%)=W%(T%)+1   :L%(U%)=L%(U%)+1   :ELSE W%(U%)=W%(U%)+1
:L%(T%)=L%(T%)+1
300 NEXT G%   :NEXT U%
302 WA%=W%(T%)-30   :IF WA%<0 THEN WA%=0   :ELSE IF WA%>100 THEN WA%=100
304 WE%=2*HG%*P(T%)-30   :IF WE%<0 THEN WE%=0   :ELSE IF WE%>100 THEN WE%=100
310 WT%(WE%,WA%)=WT%(WE%,WA%)+1
312 WD%(T%,WA%)=WD%(T%,WA%)+1
316 IF TF%=0 AND W%(T%)>WMAX%(DIVT%) THEN WMAX%(DIVT%)=W%(T%)   :
TMAX%(DIVT%)=T%   :TF%=1   :GOTO 318
317 IF TF%=1 AND W%(T%)>=WMAX%(DIVT%) THEN WMAX%(DIVT%)=W%(T%)   :
TMAX%(DIVT%)=T%   :TF%=0
318 N=N+1   :SSQ=SSQ+(W%(T%)-HG%)*(W%(T%)-HG%)   'N AND SIGMA SQUARED
320 NEXT T%

323 FOR DIV%=1 TO 3
324 F%(TMAX%(DIV%))=F%(TMAX%(DIV%))+1   'FIRST PLACE
326 NEXT DIV%

330 'NOW FIND WILD CARD (SKIP DIVISION WINNERS)
331 WMAX%=0   :TMAX%=0   :FOR T%=1 TO TC%
332 FOR DIV%=1 TO 3   :IF T%=TMAX%(DIV%) GOTO 335   :ELSE NEXT DIV%
333 IF TF%=0 AND W%(T%)>WMAX% THEN TMAX%=T%   :WMAX%=W%(T%)   :TF%=1   :GOTO
335
334 IF TF%=1 AND W%(T%)>=WMAX% THEN TMAX%=T%   :WMAX%=W%(T%)   :TF%=0
335 NEXT T%
336 F%(TMAX%)=F%(TMAX%)+1

341 FOR T%=1 TO TC%   :FOR U%=T%+1 TO TC%
342 FAI%=2*HG%*ABS(P(T%)-P(U%))   :IF FAI%>50 THEN FAI%=50
```

```
344 'EXPECTED WIN DIFFERENTIAL
346 TH%=T%  :TL%=U%  :IF P(U%)>P(T%) THEN TH%=U%  :TL%=T%  'HIGHER/LOWER
348 FA(FAI%,0)=FA(FAI%,0)+1  :IF W%(TH%)>W%(TL%) THEN
FA(FAI%,1)=FA(FAI%,1)+1
350 IF W%(TH%)=W%(TL%) THEN FA(FAI%,1)=FA(FAI%,1)+0.5  'TIE
352 NEXT U%  :NEXT T%  'SEE WHO FINISHED AHEAD

360 NEXT S%

361 PRINT#2,Y%;LG$
362 PRINT#2,"CLB    W     F";
364 FOR WA%=0 TO 100  :PRINT#2,USING "###";WA%+30;  :NEXT WA%  :PRINT#2,""
370 FOR T%=1 TO TC%
372 PRINT#2,T$(T%);
374 PRINT#2,USING " ### #### ###";TWL%(1,T%);F%(T%);T%(T%);
380 FOR WA%=0 TO 100
382 PRINT#2,USING "###";WD%(T%,WA%);
384 NEXT WA%  :PRINT#2,""  :NEXT T%
390 PRINT#2,USING "##.## #.### ###.# ##.# ###.#";SQR(SSQ/N);RF;VAT;VAC;VAS
```

To calculate the probability of a team with a given one-game winning percentage winning a series of varying length, I used the following:

```
100 OPEN "SERIES.OUT" FOR OUTPUT AS#1
105 FOR P%=1 TO 20
110 P=.500+P%/100  :Q=1-P
120 N%=1
130 PRINT#1,N%;  :PRINT#1,USING " .###   .###";P,Q
140 N%=3
150 P3=P^2+2*P^2*Q
160 Q3=Q^2+2*Q^2*P
170 PRINT#1,N%;  :PRINT#1,USING " .###   .###";P3,Q3
200 N%=5
210 P5=P^3+3*P^3*Q+6*P^3*Q^2
220 Q5=Q^3+3*Q^3*P+6*Q^3*P^2
230 PRINT#1,N%;  :PRINT#1,USING " .###   .###";P5,Q5
250 N%=7
260 P7=P^4+4*P^4*Q+10*P^4*Q^2+20*P^4*Q^3
270 Q7=Q^4+4*Q^4*P+10*Q^4*P^2+20*Q^4*P^3
280 PRINT#1,N%;  :PRINT#1,USING " .###   .###";P7,Q7
300 N%=9
310 P9=P^5+5*P^5*Q+15*P^5*Q^2+35*P^5*Q^3+70*P^5*Q^4
320 Q9=Q^5+5*Q^5*P+15*Q^5*P^2+35*Q^5*P^3+70*Q^5*P^4
380 PRINT#1,N%;  :PRINT#1,USING " .###   .###";P9,Q9
400 NEXT P%
900 END
```

—*Pete Palmer*

Top 10 Bargain Outfielders
#70 Use R and the Baseball DataBank database in MySQL to analyze statistically
the 10 most underpaid outfielders for the years 1999–2003.

The most common conversation between any two baseball fans (after argu-
ing about whose favorite team is better, of course) is what player is the best
in the game. Baseball, more than any other sport, it seems, is obsessed with
ranking players. Certainly, the fact that every player gets a turn at bat plays
into the perception that such a thing should be a "simple" matter. The ensu-
ing debate after failing to establish the proper all-time pecking order is how
high *all* players' salaries have become. Of course, both parties agree on that
and then they're friends again. But the real truth is that ranking players is
highly subjective, and the distribution of player salaries is highly skewed.
For every A-Rod making $22 million, there are 100 younger players making
a "scant" $300,000.

So, I won't even try to claim who the "best" players are; rather, I will simply
use R to help identify what players have "similar" attributes to one another
and then attempt to predict what their salary can be expected to be, based
on those attributes. Players who were paid much lower than expected given
their similarity to other players are considered "undervalued." Likewise,
players paid much more than expected are considered "overvalued." And to
help simplify things, I look only at outfielders for the years 1999–2003.

(This analysis isn't completely fair. Major league players aren't free agents
until they've played for six years, so their salaries aren't set by the market.
For the first three years, their salaries are set by their original contracts and
are often set at the major league minimum. For the next three years, players
are eligible for arbitration, and their salaries are set through negotiations
with their teams. But even if the analysis isn't totally fair, it's still interesting
to look for bargains.)

So how do you perform such an analysis using R? It's actually pretty simple,
as I will show you in this hack. The difficult part is making sure everything
makes sense and is being interpreted properly. It's really more art than science, but here are the basic steps:

1. Import raw data from MySQL into R.
2. Compress input variables to a handful of common attributes (such as
   speed, power, etc.).
3. Assign scores to all players based on these attributes.
4. Group players on these attributes based on their similarity to one
   another.

5. Predict salaries based on group membership and a few other input variables.

6. Look at actual minus predicted salaries.

Let's get started!

The Code

Prerequisites. It is assumed that you have the Baseball DataBank database loaded in MySQL [Hack #20] and that you can access this data from R [Hack #33].

Define SQL query for getting raw data. The first thing you need is a SQL query to define what raw data to get from the database. It makes sense to let R pull the data using a query because multiple tables will be joined together and we can set our criteria there. Moreover, I prefer to keep this SQL query in a separate text file because it's easier to maintain. So, use Notepad to save the following SQL query as a simple text file (in *C:\baseball_salaries\get_data.sql*):

```
SELECT
    CONCAT(M.playerID,'|',F.yearID) AS ID,
    CONCAT(M.nameLast, ', ', M.nameFirst) AS playerName,
    F.yearID,
    (F.yearID - M.birthYear) AS age,
    F.lgID,
    F.teamID,
    F.POS,
    F.G AS POS_G,
    B.G AS G,
    B.AB,
    (B.H - B.2B - B.3B - B.HR) AS X1B,
    B.2B AS X2B,
    B.3B AS X3B,
    B.HR,
    B.SB,
    B.BB,
    B.SO,
    B.GIDP,
    F.PO,
    F.A,
    F.E,
    F.DP,
    S.salary

FROM
    master AS M

INNER JOIN
    fielding AS F
    ON
        (M.playerID = F.playerID)
```

```
INNER JOIN
    batting AS B
    ON
        (F.yearID = B.yearID) AND
        (F.playerID = B.playerID) AND
        (F.teamID = B.teamID)

INNER JOIN
    salaries AS S
    ON
        (F.yearID = S.yearID) AND
        (F.playerID = S.playerID) AND
        (F.teamID = S.teamID)

WHERE
    (F.yearID BETWEEN 1999 AND 2003) AND
    F.pos IN ('LF','CF','RF') AND
    F.G >= 81

ORDER BY
    playerName,
    F.yearID
```

A lot is going on in this query. Most notable is the fact that we'll be restricting our attention to players who played defensively in at least 81 games as an LF, CF, or RF for any season between 1999 and 2003. Because 81 games are exactly half of a full 162-game season, you'll be forgiven if you assume I chose this cutoff to limit the analysis to only part- to full-time players. However, the real reason I chose this cutoff is to reduce significantly the likelihood that the exact same player will have two records for the same season on different teams or different positions. Let's say the cutoff was set to at least 40 games. We would have two records for Moises Alou for 2000: 59 games at LF and 64 games at RF. So what's wrong with that? Nothing, except the batting statistics and salary data are at the player/year/team level. That is, we don't have the data to know what Moises batted in those games in which he played LF versus RF, we have only the data to know what his final stats were for the whole season. The same is true for salary. Plus, I'm only interested in comparing players who mostly play the same position as one another. Somebody who used to play infield might claim outfield is outfield, but having played it myself a little growing up, I know there's a big difference between LF, CF, and RF. So, this analysis is constrained to only outfielders who played at least 81 games in a season at any one of the three outfield positions. I understand this systematically eliminates utility players and very versatile players, but I had to do it.

Another thing you'll notice in the query is that we're calculating singles (H-2B-3B-HR) now, rather than after we import the data into R, and that an updated ID is being constructed that takes the season into account. This will be useful for labeling and merging purposes later on. The combination of playerID and yearID should be unique (that is, we don't want more than one record for any one player for a given season), so I simply combine these into a new variable called ID.

Import data into R. Now that we have defined a SQL query for getting the data, we need to import it:

```
> # LOAD THE RODBC LIBRARY
> library(RODBC)
>
> # READ IN SQL QUERY FROM EXTERNAL FILE AND REMOVE ALL EXTRA SPACES
> queryFile <- "C:/baseball_salaries/get_data.sql"
> sql <- paste(readLines(query_file), collapse=" ")
> sql <- gsub("[[:space:]]{2,}", " ", sql)
>
> # OPEN CONNECTION TO MYSQL, RUN QUERY, AND IMPORT INTO DATA FRAME
> channel <- odbcConnect(dsn="bbdatabank")
> bbdata <- sqlQuery(channel, sql)
> close(channel)
```

If all went well, the results of the query will exist as a data frame named bbdata. To verify what was imported, we count the records and summarize the data set:

```
> length(bbdata$ID)
[1] 357
> summary(bbdata)
```

This code yields the results in Figure 6-11. This is a very quick overview of everything we will be analyzing. Notice there is never more than one ID value; this is good! The distribution of CF, LF, and RF is pretty equal, though there's slightly more CF (perhaps this player is less likely to platoon with other players or to play other positions). Also notice that slightly more NL players qualify than AL players, and notice the salary distribution. Half of all of these outfielders earned at least $3,416,667 per season, and half earned less. This breakpoint is a little higher than all players in general, which is to be expected because they're mostly full-time players, but it doesn't really matter because, remember, we'll be comparing them to one another.

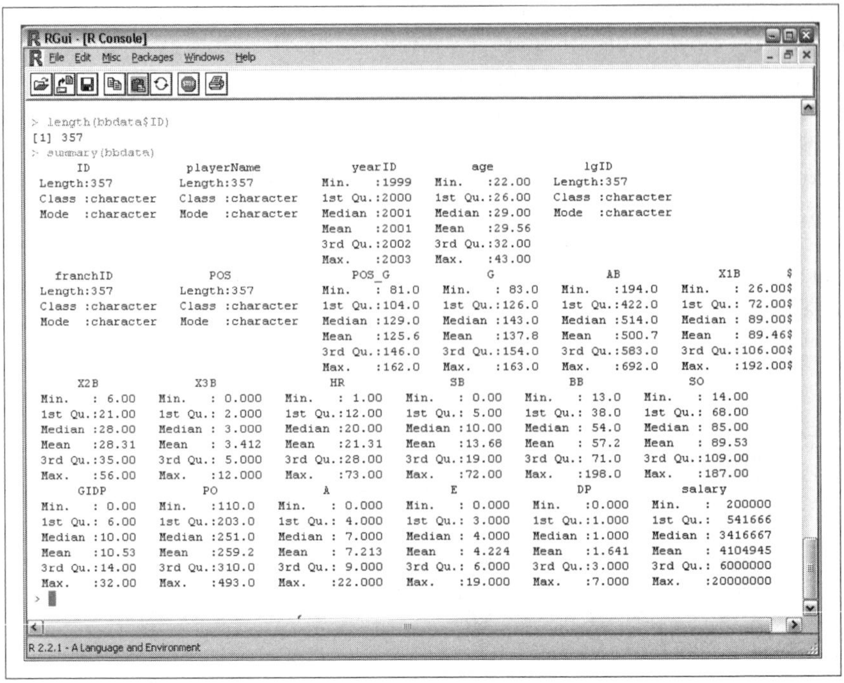

Figure 6-11. Summary of data set

Running the Hack

Identify common attributes. The next step in the process is to take the basic input variables we've imported and are quite familiar with—such as HR, RBI, and SB—and attempt to explain what accounts for them. A common statistical method for doing this sort of thing is called *factor analysis* (see *http://www2.chass.ncsu.edu/garson/pa765/factor.htm*), and R makes it very easy to perform this procedure. In a nutshell, when variables are highly correlated with each other, it's logical to assume that some underlying construct might be responsible for the correlations that you are observing. For example, a high correlation between the number of triples and the number of stolen bases is likely due to an attribute called *speed*. Of course, just because two variables have a strong correlation doesn't mean they're related. (Have you ever heard of the "Super Bowl versus stock market" correlation? See *http://www.sciencenews.org/articles/20000701/mathtrek.asp* for more information.)

Look at correlations. Let's look at the correlations of the input variables we're interested in:

```
> X <- subset(bbdata[,11:22])
> round(cor(X),digits=2)
      X1B   X2B   X3B    HR    SB    BB    SO  GIDP   PO    A    E   DP
X1B  1.00  0.50  0.31  0.06  0.42  0.04 -0.03  0.33 0.49 0.21 0.06 0.10
X2B  0.50  1.00  0.05  0.45 -0.01  0.29  0.25  0.45 0.34 0.30 0.13 0.12
X3B  0.31  0.05  1.00 -0.15  0.47 -0.05 -0.04 -0.19 0.31 0.18 0.05 0.14
HR   0.06  0.45 -0.15  1.00 -0.26  0.59  0.46  0.34 0.23 0.25 0.27 0.12
SB   0.42 -0.01  0.47 -0.26  1.00 -0.01 -0.02 -0.22 0.31 0.01 0.03 0.07
BB   0.04  0.29 -0.05  0.59 -0.01  1.00  0.32  0.08 0.13 0.13 0.18 0.07
SO  -0.03  0.25 -0.04  0.46 -0.02  0.32  1.00  0.11 0.34 0.21 0.22 0.12
GIDP 0.33  0.45 -0.19  0.34 -0.22  0.08  0.11  1.00 0.19 0.20 0.18 0.06
PO   0.49  0.34  0.31  0.23  0.31  0.13  0.34  0.19 1.00 0.33 0.14 0.29
A    0.21  0.30  0.18  0.25  0.01  0.13  0.21  0.20 0.33 1.00 0.30 0.58
E    0.06  0.13  0.05  0.27  0.03  0.18  0.22  0.18 0.14 0.30 1.00 0.13
DP   0.10  0.12  0.14  0.12  0.07  0.07  0.12  0.06 0.29 0.58 0.13 1.00
```

As expected, 3B and SB are pretty well correlated with each other ($r = 0.47$), and SB and GIDP are negatively correlated ($r = -0.22$); that is, players with high SB totals tend to have hit into fewer double plays, and vice versa.

Identify possible explanations for correlations. R's function for performing a factor analysis, factanal( ), takes a matrix of numeric values you feed it, computes their correlations, and then attempts to optimize the maximum likelihood that those observed correlations came from the specified number of factors that *you* say they did. And herein lies the art. Knowing how many factors to suggest and whether they make sense is very much an iterative and subjective process (for more background on this fascinating statistical technique, search the Web for "factor analysis"). Applying this technique to our data yields the following:

```
> far <- factanal(~X1B+X2B+X3B+HR+SB+BB+SO+GIDP+PO+A+E+DP,
+ data=bbdata, factors=5, scores="regression")
> far$n.obs
[1] 357
> print(far)

Call:
factanal(x = ~X1B + X2B + X3B + HR + SB + BB + SO + GIDP + PO + A + E + DP,
    factors = 5, data = bbdata, scores = "regression")

Uniquenesses:
  X1B   X2B   X3B    HR    SB    BB    SO  GIDP    PO     A     E    DP
0.094 0.465 0.623 0.193 0.377 0.488 0.636 0.508 0.005 0.005 0.858 0.631
```

```
Loadings:
       Factor1 Factor2 Factor3 Factor4 Factor5
X1B            0.784   0.526           0.101
X2B    0.336   0.629           0.144
X3B                    0.581   0.160   0.105
HR     0.807   0.272  -0.252   0.105
SB                     0.784
BB     0.709
SO     0.506                   0.147   0.288
GIDP   0.102   0.610  -0.301           0.101
PO     0.177   0.285   0.349   0.224   0.843
A      0.132   0.182           0.970
E      0.268                   0.253
DP                             0.581   0.136


               Factor1 Factor2 Factor3 Factor4 Factor5
SS loadings     1.666   1.583   1.521   1.484   0.864
Proportion Var  0.139   0.132   0.127   0.124   0.072
Cumulative Var  0.139   0.271   0.397   0.521   0.593

Test of the hypothesis that 5 factors are sufficient.
The chi square statistic is 30.04 on 16 degrees of freedom.
The p-value is 0.0178
```

You're looking to see that the variables that "load" into the different factors make sense and belong together, and that the higher the absolute value of the load (which ranges from −1 to +1), the more prominent a role that variable plays in the factor. So, it's fairly obvious that Factor1 equals "power," Factor2 equals "ability to make contact," and Factor3 equals "speed." Factor4 is a little harder to interpret. Is it "range" or "arm strength" that accounts for a high number of assists and double plays? Since PO and E play a small part, it might be "range." But the very high A and DP imply "arm." For now, let's simply call it "defensive prowess." And what about Factor5? Hmmm. I'm hesitant to call it "glove ability" despite the very high PO loading because there's no negative loading for E, as you would expect. Plus, some outfielders simply see more fly balls, depending on their team's pitchers. So, let's call it "fly ball opportunities." Of course, in practice, you would look at more than five factors here. Notice that the "cumulative variance" of these five factors together accounts for about 59.3% of the total variability seen in the original 12 variables, so we are losing some information. But while you could try using more factors to preserve more information, it's a balancing act because there are diminishing returns the more factors you include. Furthermore, recall that the whole point is to reduce the dimensionality of the input variables (though p-value < 0.05 suggests we should probably look at more factors). But we'll go with these five for now and see what happens. Another thing to look at is the "uniqueness" of each variable (which ranges from 0 to 1). The higher the value, the more the variable "stands on its own" and doesn't really correlate strongly enough with any other variables to suggest a common factor. For example, E is kind of high, which makes sense.

Assign attribute scores. In our call to factanal( ), we asked it to compute factor scores for the five factors. This basically multiplies the factor loadings with the players' values for each of the original variables and sums them up for each factor. Then R internally standardizes each factor based on the mean and standard deviation for that factor. The end result is five standardized factor scores for each player, where 0 suggests completely average, +2 suggests two standard deviations above the average, and −2 suggests two standard deviations below the average. So, let's label these factors and then append the scores onto our data set:

```
> colnames(far$scores) <- c("power","contact","speed","defense","flyball")
> bbdata <- data.frame(bbdata, far$scores)
```

Now, let's test this out. Which players have had seasons at least two standard deviations above average on "power"?

```
> subset(bbdata[,c('playerName','yearID','POS','AB','HR','power')],
+ power >= 2)
          playerName yearID POS  AB HR    power
40       Bonds, Barry   2000  LF 480 49 2.238885
41       Bonds, Barry   2001  LF 476 73 4.420423
42       Bonds, Barry   2002  LF 403 46 3.033495
43       Bonds, Barry   2003  LF 390 45 2.190994
131   Gonzalez, Luis   2001  LF 609 57 2.121822
305       Sosa, Sammy   1999  RF 625 63 2.644626
306       Sosa, Sammy   2000  RF 604 50 2.261168
307       Sosa, Sammy   2001  RF 577 64 3.205626
```

No surprises here! What about the players who scored *lowest* on "defense"?

```
> subset(bbdata[,c('playerName','yearID','POS','POS_G','PO',
+ 'A','E','DP','defense')], defense <= -1.5)
            playerName yearID POS POS_G  PO   A  E DP   defense
13       Anderson, Brady   2000  CF    88 230  1  1  1 -1.604664
149    Grissom, Marquis   1999  CF   149 374  1  5  2 -1.768149
162   Henderson, Rickey   1999  LF   116 167  0  2  0 -1.869917
216        Lawton, Matt   2000  RF    83 163  2  3  0 -1.508250
258       O'Neill, Paul   2001  RF   130 210  1  4  0 -1.615759
289      Sanchez, Alex   2002  CF    86 234  0  5  0 -1.648747
306        Sosa, Sammy   2000  RF   156 316  3 10  1 -1.547480
333      Wells, Vernon   2003  CF   161 383  3  4  0 -1.519429
342   Williams, Bernie   2000  CF   137 353  2  0  1 -1.523878
344   Williams, Bernie   2002  CF   147 350  2  5  1 -1.769403
```

No great surprises here either. These players have seasons with very few assist and double play totals relative to putouts, and there are some fairly high error counts.

Group players based on similarity. We could go ahead and predict player salaries based on their factor scores right now, but this isn't quite fair because not all outfielders are of the same ilk. Some are power hitters who play shaky defense, and others are fleet-footed and cover a lot of ground but are not going to hit towering 475-foot home runs. So, we shall attempt to "classify" our players into similar groups based on their factor scores to one another. One fairly simple method for doing this is to perform the k-means clustering procedure (see *http://www.statsoft.com/textbook/stcluan.html#k*). This procedure creates as many groups as *you* choose and then attempts to cluster all of the observations into these groups by seeking minimal variability *within* clusters while seeking maximal variability *between* clusters. We'll try four groups and see what happens. Note that first I'll "seed" the algorithm with what initial cluster centers to use. Because I have no real way of knowing how they'll end up, I'll simply arbitrarily choose the first four. Then, I'll allow the algorithm to use up to 10,000 "turns" for moving observations around to find the best fit (think Tower of Hanoi game).

```
> x <- subset(bbdata[,c('power','contact','speed','defense','flyball')])
> k <- kmeans(x, centers=x[1:4,], iter.max = 10^4)
> k$size
[1]  59  98  67 133
> k$centers
       power    contact      speed    defense    flyball
1 -0.4996645  0.51392727  1.2983112 -0.2806153  0.4546846
2  0.1314219  0.57052991 -0.2257822  0.9370217 -0.3982199
3  1.0818315 -0.03571007 -0.1355412 -0.2216914  1.0032891
4 -0.4201643 -0.63038395 -0.3412965 -0.4542744 -0.4136933
```

This clusters our 357 players into four groups based on the factors we found earlier. It suggests that 59 players belong to Group 1, 98 players belong to Group 2, etc. R did all of the work. All we need to do now is to attach meaningful labels to these groups somehow and see if they make sense. Looking at the mean factor scores (a.k.a. *cluster centers*) for each group, it looks as though Group 1 consists of those players with below-average power but great speed and who make good contact. They also play below-average defense, yet they record a high number of putouts. Perhaps they are leadoff-type hitters. Group 2 looks to be composed of contact hitters with average pop, slightly below-average speed, and the ability to play decent defense, despite not seeing a lot of fly balls. Group 3 comprises your typical power hitters with slightly below-average contact, speed, and defense. But they do catch a lot of fly balls—interesting. We'll see more about these players later. Finally, Group 4 consists of players that are below average all around. It also happens to be the largest group. So, perhaps these are journeymen players or platoon players. It's also worth noting that we've taken some statistical liberties in this analysis because some extremely good players (like Barry

Bonds) can count for up to five different seasons and can really raise the bar for other player-seasons. If you really wanted to be good, you'd probably want to average players' seasons so that each player appears only once. But what would you do about the fact that the player might play LF one season and RF another? Or that his salary or team might change?

Attach group membership to data set. Now we want to append group membership to our data set. This is easy enough:

```
> bbdata$cluster <- k$cluster
```

Let's take a quick look at the breakdown of clustered group versus position to see if it fits with these conjectures:

```
> table(bbdata$cluster, bbdata$POS)
```

```
    CF LF RF
  1 40 10  9
  2 12 42 44
  3 40 12 15
  4 44 42 47
```

Recall that Group 1 comprised the fleet-footed contact hitters (leadoff types) who also recorded a fair number of putouts defensively but are slightly below average defensively. Generally, center fielders are considered to be the *best* defensive outfielders, so there's probably too much thrown into that one "defense" factor (more proof that we didn't ask for enough). Group 2 consisted of contact hitters with a decent defense score despite fewer putouts. Group 3 was composed of the power hitters with average contact, speed, and defense, but a lot of putouts. I'm really surprised to see that this group is full of CF players and few LF and RF players. Finally, Group 4 consisted of the below-average all-around players, so it makes sense that it's pretty equally distributed across all three of the outfield positions. Why should there be any more or less all-around LF than RF players, for example? It's good to see this isn't the case.

Transform salary variable. Before we can accurately predict salaries for our players, we must keep in mind that salaries are not normally distributed. Specifically, taking a quick look at the distribution of salaries yields a very skewed picture, as shown in Figure 6-12.

```
> hist(bbdata$salary)
```

Let's transform the salaries into something that looks much less skewed. Let's take the natural log of salary and use it. The results are shown in Figure 6-13.

```
> bbdata$salary.log <- log(bbdata$salary)
> hist(bbdata$salary.log)
```

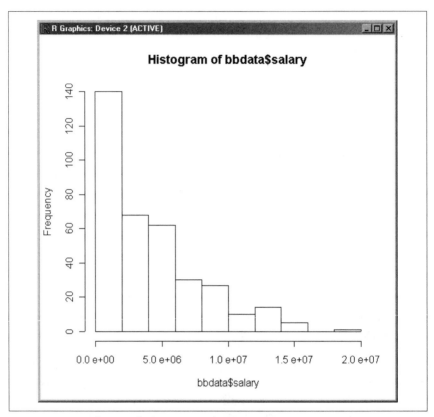

Figure 6-12. Distribution of salaries

Create linear regression model. The time has come to predict players' salaries! We will run a linear regression model for each of our four groups of players, using our factor scores, along with player age, to estimate salaries. We'll then "undo" the predicted values because, remember, we actually are predicting log(salary), so we must undo this transformation by applying exp(salary.log). We'll then stack all the subsets back into one great big data set.

```
> # BREAK UP MAIN DATASET INTO SUBSETS
> bbdata1 <- subset(bbdata, cluster==1)
> bbdata2 <- subset(bbdata, cluster==2)
> bbdata3 <- subset(bbdata, cluster==3)
> bbdata4 <- subset(bbdata, cluster==4)

> # RUN REGRESSION MODELS
> lm1 <- lm(salary.log~age+power+contact+speed+defense+flyball,
data=bbdata1)
```

```
> lm2 <- lm(salary.log~age+power+contact+speed+defense+flyball,
data=bbdata2)
> lm3 <- lm(salary.log~age+power+contact+speed+defense+flyball,
data=bbdata3)
> lm4 <- lm(salary.log~age+power+contact+speed+defense+flyball,
data=bbdata4)

> # UNDO TRANSFORMATION OF PREDICTED LOG(SALARIES)
> bbdata1$predicted <- exp(lm1$fitted.values)
> bbdata2$predicted <- exp(lm2$fitted.values)
> bbdata3$predicted <- exp(lm3$fitted.values)
> bbdata4$predicted <- exp(lm4$fitted.values)

> # STACK SUBSETS BACK TOGETHER TO FORM REAL DATASET
> bbdata <- data.frame(rbind(bbdata1,bbdata2,bbdata3,bbdata4))
```

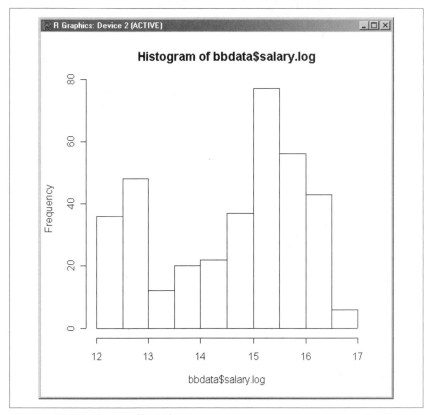

Figure 6-13. Distribution of log(salary)

Glossing over all the statistical details, such as investigating how valid these regression models actually appear to be, discussing what statistical assumptions have been violated, etc., we'll simply plot the predicted salaries against the actual salaries to see how well we did, and we'll use the players' group or cluster membership as the plotting points:

```
> plot(salary~predicted, data=bbdata, col=cluster, pch=paste(cluster,''))
> abline(lm(salary~predicted, data=bbdata))
```

As you can see in Figure 6-14, the points above the line represent players who have an actual salary higher than predicted, whereas the points below the line represent players who have an actual salary lower than predicted.

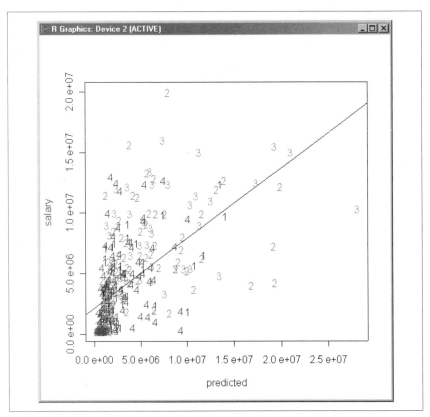

Figure 6-14. Actual versus predicted salaries

Ideally, all the points would lie on that regression line. What is the correlation between predicted and actual? We would hope it would be "high."

```
> r <- cor(bbdata$predicted,bbdata$salary)
> r; r^2
[1] 0.5861738
[1] 0.3435997
```

Again, it's OK but not great. An R^2 value of .344 means that 34.4% of the observed variability in actual salaries can be accounted for by our input variables of age, group membership, and factor scores. It's not surprising that there must be a lot more variables out there that also influence players' actual salaries than the ones we've chosen.

Compare predicted versus actual salaries. Let's compute the difference between actual and predicted salaries and save the calculation for each player. We'll then create a box plot, by group/cluster number, to see how it looks (see Figure 6-15).

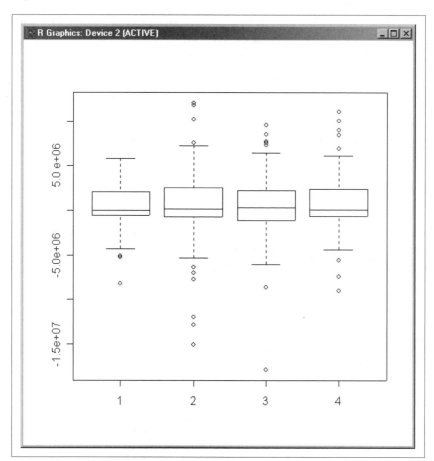

Figure 6-15. Box plot of (actual minus predicted) salary versus group number

```
> bbdata$diff = bbdata$salary - bbdata$predicted
> for(i in 1:4) {
+ print(summary(subset(bbdata[,'diff'], bbdata$cluster==i)));
+ }
    Min. 1st Qu.  Median    Mean 3rd Qu.    Max.
 -8215000 -559900  -16900  477900 2058000 5845000
     Min.  1st Qu.   Median     Mean  3rd Qu.     Max.
-15080000  -697800   181300   544600  2486000 12040000
     Min.  1st Qu.   Median     Mean 3rd Qu.     Max.
-17840000 -1099000   339000   553900 2257000  9574000
    Min. 1st Qu.  Median    Mean 3rd Qu.     Max.
 -9021000 -598800  109700  873400 2391000 11110000
> boxplot(diff~cluster, data=bbdata)
```

On average, we've undershot actual salary by about $500,000. But this could be largely due to a few extremely highly paid players "underperforming," which throws the average off for everyone. Looking at the median values, it's not quite so dire. We're only about $200,000 under for 50% of the players. And for Group 1, we've actually overestimated salary slightly for 50% of its players.

Identify most-underpaid players. It's easy enough to find which players have the very largest discrepancies between actual and predicted salaries, but let's first standardize the differences so that everybody is on equal footing, and to help eliminate some of this actual minus predicted bias that exists:

```
> bbdata$stdiff = (bbdata$diff - mean(bbdata$diff)) / sd(bbdata$diff)
```

Let's find the most relatively underpaid players; that is, those at least two standard deviations below the average (actual minus predicted) difference:

```
> underpaid <- subset(bbdata[,c('playerName','yearID',
+                    'age','POS','G',
+                    'cluster','salary','predicted',
+                    'stdiff')], stdiff <= -2)
> underpaid[sort.list(underpaid$stdiff),]
          playerName yearID age POS   G cluster    salary predicted
41       Bonds, Barry   2001  37  LF 153       3  10300000  28142677
111      Finley, Steve   2003  38  CF 147       2   4250000  19334449
133     Gonzalez, Luis   2003  36  LF 156       2   4000000  16800508
36     Bichette, Dante   1999  36  LF 151       2   7250000  19185633
163 Henderson, Rickey   2001  43  LF 123       4    300000   9321189
131     Gonzalez, Luis   2001  34  LF 162       3   4833333  13448594
152  Grissom, Marquis   2003  36  CF 149       1   1875000  10090267
328      Walker, Larry   2001  35  RF 142       2  12166667  19884406
162 Henderson, Rickey   1999  41  LF 121       4   1900000   9341312
316      Surhoff, B.J.   1999  35  LF 162       2   3705516  10697211
          stdiff
41     -5.235698
111    -4.455110
133    -3.808747
36     -3.563984
```

```
163 -2.739187
131 -2.624308
152 -2.511108
328 -2.370306
162 -2.292076
316 -2.164833
```

It's nice to see that this list contains players from each of the four identified clusters. It's interesting that all of them are older players who mostly play LF. Of course, Barry Bonds' 2001 campaign in which he broke the single-season HR and SLG records is the biggest bargain, even if he was paid $10 million, given his all-around performance relative to other players in the "slugger" cluster. It's interesting that Luis Gonzalez makes it twice—very underappreciated.

Identify most-overpaid players. At the other end of the spectrum, we have players who were actually paid more than expected, given their relative performance:

```
> overpaid <- subset(bbdata[,c('playerName','yearID',
+                    'age','POS','G',
+                    'cluster','salary','predicted',
+                    'stdiff')], stdiff >= 2)
> overpaid[sort.list(overpaid$stdiff, decreasing=TRUE),]
            playerName yearID age POS   G cluster   salary predicted
279     Ramirez, Manny   2003  31  LF 154       2 20000000   7963658
140       Green, Shawn   2003  31  RF 160       2 15666667   3818053
244      Mondesi, Raul   2003  32  RF  98       4 13000000   1890954
157 Guerrero, Vladimir   2003  27  RF 112       2 11500000   1250975
148       Griffey, Ken   2001  32  CF 111       4 12500000   2454218
191      Jones, Andruw   2003  26  CF 156       3 12000000   2425791
173   Higginson, Bobby   2003  33  RF 130       4 11850000   2852073
309        Sosa, Sammy   2003  35  RF 137       3 16000000   7435686
138       Green, Shawn   2001  29  RF 161       3 12166667   3607110
242      Mondesi, Raul   2000  29  RF  96       4 10000000   1521948
190      Jones, Andruw   2002  25  CF 154       3 10000000   2231977
        stdiff
279   3.220166
140   3.167039
244   2.957739
157   2.714350
148   2.656831
191   2.523375
173   2.360285
309   2.237571
138   2.236225
242   2.213158
190   2.012218
```

There are a lot of big salaries here, and they just didn't stand out enough from other players on the various factors.

I covered a lot in this hack, and yet, I intentionally skimmed over a lot of the underlying statistical theory to help keep the hack reasonably short. But I hope it piqued your interest to perform similar analyses using R and to learn more about multivariate statistical techniques, especially as they might be applied to baseball stats.

Hacking the Hack

Vary the numbers of factors and/or number of clusters. You can get "tighter" predictions if you ask for more than five factors (remember, using five only retained 59% of the variability), though you would need to reinterpret all of them because there's no guarantee the five existing ones would stay the same. Also, varying the number of clusters to group players would help fine-tune the predictions further, as well.

Look at different positions. This hack could certainly be applicable to other positions, as well. Obviously, what is valued in an outfielder is different from, say, a shortstop or a catcher. But it gets a little thorny if you consider some players are versatile and play a variety of positions over the course of a season (and certainly over their careers). So perhaps identify utility players in a class by themselves.

Look at different years. It would be interesting to see what mix of skills was most valued in 1985 versus 1995. Or, if you can find the salary data, you might want to look back even further.

Include more variables. The variables included in this hack only scratch the surface for drawing a "complete" picture of a player's worth. It would be much more interesting to include many more variables, such as what side of the plate he bats on; his experience, height, and weight; how good his team is; the home park he plays in; and his ground-ball-to-fly-ball tendency, just to name a few.

—*Tom Dierickx*

Fitting Game Scores to a Strength Model

HACK #71 Calculate offense, defensive, and ballpark factors simultaneously, by fitting score data to a model.

In this hack, we will introduce a mathematical model that will be fit to a simple data set that can be derived from the scores of every game in a league's season. If you have the data available, you can use this method for any league, anywhere.

We consider the list of scores for a season. Each game's results are typically represented by the home team, the visiting team, the ballpark, and the scores. For example, consider the score of the opening game of the 2004 Cincinnati Reds (CIN) campaign, in which the Chicago Cubs (CHN) beat the Reds at the Great American Ballpark, 7–4.

Within this one game's scores, we can derive five parameters and two scores. In other words, we can make the following two observations:

- The Reds' offense and the Cubs' defense at the Cincinnati ballpark led to four runs.
- The Cubs' offense and the Reds' defense at the Cincinnati ballpark led to seven runs.

You might also represent this as the following set of observations, organized as (OFFENSE, DEFENSE, BALLPARK, RUNS):

```
CIN CHN CIN 4
CHN CIN CIN 7
```

Thus, for one full season's worth of Major League Baseball games, we will have two rows of observations per game, or 15 × 162 × 2 = 4,860 total rows of data.

Our objective here is to use this data to understand the contributions each component had on the scores for the season. More specifically, we will fit this data to a model to solve for each team's offensive and defensive strengths. We will also produce a factor for each ballpark. The basic model that we will use looks like this:

```
Runs ~ Offense * Defense * BallPark
```

Assuming that each of the three terms on the righthand side is an exponential term, and adding one run to each score to avoid taking the logarithm of 0, we have the following model after taking a logarithm:

```
Log(Runs + 1) ~ O + D + B
```

where we use the notation:

```
Offense = exp(O); Defense = exp(D); Ballpark = exp(B)
```

We call this the ODB model, for obvious reasons.

Once we fit the data to this model, we will have offensive, defensive, and ballpark scores for each team and each ballpark that was used during the season. When these scores are generated, we will then be able to rank teams based on their offensive and defensive strengths in a way that indirectly takes into account the effects their ballparks and their competition might have made to their overall statistics. We will effectively be solving for the *raw* scores after removing all of these extraneous effects.

In addition to this, we will be able to go back and determine a strength-of-schedule score for each team.

The Data and the Code

For these calculations, we will use major league game scores from 2004, but note that this approach can work for any baseball league at any level, as long as you have every game from the season in your database. We will get the data for this study from the Retrosheet web site. In this hack, we'll use the Retrosheet Game Log files, as described in "Load Retrosheet Game Logs" [Hack #21]. We will also load the text files directly into R, as described in "Load Text Files into R" [Hack #34].

Using R, let's read the 2004 season data using the read.csv( ) function:

```
Scores <- read.csv("gl2004.txt", header=FALSE, as.is=T)
```

Because this datafile does not contain headers, we will need to consult the *glfields.txt* file to determine which columns we need for our calculations. In particular, the ballpark is in the 17th column, the visiting team is in the 4th column, the home team is in the 7th column, and the visiting and home scores are in the 10th and 11th columns, respectively. For ease of use, we pull those into arrays in R, as follows:

```
Parks <- Scores[,17]
VTeam <- Scores[,4]
HTeam <- Scores[,7]
VScore <- Scores[,10]
HScore <- Scores[,11]
```

From this raw data, we effectively have five columns of data—one row corresponds to one game. For example, the fourth element in each array corresponds to the game we mentioned in the introduction:

```
> Parks[4]
[1] "CIN09"
> VTeam[4]
[1] "CHN"
> HTeam[4]
[1] "CIN"
> HScore[4]
[1] 4
> VScore[4]
[1] 7
```

Recall, however, from earlier that we actually want two rows per game, with three columns of factors and one score per row. We will create the vectors we need by concatenating the appropriate vectors together in a sensible way. We create our O vector by concatenating the HTeam and VTeam vectors to each other:

```
O <- as.factor(c(HTeam, VTeam))
```

Note that we use the as.factor( ) function to preserve our desire to keep each element as one of R's factor datatypes. R's default behavior would be to assign integer values to each level during the concatenation. Continuing, because we want each element of the D array to line up with the right slot in the O vector, we will want to flip the order in which we do the concatenation. We append HTeam to VTeam as follows:

```
D <- as.factor(c(VTeam, HTeam))
```

Now, we want to build the TheScores vector and the B vector in the corresponding way:

```
TheScores <- c(HScore, VScore)
B <- as.factor(c(Parks, Parks))
```

At this point, the Cincinnati/Chicago game is represented by two rows (the 4th and the 2,432nd), as follows:

```
> O[4]
[1] CIN
30 Levels: ANA ARI ATL BAL BOS CHA CHN CIN CLE COL DET FLO HOU KCA LAN MIL .
.. TOR
> D[4]
[1] CHN
30 Levels: ANA ARI ATL BAL BOS CHA CHN CIN CLE COL DET FLO HOU KCA LAN MIL .
.. TOR
> TheScores[4]
[1] 4
> B[4]
[1] CIN09
32 Levels: ANA01 ARL02 ATL02 BAL12 BOS07 CHI11 CHI12 CIN09 CLE08 ... TOR02


> O[4 + 2428]
[1] CHN
30 Levels: ANA ARI ATL BAL BOS CHA CHN CIN CLE COL DET FLO HOU KCA LAN MIL .
.. TOR
> D[4 + 2428]
[1] CIN
30 Levels: ANA ARI ATL BAL BOS CHA CHN CIN CLE COL DET FLO HOU KCA LAN MIL .
.. TOR
> TheScores[4 + 2428]
[1] 7
> B[4 + 2428]
[1] CIN09
32 Levels: ANA01 ARL02 ATL02 BAL12 BOS07 CHI11 CHI12 CIN09 CLE08 ... TOR02
```

Finally, because we will be using the logarithm of the runs (plus one), we now create our run vector as follows:

```
lRp1 <- log(TheScores+1)
```

Now that all of the data is set up so that each row corresponds to one team's offense, one team's defense, the home team's ballpark, and the offense's total runs scored in the game, we can fit this data to our model by using R's lm( ) function:

```
a1 <- lm(lRp1 ~ 0 + D + B)
```

Once the calculation finishes, we can see the summary of the fit as follows:

```
> a1

Call:
lm(formula = lRp1 ~ 0 + D + B)

Coefficients:
(Intercept)        OARI        OATL        OBAL        OBOS        OCHA
  1.5600770  -0.2887574  -0.0008088  -0.0774623   0.0742994  -0.0699490
       OCHN        OCIN        OCLE        OCOL        ODET        OFLO
 -0.0757260   0.0397397   0.0309474  -0.0954376  -0.0035989  -0.0415393
       OHOU        OKCA        OLAN        OMIL        OMIN        OMON
 -0.0060062  -0.1322421  -0.0885335  -0.2095271  -0.0412393  -0.1604447
       ONYA        ONYN        OOAK        OPHI        OPIT        OSDN
  0.0861376  -0.1444363  -0.0442706   0.0460482  -0.0854521  -0.0119644
       OSEA        OSFN        OSLN        OTBA        OTEX        OTOR
 -0.0607188   0.0152746   0.0953595  -0.1104611  -0.0735495  -0.1939756
       DARI        DATL        DBAL        DBOS        DCHA        DCHN
  0.1380777  -0.0430947   0.0271287  -0.0363981   0.0550462  -0.0922940
       DCIN        DCLE        DCOL        DDET        DFLO        DHOU
  0.2594701   0.1539126   0.0912566   0.1255421   0.0397851  -0.0313690
       DKCA        DLAN        DMIL        DMIN        DMON        DNYA
  0.2370115   0.0086542   0.0176426  -0.0006022   0.1037448   0.1114923
       DNYN        DOAK        DPHI        DPIT        DSDN        DSEA
  0.0413074  -0.0090027   0.1163264   0.0552478   0.0534413   0.1699609
       DSFN        DSLN        DTBA        DTEX        DTOR      BARLO2
  0.0466555  -0.0309133   0.1410370  -0.0237764   0.0163193   0.2276447
     BATLO2      BBAL12      BBOSO7      BCHI11      BCHI12      BCINO9
 -0.0010244   0.1182421   0.1352769   0.0819046   0.1515526  -0.1180897
     BCLEO8      BDENO2      BDETO5      BHOUO3      BKANO6      BLOSO3
 -0.0217743   0.3030311  -0.0158623   0.0562092  -0.0442516  -0.0161868
     BMIAO1      BMILO6      BMINO3      BMONO2      BNYC16      BNYC17
 -0.1037711   0.0359219  -0.0095720  -0.0453633  -0.0331766  -0.0168252
     BOAKO1      BPHI13      BPHOO1      BPITO8      BSANO2      BSEAO3
  0.0440549   0.0236387   0.1228059  -0.0740702  -0.0695325  -0.1483783
     BSFOO3      BSJUO1      BSTLO9      BSTPO1      BTOKO1      BTORO2
  0.1029081  -0.3470711  -0.0268488  -0.0269612   0.0362239   0.1523465
```

Here is an explanation of the results:

- First, note that each of the coefficients' labels begins with an O, a D, or a B, corresponding to whether the factor came from the Offense, Defense, or Ballpark data.

- Notice that Anaheim's results are nowhere to be found here. In the case of this model, the values of the first factors are locked to 0 and all remaining coefficients are relative to this value.

- Recall that this is a logarithmic model, so a zero coefficient should be interpreted as exp(0) = 1. Positive coefficients mean that the corresponding scaling factor is greater than 1 and negative coefficients correspond to fractional scaling.

To make some of our observations a little easier to read, let's create a few vectors for each of the offensive, defensive, and ballpark scores by just reading the values directly from the coefficients of the a1 object, but continuing to bear in mind that the Anaheim scores still are not included in the resulting vectors:

```
OFF <- (a1$coef)[2:30]
DEF <- (a1$coef)[31:59]
BPK <- (a1$coef)[60:length(a1$coef)]
```

We can then proceed to sort each vector to determine who had the best and worst scores for the league. For the purposes of presentation, we used Excel to generate the following table, which represents the Offense, Defense, and Ballpark coefficients for each team. We also considered an additional quantity—the difference between the Offense and Defense scores—which we call an Overall score. We explain this score and make our observations shortly.

Team	Offense	Defense	Ballpark	Overall
SLN	0.095	-0.031	-0.027	0.126
BOS	0.074	-0.036	0.135	0.111
ATL	-0.001	-0.043	-0.001	0.042
HOU	-0.006	-0.031	0.056	0.025
CHN	-0.076	-0.092	0.082	0.017
ANA	0.000	0.000	0.000	0.000
NYA	0.086	0.111	-0.033	-0.025
SFN	0.015	0.047	0.103	-0.031
OAK	-0.044	-0.009	0.044	-0.035
MIN	-0.041	-0.001	-0.010	-0.041
TEX	-0.074	-0.024	0.228	-0.050
SDN	-0.012	0.053	-0.070	-0.065
PHI	0.046	0.116	0.024	-0.070
FLO	-0.042	0.040	-0.104	-0.081
LAN	-0.089	0.009	-0.016	-0.097
BAL	-0.077	0.027	0.118	-0.105

Team	Offense	Defense	Ballpark	Overall
CLE	0.031	0.154	-0.022	-0.123
CHA	-0.070	0.055	0.152	-0.125
DET	-0.004	0.126	-0.016	-0.129
PIT	-0.085	0.055	-0.074	-0.141
NYN	-0.144	0.041	-0.017	-0.186
COL	-0.095	0.091	0.303	-0.187
TOR	-0.194	0.016	0.152	-0.210
CIN	0.040	0.259	-0.118	-0.220
MIL	-0.210	0.018	0.036	-0.227
SEA	-0.061	0.170	-0.148	-0.231
TBA	-0.110	0.141	-0.027	-0.251
MON	-0.160	0.104	-0.045	-0.264
KCA	-0.132	0.237	-0.044	-0.369
ARI	-0.289	0.138	0.123	-0.427
San Juan			-0.347	
Tokyo			0.036	

Some observations of these results are as follows:

- Remember that these scores are relative to Anaheim's scores, which is why their scores are always zero.

- In the Ballpark factors, we included the few games that were played in Tokyo to open the 2004 season, as well as the games that the Montreal Expos played in Montreal, as well as those they played in San Juan, Puerto Rico. Because significantly fewer games were played in these stadiums, these results might have a high error rating, but we defer any further inquiry to elsewhere.

- Note that a high score means a high number of runs. In the case of Offense, this means big bats scoring lots of runs. In the case of Defense, a high score means a poor combination of pitching and fielding. In the case of the Ballpark score, a high score means that the ballpark makes a positive contribution to runs scored there.

- The Overall score is calculated as Overall <- Offense - Defense. Because we are working on a logarithmic scale, this difference is analogous to a ratio of runs scored to runs allowed (Overall ~ (RS / RA)) since, very loosely speaking, log(RS/RA) = log(RS) - log(RA), which you should recall is precisely the (O - D) term.

- It is interesting to see that the 2004 World Series did indeed consist of the two teams with the highest Overall scores.

- It is also interesting to note that the Dodgers actually finished with a lower score than both the Giants and the Padres, both of which finished below the Dodgers in the closely contested NL West Division race.
- Note that these Overall results already implicitly take into consideration the strength of schedule and the ballparks in which each team played. In fact, this really is the purpose of doing such calculations: to remove the contribution of these factors ahead of time.

Strength of Schedule

In the previous section, we illustrated how you can *simultaneously* solve for Offense, Defense, and Ballpark factors for an entire league by solving a large system for its best fit. As we noted, the results effectively take into account the schedule each team plays, as well as the net effects of all the ballparks they play in.

In this section, we have a little fun with the results of the earlier calculation to determine which Major League Baseball teams played the easiest and most difficult schedules in 2004. We will do this by calculating a schedule-strength score by summing the *Overall* score of each team's opponents. Note that adding these quantities together makes sense because we are still working in a logarithmic scale.

First, let's continue our R session by appending the Anaheim scores to the OFF and DEF vectors, and by creating the OVERALL vector:

```
OFF <- c(OFF, OANA=0)
DEF <- c(DEF, DANA=0)
OVERALL <- sort(OFF - DEF)
```

Next, let's create a function that we can use to return a list of a specified team's opponents. We'll call it getschedule( ) and define it as follows:

```
getschedule <- function(teamcode) {
  homegames <- Scores[Scores[,7]== teamcode,][,4]
  awaygames <-  Scores[Scores[,4]== teamcode,][,7]
  allgames <- c(homegames, awaygames)
  allgames
}
```

Finally, we'll define another function that will be used for display purposes. When a team code is passed to this function, it prints the team code as well as the strength-of-schedule score, which is nothing more than the sum of each of its opponents' Overall scores:

```
allD <- function (teamcode) {
  c(teamcode, sum(OVERALL[paste("O", getschedule(teamcode), sep="")]))
}
```

We'll finally loop over all of the teams and print the results of calculating their strength of schedule.

```
teams <- levels(as.factor(HTeam))

for (i in 1:30) { print(allD(teams[i])) }
```

Team	Schedule
MIL	-12.71
CIN	-12.84
SEA	-13.42
PIT	-14.54
TBA	-15.10
KCA	-15.52
ARI	-15.66
TOR	-16.15
CHN	-16.31
MON	-16.69
TEX	-17.00
HOU	-17.05
NYN	-17.09
OAK	-17.34
ANA	-17.96
BAL	-18.09
PHI	-19.00
COL	-19.38
CHA	-19.56
FLO	-19.69
SLN	-19.91
NYA	-19.92
LAN	-20.28
BOS	-20.28
DET	-20.87
CLE	-21.00
ATL	-21.14
SFN	-22.24
SDN	-23.35
MIN	-25.01

Our observations from these results are as follows:

- Again, because these scores are derived from a relative scoring system in which Anaheim's individual scores were pegged at zero, these numbers are not to be interpreted too literally. Their relative values are of interest, so they can be used for ranking purposes.

- The more negative a number is, the easier the team's schedule was. The 2004 Minnesota Twins had the easiest campaign, and the Milwaukee Brewers had the most difficult.

- Recall from the previous sections that the 2004 St. Louis Cardinals, Houston Astros, and Chicago Cubs had three of the top five Overall scores in baseball. Because of this, the remaining three teams in the NL Central Division were dealt very difficult schedules. Milwaukee, Cincinnati, and Pittsburgh had three of the four most difficult schedules in baseball.

- On the other end of the spectrum, because Arizona's Overall score was so low, the entire NL West benefited from getting to play them multiple times, so we see San Diego and San Francisco having two of the three easiest schedules.

Conclusion

In this hack, we introduced the ODB method, which has applications in many sports, including baseball. For example, you can use the results of these calculations to determine the Offensive and Defensive Schedule Strength separately. This is useful to calculate adjustments for a hitter or a pitcher, based on the strength of the teams that he faced, as well as the net effects of all ballparks that he played in. We publish such results elsewhere.

You also can use this method in any scenario in which you have offense, defense, a playing field, and two scores.

—Mark E. Johnson and Matthew S. Johnson

The Bullpen
Hacks 72–75

This chapter contains the hacks that didn't fit anyplace else in the book, including a few fun things you can do with web browsers and fantasy baseball.

 ### Start or Join a Fantasy League
HACK #72 Test your skills at picking winning players by managing your own fantasy team.

In the late 1960s, a set of professors at Harvard University (led by sociologist William Ganson) invented a new game based on baseball statistics. Each "manager" made up his own team of baseball players. The manager with the best team won. They ranked the teams based on the individual player's statistics—batting averages, runs batted in, and strikeouts.

One of the professors, Bob Sklar, moved on to the University of Michigan and passed the game on to one of his students there, a writer named Daniel Okrent. Okrent introduced this game to a set of his writer friends at a restaurant called La Rotisserie Francaise in Manhattan in 1980, and modern Rotisserie baseball was born. (Incidentally, Okrent wrote the article in *Sports Illustrated* that introduced Bill James to a wide audience. He also wrote one of my favorite books about baseball: *Nine Innings* [Houghton Mifflin], about a single game between the Milwaukee Brewers and the Baltimore Orioles on June 10, 1982.)

Today, according to the Fantasy Sports Trade Association, more than 15 million people participate in fantasy sports. There are many subtle variations on fantasy baseball games, from traditional Rotisserie–style games to sabermetric-influenced games. Some games are played for bragging rights, others for money (hence, the complicated set of fees for transactions in Rotisserie baseball).

The Basics

There are three steps to playing fantasy baseball:

1. Find or form a fantasy league
2. Pick teams
3. Rank teams

Many of the hacks in this book will help you pick teams or rank teams, and I've given some tips on how to use many of the formulas in this book to do this. Although you'll probably find or create a fantasy league before picking teams and you'll probably pick teams before ranking them, it's easier to make sense of everything if we work backward.

Methods of ranking teams. So, let's pretend you and your friends have decided to start a fantasy baseball league. One of the first decisions you have to make is how to rank everyone's teams, even though you're actually not going to start ranking teams until you've formed your league and picked your teams.

How do you decide how everyone is doing? Unless you're a real baseball team owner, you can't put together a set of players and figure out how well they play together versus competitors. But you can estimate how well a team will perform by looking at the statistics of its individual players. Here are a few popular scoring schemes:

Rotisserie–style category leagues
Each team is ranked by a few offensive categories (for example, home runs, runs batted in, stolen bases, and batting average) and a few defensive categories (for example, wins, saves, earned run average, and hits plus walks per inning pitched). Each team then receives points based on ranking. Suppose a league has 12 teams. The team with the highest number of home runs receives 12 points, the team with the second highest receives 11 points, the third highest 10 points, etc. You calculate the total score for each team by adding all the points received. For a list of popular Rotisserie–style categories, see Table 7-1.

Table 7-1. Popular Rotisserie league scoring systems

Nickname	Offensive stats	Defensive stats
4×4 (Rotisserie Lite)	HR, RBI, SB, AVG	W, SV, ERA, WHIP
5×5 (Rotisserie)	HR, RBI, SB, AVG, R	W, SV, ERA, WHIP, IP
5×5 (Alternate)	HR, RBI, SB, AVG, R	W, SV, ERA, WHIP, SO
Sabermetric League	R, RBI, OBP, SLG	W, SV, ERA, WHIP

Point-scoring leagues

As you do with 4×4 and 5×5 Rotisserie leagues, you base scores in point-scoring leagues on a team's performance using several key statistics. Unlike these leagues, however, you base points on performance rather than ranking. A league picks a weight for each statistic (say, four points for home runs, two points for stolen bases, and one point for runs batted in). To score a team, you count all the points. Suppose a team scores 10 home runs, 5 stolen bases, and 15 runs batted in. This team would score 10 × 4 + 5 × 2 + 15 × 1 = 65 points.

A popular point-scoring league is Salary Cap Baseball, available from The Sporting News (TSN) and MLB web sites. See Tables 7-2 and 7-3 for the points in this system.

Table 7-2. TSN points for offensive statistics

Statistic	Points
Outs (any at bat not ending in a hit)	-2
Run scored	5
Single	5
Double	10
Triple	15
Home run	20
RBI	5
Walk/hit by pitch	3
Strikeout	-1
Stolen base	10
Caught stealing	-5

Table 7-3. TSN points for defensive statistics

Statistic	Points
Win	30
Save	30
Loss	-15
Inning pitched	15
Hit allowed	-5
Earned run allowed	-10
Walk/hit batsman	-3
Strikeout	3

This is obviously much more complicated than the Rotisserie leagues. I don't recommend that you try one of these leagues on paper.

Head-to-head leagues

A head-to-head league works a little differently. As with the other league types, you base a team's performance on how well it fares in a set of categories. Each week, teams are paired with each other. Each pair of teams competes in each statistical category and is credited with wins or losses for the week, based on its performance. For example, suppose Team A and Team B are paired with each other. Team A has 10 home runs, 5 stolen bases, and 15 runs batted in. Team B has 8 home runs, 3 stolen bases, and 20 runs batted in. Team A will win in home runs, lose in stolen bases, and lose in runs batted in. Team B will lose in home runs, win in stolen bases, and win in runs batted in. So Team A's record for the week will be one win and two losses, and Team B's will be two wins and one loss.

Other types of leagues

You can rank teams in other ways, if you want. For example, I think it would be neat to use the linear weights scores (i.e., batter runs, fielding runs, and pitching runs) to rank a set of fantasy teams. Unfortunately, not all of the big fantasy baseball web sites let you do this.

Methods of picking teams. Once you've picked a scoring system, your next decision is how to pick teams. There are a few important decisions to make:

Rosters

Real baseball teams have 25 members (through most of the season), and fantasy teams have similar restrictions. Baseball players aren't completely interchangeable: at any time, there is one pitcher, one catcher, one first baseman, one second baseman, one shortstop, one third baseman, one left fielder, one center fielder, one right fielder, and in the AL, one designated hitter. A team's roster needs to include enough of each type of player to actually play the game: a real team with 20 pitchers and 5 shortstops wouldn't work very well.

Fantasy leagues simplify things a little by grouping outfielders together, not differentiating between the different positions. They require every team to include a minimum number of players at each position, and they place restrictions on the minimum number of plate appearances or innings pitched. (Otherwise, managers would try to include a team of elite closers such as Eric Gagne, Trevor Hoffman, Mariano Rivera, Keith Foulke, Francisco Rodriguez, and Billy Wagner.)

Traditional Rotisserie leagues include 25 players: 5 outfielders, 2 catchers, 1 second baseman, 1 shortstop, 1 other middle infielder, 1 first baseman, 1 third baseman, 1 other corner infielder, 2 utility players (who can play any position), and 10 pitchers. (For AL leagues, there are

23 players: 1 player who acts as a designated hitter replaces the 2 utility players, and there are only 9 pitchers.)

Eligible players

Will you allow players from just one of the two leagues (AL or NL) or from all of MLB? This is an issue for two reasons. First, if your fantasy league has only a dozen or so teams, it's more realistic to force everyone to pick players from the same league. Second, the designated hitter screws things up. AL-based leagues have a DH, and NL-based leagues don't; NL-based leagues might use a pitcher's batting statistics, and AL-based leagues can't. A subtler effect is that a few offensive stats (R, RBI) and a few defensive stats (ERA, SO) are affected by the DH. One out of every nine players in the NL is usually an easy out; that's not true in the AL. So pitching statistics in the NL are boosted a little bit, and offensive statistics are reduced.

Drafts, auctions, and budgets

If everyone could pick players without restrictions, almost every (AL-based) team would include Ivan Rodriguez, Alex Rodriguez, Miguel Tejada, Alfonso Soriano, David Ortiz, Manny Ramirez, and Vladimir Guerrero. To make things interesting, fantasy leagues impose auctions, drafts, and budgets to make managers compete for players.

The key part of fantasy leagues is the method used to select players. A common approach (the Rotisserie approach) is to use an auction. Each manager in the league takes turns proposing a new player for auction. Managers then bid on each player; the highest bidder wins the player.

An alternative approach is to use a draft. Managers simply take turns selecting players until each team is filled. Drafts might use preset valuations for players (for example, real salaries or values from a fantasy guidebook) to impose some restrictions on what each team can do. There are also mixed approaches—for example, a draft is used for a set number of rounds, followed by an auction.

Trades, free agents, and waivers

Just like real baseball leagues, fantasy leagues allow owners to swap players, acquire free agents, and drop underperforming players.

Keepers

Many leagues last for more than one season and include rules for retaining players across seasons. These rules place restrictions on the number of players who must be retained and the number who must be released. Rotisserie leagues require teams to keep at least 7 players between seasons, but allow no more than 15.

Minor leagues
Some fantasy baseball leagues allow teams to draft minor league players and later "call up" minor leaguers, adding them to their roster.

Find or form a fantasy league. The easiest way to start playing fantasy baseball is to set up or join a fantasy league on the Internet. The right web site for you depends on how you want to pick and score your teams. It's a lot easier to decide how to manage your fantasy league after you've figured out how you want to score and pick teams. (That's why I decided to provide this explanation last.)

Here are a few popular online fantasy baseball web sites. (The links were correct as of the summer of 2005; I can't promise that all of these links will work forever. If they fail, try going to the main page of these web sites and look for links to "sports," "MLB," and "fantasy.")

USA Stats, http://www.rotisserie.com/index.asp
This is the official web site of the Rotisserie League Baseball Association. It strictly features 5×5 Rotisserie leagues.

Yahoo! Sports, http://baseball.fantasysports.yahoo.com
This is probably the most popular fantasy baseball site. It offers a great mix of free and paid services. The options are for 5×5 leagues, point leagues, and head-to-head leagues.

Major League Baseball, http://mlb.mlb.com/NASApp/mlb/mlb/fantasy/index.jsp
Fantasy baseball leagues from MLB itself, this site offers a mix of free fantasy games and paid leagues. It features Rotisserie leagues, point leagues, and a variety of fantasy contests.

STATS Fantasy Baseball, http://fantasy.stats.com/sfbb/sfbb_promo.asp
Fantasy baseball teams from the guys who collect all the numbers, it features a points-based fantasy league.

ESPN, http://games.espn.go.com/cgi/flb/frontpage
This is my favorite site for aggregating baseball news and commentary. It provides fantasy league hosting and allows 4×4, 5×5, and sabermetric point categories, as well as Rotisserie and head-to-head leagues.

The Sporting News, http://fantasygames.sportingnews.com/crs/home.html
Here you can set up your league on the web site of the oldest and best-known baseball weekly newspaper. It uses a point scoring system.

Many of these web sites offer a mix of private leagues where only you and your friends compete, and public leagues where anyone can join. Public leagues are great for people like me who don't have a lot of friends who follow baseball.

If you're using an online service, tools are in place to help you pick and enforce rules and processes. Most leagues include rules to make the game fairer and more realistic. For example, teams are allowed to acquire a free agent (or make a trade) when one of their players is placed on the disabled list. But there are restrictions on what a team can do later. Before joining a service, look at the rules to make sure they make sense for your league. If you're starting a paper league, you might want to buy a book like *Official Rotisserie League Baseball* (Diamond Library) as a reference, or print a copy of the rules used by one of the online services.

An important consideration is the draft or auction process. Some web sites require managers to be present for drafts or auctions, or they allow auctions to take place over days or weeks. Other web sites automate this process, selecting players from a list or bidding for players automatically, according to certain restrictions.

See Also

After you've found a group of fantasy players, formed a league, and selected a service, your next step is to figure out how to beat your opponents. A lot of the techniques and ideas in this book can help you win your fantasy league, but "Draft Your Fantasy Team" **[Hack #73]** is especially relevant because it offers suggestions on what to do on draft day.

HACK #73 Draft Your Fantasy Team

Outsmart your fellow fantasy league owners and pick the best fantasy team you can.

Fantasy baseball is a lot like gambling: you have to be a little lucky to win. But it's a lot more like a poker game than a slot machine: smart players are more likely to win. This hack includes some ideas on how to be smart about drafting your team.

The Basics

You've probably noticed that I'm a modern baseball fan: I like sabermetric measurements such as OBP, slugging average, and range factor; and I don't like figures such as batting average, runs batted in, and errors. If you really want to understand the professional game and pick the winners, modern formulas work best. But if you want to win your fantasy league, they're not the best approach.

Most fantasy leagues score players by ranking them in a few categories or scoring them based on their performance in a few measurements. (See "Start or Join a Fantasy League" [Hack #72] for more information on how to score and rank fantasy teams.) These games are usually based on traditional measurements, like average, runs batted in, and stolen bases for batters; and wins, saves, and ERA for pitchers. In real games, the number of stolen bases and attempts matters (see "Measure Base Running Through EqBR" [Hack #52]), but in 4×4 Rotisserie leagues, only the number of stolen bases matters.

Here are a few simple tips on picking fantasy players.

Pick a closer. Many baseball writers think managers should try to use their best relief pitchers in key moments of the game, and not just in the ninth inning when their team is leading by three or fewer runs. But fantasy baseball owners hate to see that happen because saves are worth a ton of points. A great way to maximize your team ranking is to make sure you have a guy on your team who's going to get a lot of saves.

Pick an RBI man. To bat in a lot of runs, a player needs to do two things: bat after players who get on base, and get a lot of hits or hit fly balls to the outfield. As a measurement of player performance, RBI is overrated: players who are lucky enough to bat in the middle of good lineups bat in a lot of runs. But as a fantasy manager, it's a key measurement because you get points for runs batted in. Seek out good batters who are in the middle of powerful lineups.

Focus on AVG, not OBP. Real players who walk a lot are valuable; they don't create outs and they get on base. But 4×4 Rotisserie leagues don't directly rank players on walks. Focus on players with high batting averages. However, if your league includes runs scored and not just batting average, walks do matter because players who get on base score more runs.

Draft Tips from an Expert

It's like being on the floor of the New York Stock Exchange at 10:00 a.m. on a Monday—fast and furious—but auctions are becoming more and more popular in fantasy baseball leagues. There are some secrets to getting the most out of your money in an auction.

Be patient with your money. Rarely do owners throw out sleepers early in an auction—normally they throw out the big boys. And in a standard auction league, you have $260 for 23 players. That's $11.30 per player. So, when you shell out $34 for a player, he had better be worth three players in your league.

That isn't to say you should avoid elite players. Just beware not to over-spend or take too many of them early. You aren't putting together an all-star squad here. Your team should be a mix of studs, solid options, and sleepers. If you are more accustomed to straight draft leagues, it might help to equate each player with the round in which he would have been selected.

The second and fourth quarters of the auction are the best times to go after players. After the early spending, owners get gun-shy in the second quarter, and there still are plenty of upper-tier players left. In the fourth quarter, owners are tapped out and you can find some decent $4 to $8 players to fill your roster.

Perform the "mustard toss". Part of making your own auction money last is burning it from fellow owners' pockets. During a time of big spending (the first quarter, for example), make the player you throw on the table (to bid on) an elite player that you don't want. Then, when your fellow owners are feeling a bit shell-shocked, throw out mid-range talent you might want if the price is reasonable.

Find a bargain. You *can't* go to a draft without a proposed set of dollar values, whether you make them yourself or take along The Sporting News's *Fantasy Baseball Owners Manual*. Then you shoot to spend under those values, whether it's getting a $35 player for $28 or a $5 player for $2. It's amazing how many good players—at least statistically—there are in the majors. For goodness' sake, there were thirty-three 100-RBI guys in 2004. If the bidding goes too high for your stud RBI producer, wait for another one to be tossed. Also, note that the value of the players changes depending on what Roto categories and/or positions were taken from the pool. That's called inflation. For instance, when the top base stealers are gone, the mid-range base stealers suddenly become more valuable.

Target your favorites. Though it's nice to get good players at the right price, don't go after every player thrown. Those roster spots are coveted. High-light (literally) a handful of players at each position (obviously, many more outfielders and starting pitchers) that you really want. Make it a mix of elite players, dependable fallback options, and sleepers. If the guy tossed isn't one of your guys, let him go and hope the bid gets too high. If it's one of your boys, go after him but don't overspend. If you end up with a middle-tier guy, you'll make up for it at another position.

Know thine enemy. There are many other ways to manipulate another owner's roster. For one, you can bid up a player—$1 at a time—that you know Owner X really likes. Obviously, he must be a player that you can accept having, if it comes to that. You can toss a "theme," such as all the big-name closers or base stealers, thus placing a premium on saves and steals later. Another method is to get into a bidding war and then pull out of it, with an owner who is in a similar situation, whether it's because he needs the same positions or has an equal amount of money. It's a proven fact that owners rarely will get into bidding wars in consecutive tosses or multiple bidding wars in a short time period.

Whatever you do, keep track of what your fellow owners' rosters look like and how much money they have left. If you're bidding against a guy who is pretty strapped, bid him up, either to outbid him or to run him dry. And as in poker, the way you handle yourself is important. If you jump at a bid like a giddy puppy, it's clear to others that you are willing to spend much more. So do that, and then pull out of the bidding. Or act reluctant to make a bid, to make an opposing owner think that's your final offer.

—*Brendan Roberts*

HACK #74 Make a Scoreboard Widget

Make your own scoreboard widget for the Mac OS X Dashboard.

Apple introduced a neat new feature in OS X 10.4, Dashboard, which pops up a set of simple tools with the press of a button. The tools that come with the OS include a clock, an address book, and a stock ticker. This hack shows you how to make your own widget to display live baseball information.

By the way, if you're using a PC, an application called Konfabulator works almost exactly like Dashboard. (In fact, Konfabulator was originally written for the Mac; Apple probably got the idea for Dashboard from this application.) You can get a copy of this shareware application for about $20 from *http://www.konfabulator.com*.

The Code

A widget is really just a web page. Well, it's a deluxe web page, with background images, cascading stylesheets, and JavaScript, but that's all there is to it. If you're not afraid of a little simple code, it's pretty easy to make your own widget.

I decided to show some basic information about each game: the teams playing, the number of runs, the inning, and the number of outs. To fit all of the day's games into one window, I decided to use two different tables (and in turn, I used iFrame objects to make this work). Here are the files in this widget:

Info.plist
> An XML file containing the properties for this widget (Dashboard requires this file or the widget won't work)

Default.png
> A background graphic for the widget (also displayed while the widget is loading); just a big green box

scoreboard.html
> The main file containing the contents for the widget

scoreboard_left.html, scoreboard_right.html
> Two files containing descriptions of the two tables inside the widget

scoreboard.css
> A cascading stylesheet file containing style information for the widget

scoreboard.js
> A JavaScript file containing the guts of the widget (the code that fetches the score data)

To create this widget, start by creating a folder called *scoreboard.*

Now, we'll create the *property list* for this widget. A property list is a special XML file that describes the properties of the widget. The easiest way to create this file is through the Property List Editor, an application included with the Apple Developer tools (which are included on the Mac OS X DVD). See Figure 7-1 for an illustration of the Editor window and the keys you need to set for this widget. When you're done, save the file in the scoreboard directory as *Info.plist.*

Next, we'll create files containing the contents of the widget. We'll start by creating the *scoreboard.css* file, specifying the typefaces shown in the widget. Mostly, these specify colors for different items in the table.

```
table {table-collapse:collapse; border-spacing:0}
td {border:1px solid darkgreen; padding:2px; background-color:green;}
th {border:1px solid darkgreen; padding:2px; background-color:green;}
tr {font-size:7pt; color:white;}
td {font-size:7pt; color:white;}
.ctr {text-align:center}
body {background-color:green; font-family:Tahoma,Arial,Helvetica,
sans-serif; font-size:7px;}
```

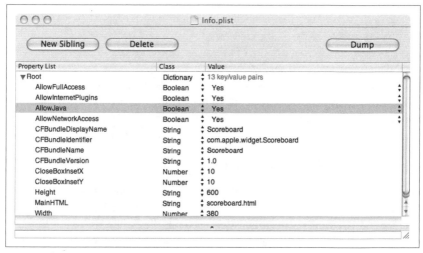

Figure 7-1. The Property List editor

Now, let's show the contents of the *scoreboard.html* file. This file will reference the stylesheet, the two HTML files with the iframe contents, and the JavaScript file. It will also load a JavaScript procedure called init( ) when it starts.

```html
<html>
  <head>
    <script type="text/javascript" src="scoreboard.js"></script>
  </head>
  <body onload="init( );">
    <title>Scoreboard</title>
    <link rel="stylesheet" id="mainStyle"
      href="scoreboard.css" type="text/css" />
    <iframe src="scoreboard_left.html" id="leftFrame" height=360
        width=180 frameborder=0 marginheight=2 marginwidth=2></iframe>
    <iframe src="scoreboard_right.html" id="rightFrame" height=360
        width=180 frameborder=0 marginheight=2 marginwidth=2></iframe>
    <div id='debugDiv'></div>
  </body>
</html>
```

The *scoreboard_left.html* file contains a single table:

```html
<html>
  <link rel="stylesheet" id="mainStyle"
    href="scoreboard.css" type="text/css" />
  <table id="todaysScoresLeft">
    <thead>
      <tr><th>Team L</th>
      <th>Runs</th>
      <th>Inning</th>
      <th>Outs</th>
```

```
        </tr>
    </thead>
    <tbody id="gameDataLeft"></tbody>
    </table>
</html>
```

Notice the id attribute in the table body. The JavaScript code uses this label
to identify where to place the score information. The *scoreboard_right.html*
file contains the exact same contents, substituting the word *Right* for *Left*
wherever it appears. Now we're ready for the interesting part of this hack:
the code that fetches the score information and populates the tables. Create
a file called *scoreboard.js* for this code.

Let's start with some basic code that describes the behavior of the widget.
We'll define two functions that tell the widget what to do when it's shown
and hidden (we don't want this widget to fetch files when we're not looking
at the Dashboard). When the widget appears, it refreshes the scores through
the refreshScores( ) function and sets a timer to refresh the scores again in
another minute.

```
var timerInterval = null;
function onshow( ) {
    refreshScores( );
    if (timerInterval == null) {
    // refresh once per minute
        timerInterval = setInterval("refreshScores( );", 60000);
    }
}

function onhide( ) {
    if (timerInterval != null) {
    clearInterval(timerInterval);
    timerInterval = null;
    }
}

function init( ) {
    // with widgets, alerts go to the console
    // let's put a debugging message here
    alert("started widget");
}

if (window.widget) {
    widget.onhide = onhide;
    widget.onshow = onshow;
}
```

Let's explain how to refresh the scores. We'll define a procedure that pulls
the latest score file from MLB.com's Gameday servers. The location of these
files changes daily, so we will make up a request name based on the date and
then call a procedure to load the file and redraw the screen.

```
function refreshScores( ) {
    var today = new Date( );
    var month, year, day, xFile;
    year = today.getFullYear( );
    month = today.getMonth( ) + 1;
    day = today.getDate( );
    if (day.length == 1) { day = "0" + day;}
    xFile = 'http://gd2.mlb.com/components/game/year_' + year +
        '/month_0' + month +
        '/day_' + day +
        '/master_scoreboard.xml';
    loadXMLDoc(xFile);
}
```

Now, let's define a procedure to fetch an XML file. I used the object
XMLHttpRequest to fetch XML files. This object includes methods for fetching files asynchronously and parsing the results into a DOM object. The
loadXMLDoc( ) function is used to load an XML file at a given URL. This
function creates a new request, sets up a handler for that request, and starts
fetching the XML document. The processReqChange( ) function is called
when the state of the request changes (most interestingly, when the file is
received). When the file arrives, this function calls the drawTables( ) function to show the results.

```
var req = null;
function loadXMLDoc(url) {
    req = new XMLHttpRequest( );
    req.onreadystatechange = processReqChange;
    alert("fetching " + url);
    req.open("GET", url, true);
    req.send(null);
}

function processReqChange( ) {
    // only if req shows "loaded"
    if (req.readyState == 4) {
        // only if "OK"
        if (req.responseXML) {
                alert("updated score file received; processing");
                drawTables( );
        }
    req = null;
    }
}
```

So, finally, we're ready to populate the HTML tables and redraw the screen.
First, we delete all the rows in the current table. Next, we read the results of
the XML file and write the results in the table. There's one clever bit here: I
alternate between the left and right tables to keep things balanced. To alternate, I count the number of games I've seen, putting the even numbers on
the left and the odd on the right.

```
function drawTables( ) {
    var trh, tra, td, i, j, tbody, oneRecord;
    var ltbl, rtbl;

    // refreshes = refreshes + 1;

    ltbl = document.getElementById("leftFrame").contentWindow.
document.getElementById("gameDataLeft");
    rtbl = document.getElementById("rightFrame").contentWindow.
document.getElementById("gameDataRight");

    // remove any rows in tables (on update)
    while (ltbl.rows.length > 0) {
    ltbl.removeChild(ltbl.firstChild);
    }
    while (rtbl.rows.length > 0) {
    rtbl.removeChild(rtbl.firstChild);
    }

    // node tree
    var data = req.responseXML.getElementsByTagName("games")[0];

    // for td class attributes
    var classes = ["ctr","","","","ctr"];
    for (i = 0; i < data.childNodes.length; i++) {
        // use only 1st level element nodes to skip
        // 1st level text nodes in NN
        if (data.childNodes[i].nodeType == 1) {
            // one final match record
            oneRecord = data.childNodes[i];

        if ((((i - 1) / 2) % 2) == 0) {
            tbody = ltbl;
        } else {
            tbody = rtbl;
        }

        trb = tbody.insertRow(tbody.rows.length);
            td = trb.insertCell(trb.cells.length);
            td.setAttribute("class",classes[trb.cells.length-1]);
            td = trb.insertCell(trb.cells.length);
            td.setAttribute("class",classes[trb.cells.length-1]);
            td = trb.insertCell(trb.cells.length);
            td.setAttribute("class",classes[trb.cells.length-1]);
            td = trb.insertCell(trb.cells.length);
            td.setAttribute("class",classes[trb.cells.length-1]);

            trh = tbody.insertRow(tbody.rows.length);
        tra = tbody.insertRow(tbody.rows.length);

            td = tra.insertCell(tra.cells.length);
            td.setAttribute("class",classes[tra.cells.length-1]);
```

```
      td.innerHTML = oneRecord.getAttribute("home_team_city")
// + " " + refreshes
;

      td = trh.insertCell(trh.cells.length);
      td.setAttribute("class",classes[trh.cells.length-1]);
      td.innerHTML = oneRecord.getAttribute("away_team_city");

ls = oneRecord.getElementsByTagName("linescore")[0];
if (ls != null) {
runs = ls.getElementsByTagName("r")[0];

td = tra.insertCell(tra.cells.length);
td.setAttribute("class",classes[tra.cells.length-1]);
td.innerHTML = runs.getAttribute("home");

td = trh.insertCell(trh.cells.length);
td.setAttribute("class",classes[trh.cells.length-1]);
td.innerHTML = runs.getAttribute("away");

td = trh.insertCell(trh.cells.length);
td.setAttribute("class",classes[trh.cells.length-1]);
td.setAttribute("rowspan", "2");

if ((oneRecord.getElementsByTagName("status")[0].
    getAttribute("status") == "Final" ) ||
    (oneRecord.getElementsByTagName("status")[0].
    getAttribute("status") == "Game Over")) {
    td.innerHTML = "Final";
} else if
    ((oneRecord.getElementsByTagName("status")[0].
    getAttribute("status") == "Pre-Game") ||
    (oneRecord.getElementsByTagName("status")[0].
    getAttribute("status") == "Preview")) {
    td.innerHTML = "Pre-Game";
} else if (oneRecord.getElementsByTagName("status")[0].
    getAttribute("top_inning") == "Y") {
    td.innerHTML = "T "
    + oneRecord.getElementsByTagName("status")[0].
    getAttribute("inning");
} else {
    td.innerHTML = "B "
    + oneRecord.getElementsByTagName("status")[0].
    getAttribute("inning");
}

td = trh.insertCell(trh.cells.length);
td.setAttribute("class",classes[trh.cells.length-1]);
td.setAttribute("rowspan", "2");
td.innerHTML = oneRecord.getElementsByTagName("status")[0].
    getAttribute("o");
} else {
```

```
td = tra.insertCell(tra.cells.length);
td.setAttribute("class",classes[tra.cells.length-1]);
td.innerHTML = "0";

td = trh.insertCell(trh.cells.length);
td.setAttribute("class",classes[trh.cells.length-1]);
td.innerHTML = "0";

td = trh.insertCell(trh.cells.length);
td.setAttribute("class",classes[trh.cells.length-1]);
td.setAttribute("rowspan", "2");
if ((oneRecord.getElementsByTagName("status")[0].
    getAttribute("status") == "Final" ) ||
    (oneRecord.getElementsByTagName("status")[0].
    getAttribute("status") == "Game Over")) {
    td.innerHTML = "Final";
} else if ((oneRecord.getElementsByTagName("status")[0].
    getAttribute("status") == "Pre-Game") ||
            (oneRecord.getElementsByTagName("status")[0].
            getAttribute("status") == "Preview")) {
    td.innerHTML = "Pre-Game";
} else if (oneRecord.getElementsByTagName("status")[0].
    getAttribute("top_inning") == "Y") {
    td.innerHTML = "T "
        + oneRecord.getElementsByTagName("status")[0].
    getAttribute("inning");
} else {
    td.innerHTML = "B "
        + oneRecord.getElementsByTagName("status")[0].
    getAttribute("inning");
}


td = trh.insertCell(trh.cells.length);
td.setAttribute("class",classes[trh.cells.length-1]);
td.setAttribute("rowspan", "2");
td.innerHTML = "0";


}
/*
    td = trh.insertCell(trh.cells.length);
    td.setAttribute("class",classes[trh.cells.length-1]);
    td.setAttribute("rowspan", "2");
    alterts = oneRecord.getElementsByTagName("alerts")[0];
    if (alerts != null) {
    td.innerHTML = alerts.getAttribute("text");
    } else {
    td.innerHTML = "";
    }
*/
}
}
}
```

The final steps in building this widget are to add a file called *Default.png* to the widget directory (preferably a green box that is 600 pixels high and 380 pixels wide) and to rename the directory *scoreboard.wdgt*.

Running the Hack

You can now run the widget by double-clicking its icon or by typing open scoreboard.wdgt on a command line. The widget is now available in your Dashboard. When you open the widget, you'll see a new box similar to the one shown in Figure 7-2.

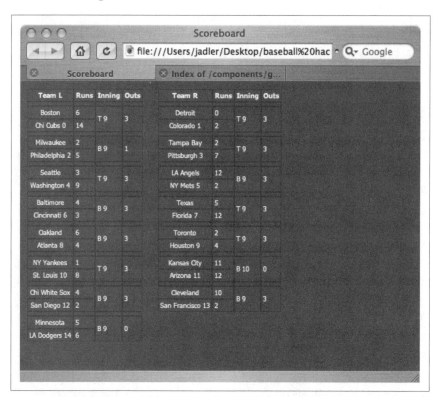

Figure 7-2. Widget illustration

Hacking the Hack

For this widget, I picked just a handful of fields describing the game in progress. I could have included the whole line score (runs per inning), the bases occupied, the name of the batter, and dozens of other fields. You can easily modify this hack to include this information from the scoreboard object. To find out what other information is available, try opening the XML scoreboard file in Firefox or Internet Explorer. Both browsers let you examine the contents of an XML file. For example, try opening: *http://gd2.mlb.com/ components/game/year_2005/month_05/day_22/master_scoreboard.xml.*

Also, there's no reason for this widget to be so ugly. Unfortunately for you, I am not a skilled web site designer, so I wrote something simple and functional but not pretty. You can use graphics to show the state of the game, change the fonts and colors, or do whatever you want to make this prettier.

See Also

I wrote the code for this hack with some help from two other O'Reilly books, *JavaScript: The Definitive Guide* and *JavaScript & DHTML Cookbook*, and with some information from Apple's developer web site, *http:// developer.apple.com/macosx/dashboard.html.*

 Analyze Other Sports

#75 Apply the techniques in this book to other sports.

This book focuses on baseball, but there is no reason you can't spider the Web for data on other sports, save statistics in a database, and analyze the game using R and Excel.

However, there are some subtle and important differences between baseball and other sports. This hack presents a few of those key differences and explains how they should affect your analyses.

Possessions

In most team sports, one side has possession of the ball and tries to score against the other side. This is true in baseball: the batting team effectively has possession of the ball. It's also true in basketball, football, hockey, soccer, rugby, cricket, and water polo—pretty much any team sport.

However, there is a very important difference between baseball and most other sports: baseball has no clock. In most other sports, the game lasts for a fixed period (unless there is a tie), and the two teams switch possession of the ball until the game is over. In baseball, the teams alternate possession for at least eight and a half innings, or until the game is delayed, the home team has had "last licks" and loses, or one team wins.

Why is this important? Well, it means some measurements work well for baseball and work poorly for other sports. In baseball, the number of points scored per plate appearance (or out, or inning) is very closely correlated with the number of points scored per game. Most games last about nine innings;

most players bat about four to five times. Points per plate appearance are usually 15% to 20% of the number of points per game.

In basketball, as in baseball, each team has almost exactly the same number of possessions. After one team has possession of the ball and scores or fails to score, the other team gets the ball. (A team can rebound a ball after a missed shot, but this just means the team retains possession.) Some teams switch possession often, not taking much time per possession, whereas other teams take more time per possession. This means the total number of possessions per game fluctuates greatly. The correspondence between points per possession and points per game is much weaker in basketball than it is in baseball. Therefore, points per possession is a much better predictor of team success than points per game. (For a more complete discussion of this topic, see *Basketball On Paper* [Potomac Books].) Be careful when choosing metrics for other sports.

Clock Strategy

There is no clock in baseball. In almost all games, each team has a realistic chance of winning the game at any time. Even if a team is down 10–0 with two outs in the bottom of the ninth, it can still come back and win the game. (This isn't very likely, but it's possible.)

In other sports, it can be impossible for one team to win or tie. Take football, for example. Suppose a team is down by 16 points with no time-outs, 30 seconds on the clock, and possession of the ball at its own 20-yard line. In this situation, it's impossible to win the game. Here are all the things that have to happen: the team has to move the ball down the field by 80 yards, score a touchdown, and score an extra point. Assuming this happens on two plays (a crazy pass or run and a two-point conversion), that's still going to eat up most of the clock. Then, the team has to have a successful onside kick and repeat the same move.

Such situations occur all the time in football, and when they occur, they're garbage time. The leading team knows it's going to win. Many teams will pull their starting players (to avoid injuries), not play very hard, and try to run down the clock. In situations like these, a team is willing to give up points and yards because doing so doesn't affect the outcome of the game.

This means players in other sports can easily accumulate individual statistics that don't truly represent their ability in a competitive game. Players can get a boost to their touchdown passes, running yards, or other stats. Likewise, teams can give up yards and points late in games that don't affect their outcome. (As an extreme example, the NFC champion Philadelphia Eagles decided to sit almost all their starters during the last two games of the 2004 season. They'd already clinched home field advantage throughout the play-offs and decided not to risk injuries, so the team gave up two whole games.) Crazy blowouts sometimes occur in baseball, but they're rare. Look critically at statistics from other sports to make sure that they truly represent a player's or a team's ability.

See Also

Basketball

If you want to learn about basketball, I recommend Dean Oliver's book, *Basketball On Paper* (Potomac Books). During the 2003–2004 season, Dean worked for the Seattle Sonics, helping the team to its best start in years. Visit *http://www.basketballonpaper.com* for more information.

Football

The best book in print on football is *Pro Football Prospectus 2005* (Workman Publishing Company). It's an annual, so you'll have to check your favorite bookstore for the latest copy. This book is modeled on the Baseball Prospectus books; it's thought provoking, unbiased, and well written. Check out the authors' web site: *http://www.footballoutsiders.com*. I think this site is actually better than *any* baseball-themed web site; the fans who read this site know their stuff and make smart comments. (KC Joyner's web site and book are also a good resource; see *http://www. thefootballscientist.com* for more information.)

You might also want to track down the book *The Hidden Game of Football* by Bob Carroll, Pete Palmer, and John Thorn (Total Sports). This is a very good introduction to analyzing football data. This book inspired Aaron Schatz to start the Football Outsiders web site. Unfortunately, it is out of print, but you can still track down copies on the Internet.

Where to Learn More Stuff

I wrote this book because I love baseball. I probably watch more than 200 baseball games every year. If you want to learn more about baseball, here are a few good places to look.

Baseball Books

Here are a few of my favorite books on baseball:

Baseball Prospectus (Workman Publishing Company)
Every year, these guys put out a giant book of forecasts, commentary, and essays on baseball. It's replaced Bill James' baseball abstracts as the best source for insightful commentary on baseball, and it's a fun read. (How could you not like a baseball book that references the Simpsons?)

Total Baseball (SportClassic Books)
If you have Luddite friends who want a gigantic, hardbound, phone-book-size reference book on baseball statistics, this is the one you should recommend. It was produced with help from Pete Palmer and John Thorn, two of the best baseball thinkers, and it includes some modern sabermetric measurements (mostly from linear weights). Even if you don't care about the vast collection of printed statistics, it is worth buying for the essays.

Nine Innings (Houghton Mifflin)
Daniel Okrent is famous (infamous?) for creating and popularizing Rotisserie baseball. He also wrote this wonderful book describing a single baseball game between the Milwaukee Brewers and the Baltimore Orioles in 1982. This is one of the best stories ever written about the game.

The Hidden Game of Baseball (Doubleday)
This is one of the greatest books ever written about baseball, by the creators of modern baseball analysis. Unfortunately, this book is out of print, so you will probably be stuck searching your library or buying a used copy. Because there's still a lot of demand for this book, used copies can be expensive.

In addition to my favorites, you also could buy the following books:

The 2006 ESPN Baseball Encyclopedia (Sterling)
This massive book of baseball statistics (more than 1,700 pages) was written by my favorite baseball writers, Gary Gillette and Pete Palmer.

The Numbers Game: Baseball's Lifelong Fascination with Statistics (St. Martin's Griffin)
If you're really interested in how baseball statistics have developed over time (both data collection and thinking), this is a wonderful history.

Eight Men Out: The Black Sox and the 1919 World Series (Owl Books)
I am kind of shocked that none of the 2005 World Series coverage talked about the 1919 World Series scandal. They wasted hours talking about the silly "Red Sox Curse" in 2003 and 2004, and in 2005, they didn't mention this story. In 1919, gamblers bribed eight players on the White Sox (the best team in baseball at the time) to lose the World Series. This is one of the best books ever written about baseball; highly recommended.

The Last Good Season: Brooklyn, the Dodgers, and Their Final Pennant Race Together (Doubleday)
In 1958, the Dodgers moved to Los Angeles, breaking the heart of everyone in Brooklyn. This is the story of the 1956 Dodgers: the team, the management, and the fans. Incidentally, there are probably more good books about the Brooklyn Dodgers than about any other baseball team.

The Neyer/James Guide to Pitchers: An Historical Compendium of Pitching, Pitchers, and Pitches (Fireside)
Bob Neyer and Bill James wrote this book to fill a specific void in baseball books: there was no guide explaining which pitches each pitcher threw. If you're wondering whether a certain pitcher from the 1950s threw a forkball, this is probably the best reference book. It also has some interesting essays on pitching.

The New Bill James Historical Baseball Abstract (Free Press)
If you've never read anything by Bill James, this is a great place to start. It's a good, opinionated book on baseball history.

Moneyball: The Art of Winning an Unfair Game (W. W. Norton & Company)
This might be the most important book written about baseball in the past 20 years. Michael Lewis is a terrific writer and baseball fan who tried to discover how the Oakland Athletics have performed almost as well on the field as the New York Yankees, Boston Red Sox, and Los Angeles Angels, but with a significantly smaller payroll. (This past year, it was less than one-third the size of the Yankees' payroll.) It's a story about the A's general manager Billy Beane, about sabermetrics father Bill James, and about baseball players such as Scott Hatteberg.

Curve Ball: Baseball, Statistics, and the Role of Chance in the Game (Springer)
If you want to see what happens when a couple of statistics professors start thinking seriously about baseball, buy this book. I especially liked their discussion of streakiness, strategy, and measuring offense.

Ball Four (Wiley)
One of the best books ever written about baseball, from a player's perspective.

Baseball America 2006 Prospect Handbook (Baseball America)
If you go to minor league baseball games, you'll find this book really useful. I like to know something about the players that I'm watching: where they're from, how they did last year, the size of their signing bonus, etc.

Baseball Web Sites

There are probably thousands of different web sites that cover baseball. Here are a few of my favorites:

Baseballprospectus.com
The most entertaining source for forecasts and commentary on baseball, with good resources for the fantasy player.

ESPN.com
The best of the big commercial sites. It has everything: scouting reports, commentary from comedy writers (like Bill Simmons) and stats geeks (like Bob Neyer and Gary Gillette), play-by-play descriptions, salary information, links to articles in local newspapers, and even sabermetric stats.

Retrosheet.org
In addition to play-by-play files, this site has the best collection of information on historic games. You can find box scores for many, many games, going back more than 100 years.

Baseballthinkfactory.org
> Another good web site in the spirit of Baseball Prospectus.

MLB.com
> The official site always has up-to-date statistics, and it has been adding lots of great stuff like spray charts, matchups, and other information.

Baseball-Reference.com
> A good site for finding baseball statistics, based on the Baseball Data-Bank database.

SABR By the Numbers
> You can get past issues of the SABR "By the Numbers" newsletter at *http://www.philbirnbaum.com*.

Works of Bill James
> Stephen Rony, a SABR member, has been collecting detailed information about Bill James's publications and has posted a guide at *http://members.cox.net/sroneysabr/JamesIndex/index.html*.

Baseball Analysts
> *http://www.baseballanalysts.com* is another well-written baseball blog.

Statistics and Data Mining Books

If you enjoy math, you might want to check out a few of these books:

Data Mining: Practical Machine Learning Tools and Techniques (Morgan Kaufmann)
> This is the most popular book on data mining. It's a nice introduction to the subject and doesn't require a graduate degree in statistics. The authors of this book developed the Weka data-mining package.

The Elements of Statistical Learning (Springer)
> The bible of data-mining techniques. This isn't an easy read if you don't know any statistics or algorithms, but it does a nice job explaining how algorithms work and when to use them.

Bayesian Data Analysis (Chapman & Hall/CRC)
> A great introduction to Bayesian data-analysis techniques. Also not an easy read if you don't know statistics, but it does provide a thorough introduction.

Databases and Computer Languages

For information on MySQL, I usually refer to the documentation on the MySQL web site, *http://dev.mysql.com/doc*.

For information on R, I refer to the R web site, *http://cran.r-project.org/manuals.html*. PDF copies of the manuals listed on the web site are usually installed with R, so check the Help menu in R to see if you already have them on your computer.

For information on Perl, I usually refer to *Programming Perl* (O'Reilly).

Abbreviations

The essence of baseball statistics is that they are countable: they're just counts of things that happen in games. Here are the common abbreviations for baseball statistics. These abbreviations are flashed on scoreboards, printed in newspapers, and used to name fields in databases. Even if you're familiar with baseball, it's worth taking a minute to refresh your memory about the common abbreviations used in this sport.

Table B-1 shows batting statistics.

Table B-1. Batting statistics

Abbreviation	Statistic
AB	Official at bat; ends in a hit, out, or error
H	Hit
BB	Base on balls, or walk
D, 2B, X2B	Double (two-base hit)
T, 3B, X3B	Triple (three-base hit)
HR	Home run
1B, X1B	Single (one-base hit)
IBB	Intentional base on balls (intentional walk)
PA	Plate appearance
SF	Sacrifice flies
SH	Sacrifice hits
SAC	Sacrifice bunts
HP, HBP	Hit by pitch
TB	Total bases
AVG	Batting average: H/AB
OBP	On-base percentage: (H + BB + HBP) / (AB + SF + BB + HBP)

Next, let's look at pitching statistics in Table B-2.

Table B-2. Pitching statistics

Abbreviation	Statistic
BFP	Batters faced by pitcher
R	Runs allowed
H	Hits allowed
HR	Home runs allowed
ER	Earned runs allowed
BB	Base on balls allowed
IBB	Intentional base on balls allowed
OBA	Opponent batting average
W	Wins
L	Losses
G	Games played
GS	Games started
CG	Complete games
SHO	Shutouts
S, SV	Saves
IP	Innings pitched
WP	Wild pitches
BK	Balks
GF	Games finished

Table B-3 shows common abbreviations for fielding statistics.

Table B-3. Fielding statistics

Abbreviation	Statistic
G	Games
GS	Games started
PO	Putouts
A	Assists
E	Errors
DP	Double plays
PB	Passed balls (for catchers)

And, finally, in Table B-4 are the official abbreviations for team names.

Table B-4. Team abbreviations

Abbreviation	Team name
ANA	Anaheim Angels
ARI	Arizona Diamondbacks
ATL	Atlanta Braves
BAL	Baltimore Orioles
BOS	Boston Red Sox
CHA	Chicago White Sox
CHN	Chicago Cubs
CIN	Cincinnati Reds
CLE	Cleveland Indians
COL	Colorado Rockies
DET	Detroit Tigers
FLO	Florida Marlins
HOU	Houston Astros
KCA	Kansas City Royals
LAN	Los Angeles Dodgers
MIL	Milwaukee Brewers
MIN	Minnesota Twins
MON	Montreal Expos
NYA	New York Yankees
NYN	New York Mets
OAK	Oakland Athletics
PHI	Philadelphia Phillies
PIT	Pittsburgh Pirates
SDN	San Diego Padres
SEA	Seattle Mariners
SFN	San Francisco Giants
SLN	St. Louis Cardinals
TBA	Tampa Bay Devil Rays
TEX	Texas Rangers
TOR	Toronto Blue Jays

Index

We'd like to hear your suggestions for improving our indexes. Send email to *index@oreilly.com*.

batting (*continued*)
   on-base percentage (OBP), 221–224
   order, 2
   outs, 2
   strike zone, 2
batting average (AVG)
   box plots, 220
   formulas, 213–221
   top 10 of all time, 216
batting statistics, abbreviations, 436
BB (see base on balls)
BBA (see base on balls allowed)
BEVENT tool, 79
BFP (see batters faced)
BGAME tool, 78
BK (see balks)
blogs, 32
book of stats, creating, 54–64
   queries, 55–60
   reports, 61
box plot
   batter runs (BR), 243
   batting averages, 220
   defensive efficiency (DER), 259
   earned run average (ERA), 249
   fielding runs (FR), 287
   isolated power (ISO), 233
   on base plus slugging average
      (OPS), 229
   on-base percentage, 223
   pitching, linear weights, 256
   runs created (RC), 237
   slugging average (SLG), 226
   walks plus hits per inning pitched
      (WHIP), 252
box scores
   A (assists), 15
   AB (at bats), 14, 15
   BB (base on balls), 14
   BBA (base on balls allowed), 15
   BFP (batters faced), 15
   BK (balks), 16
   calculating scores, 17–19
   creating, 12–19
   D (doubles), 14
   DP (double plays), 15
   E (errors), 15
   ER (earned runs), 16
   H (safe hits), 14

HA (hits allowed), 15
HBP (hit by pitch), 14
HBPA (batters hit by pitch), 15
HR (home runs), 14
IBB (intentional base on balls), 14
IBBA (intentional base on balls
    allowed), 15
IP (innings pitched), 15
K (strikeouts), 14
KA (strikeouts allowed), 15
L (losing pitcher), 16
line score, 17
LOB (left on base), 17
PB (passed balls), 15
player information, 13
PO (putouts), 15
R (runs scored), 14
RA (runs allowed), 15
RBI (runs batted in), 14
Retrosheet and, 78–83
SAC (sacrifice bunts), 14
SB (stolen bases), 14
SF (sacrifice flies), 14
SFA (sacrifice flies allowed), 15
SH (sacrifice hits), 14
SHA (sacrifice hits allowed), 15
T (triples), 14
TB (total bases), 14
TBA (total bases allowed), 15
time, 17
TP (triple plays), 15
umpires, 17
W (winning pitcher), 16
WP (wild pitches), 16
BOX tool, 79
bunting strategy, 319

C

calculations
   at bats, significant number, 332–342
   expected hits matrix, 321–329
   expected number of wins, 348–352
   hits by pitch count, 352–360
   R and, 165
   runs, expected number of, 311–321
   skill versus luck, 365–377
calls
   ball, 3
   foul ball, 3

pitching
    catcher signals and, 30
    hits by pitch count, 352–360
    identifying pitches, 28–30
    linear weights, 253–256
    Project Scoresheet codes, 25
    relief pitcher, holds, 305
    speed, 29
    statistics abbreviations, 437
    strategy, 26–28
    strike zone, 2
    top 10 of all time, 255
plate, pitch identification and, 29
platoon effects, 329–332
play codes, Project Scoresheet, 20
    base running, 23
    examples, 24
    fielding, 20
    pitches, 25
    structure, 20
play recording, traditional scoring
        and, 6–11
play-by-play data, 39
    Gameday and, 143
    hit locations, 151–157
    parser script, 147
    Retrosheet, 74–78
    spidering, 144
    updates, 142–151
    (see also statistics)
play-by-play databases, historical
        Retrosheet and, 107–110
players
    clutch players, locating, 342–348
    contributions, formulas, 212
    number on field, 2
    on base, expected runs,
        calculating, 311–321
    statistics, 39
        web sites, 31–32
players' names (see names of players)
playing information, box scores, 13
PO (see putouts)
Project Scoresheet, 19–26
    play codes, 20
        base running, 23
        examples, 24
        fielding, 20
        pitches, 25
        structure, 20

Retrosheet and, 19
Retrosheet comparison, 75
proxy servers, score applications
        and, 128
putouts (PO), 15
Pythagenport Formula, 350
Pythagorean Wins formula, 348

Q

queries, 41
    MySQL, 86–91
    SQL, Access and, 92
    stats book creation, 55–60
    web queries
        creating, 115–116
        example, 117–121
        spreadsheets, 114–121

R

R language
    arrays, 166
    assignments, 165
    calculations in, 165
    comments, 167
    data frames, 166
    formulas, batting average, 213–221
    functions, 167–168
    graphics, 169
    introduction, 162, 164–165
    ODBC and, 172–174
    outfielders, underpaid, 384–400
    packages, 162–163
    text files, loading, 180–182
R (see runs scored)
RA (see runs allowed)
ranking teams, fantasy leagues, 411
RBI (runs batted in), 14
real time charts, 193–199
regular expressions
    pattern matching, MySQL, 111–113
    Perl, 71–72
relationships, databases, 41
relief pitcher, holds, 305
reports, stats book creation, 61
resources, 431–435
Retrosheet, 1
    box scores and, 78–83
    Chadwick and, 83

transactions, databases, 41
triple plays (TP), 15
triples (T), 14

U

UltraEdit, Perl editor, 73
umpires, 17
    pitch identification and, 28
updates, databases, 131–142
    play-by-play data, 142–151
Usenet newsgroups, 33

V

variables, Perl, 68

W

W (winning pitcher), 16
walks plus hits per inning pitched
    (WHIP)
    formulas, 251–253
    top 10 of all time, 251

web queries
    creating, 115–116
    example, 117–121
    spreadsheets, 114–121
web sites
    commentary, 32
    images of stadiums, 36–38
    player statistics, 31–32
    spidering, 121–127
wild pitches (WP), 16
Windows, MySQL installation, 42–45
winning pitcher (W), 16
wins
    expected number,
        calculating, 348–352
    Pythagorean Wins formula, 348
World Series, odds of best team
        winning, 377–383
WP (wild pitches), 16

X

XAMPP, 44
Xcode, Perl editor, 73

Colophon

The image on the cover of *Baseball Hacks* is an umpire's indicator. The umpire's indicator is a handheld device that umpires use to track the progress of baseball games by recording strikes, balls, outs, and innings. Different varieties have either three or four dials and are made of plastic, aluminum, or stainless steel. Prices vary depending on make and model, but most sell for about $3 at sporting goods stores. In the early 1900s, umpire's indicators were made of celluloid and had two dials to track strikes and balls. The National Baseball Hall of Fame exhibits an umpire's indicator from 1887 with a five-ball, four-strike count (in the 19th century, the rules for walks and strikeouts varied from season to season). Antique umpire's indicators are prized by sports memorabilia collectors and can sell for as much as $5,000.

The cover image is an original photograph by Hanna Dyer. The cover font is Adobe ITC Garamond. The text font is Linotype Birka; the heading font is Adobe Helvetica Neue Condensed; and the code font is LucasFont's TheSans Mono Condensed.

Better than e-books

Buy *Baseball Hacks* and access the digital
edition FREE on Safari for 45 days.

Go to www.oreilly.com/go/safarienabled
and type in coupon code EKCH-5AZD-9E6N-WLD8-3SXU

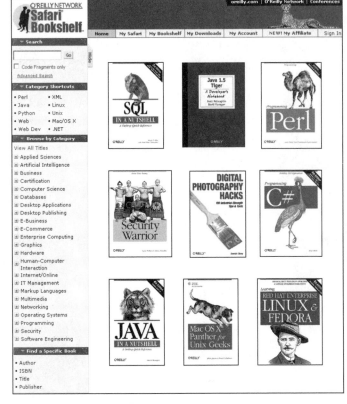

Search
thousands of
top tech books

Download
whole chapters

Cut and Paste
code examples

Find
answers fast

Search Safari! The premier electronic reference
library for programmers and IT professionals.

Related Titles from O'Reilly

Hacks

Access Hacks

Amazon Hacks

Astronomy Hacks

Blackberry Hacks

BSD Hacks

Car PC Hacks

Digital Photography Hacks

Digital Video Hacks

eBay Hacks, *2nd Edition*

Excel Hacks

Flash Hacks

Firefox Hacks

Gaming Hacks

Google Hacks, *2nd Edition*

Google Map Hacks

Greasemonkey Hacks

Half-Life 2 Hacks

Halo 2 Hacks

Hardware Hacking Projects
  for Geeks

Home Theater Hacks

iPod & iTunes Hacks

IRC Hacks

Knoppix Hacks

Life Hacks

Linux Desktop Hacks

Linux Multimedia Hacks

Linux Server Hacks

Mac OS X Panther Hacks

Mapping Hacks

Mind Hacks

Mind Performance Hacks

Network Security Hacks

Nokia Smartphone Hacks

Online Investing Hacks

Palm & Treo Hacks

PayPal Hacks

PDF Hacks

PC Hacks

PHP Hacks

Podcasting Hacks

PSP Hacks

Retro Gaming Hacks

Skype Hacks

Smart Home Hacks

Spidering Hacks

Swing Hacks

TiVo Hacks

Visual Studio Hacks

VoIP Hacks

Web Site Measurement Hacks

Windows Server Hacks

Windows XP Hacks,
  2nd Edition

Wireless Hacks, *2nd Edition*

Word Hacks

XML Hacks

Yahoo! Hacks

O'REILLY®

Our books are available at most retail and online bookstores.

To order direct: 1-800-998-9938 • *order@oreilly.com* • *www.oreilly.com*

Online editions of most O'Reilly titles are available by subscription at *safari.oreilly.com*